GW00569130

ISBN 978-1-333-65186-2
PIBN 10531254

JACOPONE DA TODI

From a manuscript in the Laurentian Library, Florence

JACOPONE da TODI

POET AND MYSTIC—1228-1306

A SPIRITUAL BIOGRAPHY

BY

EVELYN UNDERHILL

WITH A SELECTION FROM THE
SPIRITUAL SONGS
THE ITALIAN TEXT TRANSLATED
INTO ENGLISH VERSE

BY

Mrs. THEODORE BECK

J. M. DENT & SONS LTD.
LONDON AND TORONTO. 1919
NEW YORK: E. P. DUTTON & CO.

Amor che dái forma
ad omnia c' ha forma,
la forma tua reforma
l'omo ch'è deformato.

Lauda LXXXI.

Tu solus mihi ex hoc iam dulcescas
usque in saeculum; quia tu solus cibus
et potus meus, amor meus et gaudium
meum, dulcedo mea et totum bonum
meum.

De Imit. Christi, iv. 16.

PREFACE

THE object of this book is to give English readers the material necessary for a full understanding of one of the greatest and most interesting Italian mystical poets: Jacopone da Todi, the typical singer of the Franciscan movement, the first writer of philosophic religious poetry, and perhaps the most picturesque figure in the history of early Italian literature.

Three types of mind should find pleasure in Jacopone's work and personality. First, those interested in Christian mysticism; for he is among the most profound and individual of the thirteenth-century mystics. Next, lovers of poetry; who, even though they may not sympathise with his religious attitude, cannot fail to admire the magnificent poems in which it is expressed: mystical love-songs matching in the sphere of spiritual passion the most beautiful lyrics of his Tuscan and Bolognese contemporaries. Last, those who care for the Italy of St. Francis and his descendants—though without special inclination to its mystical thought or poetry —may be attracted by the human and tempestuous story of this man who was a friend of the heroes of the *Fioretti*, and who suffered in the interests of those ideals which they represent.

Yet apart from one admirable article by Professor Edmund Gardner, a few references in works on the mediæval mystics, and one or two translations by John Gray and others of his most celebrated poems, very little has been written upon Jacopone in English; and even Italian scholars have been content to leave much

v

of his most characteristic work uncommentated. This is partly due to the fact that until nine years ago no trustworthy modern edition of his poetry existed. Even now, we do not possess a complete critical text. The publication in 1910 of Dr. Ferri's excellent reprint of the first Florentine edition of the *laude*—a work of scholarship which was put into more general circulation in 1915—has alone made the present undertaking possible. This undertaking consists first of a detailed study of the man ; his mystical development, his place in history, and activities as a leader of the " Spiritual " Franciscans. Next, of a selection from his poems, chosen to illustrate the most important points of his mystical growth and outward career, and so arranged that they give some idea of his artistic and spiritual evolution. The translations into English verse should permit those who cannot grapple with the difficult language of the originals to enjoy as much of their beauty and character as may be conveyed into another tongue.

It follows from the order of arrangement, that the more crude and commonplace poems come first: moral and ascetic pieces, written soon after Jacopone's conversion, and chiefly interesting as a guide to his tendencies at that time. The mystical love-poems—part philosophic, part personal—which are most characteristic of his genius, will be found towards the end of the book. No reader should consider himself to possess any idea of Jacopone's quality who has not read at least some of the great *laude* of his middle and last years ; such as " Fuggo la croce," " Amor de caritate," " O Amor, divino amore," or " Sopr'onne lengua amore." Of all these, text and translation are here given.

Jacopone was one of the most subjective of writers. In his poetry, he admits us to close intimacy with his many-sided character, tells us of his political, social, and intellectual experiences, and all the secrets of his inner life. His *laude*, when we have learned to read them rightly, constitute a human document as complete as the *Confessions* of St. Augustine, or the autobiography of Suso; p r a more trustworthy, since they record his immediate reactions to experience, and are not—save in a few instances—the fruit of reflection upon emotions that are past. History and comparative psychology help us to fill the gaps which they leave, and to construct from them the picture of a living man, with characteristics both mediæval and universal. This man is no mere arid theologian or pious emotionalist; but a vigorous human creature, full of ardent feeling, keen of intellect though unstable and eccentric, passionately interested in the realities both of the temporal and of the eternal worlds. He touches existence at all points: is a lawyer and man of the world, a wandering missionary and didactic poet, religious reformer, politician, and contemplative friar. Often unsparing in his judgment on the follies and weaknesses of his fellows, fearless in his denunciations of sin, and full of a robust humour that is not afraid to laugh at itself, he yet never ceases to be governed by that love and wonder which Donne held to be the essence of divinity.

Both author and translator are under a deep debt of gratitude to Dr. Giovanni Ferri, the learned editor of Jacopone's *laude*, for much invaluable help. This help has been freely and generously given, out of a desire—in the donor's own words—" to contribute to the introduction of a great Italian poet to the English people." Dr. Ferri has not only permitted the use of his standard reprint of the *laude*, but has done us and our readers the great service of correcting the proofs of the Italian text; thereby giving to this part of the book an authority which it could not otherwise have possessed. The 1915 edition of his work has been used, as the slight modifications of spelling there introduced make Jacopone's Italian more intelligible to those who are not linguistic specialists. It is a source of warm gratification to us, that Italy and England should thus have combined to honour one of the great names of our common Latin inheritance.

We have also to thank Professor Edmund Gardner, the chief English authority upon Jacopone and his period, for much kind help and advice: and Mr. J. A. Herbert, Assistant Keeper of MSS. in the British Museum, for generously placing his expert knowledge at the author's disposal, and drawing her attention to a hitherto undescribed Umbrian MS. of the *laude*.

E. U.

August, 1919.

CONTENTS

PART I

PART II

LAUDE: TEXT AND TRANSLATION

CONTENTS

ILLUSTRATIONS

PART I

JACOPONE da TODI

CHAPTER I

INTRODUCTORY

Jacopone's period and personality—Sources—Early references—Self-revelations in the laude—Bonaccorsi's edition—The legendary Vita—Jacopone's historical background—Franciscan influences—Ideal of St. Francis—Dissensions of the Order—General State of Society—Summary.

JACOPONE DA TODI, the first great Italian religious poet, is also one of the most interesting and significant figures in the early history of the Franciscan Order. That Order in its first purity seemed the perfect flower of the mediæval soul. In the earlier legends, and in the pages of the *Fioretti*, we see the unfolding of the petals, and there its delicate charm still lives to delight us. But in the *laude* of Jacopone the strange fragrance of that flower, the mysterious essence which lived at its heart, has been distilled and preserved; for he is the poet and philosopher of the Primitive Rule.

Born about 1228 or 1230, soon after St. Francis died and whilst St. Clare had still twenty years or more to live, and dying in 1306—when Dante was forty-one —the span of his life covered the most impressive period of the Middle Ages: the last years of the Emperor Frederick II., and the whole reign of St. Louis, the careers of St. Thomas Aquinas and St. Bonaventura. He saw the short papacy of Celestine V., the hermit saint whom Dante placed in hell,[1] and was imprisoned for five years by his successor, Boniface VIII. We possess the poems in which he celebrates both

[1] *Inf.*, iii., 58.

3

events.[1] Living in the world until he was about forty
years of age, a brilliant lawyer, a man of strong passions,
wide cultivation and fastidious tastes, he is then said
to have experienced a sudden and dramatic conversion:
and, after following for ten years, like the English
mystic Richard Rolle, the roving career of a missionary
hermit, he entered the Franciscan family as a lay-
brother in 1278. He therefore brought to the service of
religion an acute intellect, great knowledge of the
world, and all the powers of a developed manhood.

Within the Franciscan Order, Jacopone forms a
link between the survivors amongst the First Com-
panions of Francis, and the succeeding generation,
which had never known the Founder or his friends in
the flesh. Almost contemporary with the lively chroni-
cler Salimbene (1221-88) and our own Roger Bacon
(1214-94), in his old age he may have seen Giotto paint-
ing in the great church at Assisi and heard of the build-
ing of Santa Croce at Florence. Yet two of the First
Companions — Brother Leo, the close friend of St.
Francis and witness of the Stigmata (ob. 1274), and
Rufino (ob. 1271)—were still living at the Porziuncula
at the time of his entrance into the Order; and he must
have known the last years of John of Parma (1208-87),
the great and saintly leader of the Spiritual party. He
witnessed the career of the ecstatic Angela of Foligno
(1248-1309) and the rise and disgrace of her tempestu-
ous " spiritual son " Ubertino da Casale (1259-1330).
Temperamentally inclined to that austere and thorough-
going Franciscanism of which Ubertino was the pas-
sionate defender, he took an active part in the struggle
for the observance of the Primitive Rule; and his poetry
throws much light on the ideals of the " perfect friar "
as they were understood by the rank and file of the

---

[1] *Laude LIV.*, " Que farai, Pier da Morrone? " (see p. 428): *LV.*, " Que
farai, fra *Iacovone*? ": *LVI.*, " O Papa Bonifazio " (see p. 438): and *LVII.*,
" Lo pastor per mio peccato."

Spiritual party in the generation immediately follow-
ing the death of St. Francis.[1]

Jacopone in fact, partly by reason of his poetic
genius, partly because of his special temperament,
represents better than do any other of the early writers
the characteristic blend of popular and mystical religious
feeling, the double strain of wisdom and simplicity, of
moral austerity and lyrical joy, which were the peculiar
marks of the Franciscan revival as understood by the
Founder himself. His poetry illustrates on one hand
the intimate devotion to the person of Christ, the
phases of ardent love and eager pain, of rapture and
penitence, which marked the inward growth of the
Franciscan mystic and characterised his intercourse
with God: on the other, the missionary ardour which
drove the true follower of Francis to preach to other
men the supreme duty and happiness of loving Perfect
Love. It also reveals a personality at once original,
impressive and picturesque: disclosing some at least
of the stages through which a hard-headed Umbrian
lawyer, arrogant, sensual and utterly self-centred, re-
nouncing the world in middle life, was changed into
a great Christian mystic.

The outlook for the biographer of Jacopone, how-
ever, is not a promising one. Four groups of material
are available, on which a study of his life can be based:
but none of these is adequate, and our use of them is
beset with difficulties. First, there are the few and
short references to him which are found in early docu-
ments. Secondly, his authentic poems, in so far as these
can be sifted from the mass of religious verse subse-
quently attributed to him. Thirdly, the legendary
history which grew up around his name, and which
seems at first sight to have few points of contact with
the more trustworthy statements of the first group.
Fourthly, our general knowledge of thirteenth-century

---

[1] For this see below, ch. v.

Italy, and specially of the state of the Franciscan Order
during the period in which he lived, must often be used
as a clue to the true meaning and proportion of the
facts which documents, poems and legend seem to
reveal.   To these sources of information, those in-
terested in Jacopone's mysticism may reasonably add
another: namely, the lives and works of other mystics
and " twice-born " souls.   Their declarations often help
us to elucidate the more difficult passages of the *laude*,
and to determine the relationship in which these poems
stand to the poet's inner life: assuring us that the
development which we trace in them is—allowing for
peculiarities of temperament and circumstance—the
normal development of the spiritual genius.

Beginning with material of the first class, early
references to Jacopone are with one exception[1] con-
fined to chronicles and other works written by members
of the Franciscan Order in the course of the century
following his death.   The exception, however, is of
great historical interest.   It is the manifesto[2] put forth
on May 10th, 1297, by the Cardinals Jacopo and Pietro
Colonna, denouncing as invalid the abdication of Pope
Celestine V. and election of Boniface VIII.; who " not
without the instigation of the Evil Spirit, calls himself
Roman Pontiff."   This manifesto was signed by various
ecclesiastics, including five foreign bishops, and also by
three Italian friars; of whom the first is " Frater
Jacobus Benedicti de Tuderto."   This is undoubtedly
Jacopone, whose name in the world is known to have
been Jacomo Benedetti.   This document, therefore,
coming from the lifetime or the poet, proves that he
had become in the last years of the thirteenth century
a figure of considerable importance in ecclesiastical
politics: and that he was regarded as a leading

---

[1] Possibly with two exceptions, if the person referred to in Cardinal
Bentivenga's will of 1288 be indeed the poet. See below, p. 154.
[2] Printed in *Archiv für Litteratur und Kirchengeschichte des Mittelalters*,
1889, Band V., p. 509.

man amongst those Spiritual Franciscans who had
centred their hopes for the future of the Church on the
election of the saintly hermit Celestine V. It provides
us with the reason of the imprisonment and excom-
munication which he suffered under Boniface VIII.,
and supports the statement of Angelo Clareno, the
great leader of the Italian Spirituals, who wrote, seven-
teen years after Jacopone's death, an account of the
struggles of the Franciscan extremists to obtain a papal
decision in favour of the restoration of the Primitive
Rule. Angelo tells us that " Jacobus Tudertus " was
one of the principal friars in whom " Christ and His
Spirit were firmly believed to dwell " and who fought
for the pure observance of the Rule of Poverty. This
group, shortly after the election of Pier da Morrone to
the Papacy, sent two of their number to him; beg-
ging that all those brothers who wished it might at least
be permitted to keep the strict rule as given in the
Testament of St. Francis without " molestation or
impediment " from the *relaxati* or Conventual friars,
who now interpreted Holy Poverty in a larger and more
comfortable manner.[1] Angelo was himself one of these
two delegates. His testimony therefore goes back to
Jacopone's lifetime, and ranks next in importance to
that of the Colonna manifesto.

The next notice of Jacopone occurs in the *De Planctu
Ecclesiæ* of the Franciscan Alvarus Pelagius, written
about the year 1330. He is there called "frater Jacobus
benedicti Tuderti frater minor perfectus "[2]—a phrase
which probably indicates a member of the Spiritual
group, and may be related to the title of the " Mirror of
Perfection of a Friar Minor "; that beautiful if one-
sided manifesto of the extreme Franciscan rigorists.
Jacopone's monastic virtue, especially that unmitigated

---

[1] Angelus de Clareno, *Historia septem tribulationum ordinis minorum.*
Printed in *Archiv für Litteratur und Kirchengeschichte des Mittelalters*,
Band II., p. 308.
[2] *De Planctu Ecclesiæ*, Bk. II., cap. lxxiii.

asceticism which caused him to say that the face of
the most beautiful woman was no more to him than
the head of an ass, is dwelt upon with much approval
by Pelagius, who also quotes some of the prose sayings
ascribed to him. These details are reproduced in the
well-known " Chronicle of the Twenty-four Generals,"
a *catalogue raisonné* of eminent and saintly friars
written in the mid-fourteenth century; but no bio-
graphical facts are given.

From a comparison of these documents we gain the
impression that their writers looked upon Jacopone,
not as a poet, but as an austere moralist of the monastic
type; a pattern friar of the stricter sort, an exact
observant of the Primitive Rule, and a Spiritual re-
former whose enthusiasms sometimes brought him into
collision with the higher authorities. The only early
account which corrects this, connecting the Jacopone
of spiritual politics with the Jacopone of the Spiritual
Songs, is that of Fra Bartolommeo of Pisa, who wrote
about 1385—seventy-nine years after the poet's death.
He, describing the Franciscan foundations at Todi,
says, " In Todi, not in the habitation of the friars, but
in the monastery of the sisters of S. Clare of Monte
Sancto, there lies the holy friar Jacopo Benedetti, who
was called Fra Jacopo of Todi: a man of marvellous
holiness, and wholly burning with the love of God. He
bore with patience many tribulations from our lord
the Pope Boniface, who was wrongly informed; but
afterwards he was set free. He made many songs of
praise in the vulgar tongue, which are full of high doc-
trine, and of much sweetness. Also he made manful
clamour against the life of the said Pope Boniface." [1]

These notices, such as they are, may be regarded as
authentic material for the biographer. They tell us,
however, little or nothing of Jacopone the man: the

[1] *De Conformitate vitæ beati Francisci*, Lib. I., fruct. viii., par. ii.
Printed in *Analecta Franciscana*, vol. iv.

passionate penitent, the merciless satirist, the vigorous popular preacher, the ardent mystic and profound philosopher who is so clearly revealed in the poems. It is, indeed, to those poems that we must go for all our best information about the poet. Jacopone was an intensely subjective writer, and has left in his work clear evidence of the spiritual vicissitudes through which he passed: the " many a buffeting and shrewd repulse " through which, like Jacob Boehme, he came to the heart of God. This evidence supports at least some of the statements in that Legend which is our third possible source of biographical material. These poems make it plain that their author had once lived a worldly, self-indulgent, and in his own opinion extremely sinful life: that he passed through a period of violent penitence and self-abasement. They reflect the experiences of the ten years following his conversion, during which he is said to have lived the active yet ascetic life of a missionary-hermit, subject to no rule but that of his own intense religious fervour. They disclose the moods through which he came to the conviction that true liberty was best found in the self-surrender of perfect obedience; and sought admission as a lay brother in the Franciscan convent of Todi. They record his renewal of interest in human affairs, his somewhat inimical attitude towards the " new learning," his brief and unlucky emergence into ecclesiastical politics as a leader of the Spiritual party, his attitude towards the election of Pope Celestine V., his attack on Boniface VIII., his imprisonment and excommunication. Finally, they show his growth in the mystical life; the supreme heights of contemplation to which he attained, the mysterious intercourse with Eternal Love which he enjoyed. Though perhaps the incidents of his temporal career will never be fully known to us, his spiritual adventures at least are freely disclosed in these daring and beautiful songs. " Of the life of the

aforesaid Beato Jacopone," says his first editor, " there
appears to be no certain account: but of his perfection
and transformation in the Divine Love, enough may
be seen in his works." [1] Jacopone's lyrics are indeed
faithful mirrors of their writer's mind. Through them
we come at last to some knowledge of this strange
vehement nature: this vigorous missionary and subtle
philosopher: this poet, by turns crude satirist, ardent
lover, and profound contemplative, who can sink to the
level of the popular hymnal and rise above that of St.
John of the Cross. They give us a clue on the one hand
to the full significance of those dry notices found in
early documents, on the other to the amount of truth
which may be concealed in the highly coloured and
entertaining legendary *Life*.

Many manuscripts of the *laude* are still in existence,
some dating from the early part of the fourteenth
century.[2] They were first printed in Florence in A.D.
1490 by Francesco Bonaccorsi. This edition, un-
doubtedly the best for purposes of study, was reprinted
in 1910 by the Societá Filologica Romana:[3] and again
with slight modifications in 1915. From it all my
quotations will be made. Bonaccorsi had a remarkable
critical sense, and an almost modern enthusiasm for
textual accuracy. He tells us that the poems in his
edition are based on specially prepared copies, tran-
scribed " without changing or adding any new thing "
from two ancient manuscripts of the *laude* pre-
served at Todi, which were the best and fullest to be
found in that city, " la terrena patria del auctore."

---

[1] Proem to Bonaccorsi's edition.

[2] A short account of the manuscript sources is given in Appendix I.
(p. 503).

[3] *Laude di frate Jacopone da Todi, secondo la stampa fiorentina del 1490.
A cura di Giovanni Ferri*. Rome, 1910. Reprinted in the series " Scrittori
d'Italia," 1915.

The admirable reprint of the satirical poems alone, with critical intro-
duction, by Signor B. Brugnoli (*Le Satire di Jacopone da Todi*. Rome, 1914)
is also indispensable to students: but has not the authoritative character
of Dr. Ferri's text.

These copies were collated, in order that the text, which had been much altered in many books, might be reduced to its ancient purity; and a new copy embodying the corrections was made for the use of the printer. The "exemplari Todini assai antichi" used by Bonaccorsi have since disappeared; but as he refers with less respect to the Perugian codex of 1336, from which he took certain additional poems, it seems probable that they were written at latest in the first quarter of the fourteenth century. In this case his edition represents the earliest Umbrian text of Jacopone now known. He prints one hundred and two *laude*; there being, he says, no larger number, and indeed often less, in the best and oldest manuscripts preserved at Todi, "where very many books are to be found." "Yet for this I do not say that he did not write a larger number of *laude*; nor, on the other hand, can it be affirmed that all these were made by him."—so difficult had the separation of Jacopone from his numerous imitators already become.

The first ninety-three poems in Bonaccorsi, beginning with "O regina cortese" and ending with the celebrated "Donna del Paradiso," are found in all the best manuscripts, and are certainly authentic. This, the most valuable and trustworthy part of the collection, was originally intended to be complete in itself. It therefore opens and closes with a hymn in honour of Mary: an arrangement which he felt to be "not inconvenient" since she is the "porta e inventrice di ogni gratia." The last nine *laude* are in the nature of an appendix, having been collected by him from various sources and added to the main body of the work. Amongst them two may be accepted without question:[1] of the remainder, six, which include the exquisite hymn "Fiorito è Cristo,"[2] though their history is not quite so

---

[1] *Laude XCIX.*, "L'amor ch'è consumato," and *CI.*, "Troppo perde el tempo" (p. 342).
[2] *Lauda C.* See p. 406.

good as that of the first ninety-three *laude*, have at least a reasonable claim to be treated as genuine. The last poem in the collection [1] is now recognised as apocryphal.

Later editors, however, seldom possessed Bonaccorsi's restraint and critical sense. Tresatti (Venice, 1617) prints over two hundred poems, traditionally attributed to Jacopone, and all possessing something in common with his work. Many of these are undoubtedly spurious: for the fourteenth and fifteenth centuries produced a crowd of writers of religious verse who modelled themselves upon the great Franciscan singer, and constantly reproduced his characteristic forms, phrases and ideas, though never achieving his fiery intensity. Jacopone's style lends itself to imitation, and the best of these *laude* are often hard to distinguish from his more commonplace works. The text of the authentic poems in these later editions is also corrupt; being frequently amended in the interests both of clarity and of edification, much as our own seventeenth-century editors often tampered with the style of early English mystical works. In default, then, of a modern critical text, estimates of Jacopone's genius and studies of his character and life should still be based on Bonaccorsi's edition of the *laude*. It is our second authentic source of material.

Thirdly, we have the legendary life of Jacopone; best represented by the so-called *Vita*, which was edited by Professor Tobler from a fifteenth-century manuscript and printed in 1878.[2] This vivid and amusing narrative, of which several versions are now known to us,[3] was first thought to be an early fourteenth-century work, but is now recognised as being in its present form a composition of the mid-fifteenth century:

[1] " Se per diletto."
[2] In *Zeitschrift für Romanische Philologie*, Band II., p. 26.
[3] One in the *Francheschina* of Fra Jacopo degli Oddi; another in Modio's edition of the *Laude* (Florence, 1548).

that is to say, of 150 years or more after Jacopone's time. Whatever its sources may be, they seem to have been unknown to the writers of the *Chronicle of the Twenty-four Generals* and to Bartolommeo of Pisa; who would certainly have worked into their chronicles a tale so edifying and so picturesque. Moreover the many spurious "Lives" of the troubadours which were current at this period—ingenious romances generally based upon the more personal passages in their songs—warn us against too eager and uncritical an acceptance of this biography of the great Troubadour of Christ. Yet the *Vita* may, and probably does contain some authentic elements. Although the careful Bonaccorsi forbore to make use of it, if it was known to him—saying that he found no certitude in the current stories of Jacopone's life—it was accepted without question by subsequent editors of the *laude*, and all popular accounts of the poet have drawn upon it freely. It is the only known source of the celebrated and dramatic tale of his conversion. It is, however, demonstrably wrong in several important details, gives at best a one-sided view of Jacopone's career, and falsifies the date of his death.

The Jacopone whom this legend describes is a remarkable example of the twice-born soul: a hard and avaricious lawyer, converted in middle life by crushing domestic sorrow, who renounces the world, accepts Franciscan poverty in its most drastic sense, and becomes like Brother Juniper a "fool for Christ's sake." We are given several tales of the antics of the regenerated Jacopone, "which in the sight of men seemed of extreme foolishness, but in the sight of God were of singular wisdom." These stories have a strong family resemblance to the futilities of Brother Juniper, as told in the *Fioretti*;[1] though Jacopone's eccentricities

---

[1] *Fioretti di S. Francesco: la Vita di Frate Ginepro.* The story of Juniper's antics, however, has been shown by Professor Tamassia to

struck a more savage note than those of that gentle
" fool of Christ." Whatever we may think of the truth
of these grotesque anecdotes, which must have been
very popular amongst the friars and their friends, they
are at any rate thoroughly mediæval in type, and may
indicate the kind of Franciscanism for which Jacopone
originally stood; the qualities for which he was remem-
bered and admired in the Order after his death. The
Vita goes on to tell us that for ten years after his con-
version, he wore the *bizocone*—probably the rough
habit of the Franciscan tertiaries—and lived a life of
extreme penance and self-abasement, as to which the
writer refuses details for the reassuring reason that he
had not found them to be very authentic. At the end
of these ten years he was inspired by God to enter the
Franciscan Order: and having overcome the not un-
natural reluctance of the friars to accept so eccentric
and wayward a postulant, was received as a lay-
brother, although a highly educated man. In this state
he humbly persisted till the end of his life, wholly
given up to penance, contemplation, and lowly acts of
service to his fellow men. According to the *Vita*, he
was regarded by the majority of his brethren as a holy
but " fantastic " soul, a " true son of Francis," a " man
of great penances and utmost patience, and a lover of
the Lady Poverty." But from others he suffered many
persecutions and tribulations, because of that madness
of divine love by which he was possessed, and which
was at once the source of his most annoying eccentri-
cities and his most spiritual songs. Towards the end of
his life some " viperish tongues " even accused him of
heresy; saying that he held fantastic opinions, that he
described the Godhead now in one way and now in
another, and that his mystical outpourings were but

depend on earlier tales of the same kind. The type of " Christ's fool " is
an old one in Christian hagiography. The sixth book of Cæsarius of Heister-
bach is entirely dedicated to it, and full of amusing incidents which
anticipate those of the Juniper and Jacopone legends.

" fancies founded on straw." Jacopone, having heard
this, lifted up his mind in much humility to Jesus his
love; and in the fire and fervour of the Holy Spirit
composed the poem "Sopr'onne lengua amore"[1] to
the confutation of his enemies.

The rest of the *Vita* is little more than a running
commentary on the principal *laude*, all of which it of
course ascribes to the poet's Franciscan period. It
gives, sometimes in much detail, the supposed circumstances under which each was written, and the point in
his spiritual development which it represents. Many of
the poems thus attributed to him are now regarded as
spurious. Though none can be dated with absolute
certainty, many others must be assigned, on both
critical and psychological grounds, to his missionary
period; and this part of the legend, at any rate, has
little or no historical value. As to the exact amount of
truth which the earlier narrative contains, no two
students are in agreement. Most of the earlier editors
and commentators accepted it without question. In
recent times the enthusiastic but uncritical Ozanam[2]
has followed their example; whereas the "higher
critics" of Franciscanism, such as Bertoni,[3] Tenneroni,[4]
and Ferri,[5] dismiss it as a mere legend. D'Ancona,[6]
Oliger,[7] and E. Gardner[8] take a less austere though
still critical view. They recognise the strong probability that it does preserve an old and true tradition concerning Jacopone's temperament and the circumstances

---

[1] *Lauda XCI.* See p. 474.

[2] F. Ozanam, *Les poètes franciscains en Italie au XIII. siècle.* Paris,
1859.

[3] G. Bertoni, in *Fanfulla della Domenica*, vol. xxviii., No. 23.

[4] A. Tenneroni, "Le Laude e Jacopone da Todi," in *Nuova Antologia*,
1906.

[5] In the Appendix to his reprint of Bonaccorsi's edition.

[6] A. d'Ancona, *Jacopone da Todi il giullare di Dio del secolo XIII.*
(Todi, 1914.)

[7] Livarius Oliger, art. "Jacopone da Todi" in *Catholic Cyclopedia*,
vol. viii.

[8] Edmund Gardner, "The Poet of the Franciscan Movement," in
Constructive Quarterly, June, 1914.

of his conversion; a tradition which must have been current in the Franciscan Order from early times, is supported at many points by his poems, and is not inconsistent with the references to him found in early documents. These documents, however, show plainly enough how partial a view of the real Jacopone we should get from the *Vita* alone. Though the fact of his imprisonment by Boniface VIII. is casually mentioned, without explanation of its cause, the whole of his political activity and alliance with the extreme Spiritual Franciscans is here suppressed. The date of his death is given as 1296—a year before he signed the Colonna manifesto—whereas he certainly lived for some time after his release from prison, dying about 1306.

When we see further that the writer dwells with special unction on the great spiritual advantages which his hero gained from submission to the conventual rule, and represents him as an ardent but obedient friar, we begin to suspect that the *Vita* is the official life of Jacopone as put forward by the Conventual Franciscans; who wished after his death to claim this celebrated poet and saintly soul as one of themselves. The writer, in fact, is intent on producing a work of edification; a portrait of one whose inconvenient enthusiasms had been blurred by the lapse of time, and whose memory lived in the Umbrian convents as a perfect but somewhat fantastic son of Francis, and a great poet whose spiritual songs were already known and loved throughout the whole of Italy. He chooses therefore, in the proper mediæval manner, incidents appropriate to his purpose, and omits all that interferes with it: even to the point of killing his hero before the more embarrassing events of that varied career took place. The resulting picture is of course incomplete, and in some particulars deliberately distorted; but this does not mean that it is valueless, or that all the incidents chosen are necessarily untrue. The author tells us that he is setting down things which have been told to him by " frati antichi, dingni de fede." It is indeed probable that he, or some earlier chronicler whom he reproduces, is working up into a permanent form material current in the Franciscan convents of Umbria, and that his story does contain some true elements, including the reminiscences of friars who had known Jacopone or his contemporaries. Naturally enough, those " trustworthy old brothers " remembered and loved to describe the oddities and ecstasies of their distinguished companion, and passed lightly over the more controversial aspects of his life. For them, he now shared the glamour which hung about the great Franciscans of the first generation. He was become a heroic figure, a " perfect friar," whose very peculiarities added lustre to the history of the Order: for religious communities, so intolerant of extravagances in their living members, will forgive almost any excesses in their departed saints. It was therefore possible for the original author of the *Vita*—probably a Conventual friar of real religious enthusiasm—to take pride in the Blessed Jacopone's ardours for the " true observance of the rule of St. Francis " and his tender love for Holy Poverty; whilst forgetting that this fervour had once at least led him to leave his convent, and ally himself with those insurgent friars who sought a literal fulfilment of the primitive ideal.

Taking it then as a whole, in spite of its distortions, limitations and probable accretions, the *Vita* does enrich our conception of Jacopone, and helps us to understand the personality revealed in his poems. It bears much the same relation to the historical Jacopone as the *Fioretti* does to the historical First Companions. That is to say, it is a legend, working up and elaborating older traditions, which we cannot trust as to matters of fact, but which is priceless as a record of the temperament

B

of its hero and the general impression which he left
behind. As we study this legend and these poems side
by side, the picture of a real man at last emerges
from them: a vigorous human personality, capable
both of sublime spirituality and extravagant action,
whose eccentricities and inconsistencies of character
remind us far more of the wayward creations of life
than of the pious fictions of conventional hagiography.
If the satirical poems harmonise with the known facts
of Jacopone's political career, the mystical and devo-
tional poems harmonise with the figure which the *Vita*
presents. Though our use of it, then, can only be tenta-
tive, we are justified in accepting those of its statements
which the testimony of the documents does not contra-
dict, and which agree with the evidence gathered from
the genuine *laude*.

Thus, our first three groups of material can all con-
tribute something to a reconstruction of Jacopone's life
and personality. But they must be used in relation to
one another, as mutual correctives, if we are to extract
from them all that they are able to give; and must con-
stantly be checked by the results of our general study of
the psychology of the mystics, and of the spiritual and
ascetic tradition of the Church in which they were
reared. Above all, they must be studied in closest con-
nection with the last class of material which is avail-
able; for their true meaning will only be understood,
and their proportion correctly estimated, in so far as we
are able to replace documents, poems and legend in the
surroundings among which they arose, and see Jacopone
against the background of his own time and place.
Lovers of the mystics too often forget that their lives
have a local and temporal as well as an eternal setting,
and can never be understood without reference to the
history of the world in which they lived, the peculiar
racial, intellectual and religious influences to which
they were exposed. In the case of Jacopone, such a

neglect of history is specially dangerous. He was conditioned at every point by the political, intellectual and spiritual tendencies of the life in which he was immersed; and without at least some knowledge of that life, any real comprehension of his poems is impossible. We need to know something of the circumstances in which those poems were written; the social order in which their author grew to maturity, the state of the Franciscan family when he entered it, the relation between its ideals and its average practice, the mental and spiritual food which he found there, the true condition of the Church which he so bitterly upbraided, and of the people whom he so passionately urged to a change of heart and a closer communion with God. We must remove him from the special class of " mystical poets " where so many ardent human souls are kept in spiritual quarantine, and replace him in the restless, intense, and coloured life of mediæval Italy.

Jacopone was born at Todi of an old Umbrian family, and the greater part of his life was spent in his native province. There he lived first the secular life of the crowded hill-towns; with their vigorous internal politics, perpetually tossed backwards and forwards between the Emperor and the Pope, their turbulence, luxury, and love of display, their elaborate cultivation of the senses. There he renounced the world and the social order to which he belonged, and became a roving apostle of the Spirit. There he at last accepted the organised life of religion, and entered that family of Friars Minor which has been the great gift of Umbrian religious genius to the world. His topographical background, then, is thirteenth-century Umbria; a land of violent contrasts, of strong and highly-organised material life tempered and opposed by a strong and ardent spirituality. He was conditioned, not only by the circumstances of local civic life and religious feeling, but also by the special

influences which emanate from the Umbrian landscape,
the strongly marked characteristics of the Umbrian type.
His genius, first developed by the rich human life of
the city, then enlarged and purified by years of hard-
ship, loneliness, and meditation,—when the sharp-cut
figure of the prosperous lawyer seems as it were to sink
into the landscape, and become part of the spirit of
place—reaches its height when disciplined by subjection
to the Franciscan rule, and contact with those who
still observed it in its purity. He represents the pecu-
liar tendencies and special religious temper of the
Umbrian type: its vehemence and tenderness, the
penitential and mystical moods, the reading of life at
once so intimate, so transcendental, so austere, which
is clearly expressed in its later art.

Yet this does not mean that we are to expect from
him merely the half-legendary charm which delights us
in the *Fioretti*, or the serene outlook of Perugino's
saints. That soft and dreamy quality, that deceptive
air of holy fairy tale, gives only one aspect of Umbrian
religious feeling, as its secular equivalent gives only
one aspect of Umbrian social life. There is another side
—the side which produced in Jacopone's day the great
penitential processions and savage mortifications of
the Flagellants, and afterwards found expression in the
paintings of Niccolò da Foligno, and the terrible banners
painted at Perugia during the years of pestilence. In
these we see the anguished intensity of a religious
emotion which is based upon penitence, which recog-
nises the wickedness and disharmony of human life,
and is perhaps more deeply conscious of the sin of man
than it is of the beauty of God.

Of these balanced moods of the Umbrian soul—its
instinct for purification on the one hand and for illumi-
nation on the other—St. Francis is the perfect repre-
sentative. He sums up the transcendental instincts of
mediæval Umbria, and shows in action its latent

capacity for God. Therefore, if the first great fact about Jacopone be his Umbrian nationality, the second is that he appeared in the full Franciscan epoch, at the moment when the Umbrian religious genius had flowered: that the power of the Franciscan revival was present, to condition the development of his soul. The preaching of the early friars—even of those who can hardly be said to share the Founder's peculiar secret—had an intensity, a spiritual passion, quite different from that achieved by the ordinary revivalist. Those of them who inherited the true Franciscan fervour regarded themselves as the apostles of a new dispensation. Hence their preaching—which must have been the outstanding religious phenomenon of Jacopone's youth—was always a missionary appeal; on the one hand for moral regeneration, on the other, for personal devotion, the religion of the heart. Like the early Methodists, the friars represented, in doctrine if not always in life, a return to spiritual actuality, to direct spiritual experience; and therefore drew to themselves all that was true and ardent in the religious life of their time. For all practical purposes, personal religion in thirteenth-century Italy meant a surrender to the Franciscan demand, a religion of the Franciscan type: the enthusiastic penitence and love, the renunciation and self-abasement, the simple and unquestioning response to the demands of the Gospel, the ardent devotion to Christ, which had governed the life of Francis, and which the preaching of the friars brought now into every town and village. Jacopone, brought up in Todi, where a household of Minorites had been founded by St. Francis himself, spent not merely his religious life but much of his secular life too in an environment saturated in this Franciscan spirit. It was inevitable that his conversion, when it took place, should be upon Franciscan lines. Moreover his life—intermediate between the first and second generation

of friars—coincided with the greatest, if most turbulent
period in the history of the Order; and he was con-
temporary with some of its most heroic personalities.
During his early manhood he must have heard of the
death and canonisation of St. Clare.   In later life he
may perhaps have known the last survivors of the
primitive epoch—Leo, Rufino, Illuminato—and reached
out through their reminiscences to the spirit of St.
Francis himself.   Conrad of Offida and John of La
Verna, of whom we read in the *Fioretti*, were his friends.

The influence of Franciscanism upon him was two-
fold.   First, its ideal and mystical side was a perpetual
source of inspiration to him.   The life of love and
poverty which it proclaimed was already the raw
material of poetry.   In that atmosphere his soul could
live and breathe, and all his greatest poems are satu-
rated with it.   Secondly, the actual condition of the
Order during the second half of the thirteenth century
formed for nearly thirty years the concrete setting of
his religious life.   It is the discord between the ideal and
the actual which accounts for many of the inconsis-
tencies and harsh oppositions in his works; for the
simultaneous development in them of satire and rhap-
sody, for his own alternations between the controversial
and the mystical life.

The ideal side of Franciscanism centred, of course,
upon St. Francis himself and his early companions—
first that which they really were, and secondly that
which pious admiration already supposed them to be.
Jacopone drew from both these sources.   In the first
place, he accepted the view of the Seraphic Father
which was current amongst devout souls in his day;
and this view differed so widely from our own that it
is worth while to draw attention to it.   The modern
enthusiasm for St. Francis, which focusses attention
upon the simplicity, gaiety, and sweetness of his char-
acter, upon his love of Nature and hatred of posses-

sions, but passes lightly over the supernatural aspects of his life, gives us no clue to the character of his overwhelming religious influence. If, however, we are to understand what his career meant to Catholic Christians of that time and place, we must try to see it, not with the admiring and sophisticated eyes of the twentieth century, but with the simpler and more religious vision of the thirteenth. Contemporary references prove to us that Francis, who seemed to himself "a little poor man," and to his immediate followers the "friend and servant of God," had become for the friars of the next generation nothing less than a new manifestation of the Spirit of Christ; and hence, as it were, a saviour, a renewer of God's covenant with man. "First," says the opening chapter of the *Fioretti*, "needs must we consider how the glorious St. Francis in all the acts of his life was conformed to Christ the Blessed One." [1]

There was some excuse for this startling belief. A young man of twenty-four, a soldier and a troubadour, well known for his gaiety and charm, had suddenly walked out of a prosperous house in Assisi and put into practice all the counsels of the Gospel: not in the convenient surroundings of the cloister, but in the open country-side. He lived in poverty, taking no thought for the morrow. He preached to the poor and healed the sick. He considered the lilies, and spoke to the birds of their Father's love. He spent nights in ecstatic prayer. He was both romantic and ascetic, gay and earnest, loving and austere. Disciples had flocked to him; and from these he was said to have chosen an original band of twelve followers, who received from him a dower of new life and joy, as did the little group who left all to follow Christ. Men of all types—respectable citizens, poets, peasants, learned men—had surrendered to his influence, feeling that here they touched

[1] *Fioretti*, cap. i. It is hardly necessary to say that this engaging record contains much legendary matter, and represents a fourteenth-century view of the Saint.

again the real spirit of Jesus of Nazareth. To all of them he gave the rule of Christian perfection, enforcing its practice in the most literal and rigorous sense—" If thou wilt be perfect, go and sell that thou hast and give to the poor . . . and come and follow me." To all who did this in a spirit of simplicity he communicated his own wealth of ardour, happiness, and love.

There were two sides to the vision and teaching of Francis. On that which was turned towards the perfection and beauty of God, so vividly and joyously felt by him, his whole outlook was that of a great lover and poet: on the one hand rapturously aware of the Eternal shining and sounding in created things, and making all who accepted it divine; on the other " drunken with the love and compassion of Christ "—the beginning and end of romance. But on the side that was turned toward the sin and imperfection of man, Francis shared the austere and contrite vision of the Christian ascetic and penitent; perpetually conscious of the disharmony between human nature and the glory that had been revealed.[1] Like all the great Christian mystics, he wanted to reconcile these opposites: to purify and remake human nature, since only thus could it match and comprehend the unspeakable fairness of the Divine Nature. He was therefore a stern preacher of repentance, no less than a minstrel of Perfect Joy. Love of God, he said, must involve hatred of self. Humility carried to the extreme point of self-depreciation was the only state of those who had heard the music of reality. Poverty, the keystone of the Franciscan scheme, was this humility in action, a sacrament of liberation " whereby all earthly things and fleeting are trodden underfoot, and whereby all hindrances are lifted from the soul, so that freely she may join herself to God Eternal." [2]

[1] *Cf.* T. of Celano, *Vita Prima*, caps. **x** , xi.
[2] *Fioretti*, cap. xiii. There is no doubt that this is true to the spirit of St. Francis, if not to his words.

The Franciscan idea, then, had these three essential characters. It demanded complete and uncompromising poverty from the body, penitence from the soul, mystical love from the spirit of man. All these phases in the total act of self-surrender must be taken into account, if we are to realise it as it existed in the mind of Francis: and all these form part of the spiritual atmosphere in which Jacopone's religious genius developed. When we think of St. Francis, we involuntarily lay stress on the beautiful and joyful side of his character and message, the God-inhabited world in which he lived. We remember the sweet tales of the *Fioretti*, the heavenly music, the birds and the flowers. We forget the degrading penances, the repulsive incidents connected with lepers, rags, and lice. But this one-sided appreciation distorts the real Franciscan ideal which Francis taught, which Leo and his followers maintained in the teeth of opposition, and which Jacopone celebrates in his poems: an idea which included and reconciled the extremes of "world denial" and "world renewal," of adoration and contrition, love and pain—the exaggerated mortifications of the professional penitent, the self-abasement of the extreme ascetic, no less than the merry joy of the troubadours of God, and the sweetness of friendship with all natural things.[1] Of this three-fold reaction to Divine Love, Jacopone is one of the greatest interpreters. It undoubtedly conditioned his spiritual development: each aspect of it is developed in his poems: and our understanding of these poems, with their abrupt alternations of feeling, depends on our possession of this clue—our grasp of the intimate connection which existed for him between penitential self-abasement and ecstatic

---

[1] See, amongst other places, *Speculum*, cap. lxi.; T. of Celano, *Vita Prima*, caps. xv. and xix.; *Vita Secunda*, Pars I., cap. xiv. The question of the historical value of these documents, which is still under discussion, does not affect the argument. They present a view of Francis which was certainly current in Jacopone's day, and as certainly accepted by him.

love. His Christianity is both ascetic and mystical; and as with St. Francis, the principle of Holy Poverty is the link between these two sides of his spiritual life. By turns a penitent, a " fool for Christ's sake," a missionary preacher, a popular singer, and a mystical poet, he seems to have passed through all the great phases of Franciscan feeling. In his songs we find the stern moral demands and the rapturous joy, the sense of liberation and the intimate passion for Christ, which marked the revival at its best. Above all, he is the poet of spiritual poverty, that grace of which outward poverty is the sacrament; the giving up of self-hood, all separate sense of ownership, in order that we may share everything with God. The songs in which he praises it are the best commentaries which we possess upon the Primitive Rule.

The pure Franciscanism of Francis is, then, the fountain from which Jacopone drank most deeply. But if this great source of strength and inspiration lay behind him, it was the troubled and divided Franciscanism of the second generation which lay around him; and which provided the setting of his religious career. As St. Paul was conditioned both by the primitive spirit and by the ecclesiastical developments of Christianity, so Jacopone was conditioned both by the primitive spirit and by the institutional developments of the Minorites. At the time of his admission, the Franciscan Order had already split upon the rock of poverty. The bulk of the friars, comfortably housed in convents, followed the mitigated rule of the astute Brother Elias and his successors. A handful of enthusiasts, the so-called " Spirituals " or *Zelanti*, tried in the teeth of persecution to keep alive the primitive fire.[1] To this party Jacopone belonged during at least the last twenty years of his life, and his later poems constitute the noblest and fullest expression of the Spiritual

[1] This movement is fully discussed below, ch. v.

ideals which we possess. It was for this, the pure and active spirituality of Francis, that he struggled throughout his convert-life: sometimes by the great arts of prayer and poetry, sometimes by the more doubtful methods of conflict, satire, and denunciation.

We see then that the study of Franciscan history— the immediate background of his religious career— throws considerable light upon Jacopone's life and poems. So too does a consideration of his wider environment; the world in which he lived, as it seemed to be in the eyes of his contemporaries. The thirteenth century has often been described as above all things an age of faith. We think of its saints, cathedral-builders, and theologians: of the strong religious temper of its art. But it seemed to the best of those who lived in it hopelessly corrupt; riddled with dreadful sins, given over to luxuries, formalism, heresies, violence, and intellectual pride.[1] Both the angels and the devils of the Gothic cathedrals had their counterparts in the life from which those cathedrals arose: and it was the power and prevalence of evil which chiefly impressed contemporary imagination. The religious atmosphere was full of apocalyptic fancies; many believed that such decay as they saw around them could only end in death, and that Antichrist and the last days were at hand.

> Hora novissima, tempora pessima sunt; vigilemus
> ecce minaciter imminet arbiter ille supremus.[2]

This—the recurring note of Bernard's great poem— was not a morbid fancy, but the considered opinion of serious men: a fact which helps us to understand on the one hand the love of the *macabre*, the grimly realistic treatment of death and corruption so strongly marked in much thirteenth-century art, on the other the many stories of abrupt conversion, the curious outbursts of

---

[1] See in Coulton's *St. Francis to Dante*, pp. 55–57, an ab'e if one-sided digest of the evidence on this point.
[2] Bernard of Morlaix. Cf. *Hymns Ancient and Modern*, No. 226.

penitential enthusiasm which distinguish the history of thirteenth-century religion. We have the habit of looking upon the friars as in some sense characteristic of their period. But they seemed to themselves, and to all their worthier contemporaries, to be "saviours of society," revivalists protesting against the spirit of their age. Jacques de Vitry, writing whilst St. Francis was still alive, called them "the revivers of religion, which had almost died out of a world whose eventide was come and whose sunset was near: and which was threatened by the coming of Antichrist, Son of Perdition." [1] The best of them sought to bring back the living flame of devotion to this evil and degenerate world: to redeem a time which St. Francis himself— that "sunny optimist" of modern sentimentalism— had described as overflowing with malice and iniquity.

It is true that when Jacopone was young St. Louis was King of France. But the brilliant pagan Frederick II., with his Saracens, his harem, his court of poets, his wild beasts and his dancing girls, was Emperor; and appeared in the eyes of his contemporaries a far more significant emblem of the secular power. Learning was still the servant of the Church. Albertus Magnus was at the height of his career: St. Thomas Aquinas was teaching in the schools of Paris. But though the *Summa* is the work of a great intellect wholly consecrated to the service of God, amongst theologians as a whole—even amongst the friars themselves—intellectual disputations and all the delights and subtleties of the new learning tended to obscure rather than reinforce the religion of the heart.

> O' son gli dottori pien de prudenza?
> molti ne veggio saliti en scienza;
> ma la lor vita non m'ha convenenza,
> dato m'on calci che 'l cor m'ha corato.[2]

---

[1] Jacques de Vitry, *Historia Occidentalis*, cap. xxxiii.
[2] *Lauda LIII.*, "Piange la Ecclesia." See p. 432.

Moreover, it was a time of violent and cunning political activities, of cruel and perpetual wars; in both of which the popes took a great, though not always a noble share. Jacopone, the span of whose life covered the reigns of seventeen pontiffs, from Gregory IX. to Benedict XI., saw many phases of that great but unedifying quarrel between the Empire and the Papacy which was then at its height, and which divided the whole of Italy into opposing camps. In the period before his conversion, he saw the excommunication of Frederick II. by that hard-headed Vicar of Christ, Innocent IV., his death in 1250, and the wars that followed it: the short reign of Manfred, the mad and terrible career of Ezzelino da Romano, the victory of the Ghibellines at Montaperti (1260), the coming of Charles of Anjou, and the defeats of Manfred and Corradino. War was then the normal state of the Italian cities. Each had a rival next door, and civil conflict within. The nobles and rich burgesses, who generally stood for the Empire, were opposed by the people's faction, nominally Guelph. In Todi, though it was a city of the Papal States, the dominant class was Ghibelline in its sympathies. The luxurious and secular civilisation fostered by Frederick II. appealed to the temperament of its prosperous citizens. There, the coarse jests and scandalous lampoons at the expense of the ecclesiastical party which delighted the Imperialists, must have been familiar to Jacopone from childhood. There, perhaps, he may have acquired his first bias against Papal politics, his distrust of the Curia and its works: that definitely critical attitude towards the official Church which distinguished his later career.

Though it is certain that some at least of the popes whom he knew were good men, having the interests of religion at heart and struggling against intolerable difficulties; yet the methods by which even these furthered the Kingdom of God were at best more businesslike than supernatural, and at worst shared the most vile characteristics of worldly diplomacy. Such a sudden gust of transcendentalism as that which placed the saintly old hermit Pier da Morrone upon the throne as Celestine V., only brought into sharper relief the general departure from spiritual ideals. The election of Celestine had been preceded by a long interregnum, filled by the ignoble squabbles of the cardinals. It was followed by a revulsion to ecclesiastical worldliness in the person of Boniface VIII., and by the insurrection and defeat of the Colonna cardinals—events in all of which Jacopone was intimately concerned.[1] Such things tended to discredit the Church as a spiritual power in the eyes of many serious people. It was freely criticised, even violently assailed. The average level of clerical morals was looked upon—and with good reason—as degenerate. Priests of evil life were so common, that often honest women dared not enter the confessional. Jacopone in his satires says that Christ weeps because of the ungrateful Roman Church; that her unworthy priesthood murders Him afresh, and wastes the fruits of His labours for men.[2] Nor did this represent the view of the laity alone: that which Jacopone sang St. Bonaventura had already said in equally direct and violent terms.[3] Pride, lechery, and avarice, says Roger Bacon again—writing in 1271, whilst Albert, Aquinas, and Bonaventura were still in life—are the special characteristics of the clergy.

It is true that the laments upon this subject which we find in contemporary writers must not all be taken literally. Some represent the slanders of political adversaries, others are the inevitable complaints of the enthusiastic Christian, the impassioned lover of God, against the low general level of religious ideals and

[1] See below, ch. v.
[2] *Lauda LII.*, " Jesu Cristo se lamenta."
[3] His observations will be found summarised in Coulton, *St. Francis to Dante*, ch. xxiii.

observance. Such denunciations are not peculiar to Jacopone's time, but have been common form throughout the history of Christian institutions. They represent the inevitable disparity between the ardent vision of perfection possessed by the regenerated spirit, and the tepid, imperfect practice of the crowd. Jacopone's cry, " Jesu Cristo se lamenta de la Chiesa romana," [1] might have been raised at any moment in the life of the Church. St. Bernard and St. Hildegarde scolded the twelfth century, Dante and St. Catherine of Siena scolded the fourteenth, as violently as the Franciscan Spirituals denounced their own period. At the same time, the special frequency of these passages in thirteenth-century literature, the known abuses and weaknesses of the Papal court, the appalling anecdotes in Salimbene, Bonaventura, and other writers of the time, the details of contemporary manners which are often given,[2] does suggest that ecclesiastical and social morals were not at a high level. The Catharist heresy, which infested Italy at this period, drew its strength from this general ecclesiastical and moral corruption. The heretics, as even their adversaries were compelled to admit, were distinguished by the purity of their lives, the sweetness and sincerity of their preaching, their gentle spirit of love for all living things.[3] Though the orthodox insisted that their doctrines led to a loosening of morals, they were originally puritans, whose manners contrasted strongly with the passionate cult of luxury and pleasure, the open sin and violence which characterised worldly society. The vanity and accomplished worldliness of the women of his time is the theme of one of Jacopone's most amusing satires [4]:

[1] *Lauda LII.*
[2] For instance in the terrible first chapter of Thomas of Celano's *Vita Prima*, where the Umbrian citizens are charged with deliberately educating their children in vice.
[3] *Cf.* Tamassia, *S. Francesco d'Assisi*, cap. i.
[4] *Lauda VIII.*, " O femene, guardate."

he dwells frequently on the avarice and self-indulgence
of the men. But these were only symptoms of a general
departure from Christian ideals. "Truth weeps because
Goodness is dead ": the laws of Moses and of Christ
are alike broken, the virtues forgotten, the sacraments
neglected, the gifts of the Spirit despised. The life of
the religious is as dust in the wind.[1] Strange picture of
the " age of faith " drawn by a contemporary hand!

To sum up. We see that Jacopone's life and poetry
was profoundly influenced by the time and place in
which he lived: that although a man of wide culture
and of intensely individual outlook, he is on one side of
his nature a popular poet, representing and taking
colour from the spirit of his age. We see that he was
conditioned first by his Umbrian nationality, next by
his university education and legal profession, last and
most by his connection with that Franciscan Order
which was born and developed upon Umbrian soil: that
whilst on the one hand he understood and re-inter-
preted the teaching of St. Francis, with its three-fold
demand for penitence, poverty, and adoration, on the
other hand the tension and disharmony which had
arisen within the Order—the struggle between the
primitive ideal and the institutional spirit—are also
reflected in his work. Further, as regards the wider
world of mediæval thought and life, Jacopone shows us
this both on its darkest and fairest, on its simplest and
most learned side. Its sins and fears and glooms, its
mysticism and its homeliness, its gross and its gracious
aspects are all here. His early life and probable resi-
dence at the University of Bologna—the heart of in-
tellectual Italy—the nascent school of poets with
which he must there have come in contact, his legal
training and practice, the knowledge of men and
women it brought him, have all influenced his verse.
His satirical poems and known actions prove how

[1] *Lauda LI.*, " La Veritade piange."

keenly he watched, how deeply he was affected by, the outward events of the time: the vicissitudes of the Papacy, the growth of the new learning, the general condition of the Church. He touches the common life at all points, as a good Franciscan should. In this his own life is deeply rooted, and out of it his personality develops. We must now consider, so far as the evidence will let us, what that life and personality were like.

CHAPTER II

SER JACOMO

Jacopone's origin—Infancy—Childish memories—Education—The University of Bologna—Early literary influences—Professional life —Worldly tastes—Marriage—The account of the *Vita*—Story of the death of Vanna—Jacopone's conversion.

JACOPONE was born in the city of Todi, an ancient and beautiful hill-town lying due south of Perugia on the way to Rome. He came of the family of the Benedetti; apparently members of the lesser Umbrian aristocracy, though they are called by Modio " molto nobile." His father, who is said to have been a landowner, possessing an estate—probably a farm—at Spagliagrano outside the city walls,[1] also practised as a notary in Todi: at that time not an unusual profession for persons of good birth and small possessions, for it opened the way to many rich appointments. This circumstance, coupled with the fact that Jacopone's extravagance and passion for keeping up appearances had practically exhausted the family resources by the time that he achieved manhood, suggests that the Benedetti belonged to the poorer nobility; and that life was for them, as for so many of the impoverished Italian houses, a continual struggle to adjust the claims of their rank to the facts of their income. They were probably Ghibelline in politics, and worldly rather than devout in their ideals. In the poem which we are presently to consider, Jacopone describes his father as a stern, unlovable man, very careful of his money. Of his mother we know

[1] P. Alvi, *Jacopone da Todi, cenni storici.*

34

nothing, beyond one little vivid picture of her rising in
the night to tend her fretful baby:

Con frigo suffrire
staendo a servire;—[1]

but that is surely a picture drawn by the hand of love.

Jacopone, whose true name in the world was Jacomo,
is believed to have been the eldest of their three sons.
The date of his birth is uncertain: we can only say that
it took place between the years 1228 and 1236, and
probably about 1230. We possess one poem in which
he has apparently described his own childhood and
youth, as it seemed to him in retrospect: the cele-
brated " O vita penosa," which has been freely and
sometimes uncritically used by most of his modern bio-
graphers. The exact biographical value of this *lauda*,
which describes in a mood of intense pessimism the
squalors, futilities and disappointments incident to the
whole course of human life from birth to death, is very
difficult to determine. The last half of it, at any rate,
is mere generalisation; and only in the first fifteen
verses can we reasonably look for personal remini-
scence. At best, like the earlier chapters of St. Augus-
tine's *Confessions*—upon which, indeed, it may have
been modelled—it shows us Jacomo the normal human
boy and agreeably worldly young man, as seen in
retrospect through the temperament of Jacopone the
penitent and ascetic. Yet, when we have made allow-
ance for the inevitable loss of proportion involved in
this point of view, the picture which it gives is wonder-
fully vivid, full of atmosphere, of small intimate touches.
It tallies so well, too, with our knowledge of Jacopone's
character—that vehemence, intensity of feeling, and
tendency to extravagant action which was responsible
for both the adventures and disasters of his later life—
that we cannot help feeling that he was indeed drawing

[1] *Lauda XXIV.*, " O vita penosa."

upon his own memories of the past, though purporting to give an ideal picture of the troubles and follies of man.

Life, says Jacopone in this disheartening song, is a continual worry, a perpetual disappointment; and its annoyances begin even before birth. Like Innocent III. in *De Contemptu Mundi*—a popular thirteenth-century tract which he had probably read—he dwells with unsparing realism on the circumstances of human generation, and the least agreeable aspects of infancy. This was a favourite subject with mediæval writers and preachers: but Jacopone gives it new life by treating it from the personal point of view. His own birth, he says, was hard, and his babyhood delicate. His mother had many tales to tell of the difficulty with which she reared him. Often, fearing that he must be ill, she would get up in the night to soothe his persistent cries: only to find that nothing was the matter after all.

> Ella, pensando ch'io male avesse,
> che non me moresse
> tutta tremava:
> era besogno che lume accendesse
> e me scopresse,
> e poi me mirava,
> e non trovava
> nulla sembianza
> de mia lamentanza
> perché fosse stata.[1]

> (She, deeming that I suffered from some ill,
> All trembling still,
> And fearing I must die,
> Would light her little lamp, with tender thrill,
> Turn down the coverlet, and gaze her fill,
> Seeing me sleeping lie.
> And for my cry
> No evil cause she sees;
> She heaves a sigh,
> Her heart may be at ease.)

The tiresome baby grew up to be a strong-willed and

[1] *Lauda XXIV.*, " O vita penosa."

undisciplined child; full of energy, hating all constraint.
Like the little Augustine,[1] he found the beginnings of
education excessively painful. His father's harsh
methods and constant thrashings filled him with terror:

> Se non emprenda quel ch'era emposto
> davame 'l costo
> de gran battetura.

> (Did I neglect the task he would impose,
> With heavy blows
> He made me pay the cost.)

He longed to play and fight with the other boys whom
he saw in the street; for that passion for life, which
even the cloister could not kill—the tendency to action,
conflict, self-realisation—was already beginning to stir
in him. But if he did not go to school he was caned.
" O vita penosa, continua battaglia," which presses so
hardly upon high-spirited little boys. Jacomo often
wished that his father would die, so that he might
escape these miseries and have his own way; a dreadful
crime to remember in later life. Even in these early
days submission to authority, in which at last he found
the only way of release from his turbulent self-hood,
was a difficulty to him.

When his taste for street-fighting was allowed to
assert itself, there were no half measures. The child
who was afterwards to withstand the Pope, the embryo
mystic who was to take heaven by violence in a fury of
love, already knew the charm and value of decisive
action. He fought with all his power; tore out hand-
fuls of hair, and received cuffs in exchange. Often he
was knocked down and trampled upon, " like the
grapes in the vat "—a feeling description, which cer-
tainly suggests vivid youthful memories. The picture
left upon our minds of Jacomo the boy is that of
a vehement little human animal; hard to control,

[1] Aug., Conf., i., 9.

intensely alive, violently pugnacious, full of unrealised possibilities.

Growing up, there is little doubt that he would be sent—perhaps at about sixteen or seventeen years of age, perhaps later—to the University of Bologna, since he was intended for the legal profession. This, however, is a matter of deduction, not of certainty. Since the converted Jacopone regarded learning as dangerous to the soul's health,[1] he does not mention his academic career: though the many references to the Schools which are scattered through his poems show how familiar to him were the common features of University life. He tells us only how he distressed his father by his gambling, his passion for high life, and other extravagances; tastes which were probably developed during these student years. The idle, quarrelsome, and unmanageable little boy had become a wild and high-spirited young man, loving fine clothes and costly amusements. He was vain and arrogant; and wanted to rival every one in the splendour of his dress, the feasts he gave, the fine company he kept. In the place of street-fighting there were now the quarrels and vendettas of the students. These were sometimes carried to such lengths that the victim was afraid to show himself in the streets lest he should meet his adversary on the way; and became a voluntary prisoner in his own house.[2]

Seen in retrospect by an elderly penitent, such a life seemed a mere orgy of worldliness, folly, and sin. Yet here, in this time of apparent dissipation but actual human growth—of frolics and duels, songs and satires, and every kind of excess, of intellectual keenness and exuberant physical energy—we must look for the beginnings of Jacopone's creative powers; not only for the source of that richly developed humanity, that

---

[1] *Laude XVII.*, " Frate Ranaldo," and *XXXI.*, " Tale qual è, tal è."
[2] *Lauda XXIV.*, " O vita penosa."

freakish humour, which afterwards gave such point to his satires and homilies, but also for the origin of the fine taste, the eager thirst for beauty, which flowered in his praises of the First and only Fair. That perpetual demand for completeness of life, that unquietness of heart which gave him no rest until at last it drove him back to God, was now seeking for satisfaction in worldly pleasures. The embryo poet who was afterwards proud to call himself " crazy for Messiah's sake," [1] was already intoxicated by the splendour and rapid movement of existence. The sour phrases in which Thomas of Celano describes the more innocent youth of St. Francis would probably serve for a description of him at this time. " Almost until the twenty-fifth year of his age he miserably squandered and wasted his time. Nay, surpassing all his coevals in his bad progress in vanity, he proved in more abundant measure an instigator of evil deeds, and a zealot in folly. He was the admiration of all, and in pomp of vain glory he strove to surpass the rest in frolics, freaks, sallies of wit, idle talk, songs, and soft and flowing attire." [2]

The old mystical saying that " the height of the divinity must be equalled by the deeps of the humanity " is true of every saint. Nothing less than the whole man—all his rich faculties of body, soul, and spirit tempered and matured by the pressure of existence—is needed for the achievement of Eternal Life.

> La bontate enfinita
> vol enfinito amore,
> mente, senno e core
> lo tempo e l'esser dato.[3]

(That perfect Good which hath no end
Demands of us a love complete:
Mind, sense and heart, all at His feet,
Our life in time, our very selves to spend.)

[1] *Lauda LXXXIV.*, " Senno me pare."
[2] *Vita Prima*, cap. i.
[3] *Lauda LXXIX.*, " La bontate enfinita."

A rich and complete human experience, a fully-developed
physical, emotional and intellectual life, was the founda-
tion from which Jacopone climbed up to those heights
where he had communion with the Eternal Order and
satisfied at last his craving for perfection. Thither he
carried a warmth of human feeling, a passionate energy,
a romantic fervour, which represent the spiritualisation
of qualities developed not in the cloister but in the
world.

But the colour and turbulence of student life was
only a part of the gift which Bologna could make to
him. At this time the second University of Europe,
excelled only by Paris, and far superior to Oxford both
in size and importance, it was the heart of intellectual
Italy; a forcing-house for the mental life. All new
ideas, all literary fashions, all philosophic theories,
came quickly to Bologna; and were there tested and
discussed. There, some of the first experiments in
Italian poetry were made. In Bologna, Jacomo would
study the Liberal Arts, be schooled in those rules of
logic of which he afterwards spoke with such con-
tempt, and attend lectures in literature and philosophy.
Thence perhaps come the references to the doctrines of
Plato and Aristotle which we find in his philosophic
poems. Chiefly, however, he would study Civil and
Canon Law, with their countless rules and precedents; as
contained in the Code and Pandects of Justinian, and
in Gratian's Decretals. This course lasted six years: at
the end of it, the successful student took the degree of
Bachelor of Law. To become a Doctor, further studies,
extended over six or seven years more, were necessary.
Jacomo's connection with Bologna would therefore
last until he was at least twenty-two, perhaps even
until he was twenty-eight or thirty years of age: since
Modio, who wrote in 1518, and whose biography seems
to be based upon a version of the *Vita* which has not
come down to us, speaks of him as a Doctor of Law

and a "very learned man." There, during the most formative years of life, his responsive mind would be exposed to all the influences of contemporary culture. There he would learn the arts of music and poetry. He would hear, and perhaps try to imitate, the first songs of the Sicilian school of poets; who were now applying the literary methods of the French troubadours to the Italian vernacular, and thus laying the foundations of the national literature. One of these poets, the unhappy King Enzio, was a captive in Bologna during the years in which Jacomo most probably studied there; and wrote from his gaol sweet and skilful verses in the Sicilian manner, thin perhaps in idea, but exquisite in melody, which seem like the laments of an imprisoned bird. With a pathos far removed from the usual polished insincerity of the Court poets, Enzio sang of his captivity:

> Va, canzonetta mia
> e saluta messere,
> dilli lo mal ch'i' aggio:
> quelli che m'a 'n bailia
> sì distretto mi tene,
> ch'io viver non poraggio.
>
> (Go, little song of mine,
> Go and salute my Lord.
> Tell him my grief and pain.
> So harsh is the rule and malign
> Of those who have me in ward
> I struggle to live in vain.)

Perhaps it was of this that the old poet of Todi was thinking when he wrote, long afterwards, the terrible song which celebrates his own imprisonment at Palestrina.[1]

But another and far greater poet than Enzio, Guido Guinizelli, the founder of the *dolce stil nuovo*, was now growing up in Bologna. Guido, whose early work is hardly to be distinguished from that of the Court poets, passed from this artificial style, with its perpetual

---

[1] *Lauda LV.*, " Que farai, Fra *I*acopone? "

dexterous rearrangements of emotional commonplaces, to a more real and human manner; a deeper and richer conception of the function of poetry, a fresh contact with life. He is called by Dante the father of all those who sing of love;[1] and it may perhaps have been from him that Jacomo—afterwards to become the first great Italian singer of the mystical passion of the soul—learned that Platonic doctrine of the trans-cendental character of love, which he afterwards turned to such sublime use in his spiritual songs. Guido repre-sents the transition in poetry from chivalry to idealism; from a personal and romantic to a universal and philo-sophic concept of love. Love, which was for the Sicilian school a well-understood and often a purely conven-tional relation between the poet and his lady, becomes for him a spiritual force, a holy thing, the native genius of the human heart.

> Al cor gentil ripara sempre amore
> com' a la selva augello in la verdura;
> né fe' amore avanti gentil core,
> né gentil core avanti amor, natura.

> (Within the gentle heart Love shelters him
> As birds within the green shade of the grove:
> Before the gentle heart, in Nature's scheme,
> Love was not, nor the gentle heart ere Love.)[2]

His poetry is the link between the troubadour songs and the *Vita Nuova*; beginning the process of trans-mutation which Dante was to complete.

Jacopone, in the developed work of his later life, brings to the praise of Divine Love both the accent of passionate and romantic devotion and the deep thoughts and wide vision of the philosophic poets.[3] His *laude* indicate first some knowledge of the Sicilian writers, secondly a deep and sympathetic understanding of the love poetry of Guido Guinizelli and his followers, thirdly a familiarity with metrical form which suggests

[1] *Purg.*, xxvi., 97.   [2] D. G. Rossetti.   [3] See below, ch. vi.

long practice in the writing of verse. It is reasonable to put the credit of these accomplishments to his residence in Bologna. There he would be present at the cradle of Italian poetry and spend his most impressionable years in an atmosphere of poetic enthusiasm. There he would acquire the technical dexterity and the strong philosophic bent which characterise the best of his later works. Thence too may come the memories of Romance literature which decorate some of his songs, and some of the materials for those excursions into metaphysics which accord so oddly with his later Franciscan dread of " acquired knowledge."

His university career at an end, Ser Jacomo presumably returned to Todi; to find—if we may still trust the statements of " O vita penosa "—that his extravagance, his passionate efforts to be in the best set, had exhausted the family savings. Perhaps his father was now dead. At any rate, the income of their small estate was quite inadequate to the needs of life as conceived by the brilliant and ambitious son of the house.

> Non ce bastava niente el podere
> a recoprire
> le brighe presente.[1]
> (The little manor did not near suffice
> To yield the price
> Our year's expense to pay.)

His ambitions at this time appear indeed to have been purely social:

> Asti e paraggi, calzare e vestire,
> mangiare e bere
> e star fra la gente.[2]
> (Pleasure and dress, display and rivalry,
> To eat and drink, and be in company.)

and, no longer able to live in the style which he thought proper to his rank, he was ready to die of shame.[3]

But Jacomo was now a learned man—probably a

[1] *Lauda XXIV.*, " O vita penosa."   [2] *Loc. cit.*   [3] *Ibid.*

Doctor of Law—with a lucrative profession at his dis-
posal. It was well within his power to rebuild the family
fortunes if he chose: and his own luxurious tastes,
which only money could satisfy, were a powerful in-
centive to diligence. There is therefore no inherent
improbability in the statement of the legendary *Vita*
that he now became a *procuratore*, or attorney; an
occupation which is described by the writer as " so full
of dangers, that those who have not a very keen con-
science may be brought by it to eternal damnation."
According to the same authority, Jacomo settled
down to the business of money-making with the same
zest that he had brought to the pursuit of pleasure.
The *Vita* gives a bad account of his professional years.
He was, it says, " proud and avaricious, wrapped up in
the vices and lusts of this world; the which held him
in so great a blindness that not only did he ignore God,
but was His adversary, the enemy and persecutor of
all those who would walk in godly ways." It is possible,
however, that this picture is a little overdrawn. As
Thomas of Celano exaggerates the youthful sins of St.
Francis, in order that his subsequent holiness may be
thrown into sharper relief,[1] so the author of the *Vita* is
here aiming at dramatic effect; trying to make plain
the contrast between Ser Jacomo the lover of this
world, and Fra Jacopone the child of grace. When we
consult the poems in which Jacopone pours out his
own contrition for the past, we find that he has no very
startling sins of which to accuse himself. If *Lauda XXI.*,[2]
with its description of the dying sinner's unavailing
repentance, can be taken as in any sense a personal
confession—which is extremely doubtful—he seems
there to suggest that he practised usury; lending
money to the poor, not always with a strict regard to

[1] Compare T. of Celano, *Vita Prima*, cap. i., with the " Legend of
the Three Companions," which shows us Francis as a high-spirited but
innocent and pure-minded boy.
[2] " O Cristo pietoso."

honesty. In another, more personal poem, he tells us that, like many other skilful advocates, he was not very particular as to the rights of the cases which he argued; that he often paid more attention to his clients' interests than to those of strict justice, and liked to get the criminal off when he could. Seen in the mirror of Truth:

> Iustizia mia appare
> che sia un deguastare
> de virtute e de bontate;
> l' onor de Dio furato,
> lo innocente dannare,
> lo malfattor salvare
> e darglie libertate.[1]

But apart from these professional failings, Jacomo's worldliness appears to have been more comfortable than wicked. Town life in the thirteenth century offered many opportunities for luxury and delicate living. Ser Iacomo took full advantage of them. He liked ease and pleasure, and a certain beauty and order in his surroundings: loved fine clothes and a soft bed,[2] and was very particular about the way in which meals were served.[3] The frequent and appreciative references to nice food—" viva exquisita e nuove frutta "—and magnificent dress, prove that these were subjects in which he took great interest.[4] There is no end, he says, to the worries connected with eating if one wants tasty dishes. These preoccupations seemed to him quite reasonable and harmless. Physical well-being, a " good time," represented his idea of happiness.

> Lo mangiare e lo bere
> è stato el mio deletto,
> e posare e gaudere
> e dormire a lo letto;

---

[1] *Lauda XXXIX.*, " O vita de Iesú Cristo." See p. 306.
[2] *Lauda III.*, " Audite una 'ntenzone."
[3] *Lauda XXIV.*, " O vita penosa."
[4] *Loc. cit.* The passion for clothes comes out in many places. See especially *Laude XVIII.*, "Omo, tu se' engannato"; *XXIII.*, " Omo, méttete a pensare"; *XXIV.*, " O vita penosa"; and *XXV.*, " Quando t'alegri " (p. 268).

non credeva potere
aver nullo defetto;
or so morto e decepto,
ch'agio offeso al Signore.[1]

(These things were ever my delight—
To eat and drink unfailingly,
Enjoy or rest from morn till night,
And sleep in bed full slothfully:
And deeming all I did was right,
I thought there was no fault in me.
Now blind and dead myself I see,
For I have hurt and grieved my Lord.)

The vivid description of the discomforts of asceticism, as he experienced them in later life—hard pillows, bad nights and early rising, coarse food and resulting indigestion [2]—show the direction in which Jacomo's principal weaknesses lay. He was living to the full the life of the senses and intellect, at the expense of the life of the soul.

His attitude towards religion—both the established formalism of the Church, and the missionary intensity of the friars and other confraternities—was evidently one of indifference, touched perhaps with contempt. "La legge del Signore non avi en reverenza." [3] The great religious revival of 1260, when the young hermit Ranieri led processions of flagellants through the Umbrian towns, left him untouched.[4] Church-going bored him: when the others went to Mass, or to hear a sermon, he preferred to stay at home and have a good dinner and a little music.[5] Todi was Ghibelline in sympathy: the tendency of her more cultivated citizens would be towards a critical rather than respectful view of the regular clergy and their works. Jacomo, who came of an aristocratic stock, married into a Ghibelline house;

---

[1] *Lauda XX.*, " O me lasso, dolente."
[2] *Lauda III.*, " Audite una 'ntenzone."
[3] *Lauda XXXIX.*, " O vita de Iesú Cristo " (p. 306).
[4] For this movement see G. Galli, "I disciplinati dell'Umbria del 1260" (*Giorn. stor. della Lett. Italiana*, Supp. ix., 1906).
[5] *Lauda XX.*, " O me lasso, dolente."

and there is nothing in his life or poems to suggest that he had ever taken the Papal side. On the contrary, the hostile attitude towards the temporal power, the unsparing denunciation of clerical weaknesses, which are marked features of his satires, probably represent a survival and spiritualisation of the opinions and prejudices of his unconverted days. He was, then, at this time a normal prosperous cultivated man of the upper classes; shrewd, ambitious, intelligent, robustly human. He was both sensual and artistic. Fond of physical enjoyments and of luxurious living,[1] sociable and hospitable though thoroughly selfish at heart, he yet took great pleasure in music, was keenly appreciative of beauty and refinement, and may have continued— as did so many of the great lawyers of the thirteenth century—to practise poetry in his leisure hours. He liked to pay attention to good-looking women, but cast them aside without a scruple when they ceased to please his taste.[2] Coming of a noble family, with rapidly increasing wealth and reputation, and belonging to the most highly educated class of the community, his social aspirations were now fully satisfied. He was in Todi, as he had struggled to be in his student days, a person of importance and a member of the best set. His natural arrogance had full play:

> Per la mala ricchezza
> ch'a sto mondo agio avuta,
> so visso en tanta alteza,
> l'alma n'agio perduta.[3]
>
> (Because of all the evil gold
> That I in worldly wise did gain
> So great a pride did me enfold
> My soul was nearly slain.)

The turbulent human animal of childhood and early

---

[1] *Laude XXXIX.*, " O vita de Iesú Cristo," and *XXIV.*, " O vita penosa."

[2] *Lauda XX.*, " O me lasso, dolente."

[3] *Loc. cit.*

youth, which had struggled to satisfy its Titanic crav-
ing for fullness of life, was temporarily in abeyance.
His zest for living, his demand for opportunity of self-
expression, were fully met by the varied interests of
his social and professional life.

This period of Jacomo's career seems to have ended
in either 1265 or 1267—the later date being the most
probable—when he is presumed to have been thirty-
seven or thirty-eight years of age.   In one of these
years he was married to Vanna, daughter of Bernardino
di Guidone of the house of Coldimezzo: members, like
the Benedetti, of the lesser Umbrian aristocracy, and
Ghibelline in politics.[1] From a social point of view the
marriage was therefore suitable, and may have been
decided upon for this reason alone. Jacopone has told us
what he demanded of an ideal wife.[2] She must be
beautiful and healthy, well-bred and sweet-natured.
She must have a large dowry, and must not have a
nagging tongue. But, he adds, complete satisfaction is
only found in heaven, and he who seeks it here is a
thief. This suggests that his own experience fell short
somewhere: perhaps only in the matter of dowry,
since tradition speaks of his wife as young, beautiful,
and virtuous, winning and keeping her husband's love,
and we know that she came from a noble though perhaps
an impoverished house.

As the *Vita* is our only authority for the tragedy of
Jacomo's short married life, all that we can say of it
must be deduced from this doubtful source, qualified
by the scanty self-revelations of his poems. In those
poems, he never refers directly to his marriage. We
should hardly guess from them that human love had
ever come into his life; though the intensity of his
spiritual passion gives us a measure of his emotional

[1] The certificate of marriage was still in existence in the seventeenth
century, and was seen by the local historian Guazzaroni. *Cf.* D'Ancona,
Jacopone da Todi, p. 17.
[2] *Lauda XXIV.*, " O vita penosa."

quality, and we know that the great lover and the great mystic are closely akin. His married life lasted only for a year. The *Vita*, which we have already seen cause to suspect as a conventual document, says that it was passed "in all pleasures and vanities"; perhaps, too, in great and innocent happiness.

There may be personal reminiscence in the one appreciative description of womanhood in Jacopone's poems:

> Recordo d'una femena
> ch'era bianca, vermiglia,
> vestita, ornata, morbeda,
> ch'era una maraviglia;
> le sue belle fateze
> lo pensier m'asutiglia.[1]

> (I remember a woman
> Soft, rosy, and white;
> Fairly dressed and adorned,
> A marvel to the sight.
> Now I am tormented
> By thought of her delight.)

"He loved her most tenderly," says the author of the *Vita*, here suddenly displaying an unexpected gentleness towards human affections. We can imagine the completeness with which that vehement nature, which afterwards flung itself upon God as a wave upon a rock, might surrender itself to the glamour of love: the delight of that ardent poet in its divine playfulness, its mingled chivalry and intimacy.

Ser Jacomo was a shrewd and experienced man of the world, at once sensual and keenly intelligent. Vanna is described as a young unsullied girl, deeply religious, with an almost puritanical dread of luxury: a characteristic product of the Umbrian penitential movement. Ser Jacomo, whose best ideals were of the most earthly kind, wanted to spoil and pet her: to fill her life with gaiety and amusement. His taste

---

[1] *Lauda III.*, " Audite una 'ntenzone."

for fine clothes had now a new objective. He loved to
dress his beautiful wife in magnificent garments, and
see her taking her place in those social functions which
the *Vita* curtly dismisses as " vain doings." At first,
says the legend, Vanna resisted. She " feared God "
and distrusted earthly vanities; and tried to convert
her husband to her own ideals. There were scenes which
remind us of one of Jacopone's *tenzoni* between the
body and the soul. Vanna explained the beauty of
religion; Jacopone replied by a tempting selection of
dresses and jewellery. " Quella, che temiva dio, demo-
strava nelochi del marito ciò, e ser Jacomo che cussi
se chiamava mostra de vestementi e altre vanitade del
mondo." [1] Then Vanna, because it is the duty of a
wife to please her husband if she can, submitted and
wore the beautiful clothes. Probably Jacomo thought
that his conquest was complete, for she let him go his
own way, and never spoke to him again of her religious
convictions. But she was steadfast as well as discreet,
and continued in secret her life of prayer and mortifi-
cation; never letting him suspect her private austeri-
ties, but trying to atone for her outward worldliness—
and perhaps for his—by many acts of penance. Pos-
sibly the preaching of the friars, and processions of the
flagellants, their invitations to penitence, renunciation,
and simplicity of life, had touched her; so that already,
though he knew it not, the spirit of Francis was laying
siege to Jacopone's soul. Certainly, if the story told in
the *Vita* be true, his conversion must be regarded as the
direct result of Vanna's penances and prayers.

One day, when they had been married for a year,
Vanna, because it was Ser Jacomo's wish, went to a
marriage festival, " such as are customary in that
country." She was dressed and adorned with special
magnificence in order to do honour to her hosts. There
was dancing upon a balcony. Suddenly, when the ball

[1] *Vita,* 1vo.

was at its height, the balcony broke and fell. All the dancers were injured; Vanna alone was mortally hurt. According to one account, she was already dead when her husband was brought to her. In great bitterness of spirit, because he loved her very tenderly, he caused her body to be carried home; and there stripped off the garments of vanity, that it might be prepared for the grave. According to another version, which forms the basis of Modio's biography, he found her still living, though unable to speak. She was taken into a neighbouring house, and there he wished to unlace her, that he might find out the extent of her injuries: but she resisted as well as she could, begging him by signs to let her be.

The sequel is the same in both legends. " And when they took off those garments of vanity which she had upon her, in order to make her ready for the grave, they found at last next to her bare flesh a harsh shirt of hair." Thus Vanna had obeyed at once the wishes of her husband and the secret impulses of her own soul. The beautiful girl had been an ascetic at heart.[1] Her knowledge of life had been deeper than that of the brilliant Doctor of Law: she had known how to discern the real from the sham values, and had acted upon her knowledge. Ser Jacomo, standing by the body of the woman whom he had loved but never known, saw with amazement unexpected depths of existence and opportunities of suffering opening before him. The sweet and docile wife whom he thought that he loved and understood, whose life he had filled with luxuries and amusements, had never lived. In one moment he was enlightened, bereaved, and cruelly mortified. " Ah

[1] We must remember, however, that in the Middle Ages the hair-shirt was a common instrument of mortification among devout persons, and merely meant that Vanna took her religion very earnestly. Self-expression sought more vivid forms than the modern world seems able to tolerate. Those who would now be content with the medal of a guild or the uniform of the Salvation Army then demonstrated a change of heart by public scourging of their naked flesh.

me! a woman hath deceived me; for, considering that
life which she lived in outward appearance to be but
vanity, never by the smallest act did she reveal it." [1]
Hers had been the strong nature, and his the weak.
She had behaved to him with infinite kindness and
tolerance, satisfied his demands, indulged his fancies,
and quietly gone her own way.

The shock, says the legend, not only pierced Ser
Jacomo to the heart, but drove him out of his mind.
" Now, whether because of this strange death, or
whether because of the hidden life of virtue which she
had led, Ser Jacomo was by these things so stricken in
mind, his heart so pierced, and so estranged from all
his senses, that never again from that hour did he seem
the same perfectly rational man that he was before;
but as one witless and amazed he went to and fro
amongst the people. And feeling himself so greatly
moved both in body and in soul, he retreated within
himself, and, being recollected within his own heart,
there began in a marvellous manner, and helped by
divine light, to open his eyes and consider his past life,
how far it was from God's ways: also his own salvation,
and how formerly he had been blind and mad, the
which would doubtless precipitate him into hell." [2]

As we have seen, this celebrated tale, which Matthew
Arnold has used with such great effect in his sonnet on
" Austerity in Poetry," seems to have been unknown
to the earlier Franciscan chroniclers, and to the first
editor of Jacopone's poems. Critics are sharply divided
as to its authenticity. Our only evidence for it is the
Vita ; and the *Vita* as we have it, though it may be
based on earlier material, is at best a document of the
second class. The story itself is thoroughly characteris-
tic of life in thirteenth-century Umbria as we know it,
with its mingled worldliness and missionary fervour.
At the time when it is said to have happened, the Flagel-

---

[1] *Vita, loc. cit.*   [2] *Ibid.*

lant movement—which had deeply affected the Umbrian cities—was only a few years old: and the history of other revivals assures us that in such periods secret penitents and dramatic conversions abound. Our greatest difficulty in accepting it comes from the fact that its ultimate source can only be Jacopone himself: yet his poems contain no reference to his marriage, and we could not guess from them that human love and human tragedy had ever come into his life. Nevertheless, the character of his doctrine, the temper of his religion, do suggest the possibility of such an episode, as the determining fact of that turbulent career. The " perfect friar," the man of position and education, afterwards the friend of cardinals and leaders of religion, shows in his poetry a wildness, a want of balance, an ecstasy of contrition, which surely indicate great temperamental capacity for passion, consistent with some devastating emotional experience in his past. Those *laude* which internal evidence compels us to assign to his first period are the work of a passionate convert, a " twice-born " soul. He seems always to be rediscovering, with new tenderness and remorse, the crucifixion of love, the sacrificial pain of God, suffering at the very heart of loveliness. The storms of mystic love which characterise his middle period represent the sublimation of a passion which has its erotic side. It is true that his attitude towards women, as disclosed in these poems, is hostile and even contemptuous: which seems strange if he owed to a woman his initiation into the spiritual life. But we must remember that the great revulsion of feeling which accompanies adult conversion is most strongly marked in matters of sex. The mystics who find room for women in their world—St. Francis, Richard Rolle—are those who turn to God in early life. Converted worldlings cannot act thus: their break with the past must be complete. According to the degree in which Ser Jacomo had found women

attractive, would Fra Jacopone regard them as a snare:
nor could the absorbing passion for God in which his
greatest poems were written leave room for the memory
of other loves. Moreover, his whole career consisted in
a series of breaks and renunciations: in his search for
some final objective he was always ready to leave the
past behind.

For a time, it seems likely that he was really mad:
though it is hard to say how many of the eccentricities
attributed to him are authentic, and of these which
were deliberate and which the result of a disordered
brain. Prudent persons easily confuse enthusiasm
with insanity: especially that reckless enthusiasm
which sacrifices dignity to ideal ends. He seems to
have been subject for many years to fits of nervous
irritability, freakish moods, wild alternations of ecstasy
and contrition: not perhaps exceeding those endured
by many artists and men of religious genius, yet often
resulting in foolish and impulsive behaviour. The *Vita*
suggests that there had always been in him a tendency
to extravagant action, already shown in the complete-
ness of his surrender to pleasure, vanity, worldliness,
and human love. It is probable that his marriage had
awakened some of the deeper emotional possibilities of
his nature; had provided an object on which his ardour
of temperament could spend itself. Now, disillusion
was added to bereavement. The passion and self-
surrender of the lover, fully developed, were suddenly
arrested: the woman whom he loved was removed to
an infinite distance. It was like the checking of a
river in full flood, which tears up old landmarks,
wrecks established things, and cuts new channels to
the sea.

Such an experience must mean either death or re-
birth for the self that undergoes it. It drives a man in
upon himself, confronting him with that spectre of im-
permanence which we all acknowledge but never realise

till its corrupting touch is felt on our own lives. In this moment of complete destitution only one thing could save Ser Jacomo; the discovery of some new and durable object of devotion, some new outlet for his intensity of temperament. Life he must have: he needed, as his words and acts assure us, its colour, its perpetual calls to action, its romance. Now his temporal life lay in ruins around him: but through the rents in its wall, eternal life was suddenly disclosed, grave and compelling as a sky of stars. It changed every value of existence; condemning the past, but showing a way out towards the future, a whole new order of reality waiting for his recognition. With characteristic thoroughness and zest he accepted not only the revelation but all that it implied: a practical life-changing as drastic as that undertaken by St. Francis, but infinitely harder of accomplishment. Francis, an ardent boy of twenty-four, cast off the bondage of possessions gladly and easily, in a spirit of adventure. Jacomo, a man nearly forty years of age, long past the suppleness of youth, was almost shattered by the convulsion which made possible his escape.

He emerged from the first shock of bereavement, the devastating experience of loneliness, to find himself, as did St. Francis after the Crucified had spoken to him, "another man than he was before": a man who might well seem insane to his fellows, since he no longer shared their illusions, was out of harmony with their order, and had not yet found any way of adjusting himself to the new vision which he had received. The Doctor of Law and man of the world, the delicate eater and accomplished musician, was gone. In his place was a heart-broken penitent, already conscious of the stern demands which Divine Love makes on the soul: a fanatic who sought only for opportunities of exaggerated self-abasement, for some means of atoning for the sins and follies of the past.

Ciò c'ho veduto e pensato
tutto è feccia e bruttura,
pensando de l'altura
del virtuoso stato;
nel pelago ch'io veggio
non ce so notatura,
farò somergitura
de l'om ch'è anegato.[1]

Ser Jacomo was "converted," and that in no ordinary sense. The life of the world had become meaningless to him. He gave up his establishment, distributed his wealth to the poor, exchanged his beautiful clothes for a rough tunic and hood, and was hereafter known as the mad fool Jacopone. *Incipit vita nova.*

[1] *Lauda XXXIX.,* " O vita de Iesú Cristo " (p. 306).

CHAPTER III

JACOPONE THE PENITENT

Biographical use of the laude—Jacopone's spiritual development—Its two stages—The ascetic life—Contrition—Franciscan influences—Temperament—Eccentricities—Anecdotes of the Vita—The penitential laude—Mortification—Spiritual joy—The jubilus and holy madness—Missionary career—Didactic and satirical poems—Growing popularity—Second spiritual crisis—The dark night—Surrender of the will—Close of the missionary period.

FROM the time of his conversion, Jacopone's poems become our best source for the history of his inner life; for in many of them the varied moods of the penitent, the passion for self-abasement which the quaint incidents of the *Vita* crudely symbolise, and the slow moulding of his character to the purposes of eternal life, are vividly described. It must be remembered, however, that these poems stretch over a long period: probably thirty to thirty-eight years. Many are impersonal and didactic, few bear indications of date; and all must be used with a certain reserve in our attempt to trace the story of his development. Some of these penitential *laude* seem to have been written in the years immediately following his conversion, as mental stability gradually returned to him. Others were plainly composed in later life, when he saw in a calmer light and in truer proportion the phases of mental unrest and moral purification through which he had passed. They represent, like the *Confessions* of St. Augustine, " emotion remembered in tranquillity." [1] In one of these later *laude*, Jacopone says that the revelation of reality which caused and followed his conversion was gradual.[2] Though its first onslaught seemed

[1] For a tentative chronology of the principal poems see Appendix II.
[2] *Lauda XLV.*, " En cinque modi " (p. 446).

so violent and complete, Divine Love did not at once rush in to fill his empty life with its beauty and wonder; for " God cannot lodge in narrow hearts," [1] and his had never stretched beyond the demands of selfish interests and loves. His atrophied spiritual faculties were not able to grasp the full splendour of the spiritual world. Its character changed for him as his new consciousness grew in strength and span: a process extending over many years, in the course of which his personality was cleansed, shaped, and illuminated, and at last,—after much suffering and sharp discipline—brought into perfect union with God.

> En cinque modi appareme
> lo Signor en esta vita.

These five ways, and the long growth on which they mark stages, are reflected in his poems; and it is the principal task of criticism, examining these works in the light both of religious psychology and of literary scholarship, to deduce their probable order of composition and the relation in which they stand to their author's life.

Mystics do not spring full-grown from the wreck of their worldly careers. They mostly pass through a period of spiritual childhood andy hard education, marked by the child's intensity of feeling and distorted scale of values, its abounding vitality, dramatic instinct and lack of control. The child's vivid sense of naughtiness, fear of consequences, and quick reaction to forgiveness and love, are all present in a sublimated form. Bizarre acts of mortification, world-refusal of the most extravagant kind, an overpowering sense of sin, quickly succeed the revelation of newness and joy which marks their first change of heart.

In all this, Jacopone was true to type. The divine command which he celebrates in his greatest poem—

---

[1] *Lauda LX.,* " O amor de povertate " (p. 420).

"Ordena questo amore, tu che m'ami"[1]—was really an expression of the need which governed his whole growth; the ordering and concentration on eternal reality of his vehement and disordered temperament. The process was long. We can distinguish in it two great phases: the ascetic stage, which roughly coincides with the ten years spent *en bizocone*, and in which the central interests are ethical, and the mystical stage, which seems to have begun about the time of his entrance into the Franciscan Order. In this, the central interests are those peculiar to the contemplative life.

In the early days of his ascetic life, with which we are now concerned, Jacopone's mood seems to have been dominated by an intense revulsion against all the interests of his past existence, now perceived by him to be unreal. His soul awoke to the immediate presence of God, and was filled with horror of its own record, and fear of the judgment provoked: the normal emotions of the penitent who is first touched by the overwhelming majesty, rather than the appealing beauty, of the Divine. He tells us how dreadful God seemed when He thus appeared within the soul in His richness, and how this vision made his dead spirit quick again.

> Nel primo modo appareme
> nell'alma Dio Signore;
> da morte suscitandola
> per lo suo gran valore.[2]

The supposed richness and worth of Ser Jacomo, on which he had so greatly prided himself—the comfortable poise and natural arrogance of his type—were consumed in the fire of this revelation: the " demons " of pride and luxury, which had kept him imprisoned in a world of false values, fled away. He found himself to be a naked spirit, face to face with a naked

[1] *Lauda XC.*, " Amor de caritate " (p. 362). Compare ch. iv. (p. 131).
[2] *Lauda XLV.*, " En cinque modi " (p. 446).

Reality which exhibited his own self-hood as "less than nothing." [1]

Poets share with the pure in heart an aptitude for God. The poet latent in Jacopone, perhaps long smothered by other interests, perhaps nourished hitherto upon the satisfactions of sense, now emerged from the general upheaval of his nature, and took charge of his consciousness. It recognised and responded to the vision which had broken in upon him: exhibiting in its light the meaningless folly of his worldly career. The result seems to have been one of those strange revulsions which often accompany sudden conversion: a revulsion perhaps the more violent because, always inclined to extravagant action, he was now—if we accept the traditional account of his conversion—unbalanced by the awful circumstances of his wife's death, and the loneliness and misery in which it placed him. All he had most cherished—his own dignity and self-esteem, wealth and position, the ease and refinement of existence—became hateful. He could not live the new life under the old conditions of outward luxury. A complete break was imperative; sanity could only return with the re-grouping of all his powers and instincts about a fresh centre. The old self must die that the new self might be born.

> Non posso esser renato
> s'io en men non so morto. [2]

This was the spiritual situation. Two other circumstances tended to press Jacopone towards a total and dramatic change: namely, the Franciscan atmosphere in which his enlightenment took place, and the special temperament which he brought to the service of religion. His conversion had, it is clear, a definitely Franciscan character. Though we do not know how he came first under the influence of the Order, such an influence

---

[1] *Lauda XXXIX.,* " O vita de Iesú Cristo " (p. 306).
[2] *Lauda XXXIX.*

would be hard to escape in that time and neighbourhood. It can, as a matter of fact, be detected in Jacopone's prompt revulsion from material and intellectual possessions, and his early cult of " holy folly "; as well as in the penitential love for the Person and sufferings of Christ, so strongly emphasised by the Franciscan preachers, and so dramatically manifested in the great converts who literally " left all to follow Him."

The commentator Cornelius a Lapide, who may here preserve a true tradition, says that immediately after his wife's death, Jacopone sought admission into the Franciscan convent of San Fortunato at Todi. The brothers however, unlike their Founder, seem to have distrusted sudden conversions, and reminded him of his arrogant and worldly past; saying, with a humility more professional than convincing, " If you wish to live with us, you must become a donkey; that even as a donkey you may dwell among the donkeys." Jacopone went away, stripped himself to the waist, put on an ass's skin, and returned on all fours; saying, " Brothers, here I am, become a donkey! Admit then the donkey to live among the donkeys!" This too literal fulfilment of their own demands seems to have displeased the friars, who perhaps suspected in it a satirical intention. In any event, their reluctance to admit so peculiar a novice is easily understood. San Fortunato followed the " relaxed " rule, and was hostile to the Spiritual movement. Therefore that very fervour of self-abasement in which Jacopone showed the Franciscan character of his conversion, was best calculated to alienate its sympathies. His performance pointed either to a fanaticism verging on insanity, or to an unpleasantly clear understanding of the pious shams with which the *relaxati* surrounded themselves. Either form of zeal indicated an uncompromising attitude, little to the taste of a comfortable religious house. He was refused admittance, and returned

meekly through the streets in his disguise, greatly
edifying the people.[1] . Unable to become a friar, he
joined the Third Order, accepting in its most complete
sense the rule of poverty, penitence, and continence;
and adopted as his dress the *bizocone*, or rough tunic,
which was worn by the more fervent Tertiaries.[2]

The second factor in Jacopone's life-changing was
his strongly marked and special temperament. He was
a man to whom self-expression, even display, was of
the very essence of life. A hidden devotion did not
come naturally to him. He had loved the world, and
shown it. Now he despised the world, and must show
that too. With a thoroughness and enthusiasm which
is in harmony with his vehement character, he de-
liberately sought degradation, poverty, discomfort of
every kind, as the only means of escape from the
fetters of appearance, and atonement for the mistakes
of the past. Seen from the outside, he must have seemed
at this time simply a passionate man driven mad by
grief. He was, in fact, in the grip of a mono-ideism
which came near the border-line where enthusiasm

---

[1] Cornelius a Lapide, *Comment. in Eccles.*, cap. xxxiii., v. 25. What
appears to be another version of the story of the ass's skin was used
by the writer of the *Vita* (see below), but the episode of Jacopone's rejection
by the friars of San Fortunato was, not unnaturally, suppressed. When the
Vita was written, Jacopone had become the special glory of that convent
and of his native town, and no one cared to remember that the local
Beatus had once been refused admission to the house which afterwards
claimed him as peculiarly its own.

[2] The Tertiaries, or Brethren of Penance, were now a distinct feature
in the social life of the *I*talian cities, known by their austere dress and
simple life. They formed a religious corporation, and might not plead in
civil courts nor bear arms, which they could not be forced to take up even to
defend the commune. Many, like Jacopone, distributed all their property
on entering the Order. They might not wear silk, coloured garments, or
flowing sleeves. The educated members were bound to the daily recitation
of the psalter according to the use of the Papal Court, or an equivalent
number of psalms; the others, to say a number of Paternosters at the
canonical hours. Many undertook works of charity, especially nursing the
sick poor. The tertiary congregations were nominally under the direction
of the friars. This dependence, however, was disliked by the Conventual
brothers; and their closest connection and sympathy was with the Spiritual
party, which drew some of its leading members from their ranks. See
below, ch. v. Compare Fr. Cuthbert, *Life of St. Francis*, Bk. III., ch. vi.

passes over into mania. We can imagine what the general judgment would be, did some eminent and highly-cultivated lawyer of our own day suddenly give up his practice, forsake his home, abandon every decency and convention of his class, and become an itinerant preacher: and Ser Jacomo's life-changing, as described in the *Vita*, was more thorough than this. Wearing the roughest clothes and abandoning all pretension to refinement, he now wandered about the streets of Todi, a half-crazy missionary; inviting men to repentance sometimes by words, more often by grotesquely symbolic deeds. " This man of God," says the *Vita*, " went about with so abject and foolish a mien, that almost every one regarded him as mad. And he was mocked and persecuted by the children. And all these things he seemed to enjoy, patiently enduring everything either for love of his Lord Jesus Christ who bore so many pains for sinners, or for hatred of the pride and sinfulness of his own past life." [1] Everybody gossipped of his eccentric doings, and loved to persuade him to argument: some because they found it amusing, and others because they appreciated his lofty and almost prophetic manner of speech [2]—the eloquence of the great advocate, put now to new purposes. He became a by-word in Todi, and an object of great shame and embarrassment to his unfortunate relations, who suddenly saw the wealthy and respected head of the family transformed into a religious fanatic of the most extravagant type.

" Giving himself altogether to lowliness, and to contempt of the world and of himself, his practice was to go from church to church, saying Paternosters and Ave Marias: and a part of the time grovelling upon the ground, like a fool or one who has lost his wits, according to the judgment of this world. And he gave up all intercourse with both his relations and his friends,

---

[1] *Vita*, 2vo. [2] *Loc. cit.*

and was held and reputed crazy by every one. His
relatives saw this with much shame and confusion,
reprehending him and condemning him as a madman.
And first they did all they could to recall him from
this folly, but seeing that they could in no wise move
him from his opinions, held their peace, though they
endured it with vexation and the greatest shame; since
many times he did things which in the eyes of men of
this world seemed of the utmost imbecility, though in
the sight of God they were of singular wisdom. Thus,
once when a certain *festa* was taking place in Todi,
where a great part of the inhabitants were gathered
together, he being in fervour of spirit, burning with
this shame and with love of this virtue of self-abase-
ment, stripped himself naked, and took an ass's saddle
and put it on, and the bit in his mouth, and went on
his hands and feet, ambling like an ass. And thus going
amongst the people, by this thing—Divine grace per-
mitting it—he caused such great terror and amazement
that all were moved in their hearts to compunction;
considering how Ser Jacomo, who had been so famous
a *procuratore* in that city, had given himself to such
utter contempt of the world and to lowliness. And all
who were at that *festa* were thrown into confusion, and
turned from vanities to bitterness and sorrow of heart." [1]

Jacopone's further efforts to bring compunction to
the hearts of the worldly—the pious practical jokes by
which he is said to have imparted his new convictions
—are told at some length in the *Vita*. There we read
how he went to a marriage feast in his brother's house
tarred and feathered. Entreated to behave in a normal
manner or else leave the party in peace, he said " As
my brother intends to honour the family by his wisdom,
so I wish to honour it by my imbecility." Again, asked
by a friend to carry a pair of chickens home from
market, he took them to the parish church and put

[1] *Vita*, 2ᵛᵒ.

them in the family sepulchre, explaining to the irritated owner that he had done exactly as he was asked, since the grave is the true home of man. In each case the victims were greatly edified by these tiresome performanccs. It is difficult for us to decide how many of these stories of Jacopone's "holy madness" can be accepted as substantially true; how many have been influenced by the Franciscan surroundings in which the *Vita* was composed, or by a too literal interpretation of the poems in which he praises "madness for Messiah's sake." They bear a suspicious resemblance to the now discredited tales of Brother Juniper's pious follies [1]— though Jacopone has none of Juniper's child-like charm—to some of the antics of St. Simeon Stultus, [2] and to the numerous and delightful stories illustrating *sancta simplicitas* collected by Cæsarius of Heisterbach: [3] who was one of the most popular of thirteenth-century writers. All these sources would be both accessible and congenial to the author of the *Vita*. Our suspicions are increased when we observe that the term "minstrels" (or rather "jongleurs") of the Lord, [4] which the writers of the *Speculum* afterwards put into the mouth of St. Francis, [5] is first used by Cæsarius: and that this epithet—which so excellently describes one side of Jacopone's vocation—is specially applied by him, not to missionary minstrels such as Fra Pacifico, whom St. Francis sent out to bring people to God by music and song; but to the holy simpletons whose antics entertain the angels and the saints. [6]

[1] *Fioretti : Vita di Frate Ginepro.*
[2] *Acta SS.*, T. I. Jul., 136 *seq.* *Cf.* Tamassia, *S. Francesco d'Assisi*, cap. vi.
[3] *Cæsarii Heisterbacensis Dial. miraculorum*, Lib. VI.
[4] The *jongleur*, like the nigger-minstrel, might be anything from a jester to a singer of sentimental, tragic, or even religious songs.
[5] *Speculum*, cap. c.
[6] "Simplex quandoque mimo vel ioculatori comparatur. . . . Ut sic dicam, ioculatores Dei sunt sanctorumque angelorum, quorum opera, si hi qui simplices non sunt, quandoque facerent, haud dubium quin Deum offenderent, qui in eis, dum per simplices fiunt, delectatur."—Cæsarius, *op. cit.*, vi., 8. Quoted by Tamassia, *loc. cit.*

E

Obviously, then, there were many reasons why tales of this kind should cluster round Jacopone's name. Nevertheless it cannot be denied that he did, by declaration, hold " madness for Christ's sake " to be the essence of wisdom and courtesy.   For him the true doctors of theology were those whom the world thought crazy with love; [1] and, at any rate during his early ascetic life, he regarded discretion as the enemy of true devotion.[2]   Here his views harmonised with the primitive Franciscan tradition, if not with the later Franciscan practice.   St. Francis himself seems to have put no bounds to individual self-abasement, and in his hatred of cleverness went a long way towards the deification of folly.   He rejoiced over the silliness of Brother John the Simple, and kept his disapproval for the brother who desired a psalter, not the brother who behaved like a fool.[3]   When the time came to add Jacopone to the gallery of Franciscan heroes, it was natural that those incidents which seemed to tally with this specially Franciscan view of humility should be stressed and perhaps elaborated.   They occupy in the *Vita* a far greater place than their importance can justify: but it is probable that they do represent a phase through which he passed in the early days of his conversion, when he seems to have demonstrated his contempt for earthly judgments by a deliberately assumed eccentricity.   His verses are there to prove how extravagant and unbalanced was his first mood of world-denial—so characteristic of the " twice-born " and abruptly disillusioned soul—how complete was his revulsion from the ideals of common sense: but these poems show too how many other and nobler elements entered into his penitence.

Bonaccorsi's edition of the *laude*—the only one upon which any theories can safely be based—contains a

[1] *Lauda LXXXIV.*, " Senno me pare " (p. 282).
[2] *Lauda LXXVIII.*, " L'amor lo cor sí vol regnare."
[3] T. of Celano, *Vita secunda*, cap. clxiii. *Speculum*, cap. iv.

series of poems which seem to represent the moods and phases succeeding Jacopone's conversion. Though they cannot be arranged with certainty in order of date, we shall probably be right in placing among his earliest writings those crude hymns on the commonplace themes of asceticism in which he seems to be imitating, either from humility or lack of skill, the popular verse of the *laudesi*.[1] In these there are few signs of metrical art or spiritual genius. Rhythm and thought are usually undistinguished, and often descend to the level of doggerel. It is hard to believe that Jacopone, child of a complete Latin culture, could write no better than this: and some scholars have been driven by the contrast between these raw productions and the lofty beauty of his later work to suppose that in the first agonies of penitence he abjured literary art along with material refinement, and deliberately wrote at his coarsest and worst. They would thus be an expression of the general revolt against pride of intellect which is so strongly marked in the poems of his middle period. Without adopting this extreme view, it is possible to account for these poems in two ways. First, as regards their manner, the history of literature assures us that the greatest poets may be subject to failures of inspiration and of taste, in which they descend to inconceivable depths of futility. Even Keats and Shelley— for here it is better to choose examples from those safely dead—have written doggerel which would shame the polite contributor to our literary magazines. Religious emotion is specially apt to produce this atrophy of the critical sense. Secondly, as regards their matter, we may reasonably regard these verses as the work of an over-subtle and sophisticated brain suddenly mastered by the primitive emotions and primitive truths of religion; and finding its greatest satisfaction in those simple formulæ which it once despised and

[1] See below, ch. vi.

now sees to be charged with meaning. Jacopone was in the position of the young lover who feels sure that his own understanding of the commonplaces of passion is unique; and therefore bores his acquaintances with emotional truisms, which for him are full of fragrance but for them are faded flowers. If we read these early *laude* side by side with those which contain later reminiscences of his penitential period, we find in them traces of the slow restoration of his mental balance, the movement of his consciousness from the primitive and self-regarding state of fear, in which the first revelation of God had thrown him, to the Christian attitude of humble and fervent love. This evolution was almost certainly the work of years: and we, in adopting the foreshortened view of it which his poems present, must not forget the long series of adjustments and experiences it entailed.

There are five poems of undoubted authenticity in which the moods of Jacopone's primary phases of penitence seem to be expressed. The first, "La Bontade se lamenta,"[1] is regarded by Signor Brugnoli as his earliest surviving work.[2] It certainly describes the emotions of his agony of repentance, and also contains interesting reminiscences of his legal career. But many of its verses seem to me to refer to a later state of reconciliation, when Jacopone had "learned that new language which nothing says but Love,"[3] and contain phrases which indicate the marked influence of scholastic psychology. The plan of the poem is simple. Goodness indicts the Created Affection at the bar of Divine Justice, because she has failed to love the Good; and causes her, with all her family, to be arrested and cast into gaol. Being in this misery and bondage, Affection repents; and Goodness, having mercy on her, feeds her with grace, whereby her will is changed and her whole being renewed. Though the later stanzas of

---

[1] *Lauda LXXIV.*   [2] Brugnoli, *Le Satire*, p. cx.   [3] *Loc. cit.*

this poem, and the general familiarity with scholastic language which it shows, are difficult to reconcile with the early date which Signor Brugnoli suggests for it, it does probably represent Jacopone's sophistication of his own first sense of sin—characteristically regarded by him as a perversion of the power of love—and of that sense of renovation and enlargement succeeding it, which is a well-known feature of conversion. In the next poem,[1] which can more reasonably be ascribed to his first period, the soul is again a criminal before the judge. "Hast thou not thought that I can shatter thee?" says God to the sinner who tries to explain away his past indifference to religion, and still hesitates before the hard duties of penance and confession. In the next, the beautiful dialogue between Our Lady and the penitent,[2] that sense of the inexhaustible Divine mercy and gentleness which is symbolised for Catholic Christians by the figure of the Mother of God, tempers the fear and misery of the newly-awakened conscience. In the fourth and fifth,[3] Jacopone completes the transition from a self-centred to a God-centred regret for the past; and achieves the "lofty penitence" which is grounded in self-hatred, and suffers, not for the sake of its own salvation, but because by its own imperfection it dishonours the Perfection that it loves.

> Or piagne 'l suo descionore
> e de te non gir curando.

Jacopone was an orthodox Catholic. Even in his worldly period, though indifferent to religion, he does not appear to have been sceptical. He was merely more interested in other things, and put off piety till his old age.[4] After his conversion, though his behaviour was often eccentric and he lived as a spiritual free-lance,

[1] *Lauda X.*, " Peccator, chi t'ha fidato."
[2] *Lauda I.*, " O Regina cortese " (p. 250).
[3] *Laude IV.*, " O alta penitenza," and *XI.*, " Signore, damme la morte " (p. 264).
[4] *Lauda X.*, " Peccator, chi t'ha fidato."

his attitude towards the sacraments and institutions of
the Church was always correct. During his imprison-
ment by Boniface VIII., deprivation of the sacraments
was the only cruelty of which he complained.[1] The
earlier *laude* insist frequently on the need of sacramental
confession: a dramatic act which we might expect to
appeal to him, and which he calls " a deed of truth,
bringing back hidden evils to the light and health to
the purged soul of the penitent." [2] We may accept as
probably true those statements of the *Vita* which
describe him, during the first months of his conversion,
as spending many hours at prayer in the churches: for
converts, especially at the beginning of their new life,
seem to need the still atmosphere, the long hours of
silence and recollection, if they are to reduce the uproar
of their nature to harmony, and bring into focus their
vision of truth. In a poem of great beauty, probably
written at a later date, he has celebrated the thoughts
and feelings with which he returned to Holy Com-
munion; finding his way to its hidden mysteries " like
a blind man with a stick." [3] Here he drew near " the
heavenly life of the Fragrant Rose," and by its loveli-
ness could measure the folly and sin, foul odours and
corruptions of his own past, " villana, engrata, superba."
Here that passion for the invisible which afterwards
transfigured his existence seems first to have taken
shape. Here his misery and confusion of mind began
to clear, and he perceived himself to be a " new man ";
able, to his own amazement, to feel real love for his
neighbour and accept with actual delight the contempt
of the world.

> Signor, non te veio, ma veio
> che m'bai en altro om mutato;
> l'amor de la terra m'hai tolto,
> en cielo sí m'hai collocato.

[1] *Lauda LVII.*, " Lo pastor per mio peccato."
[2] *Lauda IV.*, " O alta penitenza."
[3] *Lauda XLVI.*, " Con gli occhi ch'agio nel capo " (p. 320).

This poem seems to describe the first real expansion of Jacopone's spiritual consciousness; his complete swing-round from temporal to eternal interests. But, as against this glory of new life, in which the deprivations of poverty and chastity, the deliberate cultivation of lowliness in heart and life, were felt by the awakening spirit of the poet-mystic as actual sources of joy, there was now strongly developed in him the complementary and negative sense of the ugliness and corruption of material things; the antagonism between soul and body, the evil inherent in all flesh. The ascetic impulse kept pace with the spiritual vision, and was felt by him in its most exaggerated form. Rooted as he was in the mediæval world, it was an inevitable part of his general revulsion from the past.

The penitent in any age is almost necessarily a dualist. In his first vigorous enthusiasm for the spirit, God and His order seem to be set over against the world and its order—a pair of incompatibles. The stronger the new light, the blacker is the shadow that it throws. The wide and charitable vision which is able to harmonise matter and spirit comes only to those who have disciplined their senses, conquered the unruly elements of their own natures, and achieved the equilibrium of an " ordered love." Hence the violent physical mortifications, the distrust of human ties and natural beauty, which are such constant features in the early lives of mystics and saints. In a man of Jacopone's temperament, some conflict with the body was essential. Old strong habits, the result of years of self-indulgence, must be broken. He seems to have undertaken this work with a suddenness and vehemence untempered by common sense: impatient, in the heroic fury of his new passion for the spirit, of every limitation and natural weakness of the flesh. There was laughter and kindliness in St. Francis' view of the body. He called it Brother Ass, and restrained the zeal of those fervent

brethren who wished to chastise it without mercy.
Jacopone's early asceticism struck a more savage note.
He could not afford to make any concessions to the
senses; for they were strong and dangerous, accus-
tomed to rule his life. For the time, at any rate, he
must fight them: opposing to the beauty and colour of
existence those hideous facts of physical death and
decay waiting for all human objects of desire, which
mediæval religion tended to emphasise, and which the
special circumstances of his own conversion may have
seared into his consciousness.

Sometimes this sense of impermanence is expressed
with gentleness, and implies an invitation to perdurable
joys:

> Anema mia, tu se' eterna,
> eterno vòi delettamento;
> li sensi e lor delettanza
> vedi senza duramento;
> a Dio fa' tuo salimento,
> esso sol te può empire;
> loco el ben non sa finire,
> ché eterno è 'l delettare.[1]

(My soul, thou art an everlasting thing,
    Thy joys endure alway:
The senses, and the pleasures that they bring
    Must vanish and decay.
    To God then take thy way,
None else can satisfy;
There is a land where the Good cannot die
And happiness endures eternally.)

Sometimes the same truth is put with the uncom-
promising and minatory realism of the *Trois vifs et
trois morts*, so beloved of the thirteenth-century world:

> Quando t'alegri, omo de altura,
> va', pone mente a la sepultura.[2]

[1] *Lauda V.*, " Cinque sensi mess'on pegno."
[2] *Lauda XXV.*, " Quando t'alegri " (p. 268).

Again and again Jacopone returns to this idea of the corruption of matter and tyranny of the grave: an idea of course implicit in the mediæval view of human life, but which seems at one point of his development to have obsessed him. The body, he thought at this time, is worth nothing save as an instrument of penance. Its origin is nasty, its end is dust.[1] We have little cause for vainglory if we look facts in the face. The sheep bears wool, the apple-tree bears fruit: but what does man's body bear? Underneath his fine clothes he is swarming with nits and lice; perpetually devoured by fleas.[2]

When such doctrine takes root in an enthusiastic and unbalanced mind, as part of a general revulsion from the pride of life, it is likely to result in morbid asceticism. It induced in Jacopone a thirst for physical mortifications, which he carried to extreme and sometimes to barbarous lengths: for temperance was the last of the cardinal virtues which he learned to appreciate. Hunger, thirst, cold, and general wretchedness he felt to be essential, if he was to be freed from the tyranny of the senses: but, not content with this, he prayed that his body might be consumed by disease—toothache and asthma, epilepsy and consumption, and many other more intimate and unpleasant maladies—that he might become blind, deaf, and dumb, that men might turn from him in disgust, that his death might be lonely and bitter and the stomach of a wolf might be his tomb.

> O Signor, per cortesia,
> mandame la malsanía!
> A me la freve quartana,
> la contina e la terzana,
> la doppia cotidiana
> colla grande idropesía. . . .

[1] *Lauda XXIII.*, " Omo, mèttete a pensare."
[2] *Loc. cit.*

A me lo morbo caduco
de cadere en acqua e 'n foco,
e giamai non trovi loco
ch'io afflitto non ce sia.[1]

(I pray Thee, Lord, in courtesy
Send cruel sickness down to me,
In constant fever let me be,
—The daily fever's burning dew,
The quartan, and the tertian too,
And dropsy's misery. . . .
The falling sickness I desire,
To fall in water and in fire,
That from affliction fierce and dire
I never may be free.)

Though a merciful Providence refused to grant this
outrageous petition, and gave instead a strength of
body which survived thirty years of voluntary austeri-
ties and five years' confinement in the dungeons of
Palestrina, yet we can hardly suppose that the ascetic
life came easily to Jacopone. It must have involved
great sufferings; calling for high courage, and that
quality of dogged perseverance which had contributed
to his successful career in the world. Years of good
feeding and soft clothing had formed habits which
could only be broken at the cost of much pain, and
almost intolerable discomfort. Perhaps he was think-
ing of these sufferings when he wrote the vigorous
dialogue between the petulant body and the ardent
soul of the would-be ascetic,[2] with its realistic cata-
logue of physical miseries—the prickly hair-shirt that
never gives one a moment's peace; the soft bed and

---

[1] *Lauda XLVIII.*, " O Signor, per cortesia."
Tradition ascribes this poem to Jacopone's conventual life: but its
crudity of style and sentiment appears to me to be more consistent with
his first period of asceticism. Moreover, the prayer that he may be afflicted
with bad weather; " gelo, grandine, tempestate "—a real hardship to a
wandering hermit—loses its force on the lips of a cloistered friar. If this
poem indeed belongs to his second period, it can only refer to the moment
of despair when he says that he was driven out of the community-life.
See ch. iv., p. 118.
[2] *Lauda III.*, " Audite una 'ntenzone."

feather pillow replaced by hard stones, which bruise
the poor restless body whichever way it turns; the
enforced early rising, after a sleepless night devastated
by indigestion and cold in the head; the nasty food,
which even dogs reject; the doubtful water, which
will probably make one ill; every complaining and
unruly thought punished by some new austerity. For
a middle-aged man of luxurious tastes, to whom com-
fort has become second nature, these things represent
a hard and painful sacrifice; a heroic effort, perpetu-
ally renewed, and only made possible by the fervour of
remorseful adoration, and passionate desire to make
atonement, which now filled Jacopone's heart.

We are to think of him, then, during the first years
of his new life as developing simultaneously in these
two directions; living a hard and bracing life of stern
asceticism and perpetual self-discipline as towards the
physical order, a more joyous life of growing love,
devotion, and trust as towards the spiritual order. In
the course of that long purgation which brought him
at last to the " perfect freedom " of a surrendered
will,[1] Jacopone descended again and again to the
depths; explored without shrinking the full horrors of
death and sin. He was no easy optimist. His enraptured
celebration of Divine Love was balanced by full know-
ledge of all that opposed it in himself and in the world.
We taste in it the sharp flavour of the salt of Christ,
not the sugar of the religious sentimentalist. His early
poems show him moving in perpetual disequilibrium
between these two poles of penance and joy, and reveal
the growing intensity of his spiritual vision as de-
pendent upon the drastic purification of mind and
sense which had preceded it. They record his passage
from the first state of unrelieved contrition, with its
complete absorption in the ideas of fear, self-abasement,
sin, and death, to that ecstatic and unstable condition

[1] *Lauda XXXIV.,* " O libertá, subietta."

of intense mystical fervour in which the poems of his
middle period were composed.   The writers of the
Speculum describe St. Francis as " drunken with the
love and compassion of Christ " and breaking out like
a troubadour into " French-like rejoicings " in honour
of his Love.[1] So Jacopone seems from this time onwards
to have been subject on the one hand to wild states of
rapturous adoration, when he was " crazy for the fair
Messiah's sake," [2] on the other to profound reactions of
self-hatred and despairing grief.[3]   Like a lover at the
mercy of his passion, he was abject and exalted by
turns: for the love of life and beauty, the vehement
responsiveness, which were part of his temperament
and had been torn from their old attachments, had
found an infinitive Objective on which to spend
themselves.

It was probably about this time that he began to
exhibit the characteristic phenomena of the beginner
in the supersensual life.   That frenzy of spiritual joy
breaking out into incoherent songs and cries, which
the old mystical writers called the *jubilus* and re-
garded as a sign of ardent but undisciplined devotion,
seems at times to have seized upon him, and probably
increased his reputation for insanity.[4] He babbled of
love with " tears and laughter, sorrow and delight,"
and with gestures that seemed foolishness to other
men.   In the early stanzas of " La Bontade se lamenta "
he gives a vivid picture of the emotional fervours of
the soul touched by grace, which is probably inspired
by his own experience, and throws considerable light
upon this phase of his development.

[1] *Speculum,* cap. xciii.
[2] *Lauda LXXXIV.,* " Senno me pare " (p. 282).   Compare also *Laude
LXXIV.,* " La Bontade se lamenta," and *LXXXIII.,* " O dolce amore "
(p. 286).
[3] *Laude XI.,* " Signore, damme la morte " (p. 264), and *XXXIX.,* " O
vita de Iesú Cristo " (p. 306).
[4] *Lauda LXXVI.,* " O iubilo del core " (p. 278).   The tale in the *Vita*
which refers this poem to his conventual period (see p. 114) is not to be
taken seriously.

L'Affetto, poi che gusta el cibo
de la grazia gratis data,
lo 'ntelletto e la memoria
tutta sí l'ha renovata,
e la volontá mutata
piange con grande desianza
la preterita offensanza
e nullo consólo se vol dare.

Empreso ha novo lenguaio,
ché non sa dir se non " amore."
Piange, ride, dole e gaude
securato con timore;
e tal segni fa de fuore,
che paiono de om stolto,
dentro sta tutto racolto
non sente da fuor que fare.[1]

(For when Desire that food doth taste,
—The sweets of grace, and given for nought!—
New life in all her being wakes,
In mind, and memory, and thought.
The will to wondrous change is wrought;
Her former sins she doth lament,
With yearning grief most vehement;
She finds no comfort and no cheer.

Now a new language doth she speak,
" Love, Love," is all her tongue can say,
She weeps, and laughs; rejoices, mourns,
In spite of fears, is safe and gay;
And though her wits seem all astray,
—So wild, so strange, her outward mien—
Her soul within her is serene;
And heeds not how her acts appear.)

No doubt Jacopone's peculiar vehemence of temperament, and the mental disturbance which accompanied his conversion, tended in his case to these exaggerated transitions of feeling, and to their uncontrolled and perhaps involuntary dramatic expression. But these acute emotional reactions, often accompanied by eccentric outward behaviour, are a normal episode in the early development of many mystics; upon whom

[1] *Lauda LXXIV.*, " La Bontade se lamenta."

the beauty and wonder of the new world of spirit now perceived by them, and the Presence that fills it, have often an almost intoxicating effect. Richard Rolle, Ruysbroeck, and others have left us vivid descriptions of the *jubilus;* which seems to have been in their day, like the closely-related "speaking with tongues" in the early Church, a fairly common expression of intense religious excitement. It belongs, says Ruysbroeck, to "the first and lowest mode whereby God inwardly declares Himself in the contemplative life";[1] is one of the forms in which the "fury of love"—the first passionate response of the soul to the touch of God—makes itself felt.

"Spiritual inebriation," says Ruysbroeck, "is this: that a man receives more sensible joy and sweetness than his heart can either contain or desire. Spiritual inebriation brings forth many strange gestures in men. It makes some sing and praise God because of their fullness of joy, and some weep with great tears because of their sweetness of heart. It makes one restless in all his limbs, so that he must run and jump and dance; and so excites another that he must gesticulate and clap his hands." . . .

"Other things sometimes happen to those who live in the fierce ardour of love; for often another light shines into them . . . and in the meeting with that light, the joy and the satisfaction are so great, that the heart cannot bear them, but breaks out with a loud voice in cries of joy. And this is called the *jubilus* or jubilation; that is, a joy which cannot be uttered in words."[2]

So Jacopone:

> Parlar de tale amor faccio follia,
> diota me conosco en teologia,
> l'amor me constregne en sua pazia
> e famme bannire. . . .

[1] *The Book of the Twelve Béguines*, ch. x.
[2] *The Adornment of the Spiritual Marriage*, Bk. II., chs. xix. and xxiv.

L'abundanza non se pò occultare,
loco sí se forma el iubilare,
prorompe en canto che è sibilare,
che vidde Elia.[1]

(Crazed must I be, of such a love to speak,
For in theology my skill is weak;
Yet from the madness of Love's mountain peak,
Prophetic fury in my words must show.
Abundance cannot hide herself apart;
And joy, from out her nest within the heart,
Breaks forth in song, and in the prophet's art;
Even as did Elias long ago.)

This fury and intensity of love, the "*ebrieza d'amore*," long remained a favourite theme with him, as it seems also to have been an enduring though intermittent element of his religious experience. For this reason, the poems in which it appears are very difficult to date. He discerned it not only in himself, but in the very heart of the universe. It was, he thought, a mutual madness. Creator and creation, God and the soul, alike were possessed by the noble folly of unmeasured love,[2] "Cristo per me fo pazo";[3] and the nearest way back to Reality consisted in self-abandonment to this ecstatic dance.[4]

Poiché lo saper de Dio
è empazato de l'amore,
que farai, o saper mio?
Non vol gir po' 'l tuo Signore?
Non pòi aver maiur onore
ch'en sua pazia conventare.[5]

(For since God's wisdom, though so great,
In all intoxicate with love,
Shall mine not be inebriate?
And so be like my Lord above?
No greater honour can I prove
Than sharing His insanity.)

[1] *Lauda LXXX.*, "Sapete voi novelle de l'amore."
[2] *Lauda LXXXII.*, "O amor, divino amore, perchè" (p. 442).
[3] *Lauda LXXI.*, "Omo che vol parlare."
[4] *Lauda LXXXIII.*, "O dolce amore" (p. 286). See also *LXXXIV.*, "Senno me pare" (p. 282).
[5] *Lauda LXXIII.*, "O derrata, guarda al prezo."

Studying Jacopone in the light of his fellow-mystics, we are able to supply some of the links which connect his personal poems, and to divine the progressive character of that spiritual life which lies behind them. Whatever the date of their composition, this test assures us that it was neither a raw convert nor the initiate of an "ordered love" who described Love drawing him in its mesh like a helpless fish from the sea,[1] and sang the praises of the *jubilus* and the wisdom of folly. These are the natural expressions proper to a period of illumination, transition, and unrest, culminating perhaps in that apparent "departure of grace" which is an inevitable phase of all intense spiritual experience, and inspires the bitter lament:

> Piangi, dolente anima predata,
> che stai vedovata de Cristo amore.[2]

Poems of this type should therefore be distinguished from those other groups of *laude* which exhibit on the one hand Jacopone's complete surrender to the sense of sin, on the other his progress in the "unitive way." I do not wish to suggest that all of them were necessarily written in the period we are now considering: for it is clear that he was subject throughout his life to constant and violent changes of mood, and that the "holy madness" was—if we may say so with respect— a favourite pose. Nevertheless these are works of a transitional type. They show him to us as developing along normal lines; yet in a way which is profoundly characteristic, and helps us to understand much that is puzzling in his career. We see in them the slow and difficult emergence of a "new man": but a new man in whom all the old traits of character—the energy and

---

[1] *Lauda LXXXIII.*, "O dolce amore" (p. 286).
[2] *Lauda LXVIII.*, "Piangi, dolente" (p. 290). *Laude LXVI.*, "Or chi averá cordoglio," and *LXVII.*, "Amor, diletto amore" (p. 294) seem to be inspired by the same spiritual condition; but may have been written in later periods of destitution. See chs. iv. and v.

vehemence, the immense vitality and power of concentration which had served him so well in the old life —gradually reappear, grouped round a new centre, dedicated to new purposes. Jacopone can still love hard, work hard, fight hard. He still tends to extravagance of feeling; swings between the extremes of rapture and despair. He is still ruled by desire, though his desire is now one of the noblest which is possible to man.

To the outward world he probably appeared at this time as one of those wandering religious enthusiasts, or "free hermits" (gyrovagi), not uncommon in the Middle Ages. Some of these were mere professional beggars and vagabonds. Others were real wayside evangelists who lived a two-fold life of penance and prayer as towards God, missionary activity as towards men. In his adoption of this career, which he followed for the greater part of ten years, we may trace the continuing influence of the original Franciscan ideal: its freedom and apostolic fervour, its spirit of penitence and love, manifested through a totally different temperament. Where these years were chiefly spent is unknown to us. We gather that Jacopone did not break his connection with Todi, but made it in some sense his base; for it was here in 1278 that he at last became a friar. Some think that he visited during this period the great Franciscan sanctuaries, and entered into those relations with John of Parma, John of la Verna, Conrad of Offida, and other leaders of the Spiritual party, which counted for so much in his later life; others that he rambled through Umbria as an itinerant minstrel and preacher, a *giullare di Dio*, attracting men by his singing and then persuading them to God in the primitive Franciscan way; others that he lived much in solitude, devoted to prayer and contemplation. All these things may be true, but they are matters of conjecture. Here neither *laude* nor documents give us any information.

F

We are reduced to the frank statement of the *Vita*: "As to these things I hold my peace, that I may not be too long, and also because I have not found them to be very authentic."

But we may reasonably suppose that, with the return of mental balance and the complete establishment in him of the spiritual life, the apostolic enthusiasm which took so quaint a form in the first days of Jacopone's conversion would find more normal ways of expressing itself, and turn to its own purposes his poetic and oratorical powers: and this theory at least is confirmed by the *laude* themselves. We find in fact from this point onwards two distinct strains in his poetry. There are the lyrics—by far the more attractive—which express his own intimate experiences of penitence, love, and joy, in the period in which God began to appear to him, no longer as dreadful Judge or wise and stern Physician, but as a " noble comrade," a Wayfaring Love.[1] There are the vigorous and popular songs, plainly addressed to the people, and which the poet himself probably sang to them: rhymed sermons full of robust doctrine on morals and faith,[2] or dramatic exhibitions of human frailty,[3] which they took from his lips and sang throughout the country. In them speak by turns the experienced man of the world, with a sure knowledge of human nature: the old lawyer, familiar with the seamy side of existence, the wriggles and self-deceptions of the average easy-going man: the ardent Christian, determined if he can to bring other men to God. All are coloured by that intense asceticism which was the natural complement of his mystical life, and which was, as we have seen, specially pronounced in its earlier stages. Reading the *laude*, in fact, these two,

[1] *Lauda XLV.*, " En cinque modi " (p. 446).
[2] Good examples are *Laude VI.*, " Guarda che non caggi " (p. 274); *XII.*, " Sì como la morte face "; *XIX.*, " Figli, nepoti e frati," and *XCVII.*, " O peccator dolente."
[3] For instance *Laude VIII.*, " O femene, guardate," and *XXII.*, " Audite una entenzone."

Jacopone the embryo mystic and Jacopone the popular missionary, perpetually jostle one another. The dreamer wants to embody his dream in action, the man of action is possessed and driven by his dream: a situation not unlike that which we find in the records of the early Methodists, who combined vigorous popular propaganda with an intense devotional life and sometimes —as in the case of Wesley himself—made poetry serve the purposes of both.[1] Here too we have on the one hand the rough male brutality, the homely vigour, of the skilful advocate of heavenly causes: on the other the beauty and fervour of the lover, when he writes high poetry in honour of his heavenly love. If we are to get the real man, with his disconcerting changes, his abrupt transitions between earth and heaven, satire and prayer, we must keep both aspects of him in view: and remember that the popular poet, who bullied, amused and persuaded the people, lashing without mercy the follies and sins of priesthood and laity alike, was at the same time a humble and tormented soul struggling to adjust himself to a revelation far greater than he would ever be able to describe. A comparison of our Lord's most transcendental sayings with His scathing denunciations of Pharisees and scribes proves that this double reaction to existence does not lack the highest sanctions.

As a missionary, Jacopone seems to have had all the qualities of a successful revivalist: the fierce moral enthusiasm, the uncompromising directness, the freedom of speech of a man who knew how to speak to the people in their own tongue. His language was vigorous,

[1] The literary parallel between Jacopone and Wesley is a close one, in spite of their wide separation in time and temperament. Such poems as " Jesu, Lover of my soul," and " Come! O thou Traveller unknown," in which Wesley reveals his strong mystical bias, are very near in spirit to the great Franciscan. On the other hand. Wesley's popular hymns, often roughly phrased, but always vigorous and sincere, help us to understand the circumstances under which Jacopone's didactic *laude* were composed.

his method deliberately popular. We find in his didactic songs the " straight talk " which makes the sermons of St. Bernardino so vivid and sometimes so startling. Jacopone's object is to convict his hearers of sin, to awaken them to the real facts of life and death; and he does not mince matters. The most violent invective, the most loathsome imagery, the crudest and most audacious physical parallels, are used without stint to drive his meaning home. He knows the value of terse and pungent phrases; that where a long discourse bores, the rhyme arrests attention and is remembered.

> La longa materia
> suol generar fastidia,
> lo longo abreviare
> suole l'om delettare.
>   Abbrevio mei ditta,
> longheza breve scritta;
> chi ce vorrá pensare
> ben ce porrá notare.[2]

> (To be long-winded, I confess,
> For those who hear is weariness;
> The skilled abbreviator's art
> Will make the listener glad at heart:
> So will I shorten all I say,
> Compress my writings as I may,
> And who attends to what I tell
> Within his mind may store it well.)

The song thus introduced is a peculiarly daring and detailed description of the " Spiritual Marriage "; which can hardly be offered to the modern reader, but must certainly have entertained and impressed those who heard it. It is perhaps the most startling—and also probably one of the latest—examples of Jacopone's popular style which has come down to us. But an equally amusing and less embarrassing candour is found in those moral discussions in which his shrewd

[1] *Lauda LXXI.*, " Omo che vol parlare."

knowledge of human nature, and his memories of
worldly society, come into play, and which can more
certainly be ascribed to his missionary period. Thus
the song on the "pernicious adornments of women"[1]
is a perfect picture of feminine vanities and obliquities,
less mediæval than universal. Then, as now, we find
that women were accustomed to excuse their own
extravagance by saying that their husbands expected
them to dress well; but as a matter of fact were con-
cerned only to outvie each other, and attract admira-
tion. They wore high heels under their long trains to
make their "little persons" look taller, tampered with
their complexions, and adorned their heads with false
hair; thus presenting a very attractive appearance in
public, but preparing a painful disillusion for those who
followed them into the intimacies of private life.

> Per temporal avenesse
> che l'om la veda sciolta
> vedi che fa la demona
> colla sua capovolta!
> le trez'altrui componese
> non so con que girvolta;
> farattece una colta
> che paion en capo nate.[2]

> (For now and then, the thing hath been,
> That all ungirt she may be seen;
> An altered aspect now she wears,
> Ah! what a demon she appears!
> She twines another's tresses, see!
> —I know not half her artistry—
> With plaits and ringlets mingled so,
> On her own head they seem to grow.)

This familiar realism, turned to the purpose of demon-
strating the falsity of worldly values, is well seen in the
semi-autobiographical "O vita penosa," which we
have already considered at some length.[3] But it

[1] *Lauda VIII.*, " O femene, guardate."
[2] *Loc. cit.*
[3] See ch. ii.

achieves its greatest success in two dramatic dialogues:
the celebrated and terrible meditation upon death,
" Quando t'alegri, omo de altura," [1] with its unsparing
catalogue of the horrors of the tomb; and the viva-
cious *contrasto* between the Rich Old Man and the
Poor Old Man.[2] These poems, which are marked by
great maturity of style, represent the culmination of a
type of poetry specially characteristic of his missionary
period.

" Quando t'alegri," one of the most powerful of
Jacopone's works, achieved a swift and widespread
popularity. The early date of this poem is proved by
its inclusion in the few existing manuscripts which
may belong to the late thirteenth century—*i.e.* to the
period preceding Jacopone's imprisonment—such as
the *laudario* of the flagellants of Cortona [3] and the
contemporary codex in the archives of Pietra Ligure: [4]
its immense popularity and wide diffusion, by the
fact that it alone among Jacopone's works appears in
almost every miscellaneous collection of Italian *laude.*
In " Quando t'alegri " we see Jacopone under the spell
of that mediæval obsession which produced the Danse
Macabre and the popular poem of the *Trois vifs et
trois morts.* There is nothing original in it. It is but a
dramatic variation, of special vigour and nastiness,
upon a theme which was dear to every thirteenth-
century moralist, and which the tragedy of his own
life may have compelled him to face in its most terrible
form—the transitory character of all bodily strength
and beauty, the imminent death and decay of the flesh.

If " Quando t'alegri " be a sermon on the inevitable
horrors of death, the *tenzone* between Two Old Men
is a sermon on the preliminaries of old age, the passing

---

[1] *Lauda XXV.* (p. 263).
[2] *Lauda XXII.,* " Audite una entenzone—ch'era fra doi persone."
[3] Described by R. Renier in *Giornale Storico della Letteratura Italiana,*
xi. (1887).
[4] Brugnoli, p. cvii.

away of bodily beauty and strength. It is a vivid
picture of helpless and senile humanity, wretched
indeed if it have no hope beyond the visible world.
There is little to choose here between the lot of the
rich and the poor. The ragged old man is cursed with
a cruel son, who robs, mocks, and frightens him, and
perpetually asks him when he is going to die: but he
has a kind and pious daughter-in-law, who washes and
cleans and does everything for him, and makes his old
age at least bearable. Worse is the position of the
prosperous old man, once a gallant and handsome
knight, now reduced to the undignified dotage of the
worn-out worldling. His daughter-in-law is hard, with
a serpent's tongue and a voice like a neighing horse,
and abuses him all the time; pointing out how revolt-
ing are his weaknesses, how nasty his habits, how
hideous his appearance. The moral, as in "O vita
penosa," is always the worthlessness of earthly life
taken alone; the miseries and discomforts which out-
weigh its satisfactions, the retribution which follows
indulgence in its pleasures. It was by the negative and
ascetic way of disillusion with the here-and-now, by
perpetual demonstration of the folly of a life devoted
to mere worldly success, that Jacopone first strove to
turn his hearers to eternal things.

> O gente che amate
> en belleza delettate,
> venite a contemplare,
> ché ve porrá giovare!
> mirate en questo specchio
> de me desfatto vechio;
> fui sí formoso e bello,
> né citade né castello
> chivel non ci armanca
> ch'a me veder traea;
> or so cosí desfatto
> en tutto scontrafatto,
> onomo ha gran paura
> vedendo mia figura;

vedete la belleza
che non ha stabeleza:
la mane el fior è nato,
la sera el vei seccato.[1]

(O folk who take delight
In beauty fair and bright,
Come hither, gaze on me!
That sight may wholesome be.
Yea, in this glass behold
Me, wretched, hideous, old!
—In castle and in town,
Such beauty was my crown,
That every soul would run
To see so fair an one.
Now, how am I disguised,
Undone, deformed, despised!
My face makes men afraid,
So woful, so decayed.
Lo! beauty, fair of face,
Hath no abiding place;
At dawn the flower is gay
At dusk it fades away!)

In these poems, then, we may still see the character
of much of Jacopone's early preaching, and are able to
look at him through the eyes of those contemporaries
to whom these menacing compositions were first sung.
He was evidently at this time a blunt evangelist, who
mocked, bullied, and scolded the sinner to repentance:
unwilling, as indeed all the great missionaries have
been, to offer the sweetness of the spiritual life to those
who had not yet realised their own deep need of moral
reformation. He did not hesitate to draw in darkest
colours the horrors of sin and its inevitable result: for
he wanted his converts to follow the way he had trodden
himself, to face the stern demands of the spiritual
world, and experience to the full the purgative in-
fluence of godly fear.[2] This bracing propaganda pro-
bably had considerable success in attracting listeners,

[1] *Lauda XXII.*, " Audite una entenzone."
[2] *Lauda I.*, " O regina cortese " (p. 250).

if not in saving souls. Even in the words of the dullest
and most ignorant revivalist there is a burning sin-
cerity which arrests attention; and Jacopone was
neither dull nor ignorant. He brought from the old
life to the new a trained intellect, skilled eloquence,
and a thorough understanding of the world he had
left. The little pictures of daily life in " O femene,
guardate,"[1] " O me lasso, dolente,"[2] " Audite una
entenzone,"[3] and " O vita penosa "[4] are real con-
tributions to our knowledge of thirteenth-century
Umbria. He was by nature both fervent and acute;
sometimes exuberant, racy, even humorous, sometimes
terrible in his denunciations. Those to whom he sang
would enjoy both extremes. Moreover, even in that
time of great converts, his social position and dramatic
abandonment of the world, his first strange antics and
subsequent austerity of life, would give to him con-
siderable notoriety. Long before the end of his mis-
sionary period, he must have become a well-known and
perhaps a popular figure in the religious life of Umbria:
for so vigorous a personality could hardly pass un-
noticed, whether regarded as a fanatic, a troubadour,
or a saint.

This growing celebrity may well have been one of
the factors which brought about the second great
spiritual crisis in Jacopone's life. It might have seemed
to the outward eye that he had now achieved perfect
self-conquest; that his renunciation was complete, his
new life firmly established, and nothing stood between
himself and God. The fact remains that he was not at
rest; that he felt a growing need, as the years passed
and the powers of his soul developed, for some more
complete abnegation of self. He appeared, it is true, to
be living a life of heroic mortification. But as the
elements of that life crystallised, and it took on more
and more a professional shape, it brought into being a

---

[1] *Lauda VIII.*   [2] *Lauda XX.*   [3] *Lauda XXII.*   [4] *Lauda XXIV.*

fresh phase of the conflict between the human tendency
to action and self-expression, the mystical tendency to
humble surrender and self-mergence, which persisted
almost to the end of Jacopone's life. The records prove
to us how passionate was his interest in human affairs,
how difficult he found it to leave his fellow-men alone.
In the world he had struggled with them for profes-
sional and social supremacy. Now he struggled with
them that he might win their souls. Hence the career
of the wandering missionary, as it developed, made
ever greater calls on his attention and energy; and
ended by giving too much scope to the artist and
orator, too little to the contemplative and penitent—
a situation only too common in the lives of great
preachers, teachers, and revivalists. In one of his most
personal poems,[1] he describes the constant effort to
attain the "golden mean" of a perfectly balanced inner
and outer life, which continued to torment him even
after he had submitted to the guidance of an external
rule: the impossibility of achieving an abstinence
which will yet leave the body strong enough to bear its
burdens, a life of prayer and silence which shall yet
fulfil its duty to the world. He wants to be despised of
men, but cannot go in rags without attracting their
notice, and consequently becoming puffed up and in-
jured by vanity. When he gives himself to contempla-
tion he has a horrible fear that he is wasting his time.
He sways helplessly between these extremes of thought
and action, his emotional instability increased by this
external disharmony and unrest. We shall probably be
right in conceiving this situation, in an aggravated
form, as a dominant feature in the last phases of his
free ascetic life. He might have said with Augustine,
" I was caught up to Thee by Thy beauty, and dragged
back by my own weight." [2] Plainly he needed a rule

---

[1] *Lauda XXXVIII.*, " O megio virtuoso."
[2] Aug., *Conf.*, vii., 17.

which should be independent of his own impulses, free
him from the onus of choice, and relieve a struggle
which was steadily dissipating his spiritual energy.

That three-fold vow of poverty, chastity, and
obedience, which summarises the demands of Christian
asceticism, represents not merely three external obliga-
tions, but three essential interior conditions of the soul
which seeks for union with God. They are interde-
pendent forms of spiritual freedom, based on the
liberating virtue of humility. Now outward poverty
Jacopone certainly possessed. But interior poverty he
had not: the I, the Me, the Mine, still persisted in him,
since he kept and enjoyed his own liberty of action, his
self-chosen position in the religious world, his rapturous
and cherished communion with God. He had merely
exchanged one sort of wealth for another. Of those
three "heavens of poverty" which he describes in his
great Ode [1] he had only reached the first, the renounc-
ing of riches, knowledge, and reputation: this last,
perhaps, not quite so perfectly as he supposed, since
the "fama di sanctitate" on which he looked with such
horror in after years certainly touched, and perhaps at
one moment enticed him. The second great stage of
detachment was yet beyond his reach—the painful
renunciation of his spiritual treasure. The fundamen-
tally self-regarding hope of heaven and fear of hell,
the craving for God's sweetness and dread of His dark,
so hard to evict from the human heart, still prevailed
with him.

> Queste quattro spogliature
> più che le prime so dure;
> se le dico, par errure
> a chi non ha capacitate.
>   De lo 'nferno non temere
> e del ciel spem non avere;
> e de nullo ben gaudere
> e non doler d'aversitate. [2]

---

[1] *Lauda LX.*, " O amor de povertate " (p. 420).   [2] *Loc. cit.*

Again, outward chastity he possessed: but that interior chastity, that pure, still spirit of devotion, which Ruysbroeck defines as the casting out of all disordered love,[1] all desire for spiritual satisfaction, he had not yet achieved. He lusted after God with the fierceness and heat of his old unmortified passions turned to a supernal objective. But perhaps it is in the matter of obedience that the falling-short is most glaringly apparent. From one point of view, Jacopone's convert life had been an orgy of spiritual self-will, noble indeed, but with the untamed nobility of the wild. It had been marked first by self-chosen and immoderate asceticism, then by uncontrolled wanderings and undisciplined spiritual exaltation. He was a freelance, fervent and zealous in prayer and good works, but subject to no authority other than his private interpretation of God's will. We do not know when or how the unsatisfactory character of such a liberty became clear to him: but we have one poem which—if we can regard it in a personal light—seems to suggest the character of the danger which first led him to recognise it, and drove him to the higher freedom that consists in the total surrender of the will. In this poem he accuses himself with great bitterness of having wandered far from the pathway traced by the saints: of yielding to the temptation which dogs all professional spirituality, and desiring in his heart the deadly poison of religious popularity, the respect and admiration of men, whilst appearing to the world a humble and illuminated soul.[2]

> Molto me so delongato
> de la via che i santi on calcato.
>   Delongato me so de la via
> e storto me so en ipocrisia;
> e mostro a la gente che sia
> lo spirito illuminato.

[1] *The Seven Degrees of Love*, ch. iii.
[2] *Lauda XXIX.*, " Molto me so delongato."

Illuminato me mostro de fore
ch'aia umilitate nel core;
ma se l'omo non me fa grande onore,
encontenente me so corrocciato.

Corrocciato me so per usanza
qual om en mio onore ha mancanza;
ma quel che ci ha fede e speranza,
con lui me so delettato.

Delettato me so en mostra fare,
perché altri me deia laudare;
odendo 'l mio fatto blasmare,
da tal compagnia so mucciato.

El mucciare aio fatto ad engegno,
perché altri me tenga de meglio;
ma molto m' apiccio e destregno
ché paia ch'el mondo ho lassato.

(Very far my feet have strayed
From the road the saints have made!
Yea! far enough away, and yet I wind
A coiled hypocrisy about my mind
And strive to show myself to all mankind
With shining sanctity illuminate.
Illuminate, my lying part I play
Heartfelt humility my false array;
Yet, unless men due honour to me pay
At once I rage within, disconsolate.
Disconsolate my heart with all around
If any praise with faint uncertain sound;
But he whose faith and hope in me abound,
In him is my delight immoderate.
Immoderate is my desire to claim
The praise bestowed upon a holy name
But if instead I hear a word of blame
Straightway I turn and flee precipitate.
Precipitate I flee, with purpose clear
That worthy in men's eyes I may appear;
With many a fast and penances austere
I feign to spurn this world degenerate.)

It was, then, if we accept the evidence of this poem, the old talent for success, the old pride of life reappearing in a new disguise which first revealed to Jacopone the fact that self-love had not yet been evicted from the centre of his consciousness: that self-chosen penances

may become an indulgence, and deliberate self-abase-
ment a subtle form of arrogance, which ends by
demanding, attracting, and enjoying the dangerous
appreciation of the world. Probably the mood which is
here expressed was exaggerated: but there are other
passages in the *laude* which suggest that the danger he
describes was a real one, which tormented him through-
out his spiritual course. Again and again he names
with horror a reputation for holiness as one of the
worst weapons which Satan can use against the soul.[1]
Further, the perpetual demands made upon a well-
known and popular missionary may have starved his
contemplative life: splitting his attention, exhausting
his energies, and producing those inevitable periods of
reaction, gloom, and spiritual impotence when the
Divine Light seems to be withdrawn, which ascetic
writers call "aridity" or "loss of God." Such an
interior darkness and deprivation of God every con-
templative has to bear, sometimes for long periods, in
the course of his interior education.[2] Psychologically,
it seems to be a negative state, a reaction from the
intense exaltation felt by the growing mystical con-
sciousness; and represents the abrupt relapse of an over-
strained spiritual apprehension. Spiritually, it effects
the difficult purification of the will, which here if any-
where learns the lesson of complete surrender and
enters the "second heaven" of poverty. Always en-
tailing the most awful loneliness possible to the spirit
of man, this condition presses with special weight on
those who are subject to no rule but that of their own
enthusiastic and undisciplined wills, and who lack the
support of a solid ascetic tradition, an enclosing cor-
porate life. These are lost in the sudden darkness,

---

[1] *Cf. Laude XVI.*, " Que fai, anema predata ? "; *XXXVIII.*, " O megio
virtuoso "; *XLVII.*, " Or udite la battaglia "; *LX.*, " O amor de pover-
tate " (p. 420).
[2] See the admirable description in the *Imitation of Christ*, Bk. II.,
ch. ix.

chilled, impotent and bewildered; unable to read, to
pray, even to weep for the departure of grace. Three
of Jacopone's poems seem to describe either his actual
endurance or vivid memories of this state;[1] in which he
suffered, as only a great and impetuous lover can, from
the mysterious absence and apparent cruelty of his
Love. In these passionate songs we feel again the
alternate moods of anguish and tenderness, self-abase-
ment, entreaty, despair, through which he passed.

> Amor, di' la cagione
> de lo tuo partimento,
> che m'hai lassata afflitta
> en gran dubitamento;
> se da schifeza èi vento,
> vogliote satisfare;
> s'io me voglio tornare,
> non te ne torne amore?
>
> Amor, perché me desti
> nel cor tanta dolceza,
> da poi che l'hai privato
> de tanta alegreza?
> non chiamo gentileza
> om che dá ed artoglie;
> s'io ne parlo co folle,
> io me n'ho anvito, amore.

The answer of Love seems to point back to this period
of imperfect detachment and new yielding to the world:

> Omo che te lamenti,
> brevemente responno:
> tollendo lo tuo albergo,
> crédici far sogiorno;
> albergastice 'l monno
> e me cacciasti via;
> donqua fai villania,
> se tu mormori d'amore.[2]

---

[1] *Laude LXVI.*, "Or chi averá cordoglio?"; *LXVII.*, "Amor, diletto
amore" (p. 294), and *LXVIII.*, "Piangi, dolente anima predata" (p. 290).
But one or more of these may belong to the "second night." See
below, p. 200.

[2] *Lauda LXVII.*

Beside this we may place " Or chi averá cordoglio ? " [1] with its recognition of wrongness; representing perhaps Jacopone's awakening to the causes of his own state, to that failure in perfect gratitude for the love poured out on him, which had now " locked the door " between himself and God.

> Veggio che iustamente
> haime de te punito,
> mostrato m'hai el defetto
> perch'èi da me fugito,
> iustizia m'ha ferito
> ed hamme de te privato.[2]

> (I see that 'tis in justice thy hand hath chastened me
> In leaving me forsaken, my sin thou makest me see;
> 'Tis Justice that hath struck
> And robbed my soul of thee.)

Whether these inferences be true or not, it is at any rate certain that, about the year 1278, Jacopone awoke to the fact that all was not well with his soul. He had reached that curious spiritual *impasse* which so often occurs in the lives of the mystics, when the great thrust forward of conversion seems to have spent itself, and they can do no more of themselves. This situation, they say, marks the transition between the " first mystic life " of purgation and that " second mystic life " of illumination, which leads to divine union. Whilst the characteristic of the first life is a fully-developed personality, enlightened and supported by a strong sense of the Presence of God, which often expresses itself in lofty spiritual intuitions, vigorous individual action, and the ecstatic perception of heavenly things; the final aim of the second life is the loss of the personal self in a greater whole—a total self-abandonment to God and the movements of His will. Jacopone had completed the first cycle of the spiritual course, with its complementary states of

[1] *Lauda LXVI.*   [2] *Loc. cit.*

pleasure and of pain. He had purged his sense-life of its errors. It was the purification of the will which he needed now: its detachment from personal desire. The universe of the purified consciousness, with its fervid emotional reactions to the Presence of God, was broken up. Terrible hours of gloom in which Divine Love seemed to have forsaken him, the sharp oscillations of a consciousness moving towards fresh levels, had prepared the way for that second surrender, perhaps not less searching than the first, in which he yielded up his free will. With so clear an inward vision of the form which love should give to life, he deliberately submitted himself to its imperfect earthly imitation:

> They say, " What is love? " Say " Renunciation of will."
> Whoso has not escaped from will, no will hath he.[1]

Being the man he was, only a dramatic act could content him. He wanted to give external expression to his instinct for an ordered, balanced, and surrendered life; to obtain, in the place of the free, self-chosen, and untrammelled career of the wandering ascetic, the more perfect liberty conferred by obedience. The solution he chose was drastic, like all the decisive acts of his life. He surrendered to an authority peculiarly uncongenial to him; to the rule of a temporising religious institution which retained the outer shell of the Franciscan idea, but had lost touch with its fervour and its romance. Even the *Vita*, strongly biassed in favour of the Conventual friars, acknowledges how hard a wrench was here needed, how great a sacrifice was made.

" And when the end of ten years had come, Divine grace inspiring him, he perceived this state of freedom to be very dangerous, although it was of great perfection for the mortification of the self, and the true grounding of the spiritual life. And therefore he thought within himself that he would take up a life more certain

[1] Jalalu 'd 'Din Rūmi.

to save his soul.   And having dwelt for some time in this thought, and made much orison to God concerning it, he was at last inspired by God to enter the religion of the Friars Minor, as the religion which is the most detached and alien from the world, and nearest to the life of Christ and His holy apostles." [1]

[1] *Vita*, 3ᵛᵒ.

CHAPTER IV

JACOPONE THE FRANCISCAN FRIAR

ST. JOHN of the Cross says that human nature must pass through "three nights" in its growth towards union with the Divine order. These are the night or purification of the senses, of the will, and of the spirit.[1] In Jacopone, both senses and will were strong and highly-tempered. Life in the world had developed them and given them ample scope. His career as a penitent tertiary, now ten years old, had entailed the perpetual and at last complete mortification of the senses. The old attachments to material comfort and sensual satisfactions were broken for ever. Now, at the end of his free missionary career, he was faced by the "night of the will" awaiting him, and separating the ascetic from the mystic life.

We have seen the strong emphasis which he placed on self-abasement: how its dramatic expression and inward realisation dominated his penitential practice. From first to last, his ethical struggle was centred on the "mortal sin" of pride—the standing menace of all strongly volitional temperaments. Therefore it is not surprising that the call to a more complete spirituality which he now heard, should have taken the form of a

[1] St. John of the Cross, *The Ascent of Mount Carmel* and *The Dark Night of the Soul*.

99

call to new and more complete humiliation; a self-surrender which included the sacrifice of his personal liberty and personal will.

A parallel situation in the life of a later mystic, Suso, will help us to understand the nature of the interior crisis through which Jacopone now passed. Suso, converted in his eighteenth year, was a man of ardent temperament who at first practised, like Jacopone, intense physical mortifications. For twenty-two years he lived a life of asceticism and fervid devotion, by which he "triumphed over the unruly sensual man."[1] At the end of that time, being forty years old, "God showed him that this severity and these penances were but a good beginning"; a preparation for the "upper school of perfect self-abandonment." It was this "upper school" that Jacopone—now close on fifty years of age—sought in the convent of Todi. The words in which the angel of his vision recommended it to Suso might well be applied to him: "Examine thyself inwardly, and thou shalt see that thou hast still much self-will. Notwithstanding all the mortifications which thou didst of thy own choice inflict on thyself, thou canst not yet endure external vexations . . . when they praise thee thou art happy, when they blame thee thou art sad. Verily it is needful that thou shouldst go to an upper school."[2]

The Friars Minor of Todi, if we may here trust the statements of the *Vita*, were not greatly inclined to receive their notorious fellow-citizen; though they could no longer reject him, as in the first days of his conversion, either on the score of arrogance or on that of insanity. The convent followed the "relaxed rule," and was inimical to that movement for the restoration of perfect Franciscan poverty with which, perhaps, Jacopone had already associated himself. Its inmates had no wish for the company of extremists, or

---

[1] Suso, *Leben*, cap. **xx.**   [2] *Op. cit.*, cap. **xxi.**

inconveniently consistent observers of the Rule; for
moderate piety is apt to seem tepid when brought into
contact with the unmitigated fervour of the enthusiast.
Further, the Church as a whole, and the religious in-
stitutions living under its protection, felt no more
friendliness for the roving evangelists and *giullari di
Dio* who fed the growing hunger of the people for per-
sonal religion, than comfortable vicars of our day feel
for the "undenominational" street-corner revivalist.
The popular appeal, the ardour and directness of these
minnesingers of the Holy Ghost threw the unconvin-
cing ministrations of the professional clergy into un-
pleasant relief; and it seemed best to class them with
other minstrels as "ballad-singers and vagrants." This
feeling was particularly strong among the Conventual
friars, who regarded the continuance and success of
these primitive Franciscan methods as an implied
reproach. Therefore Jacopone's missionary life, though
completely in harmony with the spirit of St. Francis,[1]
would not recommend him to the official representa-
tives of the Order. That Order already meant many
things which had not entered into St. Francis' plan:
some, which we know that he abhorred. The freshness
of its morning hour was past; it had crystallised, lost
intensity, and sacrificed fervour to common sense. The
primitive Christian enthusiasm, the grace, simplicity,
and power which Francis had given to his little flock, was
no longer the common possession of the friars. The
family had now become a huge institution, sheltering
almost every type of character, almost every grade of
spiritual enthusiasm. We have only to read the lively
chronicle of Jacopone's contemporary, Salimbene, to
realise how far the Friars Minor had already drifted
from the unity of spirit at which Francis had aimed.
The rule of poverty was the rock on which they had
split.   Once this passed beyond the little group of

[1] See Tamassia, *op. cit.*, cap. vi.

enthusiasts to whom it had seemed the very condition of happiness and peace, it tended to encourage on the one hand a deliberate and fantastic squalor, on the other the unworthy shifts and compromises of those who could not endure its full severity. At one end of the scale there was now the exalted and sometimes absurd perfectionism of the extreme Spirituals or *zelanti*; who, interpreting the Rule and Last Testament of Francis in its most literal sense, hated the comforts and even the decencies of life as the early Quakers hated steeple-houses and sacraments, and often judged their weaker brethren with a want of charity which Francis would surely have condemned. These hot-headed lovers of Lady Poverty went to all lengths in their devotion to the accidents of destitution, and by their excesses brought into contempt the sane and moderate Spirituals of the type of John of Parma and John Parenti, who struggled to keep the Order true to those ideals of simplicity and humility of life which Francis had taught. They regarded ignorance, thriftlessness, and squalor as positive virtues, and rebelled against the most ordinary decencies of clothing and cleanliness.[1] Hence they played into the hands of the opposite party of the "wide observance," who stretched the Rule to a point at which it would accommodate all sorts and conditions of men. Many of these were Franciscan only in name, and naturally regarded the Spirituals—moderate and extreme alike—as inconvenient and disorderly fanatics.

But between these groups of zealous and of comfortable souls there was room for many shades of temperament and practice: for the ordinary human being, eager to be good, but unable to be perfect save in rare moments of enthusiasm, who must always make up the bulk of any religious society, and whose religious needs were satisfied by the wise moderation of St.

[1] Cf. *Chronicle of the Twenty-four Generals*, p. 263.

Bonaventura's rule. We read in Salimbene of learned, simple, merry, holy, and worldly friars: of theologians, visionaries, musicians, missionaries, politicians, saints. The great convents of the Order were little worlds, in which moderate men of all types could live together in peace ; as Salimbene himself, who observed the " relaxed " rule, but could admire the nobler souls who rejected it, did with the great Spiritual, John of Parma. Theoretically all—" spiritual " and " relaxed " alike—had accepted Holy Poverty ; as, theoretically, ordinary Christians have accepted the Sermon on the Mount. She was the special glory of the Friars Minor. They preached sermons and wrote hymns in her honour ; but in Jacopone's day the majority interpreted their obligations to her in a way that will easily be understood by any member of an " established church." When the Conventual party built at Assisi the beautiful and costly church of S. Francesco, the very existence of which was an infraction of the Primitive Rule and filled the loyal hearts of Giles and Leo with wrath and despair, they caused the Marriage of Francis with Poverty to be painted above the Founder's tomb. Already it had passed from the sphere of example to the sphere of myth. Already the new, vital impulse which Francis had brought into being, had lapsed into the mechanical. Only the Spiritual brothers protested with varying degrees of energy against these inconsistencies, and tried to put into practice the stern precepts of the Founder's testament. For this they were sometimes admired as saints, sometimes mocked at as eccentrics, sometimes persecuted as fanatics. Those writings, such as the *Sacrum Commercium* and the early legends now included in the *Speculum*, in which they drew attention to the more austere side of the teaching of Francis, were suppressed. Most of them had now withdrawn to remote friaries and hermitages, where they could practise the Primitive Rule in peace. In some extreme cases, the more rebellious spirits were expelled from the Franciscan family.[1]

This being the condition of the Order, it is plain that Jacopone's missionary life and passion for destitution would not be attractive to its Conventual superiors. He may already have been known as a member of the Spiritual party, for many Tertiaries held important positions in it.[2] His mordant tongue, and uncompromising devotion to poverty and penance, were certainly notorious. The relaxed houses had only lately escaped from the firm rule of St. Bonaventura, whose death in 1274 had been followed by a distinct sharpening of the hostility between the Conventual and Spiritual groups. Yet, as against all this, Jacopone was now a person of some importance in the religious world of Umbria ; a successful preacher, probably a popular poet of established reputation, and regarded by the people as a saint. In Todi, which seems to have remained his headquarters, the social standing of the Benedetti no doubt contributed to his prestige. Such a personality is not easy to refuse. His capitulation to established forms after ten years of complete spiritual liberty was itself something of a triumph for the Conventual friars ; and the acquisition of saints is a primary function of every self-respecting religious house. This difficult situation is reflected in the *Vita ;* which chronicles— perhaps from some source based on the discreetly-edited reminiscences of those who took part in it—the anxious discussion that preceded Jacopone's admission.

" He, being in this purpose and true disposition, began to reason with the friars of the Order concerning his desire ; for these hesitated to receive him, because of his vagabond life. And all differed, some praising and some abusing him ; so that they knew not what to

---

[1] For the Spirituals see below, ch. v.

[2] For instance, Pier the Combseller of Siena (*Purg.,* xiii., 124), who instructed Ubertino da Casale in the spiritual life. See E. Gardner, *Dante and the Mystics,* p. 214.

do, and discussing it, came to no decision. And at this time Jacopone made that song of contempt of the world which begins thus, " Or udite nova pazia." O marvellous thing! when he had sung this *lauda* to the brethren, inspired of God they received him into the Order, and called him Frate Jacopone. And although he had much learning, he would not be a clerk but a lay brother; and in this state he meekly lived and persevered till the end of his praiseworthy life." [1]

It is by no means certain that humility was the only, or indeed the principal, reason for Jacopone's refusal to take orders ; though the position of lay brother plainly offered special opportunities for the cultivation of meekness and self-suppression. Clearly he had no special love for the priesthood as such ; indeed, he took with him into the Order a distinct anti-clerical bias. Though his attitude to Church discipline was orthodox, and he always urged his converts to sacramental confession and reverence for religious authority,[2] his whole career as free hermit and lay-missionary constituted an implied criticism of the apathy of the professional priest as regards the saving of souls. Further, we must remember that when he became a Friar Minor, the whole question of the relation of lay brothers to professed was a controversial one. St. Francis had first planned his Order as a free community of single and married laity of both sexes, devoted to a life of poverty and penance for love of God. From this original stock the three orders of Friars Minor, Poor Clares, and Tertiaries were afterwards formed. Priests were not excluded from the

---

[1] *Vita*, 3\o and 4\ro. The attribution of *Udite nova pazia* to Jacopone is apocryphal and dates only from the fifteenth century (see Brugnoli, p. 407). This and other statements of the *Vita* concerning the circumstances in which the various *laude* were composed are valueless, and largely concerned with poems which are no longer regarded as authentic. These passages are probably late additions to the primitive legend.

[2] Cf. *Laude XCVII.,* " O peccator dolente "   *X.,* " Peccator, chi t'ha fidato " ; *IV.,* " O alta penitenza."

primitive society, but it was fundamentally a lay
movement, in which they were never intended to form
the majority. This policy had been reversed by Elias
and his successors, under whom Franciscanism became
more and more monastic and ecclesiastical, losing its
open and popular character. The Spiritual party was
now pressing for the restoration of the primitive ideal:
a restoration which involved recognition of the lay
brother as the typical friar. Jacopone's refusal to take
orders therefore suggests that, if not actually a member
of the Spiritual group, he was already in full sympathy
with its programme, and willing in his own person to
put this into effect.

From the beginning, then, his position in the Order
was paradoxical: for he stood for the Franciscanism of
Francis, the life of meekness, poverty, and love, yet
deliberately entered a convent of the wide observance,
where those who kept the Primitive Rule in its severity
were disliked. His reason for choosing San Fortunato
may have been personal. Perhaps memories of his con-
version drew him to his native city. Perhaps he had one
or more friends and sympathisers amongst the friars ;
for there were, as Salimbene shows us, saintly and
ardent spirits to be found even in the relaxed communi-
ties.[1] Almost certainly he had to endure there con-
siderable petty persecution, perhaps real ill-treatment,
in addition to the thorough training in patience, meek-
ness, trivial obedience, and good temper which is
inherent in all community life: a difficult environment
for a middle-aged man of strong character, never since
youth subjected to any rules but those of his own
making. He was like a gifted and ardent amateur
suddenly introduced into a society of rather bored
and sophisticated professionals, who had long ago re-
lapsed from the vital to the mechanical. From them he

---

[1] Thus even Ubertino da Casale, for years after his " introduction into
the mysteries of Jesus," continued to live comfortably, observing only the
mitigated rule. (*Arbor Vitæ Crucifixæ*, Prologue.)

must endure not only the inevitable jealousies and animosities which the successful free-lance evokes in the established practitioner, but also the quiet hostility of the professional point of view, with its disconcerting scale of values, its established formulæ, its hatred of the unusual or the enthusiastic. "And it was not a little difficult to him," says the *Vita*, "to submit himself altogether to obedience to his superiors; considering that he had done great things in mortification in the ten years when he wore the *bizocone*, but had never endured the subjection and mortification of his own will. And this he did greatly in these first beginnings. And therefore, now discerning in spirit true liberty from the false liberty of the world, he composed the *lauda*, 'O libertá, subietta.'[1] Then Fra Jacopone began to taste and comprehend that Franciscan liberty which before he had not truly known."[2]

Jacopone entered San Fortunato in 1278. Our next undoubted notice of him comes from the year 1294, when Celestine V. was elected to the papacy.[3] This notice assures us that he was then one of the principal leaders of the Spiritual Franciscans, that his activities and reputation had spread far beyond the limits of Umbria, and he had become a person of importance in the religious world. The outward events of these sixteen years, which separate the *giullare di Dio* from the reforming friar and ecclesiastical politician, are mostly unknown to us; though there is reason to suppose that only the first ten were spent in the Umbrian convents, the last six in or about Rome. But Jacopone's self-revelations enable us to reconstruct the general course of his inward development: a development in which we meet again, upon higher levels of activity, most of the qualities which gave peculiar flavour to his penitential life. The ardour of devotion, the freakish humour, which sometimes passed the limits of eccentricity, the

[1] *Lauda XXXIV.*   [2] *Vita, 5to.*   [3] *Vide infra, p. 173.*

vigorous spirit of criticism, the extravagant asceticism, and paradoxical exaltation of the "wisdom of folly," all reappear; gradually to be disciplined by that spirit of ordered love which he now learned to recognise as the ideal disposition of the surrendered soul.

In a long and rather uninspired *lauda*, probably composed towards the end of his life,[1] Jacopone purports to describe his own mystical development under the image of an ascent to the "three heavens": the Stellar Heaven of faith, where we apprehend God by meditation; the Crystalline Heaven of hope, where we achieve His contemplation; and the Empyrean of Love, where He is known in His essence. This conception, in which students of Dante will notice several points of contact with the *Paradiso*, and also with St. Thomas Aquinas, is of course derived through the Dionysian writings from Neoplatonism.[2] According to Jacopone, the ascent is made by way of the three trees rooted in faith, hope, and charity, which bridge the gap between earth and the Empyrean. Though we need not insist that this schematic arrangement answers in all respects to his own experience, yet the points which he chooses to emphasise, and the order in which they are placed, do give us a clue to the general trend of his inner life, as he saw it in retrospect in those last peaceful years when he had reached the summit of contemplation.

First we observe how small and unimportant the ten years spent *en bizocone* now appeared to him; how little they had done for his inward growth. Each of the trees by which the soul mounts has nine branches, answering to the nine angelic orders. There are thus twenty-seven stages between its conversion and its ecstatic union with the Godhead. But only the first three of these stages—namely contrition, satisfaction,

---

[1] *Lauda LXIX.*, " Fede, spene e caritade." Cf. *Lauda LX.*, " O amor de povertate," p. 420.
[2] See below, ch. vi.

and voluntary poverty—can be identified with his missionary career. On the fourth branch of the tree of faith we already find him entering religion, an act for which the long ascetic training that preceded it now seems merely preparatory: and in the description of its last five branches I think we can see a picture, which both the *laude* and the *Vita* support, of his early life as a friar.

He tells us here that, on his first admission to the Order, he was led to devote himself to prayer, and was drawn to the practice of silence—which can hardly have been an outstanding feature in the life of the popular preacher and *giullare*—beginning, in fact, that education of the contemplative consciousness which mediæval Catholicism had brought to a high point of exactitude. Spiritually as well as physically he had been hitherto a free-lance. His response to the supersensual had been like the response of the untrained artist to beauty: vivid, spontaneous, crude. The ordered routine of the convent, its opportunities of recollection and quiet, its set periods of prayer, would inevitably foster the growth of his inner life, perhaps starved by the demands and preoccupations of a missionary career. He now came into direct contact, possibly for the first time, with the formal side of Christian mysticism, its theory and psychology, its codified states, as worked out by Dionysius the Areopagite, Hugh and Richard of St. Victor, and other great theologians. In spite of his ostentatious disdain for learning, all the poems of his middle period prove to us the eagerness with which Jacopone fed upon these works, and the promptitude with which he responded to their suggestions. The new concentration on the inner life and new submission to established forms had therefore its intellectual as well as its practical side.

The next stage of faith, and perhaps for him one of the most difficult, was that of obedience to his superiors.

In his own words, he found it "better than sacrifice."
The *Vita* has told us how arduous conformity seemed
to him. It goes on to describe his efforts to attain
perfect humility and self-subjection; virtues which he
agreed with St. Francis in regarding as the foundations
of all spirituality—perhaps because they so directly
opposed his natural instincts. Community life, with its
many small restrictions and irritations, its indifference
to the personal point of view, now tested them to the
full. From true humility, says Ruysbroeck, comes
godliness, which makes a man gentle, patient, and
docile.[1] The most fervent admirer of Jacopone will
hardly maintain that these qualities came easily to
him ; yet his position in the convent made constant
demands upon them, his inner life was a perpetual
effort toward their attainment. Though the *Vita*
praises his swift ascent of the ladder of virtue, his own
account assures us—as indeed the vigour of his satirical
laude might make us suspect—that unmortified corners
of character long remained. The wayward ascetic was
not easily transformed into the pattern friar. Fasting
and prayer were welcome—indeed, he loved them to
excess [2]—but it was long before he learned to accept
with meekness the small mortifications of daily life,
and the disharmony between his own vision of perfec-
tion and the low level of the average practice. The
little poem on impatience,[3] which plainly dates from
the later part of his convent career—since he refers in
it to his long training in religion, and faithful recitation
of the hours—shows him still at the mercy of hot
temper and self-esteem, reacting to injustice and con-
tempt with all the old fire and promptitude.

Regarded by a few brethren as an embryo saint,
by most as a tiresome enthusiast, his position in the

[1] *The Kingdom of God's Lovers*, ch. xv.
[2] *Laude XXXVIII.*, "O megio virtuoso" (see below, p. 133), and
XLVII., "Or udite la battaglia."
[3] *Lauda XXVIII.*, "Assai me sforzo," p. 384.

convent cannot have been easy, and his own behaviour seems to have done little to improve it. His openly expressed contempt for those learned friars in whom the Order as a whole took great pride,[1] might have been tolerable in a seasoned saint, but can hardly have been attractive in a new arrival. George Fox, surrounded by the decorous amenities and pious unrealities of a cathedral close, would have been more comfortable than Jacopone in the ranks of the Conventuals. His entrance into the Order had followed close upon the death of St. Bonaventura (1274), who as Minister-General had vainly struggled to bring back the " relaxed " convents to a reasonable observance of the Franciscan ideal, and persuade them to reconciliation with the Spirituals. Bonaventura's own devotional writings prove how deep was his sympathy with the Spiritual point of view; how real, in spite of a certain academic temper, was his enthusiasm for the life of the soul. The satirical poems of Jacopone prove how small had been the success of his efforts to rekindle the primitive fire. In these poems the lack of fervour, the love of comfort, the intellectual pride of the friars are denounced with almost savage violence. Jacopone had dreamed again the lovely dream of Francis, of a community wholly surrendered to the Spirit of Love. He found instead a community full of personal ambitions, and divided by petty differences:

> Vedete el grand'amore
> che l'un a l'altro ha en core!
>
> (Behold the great and wondrous love
> That one and all their hearts doth move!)

he exclaimed in his bitterness, observing the odious pride of the more educated brothers, who ate apart and gave themselves royal airs, though often of humble

[1] See below, p. 142.

birth.[1] Though his own later works witness to deep
reading in philosophy and theology, he saw with special
distress the intellectual snobbery which had invaded
the Order, the spiritual priggishness and absurd
vanity of the learned friars, which already justified
the Founder's deep distrust of academic knowledge.
Francis, like Chaucer's parish priest, had wrought
before he taught: but his followers " voglion dir
molto e niente fare." [2] The Schools of Paris, said
Jacopone, echoing the sorrowful epigram of Giles,
have destroyed Assisi ; for logic is not religion:

> Tale qual é, tal è;
> non c'è religione.[3]

Nor was this spirit of criticism the only quality likely
to render him unpopular. We know that he shared the
enthusiasm of the extreme Spirituals for old clothes
and personal squalor:

> Lo desprezare piaceme
> e de gir mal vestito.[4]
>
> (It pleases me to be despised
> And always go ill clad.)

Contemporary documents leave us no illusions as to
the unpleasant forms which this passion assumed. The
Rule, as interpreted by Ubertino da Casale and other
rigorists, allowed for no change of garments, though a
few spare sets might be held in common, for use when
washing could no longer be deferred.[5] Frocks were
worn day and night. Conrad of Offida, Jacopone's
friend and contemporary, is said to have inhabited the

[1] *Lauda XXXI.*, " Tale qual è." Many of the descriptions in Salimbene
testify to the accuracy of this picture. Observe especially the astonish-
ment of the friars of Ferrara, when John of Parma insisted on inviting the
poorest and feeblest of the brethren to sup at his table, saying, " Go, call
me the poor brethren of the convent, for this office is one wherein all know
enough to bear their Minister company." (See Coulton, *St. Francis to
Dante*, p. 107.)
[2] *Lauda L.*, " Or se parrà."   [3] *Lauda XXXI.*
[4] *Lauda XXXVIII.*, " O megio virtuoso."
[5] *Archiv für Litt. und Kirchengeschichte des Mittelalters*, Band III.,
pp. 56, 176.

same tunic for fifty years. Though the intimate companionship of vermin was far from being a monopoly of the religious life, it was a cross which all true lovers of poverty must cheerfully accept.[1] This strenuous cult of uncleanliness had been considerably mitigated by the *relaxati*, and the friars of San Fortunato probably found Jacopone's edifying personal habits hard to bear. Moreover, the *Vita*—which of course takes the most favourable view of his relations with the community—describes at least one instance in which he relapsed, to the annoyance of the brothers, into those grotesque excesses of mortification which are said to have marked his first revulsion from the world: performances which justify Mr. Coulton's remark that " we revel in Jacopone da Todi's eccentricities, but we are glad to live 600 years to windward of him." [2] It is now impossible to determine whether these tales contain, as they may, a substratum of fact, or whether they represent an effort on the part of the next generation of friars to attribute to a hero of the Order the maximum amount of true Franciscan simplicity, and provide an appropriate setting for the largest possible number of his genuine and apocryphal poems. No biographer of Jacopone, however, can reasonably omit some reference to them ; and each reader must draw his own conclusions as to the extent to which they are consistent with the known facts of his life and work.

The story we are now to consider is presented as an example of the exactitude with which Fra Jacopone observed true Franciscan poverty, " which he loved so tenderly," says the *Vita*, " that he never wished for anything but that which the Rule allowed," being " a true friar minor, and the lover of the virtuous Lady Poverty " —a phrase in which we can detect the influence of John Parenti's beautiful allegory. " And this man of God and fervent Franciscan, Fra Jacopone, was one

---

[1] Coulton, *St. Francis to Dante*, pp. 70, 71.   [2] *Op. cit.*, p. 65.

H

day tempted to eat some liver; but he, as a true warrior
against vice, wished to hold the mean, that is to satisfy
both the body and the soul." Therefore he took the
liver and put it in the cell where he slept, and every
morning when it was time to eat, instead of eating he
smelt it and touched it ; a proceeding which naturally
became less appetising with each succeeding day. The
story gains emphasis when we remember that, on the
evidence of his own poems, the worldly Jacopone had
been very particular about his food: and after his con-
version had struggled to cure himself of fastidiousness,
first by dipping each morsel in wormwood, and then by
cutting his portion into tiny pieces and swallowing
them like pills.[1] Presently the liver went bad, and an
extremely nasty smell penetrated to the corridor,
where it attracted the attention of the friars. These,
becoming more annoyed as it grew in power, looked in
vain for its cause, until at last they traced it to its
home, and found that it issued from Jacopone's cell.
" What madness is the *fantastico* up to now?" they
exclaimed in not unnatural wrath ; and, opening the
door, saw his cherished delicacy, now completely de-
cayed and crawling with worms. Their revenge, which
was prompt and appropriate, must certainly have
satisfied to the full Jacopone's constant craving for
humiliation.[2]

---

[1] Feo Belcari, *Trattati di Fra Jacopone da Todi*, p. 73. Unfortunately,
this habit gave him indigestion ; whereupon, with surprising good sense,
he abandoned it.

[2] *Vita*, 7ro and 7vo. The rest of the story will hardly bear translation:
" Allora quelli frati reprendendolo asperamente lu pigliarono e presolo
sensa tocare terra lu portarono nelo necessario e miselo dentro en quella
puza dicendo poiche te sa cussi bona la puza toghtene e satiatene mo
quanto tu voli. La qual cosa fra Jacopone recevette con tanta alegreza
como uno goloso affamato fose stato posto ad una mensa piena de soavis-
simo cibo. Et estando li dentro tuto giubilando cantando ad alta voce
quella lauda che comenza " O jubilo de core che fai cantare damore." Et
cantando fra Jacopone en questu giubilu en quello luoco cussi fetente. Et
ecote quello consolatore vero delli aflicti e esconsulati ybu xpo beniditu
che gli apparve en quello luoco. Non temendo per la puza de consolare el
suo servo fedele frate Jacopone. Et desegli cossi frate Jacopo carissimo io
o veduto che non te sei schifato ne turbato per langiuria recevuta e per la

This outrageous anecdote is the worst the *Vita* has to tell us about the collisions of temperament which must certainly have occurred between Jacopone and the friars: but it adds that this adventure so greatly increased his love of God that he seemed almost continuously drunken with joy. " And because of this, he suffered much persecution and tribulation, and composed many songs."[1] His own account suggests that these exaggerated practices, or some other expression of unwelcome zeal, did indeed bring serious difficulties upon him; and even that his position in the Order was for a time in doubt. The growing hostility felt by the Conventuals for the friars of strict observance makes this at least probable. A further remark of the *Vita* that " because of his great zeal (for poverty), when he saw that she was little loved he grieved much, and was displeased," shows us one direction in which his critical and uncompromising temper was likely to court unpopularity.

Jacopone's only direct reference to this period is short but clear. At the seventh stage of faith, he says, he endured the contempt of his fellow-men, was beaten, and expelled; and this was to him a very heavy grief.

> Nello settimo fui tirato,
> d'uno ramo desprezato,
> fui battuto e descacciato ;
> ben me fu grave a portare.[2]

(In the seventh state, I was drawn
To the branch of scorn,
With blows thrust forth forlorn,
And this was hard to bear.)

puza dove tu stai per lo mio amore. Ora io te voglio rendere per la puza soave odore domandame quello che tu voli da me chio tello voglio dare gratiosamente."

Students of mediæval literature will not need to be reminded that the last part of this story belongs to a well-marked group of tales illustrating the homely character of the Divine condescension. I have already given my reasons for regarding the *lauda* on the *jubilus* as a composition of earlier date.

[1] *Loc. cit.*   [2] *Lauda LXIX.*, " Fede, spene e caritade," v. 14.

We have no means of knowing whether the dis-
taste felt by the Conventual brothers for the "*fantastico*"
really went to these lengths: but it is difficult to
imagine any other reason for this definite statement
than that of its truth. Perhaps Jacopone's eccentricity
may at times have passed the limits of sanity: for some
students regard the *santa pazia* as a pathological
phenomenon, and believe that he was subject through-
out his life to recurrent periods of instability, when
its frenzy entirely possessed him. Even its milder
manifestations, as we have seen, were calculated to
annoy a well-regulated community; and we can well
understand the sudden exasperation in which the
friars may have ejected this unmanageable saint. It
may on the other hand have been his uncompromising
passion for the Primitive Rule and connection with
the Spiritual party which brought Jacopone into con-
flict with his superiors. As things stand at present, we
can neither accept nor reject, date nor explain the
episode which these lines seem to describe. If the malice
of the *relaxati* really attained such dimensions, it
appears to have overreached itself; for Jacopone—
perhaps because he had accepted adversity with meek-
ness—says that he next found himself revered on
account of his great spirit of devotion, and subject to
the old temptation to allow himself to be regarded as a
saint. We can only conjecture that this indicates some
sort of reconciliation with the Order ; on the one hand,
perhaps, the temporary triumph of those brothers who
saw in his excesses a mark of special holiness, on the
other, a more complete surrender on his own part to
the principle of religious authority, a sacrifice of private
judgment which allowed him to concentrate his atten-
tion on the problems of the inner life. The turmoil of
adjustment to a new environment was now reaching
its term. He was nearing the end of a stage: the
summit of the "tree of faith." There, he says, per-

ceiving with disgust the "nothingness" of his former activities, he began to practise the art of meditation.[1]

Now since the term "meditation," as used by Catholic mystics, describes the lowest and simplest activities of the contemplative consciousness—the first stage in the education of the spiritual sense—we cannot place its acquirement very late in Jacopone's religious career. We might expect him to come to it quickly, when he ceased to be wholly at the mercy of his untamed emotions, and began that deliberate training of the will and attention which is the secret of the life of prayer. I think, therefore, that the period between his entrance into religion and learning of the art of meditation was probably short; and the incidents which marked it were merely successive phases in the difficult adjustment of a particularly inappropriate novice to the set life of a religious establishment. If the verses in which Jacopone describes how he came to the "tree of hope" be confronted with that passage in the *Vita* which deals with his first reactions to the new life, we see that the situation they describe is identical. Here either the *Vita* derives from the *lauda*, or both are recording, from independent standpoints, the same sequence of events. The *Vita* says that Jacopone, in the earlier part of his life as a friar, gave himself to prayer and contemplation. It records at some length —perhaps from a personal reminiscence—the impression made upon him by the prayer of St. Francis in the house of Bernard of Quintavalle, "*Dio mio, Dio mio! Chi sei tu e chi so io ?*" of which he now heard from the friars. "And considering this, Fra Jacopone gave himself altogether to the consideration of these words, which seemed to him of great substance. And resting for some time in this thought, he was brought by God into a marvellous light of self-knowledge." [2] Thus brooding on his own nothingness, and his many past

---

[1] *Loc. cit.*, v. 16.   [2] *Vita*, 4vo.

sins, he became possessed by a deep melancholy; being
" sometimes as full of bitterness and grief as in the first
years of his conversion, so that the friars tried to con-
sole him, thinking he suffered some temptation." [1] To
this period the *Vita* attributes the *lauda* " O Signor,
per cortesia," [2] with its passionate prayer for disease,
adversity, and death; but that poem, in its im-
moderate asceticism and marked crudity of expression,
seems to me more probably a work of his penitential
life.

In *Lauda LXIX*. Jacopone shows us from the
inside this same phase of feeling, when fresh and more
searching self-criticism brought with it a new sense of
unworthiness, and a new realisation of the superficial
character of all merely physical austerities. The standard
of purity and devotion which had satisfied the convert
and penitent, could no longer fulfil the contemplative's
growing hunger for a total self-dedication. Gazing in
his meditation at the " tree of hope "—*i.e.* at the
vision of supersensual possibilities now being revealed
to him—he says that he was filled with contempt for
his own feeble achievement.

> Allora conobbi me dolente,
> ch'io me tenea sí potente,
> e non sapea che fusse niente,
> pur al corpo facea fare.[3]

> (Then I to know my sorry state was brought
> That had myself so stalwart thought,
> Not knowing that those things were nought
> Which I had made my body bear.)

Nevertheless, to the mocking voice which asked him
how he dared try to mount further, since the way was
so steep, he answered that he " could not do otherwise ;
because his heart, burning with love, was seeking for
its Lord." " Then come," said the voice; " but first
you must abandon all things, and next you must do

---

[1] *Loc. cit.*   [2] *Lauda XLVIII.*, see p. 73.   [3] *Loc. cit.*, v. 19.

violence to yourself": that invitation to complete self-giving and heroic endurance—the final conquest over the I, the Me, and the Mine—which is a part of all virile spirituality.

Jacopone now began to climb that tree of hope which "none can see whose feet are fixed on earth," and which brings the soul to the contemplation of the Deity. The preacher, singer, and ready satirist had become a man of silence and prayer: "sappi parlare, ora so fatto muto." [1]   The energies once scattered among many objectives were gathered in, to spend all their power on that deep probing of the secrets of the spirit which is the business and justification of the cloistered life. He has recorded in a few vivid lines the vicissitudes which he endured in the course of this ascent ; the violent oscillations between rapture and anguish through which, as might be expected in a man of his unstable temperament, he moved to new levels of consciousness. We have no clue to the length of time over which these experiences stretched ; but comparison with other documents of Christian mysticism, in which we find a close parallel to the adventures of Jacopone's spirit, suggests that we have here to deal at least with a period of several years. In this he passed through those alternating states of spiritual exaltation and bitter suffering which mystical writers regard as the initiation into the illuminative way, and sometimes call the " Game of Love " wherein God by turns pursues, forsakes, and rewards the soul which desires Him. [2] This stage is commemorated by curt references in two autobiographical *laude*, but chiefly by the important group of poems which was its literary expression.

We need not be surprised that Jacopone's reaction to the vision of God which is the gift of the contemplative life, should have taken an intense emotional

[1] *Lauda XC.*, " Amor de cantate," v. 18, p. 372.
[2] Cf. St. Catherine of Siena, *Dialogo*, cap. lxxvii., " With souls that have arrived at perfection I play no more the game of love."

form ; nor that the phase of development which we
are now trying to analyse should have seen the full
flowering of his spiritual passion. As the natural artist,
once he submits himself to training, achieves a more
profound and delicate perception of beauty, so does
the spiritual genius sharpen and refine his special
faculty by education ; bringing into clear focus our
blurred human vision of that " Beauty supreme, the
absolute and the primal, which fashions its lovers to
beauty and makes them worthy of love." [1]   Towards
such a vision, as it slowly grew before him, Jacopone's
ardent nature—forced now into the single channel of
the devotional life—would rush out in a torrent of
adoration. " In the illuminative way," says Dionysius
the Areopagite, " the mind is enkindled to the burning
of love." [2]   In Jacopone this surrender to pure feeling
would be encouraged rather than checked by his Fran-
ciscan environment, and by the strong Franciscan bias
to devotions centring upon the passion and humanity of
Christ. When, therefore, he tells us that on the second
branch of the " tree of hope " he received the fruit
of love and gift of tears, he tells us in effect that he was
now experiencing in an intense degree the characteristic
mood of the Franciscan mystic. As regards the em-
phasis laid upon tears, we have to remember that these
were in the Middle Ages among the most valued graces
of the spiritual life. They played a large part in Fran-
ciscan devotion.[3]   According to Thomas of Celano, St.
Francis when at prayer " watered the ground with his
tears." [4]   The *Speculum*, a document which is valuable
as a record of tendency, if not always of fact, says that
even those " French-like rejoicings " in which he sang

[1] Plotinus, *En.*, i., 6, 7.
[2] *De mystica theologia.* Prologue.
[3] Cf. the account of the Blessed Umiliana, who tried to produce the gift
of tears by the use of quicklime, and nearly blinded herself. Wadding,
Annales Minorum, an. 1246. Quoted by Coulton, *From St. Francis to
Dante,* p. 317.
[4] *Vita Secunda,* cap. lxi.

like a troubadour to the Lord Jesus Christ, always
ended in weeping.[1]   In this extreme emotionalism the
heroes of the Order followed the example of their
patriarch. We can therefore understand why Jacopone
chooses tears as the symbol of growing fervour, and
sign of spiritual advance.[2] In another poem of personal
reminiscence, the *Tree of Divine Love*, he places them
in their proper connection with the ardent state of
feeling which now possessed him.

> Salendo su sí resedea,
> le poma scritte ce pendea,
> le lacrime ch'amor facea,
> ché lo sponso gli era sí celato,
>
> Da l'altra parte volse 'l core
> vidde el ramo de l'ardore,
> passando l'ha sentito amore
> che m'avea sí rescaldato. . . .
>
> Da l'altra parte pusi mente,
> vidi ramo ante me piacente,
> passando l'ardor pongnente
> ferendo al cor l'ha stemperato.
>
> Stemperato de tal foco,
> lo mio cor non avea loco,
> fui furato a poco a poco
> en el ramo sopra me fidato.[3]

(And climbing still, above my head
I saw love's apples rosy red,
Marked with the tears that love must shed
When her Beloved she cannot see.

[1] *Speculum,* cap. xciii.
[2] In the prose sayings attributed to Jacopone—probably a collection
made by some disciple after his death—the stages in the soul's advance
are indicated by changes in the character of her tears, which only cease to
flow when she achieves the unitive life. See Feo Belcari, *Trattati di Fra
Jacopone da Todi,* p. 71.
[3] *Lauda LXXXIX.,* "Un arbore è da Dio plantato." The " tree of
love " is a favourite conceit of late mediæval mysticism, and is often seen
in the illuminated MSS. of the fourteenth and fifteenth centuries. It is an
apt symbol of the living and fertile character of Divine Love, and the
efforts demanded from those who would experience it. This *lauda* there-
fore represents Jacopone's personal gloss upon a conventional theme.
This poem seems to be an earlier composition than *Lauda LXIX,.* as the
final stage of contemplation described in it is much less advanced.

The other side my heart I turned,
And saw a flaming branch that burned;
And passing this, my love hath learned
    To bear love's heat full joyfully. . . .

The other side I turned my mind,
And there a gladsome branch did find;
Where love surpassed that ardour blind,
    And whelmed the heart in ecstasy.

So greatly burned in such a heat,
My heart could find no sure retreat,
But step by step my eager feet
    To the tree-top must carry me.)

This great outburst of feeling, however, had its negative aspect; and seems, in its first phases, to have come near the destruction of his mental balance. He has described with great vividness the inevitable reactions in which he paid the price exacted from all highly-strung temperaments for such a surrender to unchecked emotion. These reactions, in which we recognise the characteristic symptoms of nervous disequilibrium, represent the dark—one might perhaps say the pathological—side of the *santa pazia*.

Jacopone says that the first result of that passion of love in which he received the " gift of tears " was so great a thirst for suffering and immolation that he prayed for death and hell: a form of self-depreciation which was much approved by mediæval piety. From this morbid mood he sank to a condition of acute mental distress, in which his mind was darkened so that he knew not what he did. At first he was tortured by evil dreams and fantastic visions, and afterwards by insomnia. The whole world seemed black to him; he felt that he was surrounded by enemies, and was filled with despair. But, fixing his mind on God, and clinging to the Cross, he weathered the storm; and emerged at last on more tranquil levels of experience, where this

access of misery was compensated by the gift of a
" double light." [1]

Ruysbroeck, whose detailed and acute analyses of
the inner life often provide us with an apt commentary
on Jacopone's personal declarations, has described this
unstable condition of rapture and destitution as " the
state of heavenly weal and hellish woe." " Heavenly
weal," he says, " lifts a man up above all things into an
untrammelled power of praising and loving God, in
every way that his heart and his soul desire. After this
comes hellish woe, and casts him down into misery, and
into a lack of all the comfort and consolation that he
experienced before. . . . When a man feels God within
himself with rich and full grace, this I call heavenly
health ; for then he is wise and clear of understanding,
rich and outflowing with heavenly teachings, ardent
and generous in love, drunken and overflowing with
joy, strong in feeling, bold and ever ready in all the
things which he knows to be well-pleasing to God ; and
such like things without number, which may only be
known by those who feel them. But when the scale of
love goes down, and God hides himself with all his
graces, then the man falls back into dereliction and
torment and dark misery, as though he should never-
more recover. . .. . Now if that man is to recover from
his misery, he must observe and feel that he does not
belong to himself, but to God ; and therefore he must
freely abandon his own will to the will of God, and
must leave God to work in him in time and eternity.
So soon as he can do this with an untroubled heart and
a free spirit, at that very moment he recovers his health,
and brings heaven into hell and hell into heaven." [2]

With such a passage in mind, it becomes possible
to elucidate Jacopone's rather obscure references to
this period of his career: a period in which his spiritual

---

[1] *Lauda LXIX.,* " Fede, spene e caritade."
[2] Ruysbroeck, *The Book of Truth,* ch. vi.

passion seems to have reached its fullest development.
It was the ardent Franciscan devotion to the person of
Christ which now dominated his mysticism; a passion
in which the divine and human elements, the extremes
of intimacy and worship, of awe and desire, were fused,
and which gave adequate scope to his vehement tem-
perament. Rising at times to an almost unendurable
intensity, this wild craving for a perdurable satisfaction
of desire seems to have touched at least the fringe of
religious eroticism.

> Tanto d'amor fui ferito,
> ch'en quel ramo fui rapito
> o' lo mio sponso fo apparito
> e con lui fui abracciato.[1]

> (So was I wounded by love's spear,
> There straightway I was lifted clear
> There where my Bridegroom did appear,
> And in his arms embraced me.)

This is the state which Richard Rolle, a mystic whose
temperament has much in common with that of Jaco-
pone, has described as the state of " fire and song."
" For the sweetness of Him in this degree is so com-
forting and lasting in His love; so burning and gladden-
ing; that he or she who is in this degree can as well
feel the fire of love burning in their soul, as thou canst
feel thy finger burn if thou puttest it in the fire. But
that fire, if it be hot, is so delectable and so wonderful
that I cannot tell it. . . . Then the song of praise and
of love has come. Then, thy thought turns into song
and into melody. . . . The soul that is in the third
degree is all burning fire, and like the nightingale, that
loves song and melody and fails for great love: so that
the soul is only comforted in praising and loving God.
. . . And this manner of song have none, unless they

---

[1] *Lauda LXXXIX.*, v. 30. Cf. *Lauda LXXI.*, " Omo che vol parlare."
The wound of love, of course, is a stock metaphor of emotional mysticism.
It was borrowed directly from Jacopone by St. Catherine of Genoa, but
appears independently in Rolle, St. Teresa, and many others.

be in this third degree of love: to which degree it is impossible to come, but in a great multitude of love." [1]

Such passionate apprehensions, whether of love, of beauty, or of pain, are the food of poetry: the necessary condition of greatness in the arts. When they take the mystical form of direct and ecstatic apprehension of God, as the Source and Sum of love, beauty, and truth, and of Christ as the lover and pursuer of the soul, we have the most favourable of all circumstances for the appearance of that rare form of genius, the great religious poet. We may reasonably suppose, then, that some of those wonderful outpourings of the heart on which Jacopone's poetic reputation chiefly depends, date from this time, and are the creation of those moods in which he felt himself " rich and overflowing with heavenly teachings, ardent and generous in love, drunken and overflowing with joy, and strong in feeling." [2] That wild rapture which had in its earlier phases produced the excesses of the *santa pazia* and the *jubilus,* and persuaded him that the highest wisdom was found in the folly of love, now seems to have inspired a group of poems in which his genius appears in its full splendour, and lifts the religious poetry of Italy to a level which has seldom been surpassed. In " Ensegnatime Iesú Cristo " [3] and the beautiful " Troppo perde el tempo," [4] we seem to see the preparation for this storm of feeling, the stage in which his heart was still seeking complete communion with its Love. In the dialogue upon the contemplation of the Cross [5] and in that marvellous rhapsody of spiritual passion, " Amor de caritate," [6] he achieves the complete literary expression of this phase in the mystic life: a phase corresponding to that new intensity of communion with the Divine order which in the classic code of mysticism

[1] Rolle, *The Form of Perfect Living,* ch. viii.
[2] Ruysbroeck, *loc. cit.*
[3] *Lauda XLII.,* p. 328.
[4] *Lauda LXXV.,* " Fuggo la croce," p. 356.
[5] *Lauda CI.,* p. 342.
[6] *Lauda XC.,* p. 362.

seems to mark the full establishment of the " illumina-
tive way."   Maturity of style and internal content
prevent us from attributing these poems to Jacopone's
ascetic period.   Only in the most transcendental sense
could their writer reasonably describe himself as
" diota en teologia." [1]   " Troppo perde el tempo," which
appears in one of the earliest Umbrian collections,[2]
must have been in existence well before the end of the
thirteenth century—*i.e.* before the beginning of Jaco-
pone's political activities—but its strong philosophical
colour marks it out from the works of his convert
years, and shows him already influenced by Platonic
theology.[3]   " Ensegnatime Iesú Cristo " also exhibits a
sophistication of language which we do not find in the
earlier poems.   " Fuggo la croce " is a dialogue between
two friars, of whom the poet is plainly one ; and for
this reason, apart from the very advanced spiritual
state which it describes, may be presumed to have been
written during his conventual life.[4]   " Amor de caritate,"
with its direct references to Pauline and Augustinian
theology, again shows him accepting suggestions from
the learning which he professed to despise.   There are
two conflicting traditions with regard to this poem:
one, which is probably near the truth, says that he
wrote it soon after entering the convent.   The other
ascribes it to the last years of his life.   Its vigour and
splendour, so unlike the work of an old and broken
man, are, however, difficult to reconcile with the more
gentle and contemplative character of the *laude* which
critics agree in assigning to his final period.

If, then, we take these four poems in the order
which I have suggested, we find in them distinct traces
of development.   " Troppo perde el tempo " is the

---

[1] *Lauda LXXX.*, " Sapete voi novelle de l'amore."
[2] Brugnoli, p. cxiii.
[3] Verses 6, 9, 22, etc. See below, ch. vi., p. 231.
[4] I must here register my respectful dissent from Signor Brugnoli's
dating of " Fuggo la croce," which he regards as one of the earliest com-
positions of Jacopone's penitential period (*op. cit.*, p. cxii).

work of a man who has emerged from a period of gloom into the radiance of Divine love—"letizia e gaudio de la gente"; and, finding here the strength and sweetness of existence, the reality that blazes in all beauty, and the love that leads the earth and all the stars, asks only that he may enter more and more deeply into its comprehension. Few of Jacopone's poems breathe so tranquil a spirit of happiness.

> Splendor che dona a tutto 'l mondo luce,
> amor, Iesú, de li angeli belleza,
> cielo e terra per te si conduce
> e splende in tutte cose tua fattezza. . . .
>
> O Redentore, questo è 'l mio volere:
> d'amarte e de servir quanto io potesse;
> o dolce Cristo deggiati piacere
> che 'l mio core del tuo amor si empiesse,
> quella ora, buon Iesú, mi fa vedere
> ch'io te solo nel mio core tenesse
> e tu me fussi cibo e pascitore.[1]

In "Ensegnatime Iesú Cristo" the same demand is repeated in somewhat different terms, and linked with that passion for suffering and self-abasement which was for Jacopone an essential part of love:

> Opriteme la porta,
> ch'io vogli' entrar en viltate,
> ché Iesú Cristo amoroso
> se trova en quelle contrate.

The poem is an itinerary of the soul searching for its love. It goes by way of the "valley of lowliness," by utter destitution and self-stripping, even of all spiritual goods—for these are the only treasures to which the mystic clings—until at last, mounting naked to the Cross, it there finds itself united, not with the beauty of the Universe, but with the divine type of all courage

---

[1] *Lauda CI.*, vv. 6 and 27, pp. 344, 352. The Eucharistic colour of several passages in this poem closely resembles that of *Lauda XLVI.*, "Con gli occhi ch'agio nel capo" (see pp. 70 and 320): which, though containing earlier reminiscences, may well belong in time of composition to this group.

and love. "The top of the Cross," says Tauler, "is the love of God. It has no resting-place, for at all times it is a pure, bare going-forth, forsaken of God and all creatures."[1] This then is the "food and drink" which Jacopone asked and received, and this helps us to understand the many references to self-stripping and total destitution, which are scattered through his poems.

> Cristo amoroso, e io voglio
> en croce nudo salire;
> e voglioce abracciato
> Signor, teco morire.

In "Fuggo la croce," one of the greatest expressions in literature of the agony and surrender of love, we see the next phase in this spiritual situation. Jacopone has received in its fullness the terrible grace for which he asked. Now, possessed and devoured by the fury of a love that wounds while it enslaves, he is seeking, like the soul pursued by the Hound of Heaven, escape from the fires of the all-demanding Cross.

> Fuggo la croce che me devora,
> la sua calura non posso portare.[2]

The poem is a dialogue between two friars. One is a passionate and tormented mystic, in whose person the poet surely speaks. The other is a gently devotional soul, who stands much where Jacopone did when he wrote "Troppo perde el tempo." He cannot understand the anguish of his friend, who is blinded by the light that guides him, and seared by the fire of love in which he delights:

> Tu stai al caldo, ma io sto nel fuoco;
> a te è diletto, ma io tutto cuoco;
> con la fornace trovar non pò loco,
> se non c'èi entrato non sai quegn'è stare.

---

[1] Sermon on the Holy Cross (*The Inner Way*, p. 196). This same doctrine of the Cross is expounded by Jacopone in a later poem, "L'amor ch'è consumato" (*Lauda XCIX.*, p. 470).

[2] *Lauda LXXV.*, p. 356.

For one the Cross is full of arrows, for the other it is wreathed in flowers. Reading this poem, we feel that Jacopone was now experiencing in his heart that which a later mystic called " the terrible initiatory caress of God ": [1] the same strange induction into the mystery of divine suffering which is said to have produced in the body of St. Francis the phenomenon of the Stigmata. [2] The rarity of such a state should not make us deny its reality. As a matter of fact the records of mysticism contain many examples of a similar emotional situation ; which may seem to us exotic and even morbid, but which the whole temper of mediæval piety, especially in Franciscan circles, would tend to produce. "Christ said unto me," says Angela of Foligno, the Franciscan recluse who was Jacopone's contemporary and near neighbour, ' I will give thee a sign by the which thou mayst know that I am Christ Who have talked with thee. This sign is the Cross and love of God, which I do place within thee, and which shall be with thee for ever.' And immediately I felt the Cross and the love of God within my soul and spreading throughout my body so that I did actually feel it corporeally." [3] " Turn to the heights," says á Kempis, "turn to the deeps, turn within, turn without ; everywhere thou shalt find the Cross." [4] This notion was prominent in the teaching of the Spiritual Franciscans. The earliest manuscripts of the *laude*, which first circulated among the " Spiritual " friars and Tertiaries, are expressly addressed to those who

[1] Coventry Patmore, *The Rod, the Root, and the Flower.*

[2] This notion had already been woven into the fabric of Franciscan mysticism, and probably influenced Jacopone's experience. St. Bonaventura, whose works were certainly accessible to him, says of the " ecstatic height of Christian wisdom," " Via autem non est nisi ardentissimum amorem crucifixi. . . . Qui etiam adeo mentem Francisci absorbuit, quod mens in carne patuit, dum sacratissima passionis stigmata in corpore suo ante mortem per biennium deportavit." (*De Itinerario,* Prologue.)

[3] *Visionum et instructionum liber,* cap. xx.

[4] *De Imit. Christi,* Bk. II., cap. xii.

would follow " that angelic life which is called the Way
of the Cross."

We see another aspect of the same phase of feeling
in the *lauda* which is probably Jacopone's masterpiece,
the celebrated "Amor de caritate."[1]   In this torrent
of wild loveliness, the most extravagant raptures of
the *santa pazia*, controlled by Jacopone's genius, are
captured and reduced to artistic expression; sub-
mitted to the criticism of his growing spiritual sense,
and finally brought into connection with a reasoned
philosophy of mysticism. The poem as a whole occupies
an important place in the evolution of his mystical
doctrine; and will afterwards be discussed in this
connection.[2]   Here we are chiefly concerned with its
bearing upon the development of his personal life.
From this point of view, its most important passages
are those which descant on the difference between lust
and love; a distinction which holds good as well in the
passions of the spirit as in those of the senses and the
heart. The opening stanzas continue the spiritual situa-
tion of " Fuggo la croce ":

> Arde ed incende, nullo trova loco,
> non può fugir però ched è legato,
> sí se consuma como cera a foco;
> vivendo more, languisce stemperato.

But the centre of devotion has shifted; or rather, it is
seen from another angle. It is not the awe and wonder
of the Crucified, but the beauty of the " first and only
Fair" which now possesses him. " Cristo me tra' tutto,
tanto è bello! " This is, in fact, the love-song of a great
poet and lover, addressed to the ultimate source and
object of love. Though it seems in its ardour and swift-
ness to owe little to art, as a matter of fact it is built
on a considered plan, and is a masterpiece of dramatic
construction. It consists of three movements. In the

---

[1] *Lauda XC.*, p. 362.   [2] *Infra*, ch. vi.

first, the passion of the lover ascends in a crescendo of ardour, past all lesser loves:

> Giá non posso vedere creatura,
> al Creatore grida tutta mente;
> cielo né terra non me dá dolzura,
> per Cristo amore tutto m'è fetente.

Thence it issues in that ecstatic sense of complete self-loss in the beloved which is the consummation of all mysticism of this emotional type:

> En Cristo trasformata, quasi è Cristo;
> con Dio gionta tutta sta divina;
> sopr'onne altura è sí grande acquisto
> de Cristo e tutto lo suo star regina.

This first movement ends in a magnificent string of mystical paradoxes, wherein Jacopone, by that device of antithesis which was known to the troubadour poets as the *devinalh*, struggles to communicate something of his inexpressible state:

> Sappi parlare, ora so fatto muto;
> vedea, mò so cieco deventato;
> sí grande abisso non fo mai veduto:
> tacendo parlo, fugo e so legato,
> scendendo salgo, tengo e so tenuto,
> de fuor so dentro, caccio e so cacciato.

Here, where the passion of the poet seems to have reached its height, the voice of Christ suddenly breaks in: that Christ Who is for the Christian Platonist Wisdom and Rule of the Universe, the fount and principle of ordered form, no less than Bridegroom of the soul:

> Ordena questo amore, tu che m'ami,
> non è virtute senza ordene trovata, . . .
>
> Tutte le cose qual aggio ordenate
> sí so fatte con numero e mesura,
> ed al lor fine son tutte ordenate
> conservanse per orden tal valura,
> e molto piú ancora caritate
> sí è ordenata nella sua natura.[1]

[1] *Lauda XC,* vv. 19 and 20.

In this passage, which all students of Jacopone have recognised as crucial for an understanding of his character and work, we have, I think, the record of a crisis marking his definite abandonment of the *santa pazia*. The deliberate cultivation of that holy frenzy seems to have characterised the first phase of his spiritual life:

> Chi per Cristo va empazato,
> par afflitto e tribulato;
> ma è maestro conventato
> en natura e teologia.[1]

Now he recognised the imperfection of this ideal; the need for order and stability, the difference between fervour and fanaticism, the disciplined soul and the spiritual libertine.

In the third and last movement of the poem the lover turns on the Beloved, and, with superb artistic effect, accuses Christ of Himself displaying and Himself inspiring the unmeasured love which He now rejects:

> Questo ben sacci che, s'io so empazito,
> tu, somma sapienzia, sí el m'hai fatto.

Yet we are left in no doubt as to the poet's final view. Even in the grip of his passion, he knows that it is not the norm of the spiritual life. The contrast is not between ardour and a reasonable affection: it is the deep distinction between Eros and Agape. In the place of immoderate transports, tears, rapture, despair, Jacopone now desired a deeper, sterner love; not less ardent, but more ordered. There is something deeply impressive in the spectacle of this vehement nature thus capitulating to the austere Augustinian concept of love as the very principle of order itself,[2] at the moment in which it is still swept by the tempest of feeling, and ready to justify its own impassioned state:

[1] *Lauda LXXXIV.*, " Senno me pare," p. 282.
[2] Aug., *De Civ. Dei*, **xv.**, **22**. See below, ch. vi.

Ad tal fornace perché me menavi,
se volevi ch'io fossi en temperanza?
Quando sí smesurato me te davi,
tollevi da me tutta mesuranza ;
poi che picciolello me bastavi,
tenerte grande non aggio possanza ;
onde, se c'è fallanza,
amor, tua é, non mia,
però che questa via
tu la facesti, amore.[1]

From this time the vision of " fair order " seems to
have ruled Jacopone's thought, and was the key with
which he tried to solve the problems of inward devotion
and of external behaviour. We catch many glimpses of
it in the *laude*, where it inspires passages condemnatory
of all " furious love," [2] and directly contradicting the
doctrine of the *santa pazia*:

Emprima t'è opo con Dio ordinare,
e da lui prender regola d'amare.[3]

(First you must be in God's own order set,
And then from him the rule of love must get.)

Yet we need not doubt that the establishment of this
rule at the centre of his own life was slow and difficult ;
that he had yet to experience many oscillations between
rapture and gloom, and harmonise—not always with
due regard to prudence and temperance—the opposi-
tions of his own nature. I think we can probably place
in or near this period that poem on " The Golden
Mean," to which reference has already been made: [4]
for here we see him contemplating in a critical spirit
his own unstable character, blown here and there by
every impulse, and perpetually torn between pairs of
incompatibles. Ecstasy and misery, extravagance and
common sense, the instinct for contemplation and the
instinct for human affairs, possess him by turns. How

[1] V. 24.
[2] Cf. *Lauda LXXXVII.*, " Amor che ami tanto.'
[3] *Lauda LXXX.*, " Sapete voi novelle de l'amore."
[4] *Lauda XXXVIII.*, " O megio virtuoso." See above, p. 90.

is the silence for which he craves to be reconciled with
the promotion of God's kingdom; and the love of
poverty with charity towards those brothers who fail
to observe it? All extremes, he sees at last, are a mis-
take: yet moderation is very hard to attain::

Lo delettar abracciame
gustando el desiato,
lo tristore abatteme,
sottratto m'è 'l prestato,
tristare e delettare
nello suo comitato,
lo cor è passionato
en tal pugna abitare. . . .

L'odio mio legame
a deverme punire,
discrezion contrastali
che non deggia perire;
de farme bene en odio
or chi l'odí mai dire?
altro è lo patire
che l'udir parlare.

Lo degiunare piaceme
e far grande astinenza
per macerar mio asino
che non me dia encrescenza;
ed esser forte arpiaceme
a portar la gravenza
che dá la penitenza
nello perseverare. . . .

Piaceme el silenzio,
báilo de la quiete;
lo bene de Dio arlegame
e tolleme *silete*;
demoro infra le prelia,
non ce saccio schirmete,
a non sentir ferete
alta cosa me pare.

La pietá del prossimo
vuol cose a sovenire,
l'amor de povertate
gli è ordo ad udire,

l'estremitate veggiole
viziose a tenire,
per lo megio transire
non è don da giullare.

(Whene'er I taste my heart's desire
  Delight enwraps me round,
But when the gift departs from me,
  In sadness I am drowned.
So sorrow and my heart's delight
  In interchange are found,
  My troubled heart, in torment bound,
    This ceaseless strife must bear. . . .

Mine own self-hatred urges me
  To penances austere.
" Yet pause, lest thou shouldst perish straight!"
  Discretion's voice is clear.
To spare myself, whom yet I hate?
  Whoe'er of this did hear?
  'Tis harder to the soul sincere
    Than language can declare.

So also I desire to fast
  And practise abstinence,
Keep Brother Ass in due control,
  And still the pangs of sense.
Yet to be strong is all my need,
  To lift the load immense
  Laid on my back by penitence,
    And persevere in prayer. . . .

And silence do I greatly love,
  The guard of quiet she,
Yet to God's work I am constrained,
  That takes my peace from me.
Yea! I must dwell in ceaseless war,
  For no defence I see:
  No more so buffeted to be,
    What bliss beyond compare!

Our neighbour's state with tolerance
  And pity must we view ;
And love of poverty, to him,
  Is hateful through and through.
And so I see that all extremes
  Are evil things to woo ;
  The perfect mean who would pursue,
    It is no light affair!)

Here then, in this group of poems, we seem to have the spiritual and the ethical expressions of that conflict which was the ruling fact of Jacopone's middle period. It was really a conflict between those two sides of his nature which the shock of conversion had in some sense dissociated. On the one side was the old lawyer and leading citizen, trained for years to regard law and order as the framework of society: on the other, the ardent and unbalanced lover and poet, avid of emotion. Now the two ideals were brought together in a vision which harmonised love and law.

> O caritate, vita,
> ch'ogn'altro amor è morto ;
> non vai rompendo legge ;
> nante, l'observe tutto ;
> e lá 've non è legge
> a legge l'hai redutto.[1]

(O life of love! wherein all other loves are dead,
Thou dost not break the laws, but keepst them all instead!
And every lawless thing to law hast subjected.)

On psychological grounds alone, we might expect the result of such a unification to be a general increase in efficiency; the establishment of consciousness on fresh levels, and its self-expression in new and higher ways. If the chronology I have here put forward be accepted, I think we can see evidence of such a process in two directions: first in a new and wider understanding of contemplation and mystical prayer, next in the varied group of *laude* which seem to belong to this period, and which show Jacopone's poetic genius in maturity. If we consider first the evolution of his inner life, its leading characteristic seems to be this. He now moved away from a communion with God which was primarily emotional, conceived under personal forms, and began to apprehend the real nature of contemplation ; which is not an orgy of spiritual emotions, but

[1] *Lauda XXXIII.,* " Amor contrafatto."

involves the serious activity of the whole man, reason, feeling, and will. The appearance in his work of this conception, which involved the stilling of his vehement passions and restless imagination, a sober concentration of his faculties, assures us of the death of the *santa pazia*. Whilst on the one hand we may look on this change as an essential stage in his soul's growth—for the religious amorist at the mercy of his passion is still but the " child " and not the " man " of God—on the other hand we cannot doubt its connection with his new introduction to mystical philosophy. The training in metaphysics which must have formed part of his university education would give him a deeper understanding of these works than that possessed by the average friar. The descriptions of contemplation in the works of Richard of St. Victor, where the most profound searchings into man's knowledge of God go hand-in-hand with the doctrine of " burning love," [1] the wide horizons opened to the mind by Dionysius the Areopagite and other Christian Neoplatonists, must inevitably have transformed and extended his conceptions of the spiritual world. The natural mystic, when he comes into contact with these writings, feeds upon them eagerly ; for they seem to tell him news about his home, and help him by means of intellectual symbols to describe—and so better to understand—his supernal experiences. But beyond this, these works may tempt him—as all who are conscious of the subtle movements and responses of the soul must be tempted—to new and untried forms of contemplation and prayer. He perceives himself to stand on the frontiers of a great country. He is told of the unspeakable joys, the fruition of eternity, which wait for a consciousness stretched out towards God. Innumerable opportunities of adventure entice him, for now the telescope of philosophy

[1] R. of St. Victor, *De quatuor gradibus violentia charitatis*, and other works.

seems to bring into focus that Reality which is sought
by the eye of faith; and only experience can prove the
danger of a transcendence thus deliberately sought.

Jacopone has described very vividly his own pre-
mature attempt to attain " the vision of that which
Is," [1] and the intellectual bewilderment and distress it
brought upon him. He says that when he had passed
the " time of storms, in which self-will is slain," he
came to quiet weather, and determined that all things
should now be ordered equally and according to reason;
no power lagging behind the rest in the ascent to God.
But ardour ran ahead of experience. He had yet to
learn that profound stilling of the mind which is the
essential preliminary of contemplation; and his first
experiments he compares with the flounderings of those
who " go bathing before they know how to swim." [2]
He was out of his depth: immersed in that unknowable
" ocean of the Godhead " wherein all distinctions are
transcended—the " dark silence, where all lovers lose
themselves." [3] To these lovers, such an experience of
God's silence is a perfect fruition of Reality, for that
which is dim to the intellect is radiant to the heart.
But the novice, who has not yet stripped himself of all
sensual images, or conquered the instinctive tendency
of intellect to struggle where it ought to lie still, can
only feel the terror and confusion of a child in darkness
among the waves.

> O entenebrata luce che en me luce,
> que è ch'io en te non veggio?
> Non veggio quel che deggio
> e que non deggio veggio ;
> la luce che luce
> non posso testare.

[1] *Lauda XCII.*, " La fede e la speranza." This poem appears to have
been written in his last years. Its language is so strongly personal that
we can hardly doubt it to be based upon direct experience.
[2] *Op. cit.*, v. 7.
[3] Ruysbroeck, *Adornment of the Spiritual Marriage*, Bk. III., ch. iv.

Staendo en questa altura de lo mare,
io grido fortemente:
— Succurre, Dio, ch'io sto su l'anegare! —
E per fortuna scampai malamente ;
non vadano a pescare
nell'alto de lo mare, ché fa follia
se d'onne cosa empría
non se vole spogliare.[1]

(O light so dark, that is my light,
What is it thou dost hide from me ?
What I should see I do not see,
And see what should be veiled from me.
To that enlightening light
I cannot witness be.

Tossed on the billows of that shoreless sea
I cry in my distress,
" Help, God ! or I shall drowned be ! "
And I am saved from the wave's wilderness.
They do but foolishly
Who go to fish that ocean unless they
First, of all things they may,
Strip themselves utterly.)

We have, then, at least good grounds for suggesting that Jacopone did not easily or quickly achieve that quieting and subjugation of intellect as well as will, in which the great mystics enjoy their most profound experiences of Eternity. Passivity of all kinds was unnatural to him: he was essentially an active type. The ideals of the quietist and religious emotionalist, totally absorbed in a private enjoyment of God, he came to reject as temptations of Satan ; [2] seeking in their place the rounded and balanced career of the creative mystic, who holds the golden mean of an energetic yet contemplative life. Therefore we cannot suppose that the fervours and derelictions, the progress in contemplation, described in the great poems of his middle period, filled his whole life at this time; or that his

[1] *Lauda XCII.*, " La fede e la speranza," vv. 9 and 10. The imagery is of course derived from the Fourth Gospel and Dionysius.
[2] *Lauda LXIX.* See below, ch. v., p. 177.

cherished gift of tears never failed. The poems them-
selves, with their carefully held and often elaborate
artistic form, their evidence of wide reading and re-
newed interest in the world of men, are proof to the
contrary. Human nature, indeed, cannot live continu-
ally either upon the heights of pure contemplation, or
in the ardours of emotional prayer. Even for those
absorbed by the fullest artistic vision or most intense
of earthly loves, the great moments of feeling are transi-
tory: it was only in hell that Paolo and Francesca
were eternally locked in each other's arms.[1] The most
enraptured poets, most vehement lovers, are still con-
ditioned and steadied by the wholesome demands of
diurnal life. So, too, in the passions of the soul: the
mystic who is perpetually obsessed by the ideas and
emotions of the spiritual marriage is a pathological
specimen, not a saint. Moreover, real contemplation is
an activity of the will, which involves a concentration
so complete as to be only possible for a short time;
resembling in this those brief and vivid periods of
insight when artists see the Primal Beauty in its works.
To say, therefore, that a mystic has achieved this or
that degree of contemplation, experienced this or that
spiritual state, is to give but a partial account of him:
we have still to know how this participation in Eternity
is actualised by him in the world of time, for we are
concerned with the whole man, not with one faculty
alone, however great. Hence, having followed Jaco-
pone's interior growth through those degrees of love
which the old masters called *Calidum*, *Acutum*, and
Fervidum, to his first tentative experience of ecstasy, it
remains to ask him his own question—" What fruit
dost thou bring back from this thy vision?"[2]—to see
what this long development had done for his outward
life.

In the first place, we have observed that his entrance

---

[1] *Inf.* v., 74.　　　[2] *Lauda LXXIX.*, " La bontate enfinita."

into San Fortunato was in some sense a return to the
world of culture he had left. In spite of St. Francis'
expressed dislike of books and contempt for education,[1]
the Conventual friars were already known for their
learning. Many took an important part in the work of
the Universities, and struggled with more zeal than
humility for the doctor's degree. This seemed to the
more extreme Spirituals a betrayal of the Founder's
ideal. They would gladly have condemned the whole
Order to illiteracy: and one of the most embittered
controversies between the two branches was centred on
this question of scholarship.[2] As an educated man of
keen intelligence Jacopone could not—and plainly did
not—subscribe to this exaggerated view. The best of
the Spiritual Franciscans, and especially that body of
sane enthusiasts to which he seems to have belonged,
never ran to these excesses. They had no objection to
learning if it was kept in its proper place ; the majority
of them, indeed, were men of solid intellectual gifts.[3]
But they had their eye fixed on the truth that the first
business of the friar was to live the spiritual life: and
that this was not to be effected, or indeed much to be
assisted, by arguing about it, for those who apprehend
God will seldom waste time trying to define Him. That
which they did condemn without mercy was the ten-
dency to accept theological knowledge as a substitute
for sanctity ; the absurd reverence now given to merely

[1] T. of Celano, *Vita Secunda*, caps. xxxii. and cxlvii. *Speculum*, cap.
lxxii.
[2] Thus a fourteenth-century Spiritual document preserved in the con-
vent of the Cappuccini at Foligno states that Brother Leo told Conrad of
Offida, Jacopone's contemporary, how he once dreamed he saw many
friars drowning in a river covered with leaves of books: and when he told
St. Francis of it, the saint replied to him, " Brother Leo! these are those
evil books, through which the Order shall be destroyed." (*Misc. Fran.*,
VII., pt. iv., 1889.)
[3] Pier Olivi, Conrad of Offida, Angelo Clareno, and Ubertino da Casale
were all good theologians. (See below, ch. v.) Brother Leo himself was a
man of education and an excellent scribe ; as we may see from a Breviary
which he wrote for St. Clare, now preserved at S. Damiano. (See *Speculum*,
Sabatier's edition, p. lxxxii.)

academic knowledge for its own sake. " There be many friars," says the *Speculum*, " who place all their study and care in acquiring knowledge ; leaving their holy vocation, and wandering with mind and body out of the way of humility and holy prayer." [1] Some of Jacopone's roughest and most mordant verse mocks the conceit, ill-manners, and hypocrisy of this new class of learned brothers ; eaten up by intellectual pride, and having neither spiritual nor social graces to recommend them. The picture he draws is hardly that of the scholar ; and goes far to justify St. Francis' fear of the effect of book-learning on his sons :

> Mal vedemmo Parisci
> c'hane destrutto Ascisi ;
> con la lor lettoría
> messo l'ò en mala via.

> Chi sente lettoría,
> vada en forestaría ;
> gli altri en refettorio
> a le foglie coll'olio. . . .

> Totto 'l dí sto a cianciare,
> co le donne a beffare ;
> se 'l fratecel gli aguata,
> è mandato a la malta.

> Se è figlio de calzolaio
> o de vile mercenaio,
> menerá tal grossore
> co figlio d'emperadore.[2]

> (Evil be of Paris said!
> By it is Assisi dead.
> They, with all their lettered skill,
> Set us on the road to ill.

[1] *Speculum*, cap. lxxii. The words are put into the mouth of St. Francis, but undoubtedly represent the views of the Spirituals in Jacopone's day.

[2] *Lauda XXXI.*, " Tale qual è."

If a brother's learned, he
Treated as a guest must be ;
While the other friars eat
In common hall their humble meat. . . .

Gossiping he'll stand all day,
And loves with women to be gay ;
Should some brother watch too well,
He consigns him straight to hell!

Though he be a cobbler's lad
Or call some petty shopman dad,
He looks on other folk with scorn,
As if he were in purple born.)

To call this poem, as some have done, an attack upon
learning and a defence of " holy ignorance," is surely
to misunderstand the situation.   It expresses merely
the contemptuous disgust felt by the inheritor of a
solid culture and an unassailable social tradition for the
thinly-veneered imitation—the intellectual " beggar
on horseback "—now being produced by the Paris
schools.   Nor can the other celebrated poem on this
subject, the address to the dead Friar Ranaldo,[1] really
be made to yield proof of Jacopone's hostility to learn-
ing as such.   It is pride of intellect which is here con-
demned ;   the setting of cleverness before character.
Here, however, Jacopone is supported by all consistent
Christians from St. Paul onwards.[2]   " What will it avail

---

[1] *Lauda XVII.,* " Frate Ranaldo, dove se'andato? " This poem exists
in two versions. The short form printed by Bonaccorsi is found in all the
best MSS. of Umbrian provenance. The version in *Magliabechiano, II., vi.,*
63, a Tuscan MS. of the fourteenth century, contains eight additional
stanzas: some of which reappear in the *Codex Marciano,* IX., 182, and in
Tresatti's edition of the *Laude.* These, if authentic, are of great interest.
They state that Ranaldo was reader in theology at the Papal court ; and
further that Jacopone was his godfather, and initiator into the religious life.
The poet is represented as writing in prison (*i.e.* between 1298 and 1303),
and the general tendency of the additional verses is to strengthen the note
of contempt for scholastic subtleties and academic distinctions which
inspires the whole poem. Signor Brugnoli, who prints the interpolations
with some admirable notes (*Le Satire,* p. 130), considers that it is not at
present possible to pronounce on their authenticity.
[2] Col., ii., 8.

thee to dispute profoundly of the Trinity," says the
well-read Thomas á Kempis, " if thou be void of
humility, and thereby displeasing to the Trinity ? "[1]
This is exactly the case of Ranaldo.   He has been a
fine theologian, and received at Paris his doctor's
degree, with much honour and at great expense.   He
made, to outward seeming, a good death.   Yet his friend
cannot be sure how he will stand in that School of
Reality where thought and word are exhibited in the
light of the absolute truth.

> Ché non giova far sofismi
> a quelli forti siloismi,
> né per corso né per risme
> che lo vero non sia apalato.

> (There are no sophistries that will
> Those mighty syllogisms kill,
> And there nor prose nor rhyme has skill
> To hold the truth concealed.)

All turns on one point; whether Ranaldo has been true
to the Franciscan ideal of humility, and ever esteemed
himself in the teeth of success the least and most abject
of " poor little friars." [2]   This alone can neutralise the
poison which lurks in " acquired " knowledge.

> Scienzia acquisita
> mortal sí dá ferita,
> s'ella non è vestita
> de core umiliato.[3]

> (The knowledge men acquire
> Deals them a wound most dire,
> Unless her meek attire
> Be heartfelt lowliness.)

A true grasp of spiritual values—of the vital differ-
ence between knowledge which is infused of God

[1] *De Imit. Christi*, Bk. I., cap. i.
[2] *Loc cit.* A passage in the *Speculum* (cap. lxxii.) exactly illustrates
Jacopone's view. " The blessed Father," says that work, " looking for-
ward to the future, knew by the Holy Spirit, and many times used to say
to the brethren, that friars by occasion of teaching others lose their own
vocation, that is holy humility, pure simplicity, prayer, and devotion."
[3] *Lauda LXXXI.*, " O Amor, divino amore, amor."

into the soul and knowledge acquired by the brain—harmonising lowliness of heart with vigour of mind; this seems to represent Jacopone's ideal. His writings show no trace of contempt for the traditional wisdom of the Church. On the contrary, as his genius develops it is enriched more and more by the result of his eager study of the Christian Neoplatonists and Victorine philosophers; and in one of his minatory *laude* he describes Philosophy no less than Holy Scripture as wounded by the neglect of that "most noble Goodness" which is her "treasure and her way."[1]

We need not, therefore, be surprised to find among his poems a large group which are distinguished as much by thought and skill as by ardent feeling; showing the strong influence of mystical philosophy as well as that of Franciscan sentiment. Some of these *laude* are directly inspired by the ideals of the Spiritual party, and were probably written for the use of its members or as propaganda of its aims.[2] These will best be studied in connection with his work as a Spiritual leader.[3] Others are sermons or rhymed tracts on the Christian life and the special Franciscan virtues. These show him to us continuing the missionary work which inspired the didactic *laude* of his first period; but we shall probably be right in attributing to his career within the Order those which indicate special familiarity with the language of theology, and the formal categories of Christian asceticism.[4] Some of

---

[1] *Lauda LI.,* " La Veritade piange."

[2] For instance, those against unworthy friars (*Laude XXX.* and *XXXII.*); on the corruption of the Church and approaching doom (*Laude LI., LII.,* and *LIII.*); on Poverty (*Laude LX.* and *LXI.*); and on St. Francis (*Lauda LXII.*).

[3] Ch. v.

[4] Outstanding examples of this class are the *laude* on the Seven Deadly Sins (*XIV.,* " La superbia de l'altura "); on Chastity (*XXXVII.,* " O castitate, fiore "); on the Lord's Prayer (*XLIV.,* " En sette modi "); on the Cardinal Virtues (*LXX.,* " Alte quattro virtute "); the long and tiresome allegory, " L'omo fo creato virtuoso " (*Lauda XLIII.*); and the

K

these elaborate and rather conventional works may have been written during his residence in Rome, to please the taste of his ecclesiastical friends.

But there is another group of poems having neither a controversial nor a deliberately didactic character. This group includes the beautiful Christmas carols, " O Vergine piú che femina," " O novo canto" and "Ad l'amor ch'é venuto,"[1] the celebrated drama of the Passion, "Donna del paradiso," and the *lauda* on the Incarnation, " Fiorito è Cristo."[2] In these, Jacopone appears, not as the frenzied penitent and revivalist, or the impassioned lover and contemplative; but as a great Christian poet, giving artistic form to the deepest mysteries of his faith, and the purest aspect of the Franciscan spirit. These poems are, indeed, among the most perfect creations of thirteenth-century feeling; expressing that assured faith, that tenderness and intimacy, that happy enjoyment of Christ, of which St. Francis, in such an incident as the setting up of the Crib at Greccio,[3] had been the perfect interpreter. We feel that Jacopone, when he wrote them, did indeed know " true Franciscan liberty "; and suspect in them the influence of those lofty personalities, such as Conrad of Offida and John of La Verna, who still kept unimpaired the primitive spirit, and whom we know to have been his friends.[4] They show us how far Jacopone had now travelled from the mood in which his first ascetic *laude* were composed; how imperfect a conception of his genius we should gain from these and his purely mystical poems alone. The spirit of play, the accent of romance, a new delicate joy in the human aspect of the Incarnation, in the flowering of Christ for the renewing of Man's faded fields, here replace the old

two poems on the Incarnation beginning " O Cristo onnipotente " (*Laude XL.* and *XLI.*).

[1] *Laude II,. LXIV.* (p. 412) and *LXV.*
[2] *Laude XCIII.* and *C.* (p. 406).
[3] T. of Celano, *Vita Prima*, cap. xxx.
[4] See ch. v. Cf. *Fioretti*, caps. xlii.-xliv. and xlix.-liii.

savage antithesis between God's perfection and human squalor.

> Tal amador è fior de puritade,
> nato nel campo de verginitade,
> egli è lo giglio de l'umanitade
> de suavitate
> e de perfetto odore.[1]

The poet who had dwelt with so great a satisfaction on the most unattractive details of infancy,[2] now delights in the " dear little rags " which swaddled and bound the Word made Flesh, and sees Mary burned up with joy when she first felt those lips at her breast:[3] for the divine light which once cast so black a shadow is now seen to light up with its beauty every man coming into the world.

> Accurrite, accurrite,
> gente ; co non venite?
> vita eterna vedite
> con la fascia legata.[4]

> (Come, come with me!
> Folk, why so tardily?
> Eternal life to see
> In swaddling bands.)

The road which he took to this, the centre of the Christian secret, had been a hard and costing one. In his spiritual journey he passed through the mysteries of sin, death, and redemption on his way to the greater mystery of new life and love—from the " naked embrace " of the Cross [5] to the Crib—and having found it, found there that " Love which made us all, to draw us to itself," [6] reconciling matter and spirit, and disclosing

---

[1] *Lauda C.,* " Fiorito è Cristo."   See p. 406.
[2] *Lauda XXIV.,* " O vita penosa." See p. 36.
[3] *Laude LXV.,* " Ad l'amor ch'è venuto," and *II.,* " O Vergine piú che femina."
[4] *Lauda II.*
[5] *Lauda XLII.,* p. 328.   [6] *Lauda XC.,* " Amor de caritate."

the Eternal Wisdom latent in every manifestation of growth and change:

> Ben so che, garzoncello,
> hai perfetto sapere,
> e tutto quel potere
> c'ha la perfetta etade ;
> donqua, co picciollelo
> poteve contenere
> tutto lo tuo volere
> en tanta vilitade?[1]

> (Ah, little boy, full well I know
>   Thy wisdom is a perfect thing,
>   Thy power hath as strong a wing
>   As ever rounded years possessed.
> Ah, little one, and is it so
>   That Thou canst hold unfaltering
>   The will and nature of a king
>   In such a little lowly nest?)

This close familiar contact with the Divine order, the sense that humanity—even at its simplest and most childish—was yet the veritable tabernacle of God, made on the one hand the true horror of sin as a defacement of the spiritual temple ; on the other, the high nobility and joy of the soul's inheritance:

> Se a lo specchio
> te voli vedere,
> porrai sentire
> la tua delicanza ;
> en te porti forma
> de Dio gran Sire ;
> ben pòi gaudire,
> c'hai sua simiglianza ;
> o smesuranza
> en breve redutta:
> cielo terra tutta
> veder en un vascello ;
> o vaso bello,
> co mal se' trattato![2]

[1] *Lauda LXV.,* " Ad l'amor ch'è venuto," v. 10.
[2] *Lauda XXXV.,* " O anima mia," p. 388.

These poems assure us that their author, when he came to write them, had at last healed the deep cleavage in his nature, and harmonised his outward experience with his inward conviction of God. Giles of Assisi, who possessed so great a measure of the Franciscan spirit, was accustomed to say that the Lady Quail taught him much about divinity, because instead of saying, " *Là, là* " (there, there), she always said " *Qua, qua* " (here, here). To this loving sense of the nearness of the supersensual—which is the secret of the Christian doctrine of the Incarnation—Jacopone seems to have come.

> O dolce garzoncello,
> en cor t'ho conceputo
> ed en braccia tenuto,
> però sí grido:— Amore!—[1]

> (O little Boy most sweet,
> In my heart I have conceived thee,
> And in mine arms received thee,
> Because my cry is Love!)

It is true that there is comparatively little trace in him of that deep love of Nature and wild things which shines in the acts and words of Francis, and reappears in the beautiful character of Conrad of Offida. Even his sympathetic references to flowers and gardens seem to owe less to observation than to the influence of the Song of Songs: the freedom and loveliness of birds and fishes is realised with the objective vision of the artist, not the intimacy of a friend.[2] But these poems assure us that the instinct for beauty, and the wide artistic interests of his early life, did come back to him in a transfigured form;[3] and with them the new tender

---

[1] *Lauda LXV.*, " Ad l'amor ch'è venuto."
[2] *Lauda LIX.*, " Povertade enamorata."
[3] See, for instance, the elaborate musical *schema* of " O novo canto " (*Lauda LXIV.*); the references to romance-literature (*Lauda XXXV.*, " O anima mia," p. 388); the reminiscences of the secular love-poets in " Fiorito è Cristo " (*Lauda C.*, p. 406); and other passages of this group of works.

love and reverence for human life and sorrow, which
inspires the poignant dialogue between Mary and her
dying Son,[1] and gives colour to the persistent opinion
that in Jacopone we may have the unknown author of
the *Stabat Mater*, the noblest of all Passion poems.[2]

So, during the period which is roughly covered by
his conventual life, probably between the fiftieth and
sixtieth years of his age, it would seem that Jacopone,
so far as his inward growth is concerned, experienced
all the phases of that illuminative way which lies
between the life of purgation and the life of union, and
set in order his relations with God and with humanity.
Further, that "ordered life which is the fruit of
vision"[3] found artistic and intellectual as well as devo-
tional expression. Thought and imagination were sub-
limated and given over to its purposes: his immense
temperamental energy found fresh outlets, fresh creative
opportunity. These years plainly witnessed a great
development in him, as poet, as Christian philosopher,
as mystic, and as leader of men. The despised *fantastico*
of the legend was now, to his great distress, widely
known and revered as a saint:

> Lo Nemico sí me dice:
> Frate, frate, tu se' santo;
> grande fama e nomenanza
> del tuo nome è en onne canto.[4]

(The Fiend says: Brother, brother, how great thy sanctity!
In every song, in every place, men say good things of thee.)

We shall best understand his position in the Order,
in those years before contact with Church politics
dimmed the spiritual light, if we think of him as belong-
ing to that small group of Franciscan contemplatives of

---

[1] *Lauda XCIII.*, " Donna del paradiso."
[2] This theory is discussed below, p. 202.
[3] *Lauda LXXIX.*, " La bontate enfinita."
[4] *Lauda XLVII.*, " Or udite la battaglia."

THE VIRGIN APPEARING TO JACOPONE DA TODI

From the frontispiece of Bonaccorsi's edition of the " Laude," Florence, 1490

whom we read in the *Fioretti*.[1] These still preserved
the pure and ardent spirit of the primitive Companions ;
and the chapters there devoted to them give us all that
was best in the atmosphere which nurtured Jacopone's
mystical life. One of them, the saintly John of La
Verna, is known to have been his intimate friend. We
possess the rather bracing poem of consolation which
Jacopone wrote to him when he had fever ; reminding
the patient that a high temperature is essential if the
soul is to be beaten into shape, and that therefore whilst
we lie upon the anvil every illness is a gain.[2] The *Vita*
makes Jacopone call John his " father," and here it is
certainly supported by many of the devotional *laude*.
These, when we compare them with the reports of John's
ecstasies and spiritual ardours, show how closely re-
lated were the mystical experiences of the two men,
and suggest that Jacopone's initiation into the secrets
of Divine love may have come to him through this
great Franciscan contemplative.

The account of John of La Verna in the *Fioretti*[3] is
probably based on contemporary sources. He seems
to have begun his religious career as a boy with the
Canons of Fermo ; but, wishing for a life of greater
austerity, whilst still a youth he became a Friar Minor.
He spent many years at La Verna, which was the
acknowledged refuge of those brethren devoted to the
contemplative life ; and here · Jacopone may have
visited him. His sanctity became widely recognised.
Though not a professed theologian, he was called to
speak on the divine mysteries " before the Pope and
his cardinals, the King and his barons, and the masters
and doctors," amazing all by his deep thoughts and
noble words. He was a pronounced ecstatic and vision-
ary, with a special devotion for the Person of Christ

[1] Caps. xlii. to liii. Cf. below, ch. v.
[2] *Lauda LXIII.,* " A fra Ianne de la Verna."
[3] Caps. xlix. to liii.

and for the Eucharist. His spiritual adventures, which are fully described in the *Fioretti*, give us a vivid glimpse of the atmosphere in which Jacopone's mystical life developed. Reading how Brother John in early life, "as one drunken in spirit, would run now through the garden, now through the wood, now through the church, according as the flame and the ardour of the spirit drave him," we recognise another victim of the *santa pazia*. The three years during which "his heart was kindled with the love divine" and often-times was rapt in God, "so that he seemed all on fire and burning with the love of Christ"; the six months of intolerable fervour when, "because of his great and exceeding love, he was in anguish and was altogether melted away"; the period of reaction wherein "the light and love of God departed," and "in torment he went through the wood, running hither and thither, calling with cries and tears and sighs on the beloved Spouse of his soul," help us to understand the psychological situation which produced "Amor de caritate" and its companion works. So too, in the later developments, when grace returned to him, and he received from the embrace of Christ "marvellous and celestial words that changed the hearts of men and brought forth rich fruit of souls in those who heard them," we may recognise a parallel to that "ordering of love" which appears to have preceded Jacopone's fully creative period.

There is, however, one marked difference between the lives of John and his fellow-contemplatives and that of Jacopone. In him we find hardly a trace of those visionary and other abnormal phenomena which the chroniclers so generously ascribe to them. Even the legends have little to say of visions or prophetic powers. He is nowhere credited with miracles. With many of the greatest mystics he disliked and distrusted "supernatural gifts" of this kind, condemning the state of those who

de fare signi sí son desiosi,
far miracoli, render sanetati,
de rapti e profezie son golosi.[1]

(long for a wonder and a sign,
For miracles or healing gifts,
Raptures and prophecy divine.)

No doubt his progress in the science of prayer already involved the experience of ecstasy; but ecstasy is not supernatural, it is rather a natural form taken by the mystic's complete absorption in God. Jacopone's ecstasies are known to us only through the poetry in which he describes them, for he seems to have taken special care to conceal them from curious admirers. In the revulsion from the excesses of the *santa pazia* his contemplative practice became secret, and this side of his life was probably known only to his intimate friends. We have his own assurance that he now deliberately hid his spiritual raptures, did his best to appear an ordinary friar of the stricter sort, and resisted as a temptation of Satan the suggestion that he was a "special friend" of God.[2] Here Jacopone exhibits more modesty and more common sense than his eminent contemporary Angela of Foligno, who has left it on record that the Holy Ghost loved her better than any other woman in the Vale of Spoleto.[3] His reserve is to us a guarantee that the secret for which he had agonised was now indeed his own; that his love had passed from the stage of blind rapture to that of creation: "en Cristo trasformata en mirabel unitato."[4] As it grew in depth and delicacy, it became "mute."[5] Save in those vocal prayers which the rule demanded, and which "we ought to let our brothers hear for their

---

[1] *Lauda L.*, "Or se parrá."
[2] *Lauda XLVII.*, "Or udite la battaglia."
[3] Angela da Foligno, *Visionum et Instructionum Liber*, cap. xx.
[4] *Lauda XLV.*, "En cinque modi."
[5] *Lauda LXXVII.*, "O amore muto," p. 456.

edification," [1] his communion with God was concealed from view.

> La mentale orazione
> quella occulta rendo a Dio,
> e lo cor serrat'ha l'uscio,
> ché nol vegia el frate mio.[2]

(My mental prayer I make to God in secrecy ;
And lock my heart full heedfully,
That its delight my brother may not see.)

We are not to suppose that these years, in which Jacopone grew from penitent to contemplative, and from a wandering singer to an accomplished poet, were entirely spent in the convent of Todi. The early friars were great travellers ; and it is probable that he made many journeys, at least among the Spiritual friaries and hermitages of Umbria and the Province of the March. Here we know that he had friends, and here the events in which he afterwards took a leading part were prepared. There is also evidence that the years immediately preceding his emergence into ecclesiastical politics were spent at Rome. Signor d'Ancona has drawn attention to the fact that a codicil of the will of Cardinal Bentivenga, Bishop of Albano, dated 1288, is witnessed by "frate Jacobo de Tuderto, *ordinis fratrum minorum,*" and that a further codicil bequeaths to this same friar—who is again witness—along with "others of our chaplains and household," a sum of money for books and other necessities.[3] The arguments by which that "true lover of Gospel Poverty" and professed enemy of acquired knowledge persuaded himself that he might become a legatee,[4] and came to reckon books among the necessities of life, are not

[1] *Lauda XLVII.,* "Or udite la battaglia."
[2] *Loc. cit.*
[3] D'Ancona, *Jacopone da Todi,* p. 79. Leonij, *Inventario dei Codici della Comunale di Todi,* p. 78.
[4] However, as we find even so strict an observant as Brother Leo receiving a legacy of forty *solidi* to buy a new tunic (*Speculum,* Sabatier's edition, p. lxxxiv), this may have been regarded as permissible.

known to us. Jacopone does not mention, among his
many " battles with the enemy," any struggle against
the temptation to buy for personal use a manuscript
of his well-loved Dionysius. But these few lines
strengthen our suspicion that the figure which the *Vita*
and more exaggerated *laude* put before us does not
tally in all respects with the personality of the able and
celebrated Spiritual friar, the humble mystic but none
the less expert poet and profound thinker, who was
now approaching the zenith of his career.

Cardinal Bentivenga was a native of Todi ; and it
is reasonable to suppose that his influence may have
brought Jacopone from San Fortunato to Rome. If the
poet were indeed for some years a member of his house-
hold—probably a secretary, since he was not capable
of a chaplain's post—many obscure points in this period
of his life become clear. He has told us in one of his
most personal poems that he was at one time attached
to the Papal court:

> Prebendato en corte i Roma,
> tale n'ho redutta soma;

> (In office at the court of Rome,
> Now to this my fame has come)

and that there he went perpetually to and fro, full of
gossip, flattery, and argument:[1] a surrender to old
instincts which was the prelude to the most disastrous
phase of his career. Here his connection with the
Colonna cardinals, his contact with the future Pope
Boniface, probably began. Here, perhaps, he knew
and watched the brilliant Frate Ranaldo,[2] if we accept
the notices contained in the long form of that *lauda*.[3]
Here, too, he would be prominent as a leader of the
Spiritual group.

[1] *Lauda LV.*, " Que farai, fra Iacovone? "
[2] *Lauda XVII.*, " Frate Ranaldo, dove se' andato? "
[3] *Vide supra*, p. 143.

To this Roman time we can perhaps refer the many bitter complaints of temptation which seem by their context to belong to the illuminative life:[1] especially the recurrent temptation to professional sanctity, to take pleasure in his own growing celebrity as an ascetic and contemplative. The quiet of his cell, the simplification of interests inherent in convent life, the intercourse with the hermit mystics of La Verna and the March, were taken from him. Here we see, on higher levels, the reproduction of those conditions which marked the end of his years *en bizocone:* a new yielding to the call of external life, the re-emergence of the "old Adam," not yet entirely mortified, with its instinct for successful action, its eager response to the call of men and things. Another phase in his soul's growth was now drawing to a close. But this new period of transition and the poems belonging to it will be better understood if they are studied in relation with the Franciscan Spiritual movement as it came to a head in the last years of the thirteenth century.

[1] See, for instance, *Lauda XLVII.,* " Or udite la battaglia."

CHAPTER V

JACOPONE AND THE SPIRITUAL PARTY

The Three Temptations—The Spirituals—Character of the Movement—
Brother Leo—Literature—Olivi—Conrad of Offida—The imitation of
Christ—Holy Poverty—Joachism—Apocalyptic ideas—Jacopone's
connection with Celestine V.—With Angelo Clareno—With Boni-
face VIII.—The Colonna insurrection—Jacopone's imprisonment and
laude—His spiritual progress—Poems of Divine union—Fall of
Boniface—Jacopone's last years—Death and burial.

In the autobiographical poem from which I have already
quoted,[1] Jacopone describes three temptations which
assailed him as he came to the summit of the "tree of
contemplation." In the first, the Devil, disguised as an
angel of light, shows him a ruined church and calls
upon him to restore it: an obvious reminiscence of
Christ's mandate to St. Francis,[2] placing Jacopone
upon a level with the Founder himself. In the next, the
enemy appears in the form of Christ, inviting him to
the raptures of divine communion:

> Allor m'aparve como Cristo
> e disse:—Io so tuo maistro;
> pígliate de me diletto,
> ché te voglio consolare.[3]

> (Then as Christ I him did see,
> Who said, Mine is the mastery;
> Find thou thy happiness in me,
> For I will give thee rest.)

In the third trial, Satan appears as an angel of light
within the fiery furnace, and hails Jacopone as worthy
of adoration. All these invitations to error the poet
resists; and looking neither to right nor left lest he

---

[1] *Lauda LXIX.,* " Fede, spene e caritade."
[2] T. of Celano, *Vita Secunda,* cap. vi.   [3] *Op. cit.,* v. 35.

should fall from the branches, he finishes his ascent
without further distraction.

Now this bald recital reveals under examination
several points of interest. In the first place, the device
of the three temptations suggests a deliberate parallel
with the three temptations of Christ ; and this alone
would prove how completely Jacopone now shared the
ideas of the Spiritual Franciscans. The first two
temptations show that he was, as we might expect,
successively attracted by the extreme " right " and
" left " of that movement, its reforming zeal and its
devotional intensity ; which would inevitably appeal,
the one to his active mind and love of affairs—to an
ambition purged of selfishness yet not entirely slain—
the other to his deep and growing mystical sense. There
was a moment when he was strongly drawn to eccle-
siastical politics, and history records its unfortunate
results. There was another moment when the free spirit
of Christ seemed to claim from him a devotion incom-
patible with obedience to his superiors.

The Spiritual party, which has seemed to some
historians a body of tiresome and unreasonable fanatics,
to others a band of saints of the purest Christian kind,
embraced as a matter of fact friars and Tertiaries of both
these types.[1] Historically, it stood upon firm ground.
Its members undoubtedly represented the true ideals
of St. Francis; many were the personal disciples of his
most loyal followers, Giles and Leo. The Chapter-
general of the Order, under the presidency of St. Bona-
ventura, had decreed in 1266 the destruction of all the
earlier lives and legends of the Seraphic Father.[2] This

---

[1] The best account is by Ehrle: *Die Spiritualen, ihr Verhältnis zum
Franciscanerorden.* (*Archiv für Litteratur und Kirschengeschichte des Mittel-
alters,* Band I., p. 509; II., p. 106; III., p. 553; IV., p. 1.) Good résumé
of main facts in Ferrers Howell, *St. Bernardino of Siena,* ch. i.

[2] This amazing decree was made in the interests of peace. The early
legends, says Angelo of Clareno, contained too many things " contrary to
the common course " (*i.e.* of the relaxed friars). All matter which could
serve as ammunition for the Spiritual war upon the Conventuals was

order had been carried out with considerable thorough-
ness, so that in Jacopone's time the judicious and
elegant work of St. Bonaventura was alone in general
circulation: nevertheless, he and his fellow-Spirituals ob-
tained through the personal reminiscences of Brother
Leo, who was living in old age at the Porziuncula,
a real contact with the spirit of St. Francis. Leo,
indeed, was the true father ot the Spirituals, many of
whom constantly visited his cell. He loved to declare
the prophecies of St. Francis concerning the future of
the Order; and as hostility between its two parties
sharpened, these prophecies increased in vigour and
detail.[1] His influence on Conrad of Offida and Angelo
Clareno was great, and through them it would reach
Jacopone. Some of the memories of Leo, written down
and preserved by the Poor Ladies of St. Clare, form
the foundation of the early fourteenth-century work
known to us as the *Speculum* or *Mirror of Perfection :*
and this book well indicates the view of St. Francis
which would be taken by Jacopone and his friends.
The original materials from which the lost Latin original
of the *Fioretti* was composed were also probably con-
temporary with Leo and his disciples, if not actually
drawn from their memories.

We gather from Ubertino da Casale and other
sources that in Jacopone's day the Spiritual party was
a loosely-knit community of enthusiasts, containing
both lay and clerical elements: not unlike the half-
mystical, half-ethical society of the Friends of God,
which arose in the Rhineland in the following century

eliminated from Bonaventura's official life. Luckily a few copies of the
condemned documents were preserved in remote friaries. Yet much of
St. Francis' own writings and of Leo's original memoirs perished ; the
Second Life of Celano—which contains a large amount of material con-
tributed by Leo—survives only in two copies, and his *Book of Miracles*
only in one.

A good account of this episode in Coulton, *Christ, St. Francis, and
To-day,* pp. 45 *et seq.*

[1] *Speculum,* Sabatier's edition, p. lxxx.

under the influence of the Preaching Friars.[1]   There
were three main groups, centred in Provence, in Tus-
cany, and in the March of Ancona. "The Province of
the March ot Ancona," says the *Fioretti*, "was in olden
time adorned, even as the sky with stars, with brothers
that were a pattern of a holy life."[2] Among these were
Conrad of Offida, his friend Peter of Monticello, and
the other great visionary friars whose deeds and dreams
it proceeds to describe. Jacopone was intimately con-
nected with this group, which had a marked mystical
bias.   Some of the Spirituals, such as Pier Giovanni
Olivi and his followers,[3] were zealous reformers, much
influenced by the prophecies of the Abbot Joachim.
These politically-minded brothers believed that they
had a mission to force the whole Order to the unmiti-
gated poverty of the First Companions, and purge the
Church of its luxuries and sins. Although under per-
secution, some of these extremists afterwards wandered
off into revolt and even schism, finally degenerating
into the *fraticelli*—a heretical body of doubtful morals [4]
—in Jacopone's day they were mostly genuine Christian
enthusiasts. Their courage in the teeth of opposition,
like that of the great early Quakers, was nourished by a
life of prayer and spiritual exaltation ; for they sought
to carry out the dual ideal of St. Francis—adoration
towards God, missionary activity towards men.   All
those works which we now regard as most typical of
the pure Franciscan spirit—the *Little Flowers*, the
Mirror of Perfection, the *Legend of the Three Com-*

[1] A good description of this movement will be found in Rufus Jones,
Studies in Mystical Religion, ch. xiii.
[2] *Fioretti*, cap. xlii.
[3] Pier Giovanni Olivi (1248-98), a man of much learning and of devout
life, was one of the most extreme among the Spiritual leaders, and head of
the *zelanti* of Provence. He was a convinced believer in the prophecies of
the Abbot Joachim, and preached the doctrine of poverty in its most
rigorous form. See Ehrle, *Petrus Johannes Olivi* (*Archiv für Litteratur
und Kirschengeschichte des Mittelalters*, Band III. (1887), p. 409).
[4] For the *fraticelli* see Tocco, *L'eresia nel medio aevo*, and *Studi fran-
cescani*.

panions, the *Visions* of Angela of Foligno, and poems of Jacopone and his closest imitators—emanate from the Spiritual group and represent the Spiritual point of view. Among them the mystical life was cherished; and was practised and taught in its most exalted form by many forgotten saints. Thus Ubertino da Casale says that the chief among those " great practisers of seraphic wisdom " who instructed him in "the whole art of the higher contemplation " were the Tertiaries Cecilia of Florence, a devout virgin of whom nothing more is known, and Pier Pettignano of Siena, whose gift of prayer is celebrated in the Divine Comedy.[1] These " introduced him into the mysteries of Jesus," and prepared him to appreciate the lofty teachings of Angela of Foligno, who afterwards " changed the whole face of his mind." [2]

The Spiritual movement had therefore its definitely mystical side, and fostered that peculiar blend of religious illuminism and reforming energy which has so often appeared to trouble the stagnant waters of in-stitutional religion. The *Speculum*, which is a mani-festo of the Spiritual party, says that Francis had wished his brothers to be " like the little bird which is called the lark "; their earthly life poor and humble, clad in grey feathers and nourished on the meanest things, their celestial life joyful, musical, and free.[3] The insistence on outward austerity was therefore only half their secret ; and was cherished as a condition of inward wealth. A comparison of Jacopone's most ecstatic odes with the highly-metaphysical " revela-tions " of Angela of Foligno, shows how advanced was the mystical doctrine then current in Spiritual circles. Some of the greatest Spirituals—both Tertiaries and

---

[1] Cf. *Purg.*, xiii., 124-9. Peter the Combseller, who was deeply venerated in Spiritual circles, lived till 1289, and may have been known to Jacopone.

[2] *Arbor Vitæ Crucifixus*, Prologue.

[3] *Speculum*, cap. cxiii.

L

friars—were hermits and visionaries who continued the Franciscan tradition of ardent devotion to the Crucified, practising in seclusion the primitive life of poverty and prayer. Many of the *laude* show how strong an appeal the ideals of this group must have made to Jacopone. But, refusing the invitation to lead the movement of reform lest he should " fall from the life of contemplation," he also refused the other temptation to devote himself wholly to the ecstatic life of intercourse with God, because such a career was " an anticipation of heaven," illicit whilst he still had work to do on earth.

His original place in the party, and attitude to its policy, were probably much like that of Conrad of Offida, with whom we know that he was closely associated.[1] Conrad is described in the *Fioretti* as a " marvellous zealot of Gospel Poverty," and is said by Angelo Clareno to have worn the same tunic from youth to extreme old age. In him, as in Jacopone, this taste for squalor was combined with a fine and cultivated intellect and soaring mystical powers. Though a man of much learning, and in after life a celebrated writer and preacher, he was for ten years a voluntary mendicant and cook of the community. Drawn to the life of pure contemplation, he yet took an active part

---

[1] Conrad of Offida (*c.* 1237-41-1306) is one of the most beautiful figures in Spiritual annals. He was a mystic, a lover of nature who " got more solace in the woods than at the altar," and is credited with the Franciscan power over animals. He is an important link between the First Companions and the Spiritual rank and file of his day. Shortly before Brother Leo's death in 1271, but after the destruction of the early records and lives, he sent for Conrad and told him " great things in words and writing." The substance of these communications is supposed to be preserved in the *Arbor Vitæ* of Ubertino da Casale, and probably tallies with much in the *Speculum.* Conrad was intimate with John of Parma and had recourse to Margaret of Cortona. Becoming celebrated for holiness he was sent to La Verna; a privilege reserved for the most saintly souls. His last years were spent at the Convent of S. Croce near Assisi, and devoted to the life of contemplation. See *Fioretti,* caps. xlii.-xliv.; A. Clareno, *Historia Septem Tribulationum* (*Archiv für Litteratur und Kirchengeschichte des Mittelalters,* Band II.); *Memorie storiche del B. Corrado da Offida* (*Misc. Franc.,* XV., 1914, pt. ii.).

in the crusade for the restoration of the Primitive Rule ;
and was with Jacopone one of the signatories of the
manifesto which Angelo Clareno presented to Celes-
tine V. After this event his attitude seems to have been
much like that of the poet.   Neither of them took
advantage of the Pope's permission to dissociate them-
selves from the main order of the Friars Minor : whilst
never ceasing to preach and practise the Primitive Rule,
they remained till their deaths under the formal
authority of its superiors.   Conrad's connection with
Clareno and the extreme *zelanti* must indeed have been
very short.   Though accused by the *relaxati* of disloyalty
and of encouraging the Spirituals to leave the Order, he
yet remained within its fold ; and from 1294 onwards
was in constant request as a Franciscan preacher,
" coming forth from his contemplative solitude out of
burning love for his fellow-men." He is a characteristic
figure of the Spiritual centre ; bold yet submissive,
active yet ecstatic, a practiser of that golden mean
which Jacopone extolled as the true expression of an
" ordered love." A study of his life and position helps
us to understand what was the temper of that inner
company of practical mystics, swaying between raptur-
ous love of heaven and bitter consciousness of the dis-
harmonies of earth, who formed the heart of the
" Spiritual " group.

Now, if we consider these points in more detail, we
observe that the three-fold character of Jacopone's
temptation strikes a definitely " Spiritual " note.   It
was the official doctrine of the whole Order that in St.
Francis the life of Christ had been lived again.   Fran-
ciscan literature, especially that emanating from the
Spiritual side, is full of details establishing the con-
formity of each act of the Founder with some act of
Christ.   Stories were told of the devils who tempted
him, of his forty days' fast on an island of Lake Thrasy-
mene, of how he had been uplifted from the earth and

transfigured by celestial light. The miracle of the stigmata, at that time unique, set the seal upon this interpretation of history. We find this belief, which to the modern mind seems bizarre, if not blasphemous, assumed as a matter of course in Jacopone's ode to the Seraphic Father:[1]

> O Francesco, da Dio amato,
> Cristo en te s'ène mostrato.

> (Thou, Francis, dear to God must be,
> For Christ hath shown himself in thee.)

And again, even more strongly:

> Lo Nemico s'atremío,
> vedendo lui s'empaurío,
> parvegli Cristo de Dio
> che en croce avea spogliato.

> (The Foe, aghast and terrified,
>   Gazed on his face and trembling stood.
> He seemed that Christ of God who died
>   Despoiled of all upon the Rood.)

This, then, was the general view of all clients and followers of Francis—a view which finds elaborate expression in the Book of Conformities of Bartolommeo da Pisa,[2] where every incident in the life of the Founder is set beside its Gospel archetype. But whilst the "relaxed" friars were content to accept and admire, extolling a heroic virtue which they did not attempt to imitate, the Spirituals, with the deadly logic of the enthusiast, insisted that every true follower of St. Francis—lay or religious—was called in his turn to the reproduction of this Christ-life; and that this could only be done by a literal fulfilment of that Primitive Rule which St. Francis had laid as a solemn charge on his followers. This Rule meant simply the uncompromising acceptance of those " evangelical counsels "

[1] *Lauda LXII.*
[2] Printed in *Analecta Francescana*, vol. iv.

of poverty, chastity, and obedience on which all Chris-
tian monasticism is supposed to be based.[1]   But its
special character lay in the peculiar emphasis placed on
poverty; which was to St. Francis and his true fol-
lowers an actual sacrament of liberation, the outward
and visible sign of the spiritual life.

If we wish to realise all that poverty meant to the
noblest souls among the Spirituals, we have only to
read Jacopone's two *laude*, " Povertade enamorata," [2]
and "O amor de povertate ": [3] for these poems are the
battle hymns of the strict observants.   Already in the
Sacrum Commercium, which may have been written
within a year of St. Francis' death, Poverty appears in
apotheosis as Lady of the Nations, " preventing with
the blessings of sweetness " those who come to her
embrace,[4] and invested with the romantic beauty
which the troubadour poets gave to the Lady of their
songs.   It is not improbable that this conception comes
from the Seraphic Father himself, for it is in harmony
with all we know of his temperament.   Jacopone's poem
to Beloved Poverty is an elaboration of these passages
in Parenti's exquisite work.   In a series of verses which
seem to unroll before us the quaint picture-maps of
mediæval cartographers, it proclaims the realm of the
Lady of the Nations;   a dominion which stretches
from " Francia ed Inghilterra " to " India e Barbaria,"
and includes the " renno Teotonicoro," " Scozia e Fre-
sonia."   The world is her manor, the freedom of all
living things—the running of waters, the swimming of
fishes, the moving winds and the flying birds—the
essence of her delight.   " Blessed are the poor, for they
shall inherit the earth."   The Spiritual Franciscans did
not merely admire the Beatitudes: they accepted them
as statements of fact.

[1] Hannay, *Spirit and Origin of Christian Monasticism*, pp. 246 *et seq.*
[2] *Lauda LIX.*
[3] *Lauda LX.*, p. 420.
[4] *Sacrum Commercium*, caps. iii. and iv.

Terra, erbe con lor colori,·
arbori e frutti con sapori,
bestie, miei servitori,
tutte en mia befolcaría.
    Acque, fiumi, lachi e mare,
pescetegli e lor notare,
aere, venti, ucel volare,
tutti me fonno giollaría. . . .

    Poi che Dio ha 'l mio velle,
possessor d'onnecovelle,
le mie ale on tante penne
de terra en cielo non m'è via.[1]

(The earth and all the plants that grow,
The trees, and all the fruits they show,
The very beasts, my yoke that know—
    All in my homestead I unite.
The running waters, lake and sea,
And all the fishes swimming free,
The birds in windy air that be—
    These are the stuff of my delight. . . .

Since to God's will my being clings,
I am possessor of all things ;
So many feathers have my wings,
    To heaven it is an easy flight.)

In the great *lauda*, "O amor de povertate," [2] we see
some of the implications of this mystical doctrine of
poverty: all that its practice meant for the "perfect
friar." The outward destitution he cherished was
merely the matter of a sacrament which made him
perfectly receptive of Christ. Poverty, says Jacopone,
considered in this deep sense, is "highest wisdom." It
is the secret of perfect liberty, a "hidden heaven " ; one
phase in that process of abnegation whereby the soul
at last gives up her very self-hood, and in so doing
perfects her personality in God.

[1] *Lauda LIX.*, "Povertade enamorata." The "many-feathered soul "
is a favourite image with the mediæval mystics. Since its ultimate source
is Platonic (*Phædrus*, 246 b), its presence here may be accepted as another
proof of Jacopone's indulgence in "acquired knowledge."
[2] *Lauda LX.*, p. 420.

Povertate è nulla avere
e nulla cosa poi volere ;
ed omne cosa possedere
en spirito de libertate.[1]

We cannot be surprised that minds possessed by so sublime a vision should have failed to see in sharp focus the obstacles to its translation into fact; or that the more extreme *zelanti*, such as Olivi, should have interpreted that vow of poverty which was to them the outward sign of grace, in its most literal and impossible sense. These rigorists held that it forbade not merely ownership of property, but the use of cellars and storehouses and the purchase of goods ; and opposed, as contrary to the Franciscan idea, the growth of the big town convents with their libraries and frescoed churches. The term *usus pauper*, indicating the minimum use of essential material things, was their watchword. The least attractive chapters of the *Speculum* show what this involved in the way of squalor and thriftlessness.[2] They further declared that obedience to this rule constituted the only life of perfection ; since it was the life of Christ Himself, and all Christians are called to imitate Him as closely as they can. The " strict observants," tracing their descent through Giles and Leo from St. Francis, were the " little flock " through whom this new evangel should spread through the world. We now see the true meaning of Angelo Clareno's description of Jacopone as one of those friars " in whom Christ and His Spirit were most firmly believed to dwell." [3]

Some extremists, such as the fanatical group known as the " Beghini della Povertà," went further : claiming that the Primitive Rule had equal authority with the Gospel, and that no Pope or Council could change it

---

[1] *Loc. cit.* On account of the advanced mystical state described in its concluding verses, I am inclined to place this poem in Jacopone's last period ; but it certainly represents the Spiritual ideals in their purest form.
[2] Caps. v., xix., lviii.   [3] See above, p. 7.

without falling into heresy.[1]   This sort of thing, of
course, played into the hands of the " relaxed " party,
whose deep hostility to the Spirituals was based on
their claim to such a special possession of the Spirit of
Christ.   These Spirituals might have been cherished as
ornaments of the Order had they been content to
remain exceptions, instead of preaching a doctrine
which was an implied censure upon the larger and more
influential part of the community.   We have already
seen some of the excesses and absurdities in which this
doctrine involved them: yet it is impossible to refuse
admiration to an ideal so lofty, a courage and self-
denial so heroic.   The best of them—and among these
were Jacopone and his friends—were practical mystics,
who attached literal meanings to the New Testament
demand for a transmutation and intensification of life.
Christ was to them a " vigorous lover," giving freedom
and vitality, but accepting no half-measures in return.
This we must keep in our minds, and remember as
their constant inspiration, when we try to judge their
political acts.

At the close of the thirteenth century, the difference
between the two branches of the Order had become
acute, in spite of the efforts towards reconciliation
made by St. Bonaventura as Minister-General, and by
Pope Nicholas III. in his reinterpretation of the Rule.[2]
In this decretal, written after consultation with the
last surviving companions of the Saint, the Pope de-
clared that the Testament of St. Francis, containing his
most extreme injunctions upon poverty, was not bind-
ing upon the Order ; though obedience to it was holy
and meritorious.   But all superfluities, and everything
derogating from real poverty, were utterly forbidden
to all, and the spirit of the Rule was to be safeguarded
on every side.   Had both parties been reasonable,

---

[1] P. Ciro da Pesaro, in *Misc. Franc.*, XV. (1914) pp. 4 and 43.
[2] In his Decretal *Exiit qui seminat*, 1279.

this compromise might have formed the basis of a
settlement.   It was promulgated immediately after
Jacopone's admission to San Fortunato, and was pro-
bably regarded by him as an implied permission to
keep the rule of poverty in its most drastic form.   Un-
fortunately, the Generals of the Order during the first
ten years of his religious life were hostile to the Spiritual
movement ; and did nothing to protect even moder-
ate men of this type.   During this period, Jacopone
and his friends almost certainly endured a good deal
of persecution ; only mitigated by the election in
1287 of Matteo d'Acqua Sparta, a tolerant ruler,
who protected Olivi and the rigorists, but permitted
the " relaxed " friars to continue their evasion ot the
Rule.

The extreme Spirituals, however, were not content
with the measure of freedom given by the decretal
Exiit qui seminat, and by the protection of the new
General.   They had now reached the fanatical stage,
where ardour becomes tainted with acrimony.   More-
over, many believed themselves called not merely to
restore the Order to its primitive purity, but also to
reform the whole Christian Church, by bringing in the
Reign of the Holy Ghost as announced by the Abbot
Joachim.[1]   The prophecies of Joachim, who had pre-
dicted the fulfilment of the signs of the Apocalypse, the
reign of Antichrist—first identified with the Emperor
Frederick II. and afterwards with Pope Boniface VIII.
—and passing away of the present age, must have been
well known to Jacopone.   It is probable that the tem-
tation to " restore the Church " first came to him by

---

[1] The Abbot Joachim of Fiore (1168-1202) had prophesied that the
reign of the Son—identified with the Roman Church—was to be succeeded
by the reign of the Holy Ghost, when the gospel would be " spiritually
understood " and its ministers would be religious, living a life of prayer
and contemplation. This change was to take place in 1260, or according
to the calculations of Ubertino da Casale, reckoning from the Ascension
instead of the Nativity, in 1294. The Spirituals claimed that the mendicant
Orders were destined to bring in this new era.

way of an invitation to throw in his lot with the Joachist
group among the Spirituals: who, like all oppressed
and enthusiastic minorities, looked eagerly to a coming
day of freedom and full life. Now far advanced in the
way of contemplation, with an ever clearer vision of
eternal values, a noble sense of social duty—and of the
claim which the earth life and its problems still make
on spirits immersed in the Love of God—urged him to
take his part in the struggle to actualise those values
in the world of time. The " love which gives all things
form " shapes human history through human instru-
ments. In Jacopone the old vigorous combative nature,
the fearless spirit of criticism, sublimated but not
killed, were tools ready to hand; and under the
pressure of events—probably, too, under the influence
of his Roman environment—came once more into the
foreground of his consciousness. His minatory poems,
with their violent denunciations of social and clerical
corruption, show how intense was his reaction to this
call upon him. They must be read side by side with
the mystical *laude* if we are to obtain a clear view of
him as he was in this moment of his career; when the
denunciatory prophet was doubled with the humble
and adoring saint.

In Spiritual circles the air was full of hints and
prophecies concerning a redemption near at hand.
Sayings foretelling the future tribulations of the Order,
and the final victory of the Primitive Rule, began to be
attributed to St. Francis himself. Conrad of Offida is
said to have obtained from the aged Brother Leo a
number of such prophecies, many of which have a
decidedly Joachist air. According to them, Francis
declared that a time was coming when the Order should
forsake the true path, and demons should seize power
therein: and in those days, some brothers should flee
to heathen countries and there find rest, and others
should hide in desert places. " And after these things,

I will build up the Order in its first and perfect state." [1]

Not only by the *zelanti* was the need for such a revival felt. All spiritually-minded men were dissatisfied with the state of the Church and the world. As the thirteenth century drew to a close, the disharmony between the ideal and actual became too violent to be ignored. The general sense of a social order running to seed—of sin, confusion, and religious indifference fast approaching their term—encouraged the belief that the fulfilment of the signs, and passing away of the present age, were indeed at hand. In Jacopone's sombre apocalyptic poem, " Or se parrá chi averá fidanza," [2] we see the reflexion of these ideas. It paints in the gloomiest colours the " coming of the tribulations that have been foretold ": the Sun of Christ darkened, the Moon of the Church obscured, the Stars of the religious life fallen from their heaven, all men bearing the sign of the Old Serpent, and eaten up by the three great sins of body, mind, and spirit—avarice, intellectual pride, and that false spirituality (always feared and detested by the mystics) which clamours for signs and is greedy of raptures, prophecies, and miracles.

> Tutto el mondo veggio conquassato
> e precipitando va en ruina ;
> como l'omo che è enfrenetecato,
> al qual non può om dar medicina,
> li medici sí l'hanno desperato,
> ché non glie giova encanto né dottrina,
> vedemolo en extremo lavorare. [3]

> (I see this world a shattered heap
> Hastening its ruin to fulfil,

---

[1] It is hardly necessary to say that these prophecies are " tendency literature," only valuable as a record of Spiritual opinion at the close of the thirteenth century. The references to the exile of Angelo Clareno and his companions and the secession of the Celestine hermits are fairly obvious. They are preserved in a fourteenth-century MS. in the convent of the Cappuccini at Foligno. See *Misc. Franc.*, VII. (1889), pt. iv.

[2] *Lauda L.* · [3] *Lauda L.*, " Or se parrá."

As doth a madman, frenzied, leap,
  Nor is there medicine for his ill:
Physicians in despair must weep,
  No use in magic nor in skill—
In pangs of death it laboureth.)

These were the kind of notions current among serious
and religious men ; when, in 1294, one of the most
dramatic events in the history of the Roman Church
appeared to justify the faith and hope of those who
had clung to the Joachist belief, and held that a more
spiritual era was about to be born from the ruins of the
old. This event was the election to the Papacy of the
hermit Pier da Morrone as Pope Celestine V.

Pier da Morrone was born in 1215 of a peasant
family. He retired as a young man to the Abruzzi,
where he afterwards founded an Order of hermits ; the
Rule being confirmed by the Council of Lyons in 1274.
He was by this time a person of great importance,
venerated throughout Italy as a saint, and protected
by the powerful Colonna cardinals.[1] In sympathy, and
probably in touch with the Spiritual Franciscans—for
the reform of the religious life was one of the objects of
his foundation—he seems to have been among Jaco-
pone's personal friends. In 1293, being seventy-eight
years of age, he gave up the government of his Order
and retired to a solitary hermitage to spend the rest of
his life in contemplation. The papacy was at this time
vacant ; Nicholas IV. had died in the previous year,
and the quarrels of cardinals and politicians frustrated
each attempt to elect his successor. In 1294, the con-
tinued interregnum having become a scandal, Pier da
Morrone is said to have written a letter in the fashion-
able apocalyptic vein to the Cardinal Latino Mala-

---

[1] Cardinal Jacopo Colonna, one of the most powerful princes of the
Church and a member of a noble and wealthy Roman house, was the
friend and patron of the Spiritual Franciscans. With his nephew, Cardinal
Pier Colonna, he afterwards led the opposition to Pope Boniface VIII.
See below.

branca ; predicting the vengeance of God if the election were longer delayed. It was the authoritative letter of an established saint and visionary, and made a profound impression ; though of a kind undreamed by its writer. A sudden enthusiasm for a candidate outside the range of party quarrels, and possessing the unusual recommendation of personal holiness, seems to have seized on the Conclave, which was now reduced by sickness to eight cardinals. The name of Pier was proposed as Pope. The most astute and powerful member of the college, Benedetto Gaetani, unable to secure his own election, was glad to support an outsider whom he expected to be able to rule. The formal election took place on July 5th, 1294. Pier da Morrone received the news with consternation, and was with difficulty persuaded from his hermitage and brought to Aquila to be crowned.

The event caused an immense sensation among the Franciscan Spirituals, and all who looked for the reform of the Church. To the Joachists, it seemed that the epoch of the Holy Ghost, when "the ministers of God will lead a spiritual life, dwelling in prayer and contemplation," was indeed about to begin. Jacopone's view is seen in the vigorous letter which he afterwards addressed to Celestine.[1] This election may work the salvation of the Church, if the new Pope's will and courage equal his sanctity. It is certain to work misery for the contemplative, forced to leave the only life of happiness and take upon himself this deradful responsibility.

> Grande ho aúto en te cordoglio
> co te uscío de bocca: — Voglio; —

But he has no illusions about the difficulties that lie ahead: the clash and variety of types and interests,

---

[1] *Lauda LIV.*, " Que farai, Pier da Morrone? " p. 428.

the bewildering complexities of policy, the conflict between expediency and Christianity.

> Grand'è la tua degnitate,
> non è meno la tempestate ;
> grand'è la varietate
> che troverai en tua magione.

This poem gains weight when we remember that Jacopone probably wrote it from Rome, after an experience, stretching over several years, of the corruptions and entanglements of the Papal court. He knew but too well the sensations of the contemplative compelled to breathe that air.

For a little time perhaps Celestine may have believed himself supernaturally called to steer the ship of the Church through the storm. His first acts, at any rate, show some courage and initiative, and are more like those of a monastic superior than of a mediæval Pope. He made his own decrees and decisions—thirty between September 1st and 17th—without consulting the cardinals ; generally using as his principal mouthpiece his old friend Cardinal Jacopo Colonna, for his knowledge of Latin was slight. He cared nothing for politics ; and, bewildered by the intricacies of Papal administration, fell into mistakes and confusions from the first. The various reforming, dissident, and oppressed religious bodies and individuals, *zelanti*, *fraticelli*, and other more fanatical groups, feeling that their day was indeed about to dawn, hurried to demand his support. Among others, Angelo Clareno the famous leader of the *zelanti*, with his bosom friend Fra Liberato, came to Aquila towards the end of September, 1294, at the instance of the Minister-General of the Order; to beg the Pope's protection for those who wished to observe the Primitive Rule in its rigour. One of those who signed Angelo's petition was Jacopone, who now first appears in history as a leader of the Spiritual friars. " In the time when Fra Pier da Morrone assumed the pontificate,'" says Angelo, "it seemed good to the Minister-General and all those principal friars in whom Christ and His Spirit were most firmly believed to dwell—and especially *frati* Conrad of Offida, Pietro Monticello,[1] Jacopo of Todi, Thomas of Trivio, Conrad of Spoleto, and others—who aspired to the pure observance of the Rule, that Fra Pietro of Macerata and his companion [*i.e.* Angelo himself] should go to the most holy Pontiff and ask of him, for themselves and other brethren who were eager and willing to observe the Rule, direction and licence to undertake this observance without molestation and impediment from those others who had deliberately declined from the faithful and pure observance of that Rule which St. Francis enjoined in his Testament and other of his writings." [2]

Angelo Clareno and his little band of *zelanti* were already well known. He was a man of considerable culture, who is said by Bartholommeo of Pisa to have translated from the Greek the works of St. Macarius and St. John Chrysostom. Entering the Franciscan Order in 1260, he imbibed Spiritual ideas from some of the First Companions, and became the friend of the saintly John of Parma, and of the great visionary, Jacomo della Massa, whose mystical experiences are celebrated in the *Fioretti*.[3] In 1274, with his friend Fra Liberato, and other *zelanti*, Angelo was charged with heresy and schism ; and was condemned by five Provincial Ministers to perpetual and solitary imprisonment with privation of the Sacraments. This sentence, which was read aloud every week in every convent of the Order, was alone enough to keep Angelo in the affectionate remembrance of his fellow-observants, including Jacopone, who may have known him before his condemnation. When the Spiritual friar

---

[1] See *Fioretti*, caps. xlii.–xliv.
[2] Angelo Clareno, *Historia septem tribulationum* (*Archiv für Litteratur und Kirchengeschichte des Mittelalters*, Band II., p. 308).
[3] Cap. xlviii.

Raymond Gaufridi became General of the Order in 1289, one of his first acts was to re-examine the case of Angelo and his companions. As a result he released them, declaring their only offence to be " love of the Rule in its rigour and vigour," and sent them out of harm's way on a mission to Armenia. From this they returned to Italy in 1293, owing to the persecution of the Syrian friars. Their personal contact with Jacopone and his friends must therefore have been brief. Being excluded from all the convents of the March of Ancona by order of the Provincial Minister, they were advised by Gaufridi to appeal direct to the Pope, who already knew and admired them. Therefore, the movement with which Jacopone now identified himself was not that of dissidents and schismatics ; but had the support and approval of the General of the Order, and of the most holy and responsible minds among the Spiritual friars.

Angelo's petition did not ask for separation from the Minorite Order, but merely for authority to observe unhindered the Primitive Rule. Celestine's decision on this point shows that his enthusiasms were tempered by much common sense. He recognised both the beauty and the extravagance of the Spiritual ideals, well fitted to a handful of heroic souls, but impossible of general realisation. He therefore proposed to remove Angelo with his followers from the control of the Franciscan Provincials, placing the congregation thus formed in direct obedience to himself: an act in which we see the instinct of the old religious founder still at work. He gave them the name of Poor Hermits of Pope Celestine—a foundation which must not be confused with that of the Celestine monks—and made Liberato their first Superior: recommending them to increase rather than detract from the severity of the Rule and Testament of Francis, so far as their strength allowed it. The Superiors of his own Celestine Order—a branch of the reformed Benedictines—were directed to give them help and protection.

This solution of their problem did not satisfy the best of the Spirituals. The dream which inspired them was a dream of unity; a unity embracing not merely the Order, but Christendom itself. Therefore this permitted secession from the main body seemed like a denial of their central proposition: namely, that the life of Francis should be lived within, not without, the Minorite fold.[1] We possess the letter which Olivi wrote in 1295 to Conrad of Offida, protesting against the creation of the Celestine hermits, and censuring their leaders, whom he calls "sheep wandering in steep and desert places."[2] It is fairly clear from this letter that Conrad, whom we find preaching for the Order in the following year, did not join them: nor have we any evidence that Jacopone did so.

Jacopone's position at this time is obscure. It was now, perhaps, that he experienced his second temptation,[3] when Satan appeared disguised as Christ to claim his total devotion. We can well understand the weariness and impatience with which years of friction and perhaps serious persecution among the Conventuals, or the alternative of service in a cardinal's palace at Rome, must sometimes have filled him: the difficulties of communion with that "Love whose only name is 'I love'"[4] in such surroundings. The creation of the Celestine hermits offered him the opportunity of recapturing the secret of happiness ; living without hindrance the contemplative life, and observing poverty and self-abasement in their extreme form. The prospect must inevitably have enticed one side of his nature. Yet the other, the combative side, protested against retirement from a battle in which he believed that the very

[1] See Tocco, *Studi Francescani*, p. 274.
[2] Seiler, *Hist. Jahrbuch*, Band III., p. 649.
[3] See above, p. 157.
[4] *Lauda LXXXV.*, "O amor che m'ami."

M

foundations of the spiritual life were involved; in which, too, we cannot doubt that he found a certain enjoyment.

We can hardly suppose that so active a Spiritual, now publicly associated with the notorious Clareno, could continue to live at peace with his Conventual superiors: but the protection of Celestine and of Gaufridi must now have assured Jacopone against serious persecution. He may perhaps have found shelter for a time in one of the hermitages where the Primitive Rule was still in force: but it is more likely that he continued to live in Rome, since we find him in 1297 deeply involved in Roman politics. It must soon have become clear to him that the hopes which his party had placed in Celestine could never be realised, and that the Epoch of the Holy Ghost was still delayed. In November, under the influence of Charles II., the unfortunate Pope allowed himself to be taken to Naples; where, surrounded by political intrigues, yet struggling still to live the ascetic life, his "testing" in its full rigour began. It is at this time that Jacopone is said to have addressed to him that blunt and candid epistle which shows how accurately the more acute minds among the Spirituals already estimated Celestine's difficulties and chances of success; with how great a dismay they regarded the ascendancy of Charles II., how doubtful they were of his power in such surroundings to "hold the balance straight." "*Now* we shall see what deeds you dreamed in your cell—*now* we shall know indeed whether you are gold, iron, or brass."

> Questa corte è una fucina
> che 'l buon auro se ci afina ;
> se llo tiene altra ramina,
> torna en cenere e carbone.[1]

---

[1] *Lauda LIV.*, " Que farai, Pier da Morrone? " p. 428. Signor Bruguoli (*Le Satire*, pp. 301-2) gives reasons for supposing that the last ten lines of this poem, from " Se non hai amor paterno," are spurious, since they are not found in the best Umbrian manuscripts.

Bold words for the " least of despised little friars " to address to the Vicar of Christ ; and a measure of the position which Jacopone now held in the religious world. He had become the mouthpiece of a party more remarkable for earnestness than for tact ; and under stress of the situation in which he found himself some of those qualities which had distinguished his worldly career, the old shrewd judgment of men, the old fear-less spirit of criticism—mortified but not killed by convent life—reappeared in the foreground of his consciousness.

At Naples the fears of the Spirituals were soon ful-filled. Difficulties and confusions entangled more and more the unhappy Celestine, bewildered by problems far beyond his grasp, and by the multitude of coun-sellors " che 'l ner per bianco fon vedere." A few weeks' experience were enough to prove the completeness of his failure as a Pontiff and induce Cardinal Gaetani —the strongest personality in the Sacred College, and reputed the greatest jurist of his age—to encourage his timid thoughts of abdication ; an act hitherto unknown in the history of the Papacy. In December, to the wrath and despair of the Spiritual Franciscans and Celestine monks, the Pope laid down the tiara, " moved by lawful reasons: namely by humility, the desire for a better life and tranquil conscience ; and likewise because of my weakness of body and want of know-ledge, the maliciousness of the people, and infirmity of my person ; and that I may regain the peace ot my aforetime consolations." Appearing before the car-dinals, he made his formal act of abdication ; and resumed his hermit's dress after a reign of five months and nine days. For a moment, the pathos of the situa-tion—perhaps the uneasy suspicion that there was something wrong with a Church which could no longer be governed by a saint—obscured the general feeling of relief. All wept. Their recovery, however, was rapid.

The Conclave met immediately. On Christmas Eve, 1294, Benedetto Gaetani was almost unanimously elected Pope, and was crowned at Rome on January 23rd, 1295, as Boniface VIII.

Jacopone's disastrous conflict with Boniface occupies so important a place in his life and poetry, that these cannot fully be understood unless we know something of his principal enemy.[1] Gaetani, however, is not an easy person to know. There are few great figures in history upon whom more contradictory judgments have been passed. Born about 1217, he was closely connected with Todi, where his uncle was bishop. Here in 1260 he obtained a stall in the Cathedral, although not yet in orders: an infraction of the Capitular constitutions for which his uncle obtained a dispensation from Alexander IV.[2] He added to its emoluments those of the rich commandery of San Illuminato at Todi. Though during his papacy he gave many gifts and privileges to the Chapter, his reputation in Todi seems to have been bad. Doubtless his greedy accumulation of benefices was remembered; for at the process against his memory instituted by Philip the Fair, the friars and clerks of the city were called to witness against him. It has been suggested that Jacopone's knowledge and dislike of Gaetani may have begun in these early years, when the rising Ghibelline lawyer and the brilliant and avaricious ecclesiastic were fellow-citizens.[3] This would account for the familiar tone and unbridled language in which the old poet afterwards addressed his adversary; heightening a temperamental hostility by memories of the ancient civic conflicts between Ghibelline noble and Guelph prelate. The two men were made to misunderstand each other. Both were skilled jurists: but that instinct

---

[1] The best account of Boniface is by H. Finke, *Aus dem Tagen Bonifaz VIII.*
[2] Tosti, *Storia di Bonifazio VIII.*, Doc. A e B.
[3] D'Ancona, *Jacopone da Todi*, p. 81.

for law and order which Jacopone applied wholly to
the life of the soul, and not always sufficiently to its
material setting, Gaetani applied to the temporal life
of the Church.   Remarkable for his energetic and
masterful character, acute intellect and wide know-
ledge of the world, he was a typical ecclesiastical politi-
cian.   Regarded by his enemies as a monster of greed,
cruel, avaricious, and unscrupulous, Dante consigned
him to hell for the sin of simony.[1]   His apologists
exhibit him as a strong ruler, doing his best for the
Church in a period of peculiar difficulty.   The first of
the great art-loving popes, the patron of Giotto, and
chief builder of Orvieto Cathedral, he stood for the
perfection of that culture which Jacopone renounced
on his conversion ; and for a church policy which we
need not condemn as entirely ignoble, but which was
totally inconsistent with the transcendental dream of
the Spiritual friars.

At first, though he promptly revoked the decrees
which Celestine had made " in the fullness of his sim-
plicity," Boniface treated the Spirituals with tolerance:
and to those who brought accusations against them,
replied " Let them alone! they do better than you."
His difficulties, however, were great.   Considerable
doubt hung over the validity of his election, which was
bitterly attacked by the more extreme Spirituals and
by the Celestine monks, many of whom were more
given to political agitation than to asceticism.   All these
insisted that the Papacy, once accepted, cannot be
renounced ; since it is in essence a spiritual power given

---

[1] Se' tu sì tosto di quell'aver sazio,
   per lo qual non temesti torre a inganno
   la bella Donna, e di poi farne strazio?
                                (*Inf.*, xix., 55).

Dante's eagerness to declare the damnation of Boniface is shown by the
device to which he resorts.   When he wrote the *Inferno* the Pope was some
years dead ; but since the ideal date of the vision is 1300—the year of the
Papal Jubilee—he could not in his own person be placed in hell.   Therefore
Nicholas III., also doomed for simony, is made to mistake Dante himself
for Boniface coming to share his fate.

by God, and God alone can take it away. Any election
made during Celestine's life was held by them to be
invalid,[1] and it soon became evident that a movement to
restore him to the throne was probable. Boniface, whose
outward boldness seems to have veiled a secret sense
of insecurity, therefore placed his unhappy prede-
cessor in a custody which was nominally honourable,
but actually indistinguishable from imprisonment.
This shocked many consciences, and increased the
hostility of Spirituals and Celestines. The political
situation was also bad. Philip the Fair of France was
actively inimical. In Italy there was general unrest.

The uneasy and suspicious state in which these
complications kept the new Pope gave an opportunity
to the Franciscan Conventuals, anxious to find a weapon
against their Spiritual enemies. They accused the
Celestine monks and hermits of spreading doubts about
the validity of Boniface's election, and secretly pre-
paring the restoration of Celestine. Boniface fell into
their trap, and issued a violent decree against the
Spirituals, withdrawing all the privileges given by
Celestine: thus forcing into opposition even the more
moderate among the strict observants. He also
alienated—though ostensibly for reasons which compel
our respect—the powerful cardinals Jacopo and Pietro
Colonna, who had always been in some sort the friends
and protectors of the Spiritual group. These great and
wealthy Ghibelline princes were at first supporters of
Boniface. They had perceived the hopeless character
oi Celestine's reign, and voted for his abdication. They
found room, however, in their busy lives for more than
purely spiritual interests. Shortly after Boniface's

[1] This is the argument of the Colonna manifesto. See below. Olivi
and others, however, protested against the view that the Pope is irrevo-
cably wedded to the Church—" pate e marito " (*Lauda LIII.*), which
Jacopone seems to have shared with Ubertino da Casale (*Arbor Vitæ*, v.,
cap. v.). Olivi observes with much good sense that such a doctrine would
prevent the deposition even of a heretical pontiff. See letter to Conrad of
Offida quoted above, p. 177, and Tocco, *Studi Francescani*, p. 278.

election, Cardinal Jacopo, that friend of Poverty, seized the family estates belonging to his brothers and distributed them among his nephews. Doubtless he thought that Boniface would see the propriety of supporting his powerful friend. But he reckoned without the Pope's strong instinct for the law: perhaps, too, without the superior cunning of his victims, and the cupidity of their judge. At any rate, when the dispossessed Colonna appealed to the Pontiff for support, Boniface gave judgment in their favour.

It seems to have been this act of apparent justice—though Jacopone hints at less disinterested motives for Boniface's decision—which first made the Colonna suspect the validity of Gaetani's election. They refused to restore the property, and presently entered into relations with his known enemies, Frederick III. of Sicily, and James II. of Aragon. On detection of this intrigue Boniface, for his own security, ordered them to receive Papal garrisons in their stronghold of Palestrina and other fortresses. Therefore the movement with which Jacopone was now associated—for we next hear of him as a member of the Colonna party—had a definitely political side. No doubt he, and those other Spiritual friars who afterwards joined the insurgent cardinals in denouncing Boniface's election, did so from motives of a spiritual kind. They were possessed by that dream which Celestine had failed to realise, and by a transcendental view of the Church which was hardly appropriate to their associates. To them, the Church of Christ was still the " noble Mother " of the soul, though now reduced to evil state and deprived of her " father and spouse," *i.e.* the lawful Pope. They were her " legitimate sons," born of her union with Christ ; but those now in power were bastards, distinguished by greed, cowardice, and disharmony, united only in their determination to destroy the " true heirs " of the Spirit.[1]

[1] *Lauda LIII.,* " Piange la Ecclesia," p. 432.

> Piangon le Relione
> e fanno gran lamento:
> — Aguardace, Signore,
> a lo nostro tormento ;
> poi che Bontate è morta,
> semo en destrugemento ;
> come la polve al vento
> nostra vita è tornato.[1]

(The true Religious sorrow and complain:
Behold and see, O Lord! how sharp our pain.
Since Goodness now is dead, we shall be slain:
Our life is as the dust upon the wind!)

They heard Truth mourn the death of Goodness and demand the drastic purification of the Church:

> Purgata questa ecclesia
> e quel che ci è mal visso
> sia en tal loco misso
> che purge i soi peccata.[2]

(O cleanse the church! and him of evil fame,
Send to assoil his sins within the flame.)

They heard, too, the less disinterested cries of those who proposed to further heavenly causes by very earthly means. We cannot deny that Jacopone again dallied at this time with that temptation to undertake the " rebuilding of the Church " which finally disclosed to him its Satanic character.[3] Pushed by that longing to mend a tattered world, and make it once more the fit vesture of God, which haunts all mystics of the active type, he deliberately re-entered the world of conflict. The vigorous and even venomous quality of the satires which he now produced, show that this return was not wholly disagreeable to him. Signor Brugnoli justly observes that at this period of his life " the old Adam and the new found themselves in perfect harmony." [4] Ancient instincts reasserted themselves. The Ghibelline noble was doubled with the reforming friar.

---

[1] *Lauda LI.*, " La Veritade piange."　　[2] *Loc. cit.*
[3] See above, p. 157.　　[4] *Le Satire*, p. cxxvi.

In his heart we may be sure that Jacopone, like a later mystic, wished only to " be to the Eternal Goodness what his own hand is to a man "[1]—a skilful, supple, and vigorous tool of the Divine Will—but for a time he seems to have forgotten that the hand of Love redeemed the world by accepting, not inflicting a wound. He was now deep in political intrigue, though he might still suppose that intrigue to have a spiritual aim. His companions were no longer the mystics and visionaries of La Verna and the Province of the March, but the Ghibelline nobles of Rome, and French prelates who supported the policy of Philip the Fair. The stages of his transition from the purely religious movement led by Angelo Clareno to this more sophisticated company are not known to us. We do know, however, that in the spring of 1297 he was at Longhezza ; a Colonna stronghold, lying east of Rome on the road to Tivoli. Here upon May 10th a manifesto was issued, declaring that Boniface, who, "not without the encouragement of the Evil One," called himself Roman Pontiff, was not legitimate Pope ; since, Celestine's resignation being brought about merely by human machinations, it and his successor's election were void.[2] In the picture of the evil pass to which these events have brought the Church— the sacraments profaned, the Apostolic succession broken—we seem to see a reflection of Jacopone's laments. The signatories beg that Boniface lay down his powers, and that all his acts and proceedings may be suspended till a General Council shall declare the truth, " remove abuses, and find a true Shepherd for the Church, without spot or stain." Should he refuse their petition, they threaten that " in so far as in them lies they will keep him from exercising all pastoral power."

This manifesto is declared by the Colonna to have

---

[1] *Theologia Germanica*, cap. x.
[2] The full text is given by Denifle in *Archiv für Litteratur und Kirchengeschichte des Mittelalters*, Band V. (1889). p. 509, *Die Denkschriften der Colonna gegen Bonifaz VIII.*

been drawn up in their presence by a notary. It was signed by them, by five prelates, of whom the majority were French, and by three Spiritual Franciscans; Jacopone—" Frate Jacobo Benedicti de Tuderto "— being the first. . The others were Fra Benedetto of Perugia and Fra Deodato Ricci of Monte Prenestino. It is therefore clear, not only that Jacopone was now one of the most eminent among the Spiritual friars, but also that he shared the most extreme view of Boniface's position, and of the measures which might properly be taken against him. On the day of signature, this mani-festo was laid on the High Altar of St. Peter's, and also nailed on the door of the principal churches of Rome. On the same day, Boniface excommunicated the Colonna cardinals, giving them ten days in which to make their submission. They at once retreated with their followers to their fortress of Palestrina; whence, on May 16th, they issued another and more violent manifesto, directly charging Boniface with the murder of Celestine, who had died in his prison in May, 1296. With this document Jacopone was not concerned: but he seems to have remained with the Colonna rebels in Palestrina, at least from September, 1297, when the Pope declared war upon them, to September, 1298, when the fortress fell before the Papal troops.

Though we need not suppose that Jacopone ever lost his grip upon eternal realities, the life of a partisan in the Colonna fortress—worse, of a partisan who was in some sort their official saint—can hardly have been favourable to the spiritual life: and it is not in this period that we must look for his most beautiful, most mystical, or most Christian poems. When imprison-ment brought space for reflection, he called Palestrina *loco malino :* that " unwholesome place." [1] Perhaps it was not only of bodily health that he thought. History assures us how easily and promptly the bitterness of

[1] *Lauda LV.*, " Que farai, fra Iacovone? "

conflict poisons the spirits of those who struggle for
ideal ends: how venomous the most righteous indig-
nation becomes, once permitted to dominate the mind.
This is the tragedy of every religious revival, and of
every saint who has fought for the triumph of his
dream. St. Francis eluded it by resigning to the un-
saintly Elias the control of his Order, when its policy
approached the controversial stage. Jacopone was
made of different stuff. He responded only too easily
to any call upon his militant instincts: and the effect
upon him of this descent into an arena where neither
lions nor Christians were quite at their best, may be
estimated by the poems which both criticism and
tradition assign to this year of his life. These poems
are the three laments upon the Church,[1] and—if that
lauda be indeed authentic in substance—his violent
attack upon Boniface VIII.[2] In none of these songs do
we find that profound and joyful consciousness of God
in the world and in the heart which transfigures Jaco-
pone's greatest poems. The focus is narrowed and the
prospect blurred. The dust of the arena hides the stars.
He sees no more the " wise and jocund Love . . .
liberal, courteous, spendthrift Love," infinite in
patience and mercy, impressing the pattern of God on
recalcitrant life.[3] His vision is filled by the failures and
degradations from perfection which surround him, the
dreadful strength of Evil, the apparent death of Good:
the deformed and adulterated substitutes that now
replace the faith and hope, the fervour and strength,
which were once the marks of Christianity. Grief and
disgust are turned to fury and bitterness. " Those
who call themselves the Church are the members of
Antichrist " ;[4] a direct reference to Boniface, which

[1] *Laude LI.*, " La Veritade piange " ; *LII.*, " Iesú Cristo se lamenta " ;
and *LIII.*, " Piange la Ecclesia," p. 432.

[2] *Lauda LVIII.*, " O papa Bonifazio, molt'hai iocato al mondo."

[3] *Lauda LXXXI.*, " O Amor, divino amore, amor," p. 460.

[4] *Lauda LI.*

supports the theory that Jacopone wrote at this time
the most terrible and violent of the satires attributed
to him: the savage address to his enemy which begins,
" O papa Bonifazio, molt'hai iocato al mondo." [1]

Fra Bartolommeo of Pisa, in his eulogy of Jacopone,
says that he " made manful clamour against the life of
Pope Boniface." [2] Though modern criticism has estab-
lished the strong probability that the most virulent
passages in this horrible poem—and especially those
verses which prophesy the downfall of the Pope—are
later interpolations, and must not be charged to Jaco-
pone's account,[3] a good case can be made out for the
authenticity of the rest. It was probably written about
1298, during his association with the Colonna insur-
gents ; [4] when the stress of a situation daily becoming
more hopeless had sharpened tongues and tempers, and
the cardinal virtues of prudence and temperance were
wearing rather thin. We can measure by it the distance
which now separated Jacopone from that " Kingdom of
Tranquillity which knows neither rancours nor dis-
putes." [5] The chief accusations which he brings against

[1] *Lauda LVIII.*
[2] *De conformitate*, Lib. I., fruct. viii., pars 2. (*Analecta Francescana,*
vol. iv.)
[3] According to Signor Brugnoli, who has subjected this poem to a critical
examination (*Le Satire*, pp. cxlvi and 322), vv. 13-17 and 20, which fall
much below the level of the rest in execution, and are lacking in the early
Codex *Magliabechiano*, must be regarded as spurious. These stanzas are
probably the work of some fourteenth-century Spiritual extremist or
Celestine monk, anxious to vent the hatred of his party for the memory
of Boniface, and to condemn him out of the mouth of the great poet of the
Strict Observance. This view, if accepted, removes a difficulty felt by all
careful students of Jacopone: namely, the inconsistency of those lines
in which the poet calls Boniface a " new Lucifer poisoning the world "
(*Lauda LVIII.*, v. 14) with the probably later and certainly authentic
lauda appealing to him as Shepherd of the Church (*Lauda LVII.*, " Lo
pastor per mio peccato ").
[4] The tradition which assigns this poem to Jacopone's last years,
after the fall of Boniface, seems to me impossible of acceptance. Such
gross abuse of a fallen enemy is utterly inconsistent with the temper of
those poems which describe Jacopone's spiritual state at that time ;
whereas the invective of the authentic verses, if addressed to a living and
powerful enemy, is thoroughly characteristic of his courageous and vehe-
ment temperament and accords with his position in the Colonna group.
[5] *Lauda LX.*, " O amor de povertate," p. 420.

the Pope are those of pride, avarice, worldliness, and
cruelty. He is " covetous of nature " and has " cast all
shame away." Like a salamander in the fire, the hotter
the scandal, the better he flourishes. Evil from the
first, when he said his first Mass darkness fell on the
country-side—perhaps a reminiscence of old gossip at
Todi—and misfortune attended his coronation, where
forty men were killed " to show the pleasure of God."
Once Jacopone seems to make an indirect allusion to the
circumstances of the quarrel between Jacopo Colonna and
the Pope, in terms which suggest that the decision of
Boniface may have had more than pure justice behind it.

> Quando nella contrata
> t'aiace alcun castello,
> 'nestante metti screzio
> entra frate e fratello ;
> a l'un getti el brazo en collo,
> a l'altro mostre 'l coltello,
> se non assente al tuo appello,
> menaccel de ferire.[1]

> (Some demesne would you possess,
>   Kin with kin you set at strife ;
> For the one your love profess,
>   To the other show the knife.
> If he's tardy to submit,
> Swift you threaten him with it.)

If this represents the sort of propaganda which Jaco-
pone produced for the Colonna, and whereby he sought
to " rebuild the Church," we can well understand both
his growing notoriety and the desire of Boniface to
silence so bitter and formidable an opponent. The Pope
had declared war on the Colonna in September, 1297,
and in December preached a crusade against them. In
September, 1298, the fortress of Palestrina in which
they had taken refuge fell before the Papal troops,
which were led by Landolpho Colonna—that brother of
the Cardinal Jacopo whom Boniface had taken to his

[1] *Lauda LVIII.*, " O papa Bonifazio," v. 8.

bosom. The cardinals, clad in mourning, went to Rome, where they made their submission. Boniface absolved them, but they were deprived of the purple. Palestrina was razed to the ground and its site sown with salt. Jacopone was seized, and by the order of Boniface— who was, says Bartolommeo of Pisa politely, " ill-informed "—was condemned to perpetual imprisonment; it is believed, in the dungeons beneath the castle. We know from his own account that his prison was a narrow, evil-smelling, subterranean den.[1] There he remained for five years, from October, 1298, to October, 1303.

Our knowledge of Jacopone's inner life, which is veiled during his political period, begins again with his imprisonment. In three of his most intimate and human poems [2] he tells us of his inward and outward sufferings at this time, and of the spirit in which he met them. At first his disaster must have seemed complete. It was to no purpose that he had departed from the " golden mean," and tried to work with the unclean tool of politics the fulfilment of his ideal. The Colonna rebellion had injured rather than helped the Spiritual cause, and he seems soon to have repented his part in it. Now he was back again on that sixth branch of the " tree of hope," where the world looks dark and hostile. But in the silence and solitude of his dungeon, the blessings of adversity gradually became clear:

> Nel sesto perdei el sonno,
> tenebroso vidde el monno,
> furome nemici entorno
> vòlserme far desperare.
>
> La memoria m'aiutòne
> e de Dio me recordòne,
> lo mio cor se confortòne
> e la croce volli abracciare.[3]

[1] Lauda LV., " Que farai, fra Iacovone ? "

[2] Laude LV., " Que farai, fra Iacovone ? "; LVI., " O papa Bonifazio " (p. 438) ; LVII., " Lo pastor per mio peccato."

[3] Lauda LXIX., " Fede, spene e caritate." I cannot help thinking that these lines, though their position suggests that they refer to an earlier time, are inspired by memories of his imprisonment.

(Of my dream now dispossessed,
The world I saw in darkness dressed,
And was by enemies oppressed
  Who sought to drive me to despair.

Remembrance came to help my pain,
With thoughts of God my strength sustain,
And courage urged my heart again
  Upon the Cross His grief to share.)

We can hardly think that his connection with the Colonna had proved favourable to the mystic life. The encouragement given to his instinct for controversy, his taste for criticism and denunciation, the mingling of ancient political traditions with new religious aims; all these fostered the re-emergence of old characteristics, not slain though long suppressed, but scarcely the growth in him of the spirit of lowliness, self-surrender, and " silent love."

Tanto so gito parlando,
corte i Roma gir leccando,
c'ho ragionto alfin lo bando
de la mia presunzione.[1]

(Ever talking to and fro
About the court of Rome I'd go ;
My reasoning brought my overthrow,
And earned presumption's penalty.)

Boniface, seeking to destroy his enemy, had perhaps saved him from a more complete disaster. Shut in the dungeon, loaded " like a lion " with chains that clanked as he moved and bruised his body when he turned on his bed,[2] Jacopone began to see his life in true proportion. The Pope had done his work thoroughly. To bodily torments—scarce and filthy food, bitter cold, rats, evil smells—he added spiritual penalties; depriving his victim of the Franciscan habit, and of the sacraments. All these trials the old man bore at first with a high heart, recognising in them a test of patience and courage.

[1] *Lauda LV.,* " Que farai, fra Iacovone ? "   [2] *Loc. cit.*

Que farai, fra Iacovone?
se' venuto al paragone.[1]

(Fra Jacopone, what wilt thou do?
Thou art come to the testing too.)

The terms in which he had admonished Pope Celestine
were now applied to himself.

The poem introduced by these lines describes his
imprisonment, often with a gay humour which is in
strong contrast to the bitter satires he wrote during his
association with the Colonna.   Though kept like a
Christmas pig in its sty, he says that he is not fattening
very rapidly:

Iaci, iaci, en esta stia
come porco de grassía!
lo natal non trovería
chi déme lieve paccone.

(Although by day and night I lie
As fattening pigs within their sty,
I fear the Christmas is not nigh
When they shall make good pork of me.)

His food consists of yesterday's crusts, with a few
onions to give them a relish. These delicacies he keeps
in á little basket out of the way of the rats. By eating
every scrap he can just sustain life: if he wants more,
the price is eight Paternosters. He had no money, but
his gaoler was apparently glad to purchase so reason-
ably the prayers of an authentic though insurgent
saint. "If only the friars who come to Rome in search
of bishoprics were put on this diet," says Jacopone,
"their sermons would not be so long!" As for himself,
he finds no cause for complaint. For thirty years he has
asked that he might be, like his Master, despised and
rejected of men. Now the prayer is heard, and his old
passion for self-abasement comes to help him bear it.

[1] *Lauda LV.*

O mirabel odio mio,
d'omne pena hai signorío,
nullo recepi engiurio,
vergogna t'è esaltazione.
  Nullo te trovi nemico,
onnechivegli hai per amico ;
io solo me so l'inico
contra mia salvazione.[1]

(O self-contempt! how great thou art,
That so dost conquer every smart ;
Nought dost thou take in evil part,
  Shame is an honour unto thee.
Nought dost thou hold of ill intent,
All is to thee beneficent,
'Tis but myself that can prevent,
  I know, my own felicity.)

This is the tone of the first poem of his imprison-
ment, which he seems by some means to have sent to
Rome, that it might be circulated " among nations,
tribes and tongues "—namely, the scattered Spirituals
and their friends. But as time passed, the excommuni-
cation which was part of his sentence began to weigh
on him heavily. We know how great was his devotion
to the Eucharist, how deeply ingrained in him was the
need for some dramatic expression of his spiritual life.
The Franciscan mystics, whose love and adoration were
centred upon the Person of Christ, found in the Holy
Communion a perfect means and expression of closest
intercourse with Him. To Jacopone, old and feeble,
shut off from the corporate life of his Order and his
faith, it seemed that Boniface was determined to starve
not merely his body, but his soul. When the Papal
Jubilee of the year 1300 brought an indulgence for all
who lay under the ban of the Church, he addressed to
his old enemy a humble entreaty for forgiveness.[2]
Freedom he neither asks nor expects: protected by his

[1] *Loc. cit.*
[2] *Lauda LVI.,* " O papa Bonifazio, io porto el tuo prefazio," p. 438.

N

two shields, self-hatred and charity, he can meet all outward trials, and if Boniface wishes further to torment him, there are plenty of opportunities. Only he begs the " one word "—absolution—which can heal his spiritual wound.

We observe that Jacopone now addresses Boniface with the reverence due to the true successor of St. Peter, the holder of the " power of the keys." All those doubts about the legitimacy of his election which " earned presumption's penalty " seem to have vanished away. But Gaetani, though occasionally just, was seldom generous, and had expressly excepted the Colonna and their supporters from his amnesty. The Jubilee came, and Jacopone was still left outside the fold. Some concession—some " healing poultice "— was indeed offered to him, but at a price he could not pay.[1] It was then that he sent to Boniface a second petition,[2] the most piteous of his writings; reminding him of the previous letter, written " a long time ago with my own hand," and begging in the humblest terms that he may be absolved and " given back to St. Francis, so that he shall set me again at the table whence I receive my meat." A dreadful stagnation seems to weigh on him: he feels blind, dumb, paralysed, sick of spirit, locked up as in a tomb. It is his nearest approach to despair. As the blind man at the wayside, the Centurion's servant, the dumb possessed of a devil, the daughter of Jairus, Lazarus four days dead, he vainly waits that healing touch of Christ, which the Pope has power to confer.

> Deputato so en enferno
> e so gionto giá a la porta ;
> la mia mate Relione
> fa gran pianto con sua scorta ;

---

[1] *Lauda LVII.*, " Lo pastor per mio peccato," v. 12. The nature of this boon is unknown.

[2] *Op. cit.*

l'alta voce udir oporta
che me dica: — Vechio, surge!—
Ch'en cantar torni luge,
che è fatto del senile.[1]

(Thou hast consigned me unto hell, before its gate thou seest me.
My mother, that Religion is, makes moan with all her company.
    O let me hear, I beg of thee,
    The voice that says, " Old man! arise,"
    Then may I sing, and dry the eyes
    Of age, that weeps in misery.)

Had Jacopone been at this time in that condition of glad illumination, vividly conscious of the companionship of his Love, which inspired some of the most beautiful poems of his middle period—had he even retained in its fullness that other mysterious sense of identification with the Passion and sufferings of Christ which was so characteristic of the more advanced Franciscan mystics—we can hardly suppose that imprisonment and solitude, even deprivation of the outward means of grace, would have reduced him to this derelict state. We must seek its origin partly in his unfortunate descent into the arena of Roman politics, a departure from the way of faith and love for which his outraged spirit was now wreaking its revenge: partly in those strange laws of the mystical life, whereby the soul discovers, in each new ascent, that death must be to it the gate of life. Jacopone had now come to that terrible "night of the spirit" which St. John of the Cross describes as the last and most drastic of its gradual purifications: when the soul "seems to perish and waste away, by a cruel spiritual death, as if it were swallowed up and devoured by a wild beast, suffering the pangs of Jonas in the belly of the whale. For it must be buried in the grave of a gloomy death, that it may attain the spiritual resurrection for which it hopes."[2] We know that a phase of psychic disequilibrium,

[1] *Loc. cit.*
[2] St. John of the Cross, *The Dark Night of the Soul*, Bk. II., ch. vi.

depression, heart-searchings, and unrest, seems always
to precede each new stage of man's spiritual advance.
Again and again he is compelled to face the facts
of his own nature, the unresolved discords, prefer-
ences, and desires which still keep him from perfect
union with God. His dungeon seems to have been for
Jacopone a " cell of self-knowledge " in which he
endured this purging experience, and once more set in
order his disordered love. He had been victorious in
two conflicts: with Satan, who had tried to lead him
astray; with other men, who would corrupt him with
praise. Now he was forced to the hardest of his battles;
the final struggle with his own self-hood.[1] His mind
must be cleansed of every passion—hope and fear, joy
and grief [2]—above all from that spirit of violence which
the world had revived in him.[3] Thus only could he
ascend the " tree of charity," and enter that heaven of
purified love where all oppositions are transcended,
and we with our self-hood die into God.

Though Jacopone's brave spirit may for a time have
flickered in the human and spiritual misery of his im-
prisonment, where no man broke with him either the
bread of fellowship or the Bread of Life,[4] yet he faced
his testing, once he realised its meaning, with all his old
courage. In after-life he saw it above all as a demand
upon his valour: a struggle, hard indeed, but in which
he was not wholly without light. That light shielded
him from complete destruction. But spiritual darkness
—last test of the soul's unselfish love—was the weapon

---

[1] *Lauda LXIX.*, " Fede, spene e caritade," v. 45.

[2] *Lauda LX.*, " O amor de povertate," p. 420.

[3]   Io respusi con amore:
       — Io so libero de furore. — (*Lauda LXIX.*, v. 46.)

   (With eager love I then replied,
    " All violence in me has died.")

For Jacopone, as for Dante, the world of action was above all " l'aiuola
che ci fa tanto feroci " (*Par.*, xxii., 151).

[4] *Lauda LVII.*, " Lo pastor per mio peccato," v. 7.

with which he attacked his interior enemies, the cutting-point which forced his forward path. Holding his mind steadfastly between the two extremes, he " made of the light his shield, of the darkness his lance ": and thus, armed and mounted as a true knight of the Holy Ghost, he entered on the last stage of his spiritual quest.

> De la luce facea la tarza
> e de la tenebra la lanza,
> posi mente a la bilanza
> e comenciai a cavalcare.[1]

> (Of light my buckler I did make,
> And for lance the darkness take:
> In balanced quiet my mind abode,
> And thus upon my way I rode.)

To those who watch it, the spiritual life often seems to consist in a series of repetitions. *Gyrans gyrando vadit spiritus.* Each period of enlightenment—apparently so complete—is succeeded by a period of instability and gloom. In some minds these alternations are rapid, others describe a wider curve: but each turn of the spiral lifts the soul to a higher plane, until at last it achieves equilibrium. In Jacopone's life, this law is clearly exhibited. He passed from his ascetic period through a stage of intense psychic unrest to the state of "ordered love" which marked his establishment in the "first mystic life" of illumination. Now, the still unresolved though suppressed antagonism between the active and contemplative sides of his nature was once more revived by his entrance into politics. It brought him, in the solitude of Palestrina, to another, more terrible crisis, in which he was called to the perfect self-naughting that prepares the soul for the unitive life. The spiral had completed its second turn.

[1] *Lauda LXIX.,* " Fede, spene e caritade," v. 47.

> Spogliar se vole l'omo d'ognecovelle,
> cioé en questo stato,
> e ne la mente non posseder covelle ;
> se nell'altro vuole essere chiamato,
> dé' esser purgato dal fuoco ;
> quello è luoco da paragonare.[1]

> (A man shall strip himself of all
>   He won, to win this grace,
> And nothing his possession call.
> If to the next he lays a claim,
> He must endure the purging flame—
>   This is the testing place.)

Ruysbroeck has spoken of the three states of the awakened spirit as those of the " faithful servant," the " secret friend " and the " hidden child " of God. Certainly Jacopone during his penitential life had been the faithful servant of the Eternal Goodness. The ardent love and passionate thirst for suffering of his middle period were those of the " secret friend " of Christ. " These," says Ruysbroeck, " though they feel themselves uplifted to God in a mighty fire of love, yet keep something of their own self-hood, and are not consumed and burnt to nothingness in the unity of love. Though they may long to live for evermore in God's service and eternally please Him, they will not die in God to *all* the self-hood of their spirit, and receive from Him a God-formed life." [2] These words might have been written of Jacopone the fervent lover, relentless fighter, and self-chosen champion of the Primitive Rule. Now, in the final destitution of spirit which coincided with his imprisonment, he learned the secret of that perfect death of self-hood—the three-fold annihilation " [3]—which is the soul's introduction to that Eternal Life " where purified love dwells within the truth." [4]

[1] *Lauda XCII.*, " La fede e la speranza." Cf. *Lauda LX.*, " O amor de povertate," p. 420.
[2] Ruysbroeck, *The Sparkling Stone*. ch. viii.
[3] *Lauda XCII.*, " La fede e la speranza."
[4] *Lauda LX.*, " O amor de povertate," p. 420.

Viver io e non io,
e l'esser mio non esser mio,
questo è un tal trasversio,
che non so diffinitate.[1]

This union, says Jacopone, is the child of " con-
summate love which looks not for reward, but seeks
only to share the sufferings of the Cross." That loyal
passion, caught up to the Uncreated Charity, gives
birth through Its embrace to " beatific love," wherein
" we feel continuous union with God and taste Eternal
Life." [2] Here oppositions are at last transcended: " I
have destroyed the Yes and No." [3] The small and
separate activity of the finite will is fully conformed to
the rhythm of the Infinite, and merged in the great
action of Divine Love. Hence the strange, bold
language of the mystics concerning the unitive life:
language which we may try to understand, but are not
competent to criticise.

Jacopone is at one with the greatest Christian con-
templatives in all that he has to say about this state;
but his words have a personal stamp, a peculiar quality,
which excludes the possibility of plagiarism. He tells
us, as they have often done, that his ethical struggle is
now over:

La guerra è terminata,
de le virtú battaglia,
de la mente travaglia,
cosa nulla contende.[4]

Possessing God, he can say " All is mine " [5]: or, equally,
that he has ceased to be, since all his self is emptied into
God. Personal likes and dislikes are transcended, finding
their reconciliation in the good-pleasure of Infinite Love.

Piacer ciò che gli piace.

[1] *Ibid.*
[2] Feo Belcari, *Trattati di Fra Jacopone*, pp. 71, 73 ; and *Lauda XCIX.*,
" L'amor ch'è consumato," p. 470.   [3] *Lauda XCII.*
[4] *Lauda XCI.*, " Sopr'onne lengua amore," p. 474. Cf. the contem-
porary French mystic who wrote the *Mirror of Simple Souls*—" Virtues,
I take my leave of you for evermore ; now shall my heart be more free
and more in peace than it hath been."   [5] *Ibid.*

In another, more homely passage, he says that now
he is no longer troubled by his old temptation to take
an interest in his food: when it is nice, he refers its
flavours to God, and gives Him thanks therefor. But,
he adds, such practices are not for every one; only for
those who feel continuous union with God, and are able
to refer everything to Him.[1]

The period at which Jacopone achieved this state of
equilibrium, the extent to which his complete spiritual
emancipation preceded his bodily release, cannot of
course be determined. Neither can we tell how many
of the poems referring to this last period were com-
posed during his imprisonment. The letters to Boniface
prove that he was deprived neither of the power or the
means of composition: the long form of the *lauda* upon
Frate Ranaldo, if authentic,[2] describes that poem also
as a work of his captivity. Perhaps, too, one or more
of those laments for " departure of grace " which are
generally ascribed to an earlier period[3] may have been
written at this time, during the hours of spiritual dark-
ness to which he has confessed: for there is little to
distinguish between the emotions which accompany
the " first " and " second " nights of the mystic way.
When, on September 17th, *1303*, the lilies of France
entered Alagna, and the long-prepared revenge of
Philip the Fair and the Colonna was achieved, we may
believe that the old poet had indeed reached the " king-
dom of tranquillity " wherein outward events—even
the fall of his enemy Boniface—no longer ruffled the
waters of his soul. In October Boniface was dead; and
on the 23rd of that month, Jacopone received from the
new Pope, Benedict XI., his absolution and release.

It is said that when he came out from his prison,
and the glory of an Italian autumn met eyes which for
five years had seen only the walls of his underground

[1] Feo Belcari, *loc. cit.*   [2] See above, p. 143.
[3] Especially *Lauda LXVII.*, " Amor, diletto amore," p. 294.

den, he composed and sang the beautiful *lauda* which praises the Love of God as revealed in Creation; seen, heard, and tasted in all lovely things.

> Se io esco per lo viso,
> ciò che veggio è amore,
> en onne forma èi pento,
> ed en onne colore ;
> represèntime allore
> ch'io te deggia albergare.
>
> Se esco per la porta
> per posarme en audire,
> lo sono e que significa?
> Representa te, sire ;
> per essa non può uscire
> ciò cche odo è amare.
>
> Se esco per lo gusto,
> onne sapor te clama:
> —- Amor, divino amore,
> amor pieno de brama;
> amor preso m' hai a l'ama
> per potere en me regnare.[1]

The legend is so charming that we should like to believe it. At least all indications encourage us to place this poem somewhere in the last period of Jacopone's life. If we wish to measure his growth in the understanding of love, we have only to compare its " intimations of divinity " with the bitter distrust of the senses and contempt for their reports which inspires some of the fiercely ascetic *laude* of his early period.

> O frate, guarda 'l viso,
> se vuoi ben riguarire!
> ca mortal ferite a l'alma
> spesse fiate fon venire.[2]

> (O brother, guard thine eyes
>   If thou wouldst be made whole ;
> For mortal is the hurt
>   Which they can deal the soul.)

[1] *Lauda LXXXII.*, " O Amor, divino amore, perchè," p. 422.
[2] *Lauda VII.* Cf. *Laude V.*, " Cinque sensi mess'on pegno," and *VI.*, " Guarda che non caggi," p. 274.

Jacopone could now receive the wholesome doctrine of
St. Augustine: " There is no health in those who find
fault with any part of Thy creation." ¹   The state of
world-refusal wherein his spiritual life had begun was
merged in that condition of peaceful charity for which
" all creatures are pure to enjoy, since it enjoyeth all
creatures in God and God in all creatures." ²

After his liberation, some at least of the Conventual
Franciscans seem to have received Jacopone into their
convents.   According to an early biography,³ he went
first to Pantanelli, a little hermitage upon the Tiber,
three hours from Orvieto, and subsequently to Fon-
tanelli and other Umbrian houses.   He had now but
three years to live; and these he passed wholly in
contemplation, and in the writing of mystical poems.

A manuscript legend, now in the Communal Library
at Todi, ascribes to this period the writing of the
Stabat Mater, a poem which has persistently been
attributed to him at least from the fifteenth century.
" Giving himself to holy contemplation," says this
document, " he also composed many sacred songs ;
and one day, considering how the Blessed Virgin Mary
stood at the feet of her Son Jesus Christ hanging on the
Cross, he composed the hymn which begins, " Stabat
Mater dolorosa." ⁴   This noble hymn has been given to
many writers, from Gregory the Great downwards ;⁵ but
only two of these ascriptions—those to Pope Innocent III.
and Jacopone—are worth serious consideration.   There
is little positive evidence in favour of either candidate.
Though we have no reason to suppose Jacopone in-
capable of Latin verse, no other poem by him in that
language is known ; ⁶ whereas Latin poetry of a high

---

¹ *Conf.*, vii., 14.
² Meister Eckhart.   Quoted by Wackernagel, *Altdeutsches Lesebuch*,
p. 891.
³ Quoted in D'Ancona, *Jacopone da Todi*, p. 97.
⁴ Tenneroni, *Lo Stabat Mater e Donna del Paradiso*, p. 13.
⁵ The best discussion is in Julian, *Dictionary of Hymnology*, p. 1081.
⁶ It is true that some writers have attributed to Jacopone the Christmas

order was certainly within the powers of Innocent III., the probable author of *Veni Sancte Spiritus.* On the other hand the *Stabat*, which was a favourite processional hymn of the fourteenth-century Flagellants,[1] has certain marked Franciscan characters. Two verses especially, which have been held to refer indirectly to the Stigmata, are inspired by a view of the Passion which, though not peculiar to Jacopone, was specially dear to him, and could be matched by several passages in his works:

> Fac ut portem Christi mortem
> passionis eius sortem
>   et plagas recolere.
> Fac me plagis vulnerari,
> cruce fac inebriari,
>   in amore filii.

> (Make me in mysterious fashion
> Share my Saviour's death and passion,
>   Bear the wounds He bore for me:
> In those wounds be my salvation,
> In His Cross my exaltation,
>   In His love mine ecstasy.)

This argument, however, is not convincing. The "Franciscan" devotion to the Passion and sacred wounds cannot be proved to originate with St. Francis, though the preaching of the friars and miracle of the Stigmata had greatly popularised them. So, too, the likeness discovered by some critics between the "Donna del Paradiso" and the *Stabat Mater* appears to me to be overdrawn. The one is deliberately popular and crudely dramatic, expressing the vivid and unrestrained

hymn, *Stabat Mater Speciosa* (printed by Tenneroni, *op. cit*). But no admirer of his poetry will consent without absolute proof to ascribe to him this tame and servile imitation of the *Dolorosa*. Both *Stabats*—with five other Latin hymns by various authors—are given as his work in the Brescia edition of the *laude* (1495).

[1] It was originally a popular hymn, and was not incorporated into the Roman Missal till 1727. The liturgic version, which differs considerably from the older texts, forms the Sequence for the Friday following Passion Sunday (Seven Sorrows of the B.V.M.).

emotion of the people in the people's tongue. The grief of Mary is the noisy grief of any peasant mother watching the torture of her child. In the other the same anguish of love is sublimated, and made part of the mystery of redemption, the history of the universal soul. Instead of sharp action, profound meditation. Instead of cries of anguish, insistence upon physical pain, a prayer for participation in the saving sorrow of the Cross. In art and feeling, a wide space seems to separate the two works.

True, it might be argued that this is also the distance which separates the passionately emotional Jacopone of the middle period, Franciscan missionary and Spiritual poet, from the profound contemplative who returned to the world from Palestrina. Jacopone's connection with the popular side of Franciscanism was now over. He lived, as did so·many old friars of the contemplative type, in great retirement; immersed in loving communion with that " Infinite Light " which now irradiated his soul.[1] If, then, he wrote in old age a poem upon the Passion, we might expect it to be such a poem as this. The real difficulty in attributing it to him comes rather from the fact that he seems at this time to have moved away from the type of religious emotion which it represents, and that his meditations— as expressed in the authentic poems of his last period— had become more metaphysical and less Christo-centric. If his claim to its authorship is to be upheld, it would be easier to think of the *Stabat* as a late work of his middle period, when thoughts of the Passion certainly engrossed him and his technical powers were at their height.

When we turn from speculation to Jacopone's undoubted works, we are able to form a fairly clear idea of his spiritual position during these last years. It is at this time that he must have written the dull but

---

[1] *Lauda XCI.*, " Sopr'onne lengua amore," p. 474.

important autobiographical *lauda* from which I have already quoted,[1] since the development described in it is carried up to the unitive life. More important and characteristic are the three famous *laude* in which he tries to describe his ultimate fruition of Reality:[2] and the beautiful praises of Divine Love which were its artistic expression.[3] Here we can see the full transformation of his consciousness, the rich completeness with which he now lived the infinite life.

> Tutti gli atti vecchi e novi
> en un nichilo son fondate,
> son formati senza forma,
> non han termen né quantitate,
> uniti con la veritate ;
> coronato sta l'affetto,
> quietato lo 'ntelletto,
> nell'amore trasformato.[4]

(Now every act both old and new is based secure on Nothingness,
And without form a form doth take, unmeasured in its endlessness,
Made one with Truth in singleness;
Now is the heart to kingship brought,
And stilled is every restless thought
By love in transmutation wrought.)

The old subject-object relation between the soul and its Divine Lover, which inspired the great poems of his middle period, was now transcended: and Love was perceived as the very substance of Reality, the nature of God.[5]

The state of Jacopone in this last phase of his earthly life is that state of immediate union with the Absolute which Dante describes at the end of the *Paradiso*, and which forms the crown of the system of Plotinus. He has passed, he says, above the Stellar

---

[1] *Lauda LXIX.*, " Fede, spene e caritate."
[2] *Laude LXXIX.*, " La bontate enfinita," p. 450 ; *XCI.*, " Sopr'onne lengua amore " ; and *XCII.*, " La fede e la speranza."
[3] *Laude LXXXI.*, " O Amor, divino amore, amor," p. 460, and *LXXXVII.*, " Amor che ami tanto."
[4] *Lauda LXXXVII.*
[5] *Lauda LXXXI.*, " O Amor, divino amore, amor," p. 460.

and Crystalline heavens and has reached the Empyrean, where even the music of the spheres is transcended in the awful silence of Eternity.[1] To the heart this is a region of " love beyond all saying." To the baffled intellect it is a " radiant dark," a " soundless sea," overwhelming the spirit that it allures.

> O profondato mare,
> altura del tuo abisso
> m'ha certo stretto a volerme anegare.[2]

(O mighty sea l thy billows steep
Have seized me ; I would drown within that deep.)

His legend tells us that trying, as all true lovers must, to tell something of the ineffable Truth, and snatching for this purpose at vivid images and suggestive phrases, Jacopone alarmed those timid souls who preferred the neatness of a rigid faith, and did not like to hear God defined " now in one way, and now in another." [3] Accused, as many other mystics have been, of " fantastic and even heretical opinions," he therefore composed the great *lauda* " Sopr'onne lengua amore " [4] for the express purpose of confuting his critics. We may well doubt whether it achieved its object. Though full of reminiscences of earlier mystics, and especially of his well-loved Dionysius the Areopagite,[5] it is one of the most remarkable first-hand descriptions of ecstasy —the Plotinian " flight of the Alone to the Alone "— to be found in Christian literature. In language of the utmost conviction and ardour, with a constant and various appeal to concrete image and to the favourite mystical device of paradox, Jacopone struggles to describe the ineffable state in which he lives. He says that all his old conceptions of God and apparent attain-

---

[1] *Lauda XCII.*, " La fede e la speranza." The " stellar heaven " of the virtues is entered when the ethical purifications are over. The " crystalline heaven " is the sphere of contemplation, as enjoyed in the illuminative life. The " empyrean " is reached only in ecstasy. See below, ch. vi.

[2] *Lauda XCII.*
[4] *Lauda XCI.*
[3] *Vita*, 14ro. See above, p. 14.
[5] See below, ch. vi., p. 238.

ment of Him were illusion; or, at best, truth contami-
nated by human error. The rapturous intercourse with
Christ his love, the Franciscan self-identification with
the Passion, the sweet meditations before the Crib—all
these belonged to the world of image. " Things are not
what we thought or firmly held ":

> Or, parme, fo fallanza,
> non se' quel che credea,
> tenendo non avea
> vertá senza errore.[1]

Now, high Nothingness—pure poverty of spirit—has
opened all the doors, and he has " entered the Infinite."
He possesses and is possessed, drinks and is drunken,
climbs by sinking, and is engulfed in the Supreme.[2]

In these poems, Jacopone appears not only as a
poet and mystic, but also as a Christian philosopher of
high attainment. In them his soaring genius for divine
things, his remarkable hold upon metaphysical reality,
find full expression. Students of the mystics will note
with interest the many points of contact between his
vision of the Absolute and that of Plotinus.[3] Plainly
he obtained through St. Augustine and Dionysius the
Areopagite many Neoplatonic ideas; but the practical
and personal character of his teaching assures us that
he took from them nothing which had not been tested
in the fires of his own spiritual life. Moreover, he
brought to these doctrines a personal contribution:
that contribution which the religion of Jesus made and
still makes to the intuitions of philosophy. Half Neo-
platonist, he is half Franciscan too. So " that Love
whose name is ' I love' "[4] remains for him the primal
attribute of the Perfect; and the sinking of the soul

---

[1] *Lauda XCI.*, v. 1, p. 474.
[2] *Op. cit.*, vv. 33 and 35. With these stanzas should be compared the
less successful, but still important *Laude XCII.*, " La fede e la speranza,"
and *XCV.*, " Que farai, morte mia."
[3] See below, ch. vi., p. 231.
[4] *Lauda LXXXV.*, " O amor che m'ami."

into the sea of Being is seen to be the fulfilment of true life —the consummation of that love-quest which is its " way and term." The " liberal and jocund Love " which caught him in its net, maddened him with its delight, and burned him in its inexorable flame, is revealed as the light upon the face of the Absolute. His final vision, like that of Dante, is the vision of One who loves and smiles.

> —O alma nobilissima,
> dinne que cose vide!
> — Veggo un tal non veggio
> che onne cosa me ride.[1]

> (Most noble soul, now tell me what you see.
> I see, yet I see not, how all things smile on me.)

According to the best authorities, Jacopone died on Christmas Eve, *1306*, in the convent of Poor Clares at Collazzone; a small hill-town between Todi and Perugia. The *Vita* gives an account of his death-bed which may derive from a genuine tradition. It tells us that when the friars knew him to be dying, they wished to give him the last sacraments, but he refused them: and they, much scandalised, said: "Frate Jacopone, wouldst thou die like a heretic, since thou sayst thou dost not desire the holy sacraments?" Then Jacopone, raising his eyes to heaven, declaimed his creed in song; but, the friars still pressing him, he presently said that he awaited his brother John of La Verna, since he wished to take the viaticum from his hand.

"Now since it is a long journey from La Verna to Collazzone, where Jacopone lay sick, the brothers made light of his words; for the thing seemed to them impossible, since Brother John had not been informed, and none thought that he would come. And they, being troubled by his obstinacy, continually pressed him to take the sacraments. Then Jacopone in great fervour

---

[1] *Lauda LXXIX.,* " La bontate enfinita."

of spirit began the *lauda* that is called " Anima bene-
detta dall'alto Creatore." And as he finished this song,
one of the friars looked out towards the plain, and he
saw two strange friars approaching. And when they
drew near, it was seen that one was that holy brother,
John of La Verna, who had been inspired of God to
come and console his dearest brother in Christ, Fra
Jacopone. And when the friars saw this miracle, they
knew that Fra Jacopone had the Spirit of God in him
and was most acceptable in His sight ; since He con-
descended so kindly to his holy desires. And so soon
as Brother John had come to that servant of God, Fra
Jacopone, and they had together enjoyed spiritual
consolation, Fra Jacopone received at his hands the
sacraments of Holy Church, as he had wished and
waited to do. And thus comforted in the Lord, he
began the song which says:

> Iesu nostra fidanza
> del core somma speranza.[1]
>
> (Jesu, in Thee is all our trust,
> High hope of every heart!)

When he had finished this song he turned to the friars,
who stood round him weeping for devotion: and
finally lifting up his eyes, his hands, and his mind to
Jesus Christ his Love, that happy soul was gathered to
Christ his delight." [2] According to another tradition, he
died as the priest began to sing the *Gloria in excelsis*
of the midnight Mass for Christmas Day.

" It is said and believed," says Feo Belcari, " that
this blessed Jacopone died for love of Christ, and that

---

[1] Though constantly ascribed to Jacopone, neither this poem nor
" Anima benedetta " is found in the most authoritative collections of
his works. Signor D'Ancona regards them as genuine (*Jacopone da Todi*,
p. 98), but their authenticity is not generally admitted. Cf. Brugnoli,
p. clv.

[2] *Vita*, 14vo–15vo. In order to avoid reference to the political side of his
career, the *Vita* dates Jacopone's death March 25th, 1296. We observe in
both traditions a deliberate effort to make his heavenly birthday coincide
with a great moment of the Christian year.

by excess of love his heart was broken. It is known that for many years before his death he did not cease to weep; and when he was asked wherefore he wept he replied, ' I weep because Love is not loved.' [1] And again he said, ' The greatest blessedness a soul may have in this life is when she is continually occupied with God.' And to this state we believe that his soul had come." [2]

Jacopone's remains were taken from Collazzone either to the convent of Monte Cristo or to that of Monte Santo, outside the walls of Todi. Here they were discovered in 1433, and translated to the Church of San Fortunato, where in 1596 Bishop Angelo Cesi enclosed them in a magnificent tomb. This tomb, which still exists, bears the inscription: " Ossa Beati Jacopone de Benedictis Tudertini, Fratris Ordinis Minorum, qui stultus propter Christum, nova mundum arte delusit et cœlum rapuit." [3]

Jacopone has never been beatified, though several attempts have been made to introduce his process at Rome: the last, in 1868-9, by the heads of the Franiscan Order. Evidence was collected, proving that he had been since his death the object of a persistent veneration: but his conflict with Boniface VIII., and the independent spirit of criticism which his more vigorous satires display, were regarded as inappropriate features in the history of an accredited saint. Hence the great poet and greater mystic who was lifted through lowliness to the ultimate vision of God has yet

---

[1] See *Lauda LXXXI.*, v. 1. The extreme emotionalism here described, however, seems incompatible with those profound contemplations which we know Jacopone practised in his last years. The " gift of tears " belonged to an earlier stage. He tells us himself that in " the state of achievement " the tears of the soul are dried. (See Belcari, *op. cit.*, p. 71.)

[2] *Op. cit.*, p. 87.

[3] " The bones of the blessed Jacopone dei Benedetti of Todi, of the Order of Friars Minor; who, a fool for Christ's sake, by a new artifice cheated the world, and took heaven by storm." This, as we have seen, gives only one side of the real Jacopone, and commemorates merely the holy eccentric of the *Vita*.

to be raised to the altars of the Catholic Church. Called, like Dante, from illusion to reality " in the middle of the highway of our life," and passing through a purging experience not less searching, an initiation into heavenly secrets not less complete, he solved in the same sense the problem of Being ; finding, as the fount and origin of all that is,

L'amor che move il sole e l'altre stelle.

CHAPTER VI

JACOPONE AS POET AND MYSTIC

I. Jacopone's place in *Italian* poetry—Influences—Secular love-poets
—*Dolce stil nuovo*—Didactic poetry—The *laudesi*—Dramatic poetry
—Donna del Paradiso—Special qualities—Summary. II. Character
of Jacopone's mysticism—Empirical sources—Literary sources—
Scripture—Franciscanism—Platonism—St. Augustine—Dionysius the
Areopagite—Personal experience—Three phases—Summary of his
teaching—Doctrine of poverty—Conclusion.

I

APART from his literary significance as a representative
of Franciscan feeling, Jacopone has an important place
in the evolution of Italian poetry. In him two lines of
development meet. On the one hand he is conditioned
by the current secular poetry: both the professional
and somewhat artificial tradition of the Sicilian school,
and the young poets of the *dolce stil nuovo,* such as
Guido Guinizelli and his followers. On the other hand
he has received many suggestions from the popular
religious verse of the *laudesi.* From the marriage of
these two factors Italian religious poetry, of which he
is the earliest worthy representative, was born.

No doubt Jacopone's familiarity with the Court
poets, and with the younger school of Bologna, was
obtained during his life in the world, when he may
have written secular verse in one or the other manner.
But these memories of profane literature influenced
him till the end of his life, and many plain traces of
them appear in the *laude.* The romantic colour which
he gives to his conception of Christ the lover—

Tal amador è fior de puritade,—[1]

[1] *Lauda* C., " Fiorito è Cristo," p. 406.

his description of the Blessed Virgin as Queen of
Courtesy,[1] the very opening phrases of such poems as
" Sapete voi novelle de l'amore " or " amor che non
se' amato "[2] represent the tone and attitude of the
secular love-poets carried up into the religious sphere.
As we read the best of this secular poetry we are often
reminded that Jacopone, too, on one side of his nature,
is an Italian love-poet of the thirteenth century, who
has taken from the contemporary praises of Profane
Love many suggestions for his addresses to Love
Divine.

> Vostro amore mi tiene in tal disire,
> e donami speranza con gran gioi,
> che non curo s'io doglio od ho martire,
> membrando l'ora ch'io vegna a voi.
> Chè s'io troppo dimoro, aulente cera,
> sarà ch'io pera, e voi mi perderete.
> Adunque, bella, se ben mi volete,
> guardate ch'io non mora in vostra spera.[3]

> (In such desire your love has fettered me,
> And given me such a hope, so great delight,
> I care not what my grief or torment be
> Remembering how I came into your sight.
> But if too long I lack your sweet presence,
> Then must I die, and you shall lose me quite,
> So, Fairest One, if you would love requite,
> Let me not perish of this abstinence.)

No great distance separates such a poem as this from
the spiritual love-songs of Jacopone's middle period:

> Amor, tua compagnia
> tosto sí m'è falluta,
> non saccio do' me sia,
> facendo la partuta ;
> la mente mia smarruta
> va chedendo 'l dolzore,
> che gli è furato ad ore
> che non se nn'è adato, amore.[4]

[1] *Lauda I.*, p. 250.
[2] *Laude LXXX.* and *LXXXI.*, p. 460.
[3] Pier della Vigna (c. 1180–1249). See Dante, *Inf.*, xiii., 58.
[4] *Lauda LXVII.*, " Amor, diletto amore," p. 294.

In this, and other laments of the soul for its absent
Love,[1] he seems indeed to be directly imitating on new
levels of feeling the popular type of troubadour song
in which the lover bewails his separation from Madonna,
or the Lady that from her love.[2] Though such adoption
of the conventions of earthly passion seems inconsistent
with his bitter asceticism, we must remember first the
erotic element in Jacopone's early mystical transports,
and next the extent to which his Franciscan environ-
ment would encourage spiritual romanticism.   St.
Francis, a natural poet and skilled musician, had
brought the methods and feeling of the troubadours to
the service of God. He knew and loved the romances of
chivalry, and saw nothing inappropriate in an appeal
to the example of " Charles the Emperor, Roland and
Oliver, and all the paladins and strong men " [3] when a
novice needed to be rebuked. His cult of Madonna
Poverty, continued by Jacopone, is undoubtedly re-
lated to the troubadour convention of "Madonna."
The " French speech," in which the early legends say
that Francis was accustomed to " sing to the Lord
Jesus Christ," was the language of the troubadours
applied to the purposes of devotion.[4]

In his finest work, however, Jacopone passes far
beyond this spiritualisation of personal passion, to a
profoundly philosophic conception of love as the sub-
stance of reality, in which the ardour of each lover
becomes a manifestation of the one primal Energy,
" ever active, never still."

> Amor c'hai nome amo
> plural mai non trovamo.[5]

> (Love which hath " I love " for name
> No plural has, but ever is the same.)

[1] *Lauda LXVIII.*, " Piangi, dolente," p. 290.
[2] Cf. Caspary, *Early Italian Literature*, ch. ii.
[3] *Speculum*, cap. iv.
[4] See Della Giovanna, *S. Franceso d'Assisi Giullare* (*Giorn. stor. della
Lett. Italiana*, vol. xxv., 1895).
[5] *Lauda LXXXV.*, " O amor che m'ami."

This love is so irresistible a force that Omnipotence
cannot oppose it.[1] It gives itself without stint, and
draws all things to itself.[2] It has struck at the heart of
the Infinite Beauty.[3] It is wise and gay, courteous and
compelling:[4] at once the divine madness and divine
reason of the world.   Here, in spite of his obvious
dependence on the Christian Platonists,[5] Jacopone
surely discloses a debt to the poets of the *dolce stil
nuovo*.   These passages, and others like them, seem to
represent the ruling conceptions of Guido Guinizelli[6]
and his followers, transmuted to the purposes of the
religious mystic ; striking again upon a new instru-
ment their peculiar note of philosophic romanticism.
The strong probability that Jacopone was living in
Bologna when this school first appeared,[7] encourages
the supposition.   Did we possess the poems he must
surely have written during his life in the world, those
" canti novelle " which he loved to sing at the as-
semblies of ladies and young maidens,[8] we could fix
more positively his debt to his predecessors and con-
temporaries.   Now we can only be sure that his genius
did not spring from an unploughed field, but was
nourished by the life out of which it grew.   The intel-
lectual and æsthetic enthusiasms of youth fed the
mystical ardours of the man who supposed that he had
renounced them.

In his moral and satirical, no less than his mystical
laude, Jacopone discloses many points of contact with
contemporary writers.   A secular didactic poetry, in

---

[1] *Lauda LXXXIII.*, " O dolce amore," p. 286.
[2] *Lauda XC.*, "Amor de caritate," p. 362.
[3] *Lauda I.XV.*, " Ad l'amor ch'è venuto."
[4] *Lauda LXXXI.*, " O Amor, divino amore, amor," p. 460.
[5] See below, p. 231.
[6] Guido Guinizelli (c. 1240–76) had produced much of his characteristic
work before Jacopone renounced the world.
[7] See above, ch. l., p. 40. Jacopone, of course, drank from the same
philosophic sources as these learned poets; but their direct influence can be
detected in the use which he makes of his material.
[8] *Lauda XXI.*, " O Cristo pietoso."

which the personified vices and virtues took an almost
dramatic part, was already developing ; and from this
came the convention which he uses in such poems as
" La Veritade piange," " La Bontade se lamenta," and
" Udite una entenzone ch'è fra Onore e Vergogna." [1]
In this last *lauda* we have also a good example of his
use of the *tenzone* or *contrasto* : [2] a literary form, peen-
liarly congenial to his dramatic instinct, in which
modern critics have found the germ of the Italian
theatre. [3]

In this group of *laude*, however, we come into
contact with the second great influence which deter-
mined the character of Jacopone's verse. Its form is
controlled on one side by his knowledge of secular
poetry ; but on the other by that popular demand for
vernacular moral and devotional songs which the peni-
tential movements of the thirteenth century—especially
the Franciscan revival—had created and developed.

Though it is an exaggeration to describe Jacopone
as a characteristic example of the *giullare di Dio* or
itinerant religious minstrel, who was a common figure
in thirteenth-century Italy, he was certainly in his first
period a popular poet. His songs, which had a deliber-
ately didactic intention, were probably sung by him
in the course of his preachings. Francis, himself a
musician, had strongly encouraged such minstrelsy
among his friars. [4] In Jacopone, this side of the Fran-
ciscan propaganda joins hands with the popular move-
ment represented by those companies of *laudesi* who
were, at the time of his conversion, a prominent feature
in Umbrian religious life. These confraternities, which
came into being late in the twelfth century, were at

---

[1] *Laude LI., LXXIV,. and XCIV.*

[2] The *tenzone* was originally a troubadour form, and arose as a dialogue
between Madonna and the lover. It was considerably developed in *I*taly ;
its final phase being the elaborate *tenzoni* which reproduced the discus-
sions of a group of poets.

[3] See D'Ancona, *Origini del Teatro in Italia*, vol. i., p. 141.

[4] See Della Giovanna, *op. cit.*

first informal gatherings of singers. They went in pro-
cession through the towns, or met in the evenings in
the piazza or before some favourite shrine, to sing
hymns of penitence or adoration. By the second half
of the thirteenth century they had become organised,
and possessed chapels or other fixed meeting-places
and written constitutions. Many of their manuscript
collections of hymns, or *laudarii*, are still in existence;
but those now extant mostly date from the fourteenth
and fifteenth centuries, and therefore only give indirect
information as to the state of the *lauda* in Jacopone's
day.

These singing guilds played an important part in
the beginnings of Italian poetry; for they created a
demand for religious lyrics written in the vernacular,
at a time when Latin was still regarded as the only
language of devotion.[1] The secular poets were just
beginning to use the vulgar tongue, when this great
popular outburst of religious song offered a new field
to the growing national genius for literature. If the
highly-finished futilities of the Sicilian school of poetry
represent the ideals of the Court, and the lyrics of the
dolce stil nuovo those of the learned classes, the *laude*
come from, and were written for, the people; and
represent the vision and the need of the ordinary God-
fearing man. We may hear them still, rough, vigorous
rhymes set to easy melodies, on popular festivals in
many Italian towns. In Siena on St. Catherine's day,
in Santa Croce at Rome on Good Friday, we touch
again the public for which Jacopone and his followers
wrote many of their poems, and re-enter the circle of
feeling within which these creations were produced.
The hymns which the *laudesi* sang were of many kinds;
moral, ascetic, mystical, liturgic, descriptive. They
told in verse the histories of Christ and the Saints,
they celebrated the great festivals, they had songs of

[1] Galli, *I Disciplinati dell' Umbria del* 1260.

adoration, admonition, penitence, and love. In Tuscany the lyric was most popular, in Umbria the narrative poem. These works expressed sometimes the simplest, sometimes the most profound religious ideas; for their appeal was both to the educated and uneducated class. Jacopone's two hymns to St. Francis [1] are *laude* of the traditional type, comparable with many of the hymns to the saints found in the great manuscript collections. His Christmas carols,[2] and some of his *tenzoni*,[3] are also characteristic *laude*, though far above the average level of these works.

Probably the *laudesi*, especially those guilds attached to the Third Order of St. Francis, were the first singers of Jacopone's songs. We know that within a few years of his death he had become their favourite poet; and that imitations of his manner quickly appeared in Umbria, and thence spread to other parts of Italy. His constant employment of the *ripresa* or refrain—the rhymed couplet or triplet with which each *lauda* begins [4]—shows that many of his most personal and philosophic poems were regarded by him as hymns; and the uncritical enthusiasm which impels a modern congregation to shout its way through such personal confessions as "Abide with Me!" or "Lead, kindly Light!" suggests that the choral rendering even of "Amor de caritate" or "Fuggo la croce" was not beyond the range of possibility. In this connection we must remember that the inner circle of Spirituals to which Jacopone belonged—of which, indeed, he is the representative poet—practised a mystical devotion of

---

[1] *Laude LXI.*, "O Francesco povero," and *LXII.*, "O Francesco, da Dio amato."

[2] *Laude II.*, "O Vergine piú che femina"; *LXIV.*, "O novo canto," p. 412; and *LXV.*, "Ad l'amor ch'è venuto."

[3] *Laude III.*, "Audite una 'ntenzone"; *XXV.*, "Quando t'alegri," etc.

[4] The *ripresa*, in which the mood of the whole poem was expressed, was intended to be sung or repeated after each stanza: a fact which should be borne in mind when reading Jacopone's *laude*, for it greatly enhances their dramatic effect.

an exalted type.[1] Among these ardent " lovers of the
mystery of Jesus "—many of them Tertiaries—his
most difficult and passionate *laude* would be under-
stood, and they may have been sung at gatherings of
zelanti of this kind.

Jacopone's contact with the *laudesi* is not confined
to the purely lyrical side of his genius. In Umbria,
which was specially the home of the narrative *lauda*,
there was developed under the influence of the singing
guilds a type of dramatic dialogue dealing with moral
problems, as did the later " Mysteries " and " Inter-
ludes," and usually written in the rhymed stanzas
called *sestina ottenaria* and *ballata maggiore*. Its form
was originally borrowed from the *tenzoni* of the secular
poets. This first dramatic phase of Italian literature—
the germ from which the elaborate miracle plays and
moralities of the fifteenth century afterwards developed
—is well represented in Jacopone's works: in the
didactic dialogues between body and soul,[2] between
the poet and the dead nun,[3] and between the rich and
poor old man.[4] His masterpiece in this manner, the
terrible " Quando t'alegri," [5] quickly became a favourite
with the *laudesi*, and is found in nearly every Italian
laudario of the fourteenth and fifteenth centuries. In
his poem on the Last Judgment,[6] where speaking parts
are allotted to Christ, Satan, and the angels, a further
advance in the direction of drama is made; whilst
"Donna del paradiso," the most elaborate example of
his popular style, completes the transition from *tenzone*
to passion-play.[7] Here, the whole movement of the

---

[1] See above, ch. v., p. 161.
[2] *Laude III.*, " Audite una 'ntenzone," and *XV.*, " O corpo enfrace-
dato."
[3] *Lauda XVI.*, " Que fai, anema predata? "
[4] *Lauda XXII.*, " Audite una entenzone."
[5] *Lauda XXV.*, p. 268.   [6] *Lauda XXI.*, " O Cristo pietoso."
[7] *Lauda XCIII.*   The constant intercourse of the Spirituals with
Southern France may have some bearing on the fact that this, the earliest
known *I*talian vernacular play, is of Franciscan origin ; for in France the
vernacular passion-play was already established. Sacred plays in Latin

tragedy is suggested by the introduction of additional
voices; a device probably modelled on the liturgic
singing of the Passion, in which three voices and chorus
are always employed.[1] This poem may have been com-
posed for representation or recitation in Holy Week by
one of the Tertiary guilds. It is a deliberate and skilful
appeal to crude emotion, which falls far below the level
of thought and feeling achieved in Jacopone's best work,
but still impresses us by its tragic intensity. In it we
see the popular theatre, the natural expression of the
people's dramatic instinct, emerging from the popular
song. The vehemence of the phrasing, the vivid imagery,
on the lips of a people so naturally dramatic as those of
central Italy, would almost evoke the scenes which they
depict: and as we read, we can still conceive the cres-
cendo of emotion which would accompany the recitation
and inevitably add gesture to words:

> Donna del paradiso,
> lo tuo figliolo è preso,
> Iesú Cristo beato.
>
> Accurre, donna, e vide
> che la gente l'allide!
> credo che llo s'occide,
> tanto l'on flagellato. . . .
>
> O figlio, figlio, figlio!
> figlio, amoroso giglio,
> figlio, chi dá consiglio
> al cor mio angustiato?
>
> Figlio, occhi giocondi,
> figlio, co non respondi?
> figlio, perché t'ascondi
> dal petto ove se' lattato?

were performed in Italy as early as 1244. The transition represented by
"Donna del paradiso" was quickly completed; developed vernacular
plays, with Latin stage directions, are found in several Umbrian *laudarii*
of the fourteenth century. See D'Ancona, *Origini del Teatro*, vol. i., and
Monaci, *Appunti per la storia del Teatro Italiano.*

[1] The Passion according to the four Evangelists is thus sung in the
Roman Church at High Mass on Palm Sunday, and the three succeeding
days. Students are generally agreed in finding in this ceremony the
origin of the passion-play.

Madonna, ecco la cruce,
che la gente l'aduce,
ove la vera luce
déi essere levato.

O croce, que farai?
el figlio mio torrai?
e que ci aponerai,
ché non ha en sé peccato?

Succurri, piena de doglia,
ché 'l tuo figliuol se spoglia ;
e la gente par che voglia
che sia en croce chiavato. . . .

Mamma, perché te lagni?
voglio che tu remagni,
che serve i miei compagni
ch'al mondo agio acquistato.[1]

(*Nuncio.* Lady of Paradise,
Thy son a captive lies,
 Jesus Christ the blest.

Haste! see! the folk are fain
To do Him grief and pain;
Meseems He will be slain,
 Of their stripes oppressed. . . .

Virgin. O son, my son, my son!
Of lilies loveliest one!
Help, counsellor is none
 For my heart distressed.

Son, with sweet eyes that smiled
Where now Thine answers mild ?
Why dost Thou hide, my child,
 From Thy Mother's breast?

Nuncio. My Lady, see!
They lead Him to the Tree
Where the true Light must be
 Made manifest.

Virgin. O Cross, is this thy skill,
My Son to take and kill;
On Him to work thy will,
 That did no man molest?

[1] *Op. cit.*, vv. 1-2, 11-15, 24.

Nuncio. Help! Lady full of woe ;
 For see, they strip Him now
 And on the Cross bestow,
   With nails, that Body blest. . . .

Christ. Mother, why do you weep,
 Nay, you shall serve and keep
 My dearly-loved, the sheep
   I from the world did wrest.)

Yet in spite of this successful cultivation of the
popular manner, it would be a mistake to classify
Jacopone among the mass of anonymous versifiers who
wrote for the *laudesi* and flagellants. No doubt he had
characteristics in common with them, and especially
during his missionary career deliberately imitated their
methods. The worst poems of his first period may
reasonably be regarded as prentice efforts in the *laudesi*
style. But the best already belong to a world into
which those writers could not penetrate, whilst the
mystical poems of his later life have no parallels among
contemporary *laude*. Moreover, Jacopone has a metrical
range much wider than that of the *laudesi*. Whilst their
most common stanza, the *ballata maggiore*,[1] is never
employed by him, he adapts to his purpose several
other types of *ballata*.[2] His favourite form is the true
lauda, a derivative of the *ballata* which was reserved for
religious verse.[3] He also employs several varieties of
the *serventese*,[4] the common stanza of early Italian

----

[1] The true *ballata maggiore* has an eight-line stanza with a four-line
ripresa. The lines are alternately of eight and eleven syllables.
[2] *E.g.* in *Laude LXV.*, " Ad l'amor ch'è venuto " ; *XC.*, " Amor de
caritate," p. 362 ; and *XCI.*, " Sopr'onne lengua amore," p. 474.
[3] The *lauda* has a four-line stanza. The first three lines rhyme together,
the fourth with all other fourth lines in the poem. Good examples are
Laude XXV., " Quando t'alegri," p. 268 ; *LIII.*, " Piange la Ecclesia,"
p. 432 ; and *LXXV.*, " Fuggo la croce," p. 356.
[4] The most common type of *serventese* is written in rhymed couplets
(*Laude XXXI.*, " Tale qual è," p. 142, and *LVI.*, " O papa Bonifazio,"
p. 438). The *serventese encrociata* has a four or eight-line stanza with alter-
nate rhymes (*Lauda XLIII.*, " L'omo fo creato virtuoso "). The *serventese
caudato* resembles the *lauda*, except that the fourth line of each stanza
rhymes with the body of the stanza following (*Lauda LXXX.*, " Sapete
voi novelle de l'amore "). Cf. Casini, *Le forme metriche italiane.*

narrative and satirical poems. As regards metre, he nearly always adopts the eleven-syllabled line, the most usual measure of early Italian verse ; but obtains a considerable range of effect by variation of the stresses. Thus he frequently writes sapphics, with the accent falling on the fourth and sixth syllables :

> Sapete voi novelle de l'amore,

sometimes dactyls, stressed on the fourth and seventh :

> O vita penosa,
> continua battaglia,

sometimes six-syllabled couplets, stressed on the fifth and eleventh :

> Arde et incende, nullo trova loco.[1]

Sometimes he adapts to the vernacular the metre of Latin hymns. No new metrical forms are found in his works.

Of Jacopone as a poet, we may say generally that in him poetry turns towards the people but does not capitulate to them. As the religion of St. Francis embraced both the ineffable experiences of La Verna and the sweet homeliness of the Crib at Greccio, placing the humblest peasant—more, the birds and animals— on the highway of the Holy Cross, so Jacopone's *laude* touch the extremes of the spiritual life. They form an unbroken chain from the sinner to the seraph ; linking the least impressive aspects of folly and sin, the plain rules of Christian ethic, with man's loftiest intuitions of Eternal Love. Every side of his complex nature, wide range of interest, and spiritual vicissitudes, is represented in these songs, which include drama, satire, sermon, and rhapsody. Many, it is true, are disfigured by crudities, often resulting from an unsuccessful struggle to express new truths and contacts inwardly

---

[1] See J. Schmitt, "La Metrica di Fra *Iacopone*" (*Studi Mediavali*, I. (1904), p. 515).

felt.[1] Some of the more formal and elaborate pieces, in which he tries to extract poetry from the conventional categories of theology and ethics, are tedious and unreal.[2] Yet even in these, sudden flashes of beauty remind us that Jacopone is a true poet, if an unequal one.

> Standoce gli ucelli, loco canta,
> esbernace con grande suavitate,
> nascondece lo nido e si l' amanta,
> che non se veggia a sua contrarietate.[3]

> (Here dwell the birds and sing all day,
>   Here sweetly through the winter rest ;
> From envious eyes within the spray
>   Safely they hide the secret nest.)

This exquisite picture, which inevitably recalls Guido Guinizelli's image of love, like a forest bird, sheltering in the gentle heart,[4] suddenly redeems one of the longest, latest, and most tiresome of Jacopone's didactic poems. His rare use of natural imagery, which increases as his life goes on and his " narrow heart " expands to embrace created loveliness, is always vivid and exact, and shows him to us as possessing in a high degree the artist's power of visualisation :[5] a power exhibited indeed more completely and less pleasingly in many of his ascetic and minatory poems, with their brilliant and unsparing pictures of vanity, corruption, and death.[6] On two sides he is supreme. First, in that dramatic sense which appears to have developed early, and is seen at its height in such *laude* as " Quando t'alegri "

---

[1] *E.g. Lauda XCII.,* " La fede e la speranza."
[2] *E.g.* the tiresome *Lauda XLIII.,* " L'omo fo creato virtuoso " ; *LXX.,* " Alte quattro virtute " ; *LXXXVIII.,* " L'omo che può la sua lengua domare " ; *LXXXIX.,* " Un arbore è da Dio plantato."
[3] *Lauda LXXXVIII.,* " L'omo che può la sua lengua domare."
[4] See above, ch. ii., p. 42.
[5] For instance in *Laude II.,* " O Vergine più che femina," with its sharply-seen picture of the Mother and Child ; *LIX.,* " Povertade enamorata " ; or C., " Fiorito è Cristo," p. 406.
[6] *E.g. Laude VIII.,* " O femene, guardate " ; *XXII.,* " Audite una entenzone " ; *XXIII.,* " Omo, méttete a pensare " ; *XXIV.,* " O vita penosa."

or "Donna del paradiso." [1] Secondly, in the power of giving artistic expression to the most advanced doctrines of mysticism, the strange secret history of the " soul that is feathered with fine love." [2] In his greatest poems, these doctrines and that experience first emerge from the Latin into the vulgar tongue, and are placed at the disposal of all who are able to receive them. Thus as a missionary of the spiritual life Jacopone carries on the work which St. Francis began, and as a poet initiates the movement which Dante was soon to perfect.

II

The mysticism of Jacopone is so closely interwoven with his own experience, so full of the spirit of growth and change, that any attempt to reduce it to a logical system and exhibit him as the creator of a consistent doctrine of God and man will hinder rather than help our understanding of his work. That work is the self-expression of a singularly true and vital soul, led by grace but subject to succession, and registering at every point its changing reactions to unchanging Eternity. Of these mutations and reactions we have obtained a general view, as we followed the course of Jacopone's life ; and the curve of this life must never be forgotten in our attempt to estimate the character of his mysticism.

We have observed the profound changes which his doctrine underwent, as he moved gradually from the purely ascetic conception of religion which governed his convent years to that ecstatic vision of Divine Reality, " Love beyond all language, imageless Good," which crowned his long quest of perfection. In considering this development we have to remember that

---

[1] *Laude XXV.*, p. 268, and *XCIII.*
[2] See, for instance, *Laude LXXXI.*, " O Amor, divino amore, amor," p. 460 ; *LXXXV.*, " O amor che m'ami " ; *XC.*, " Amor de caritate," p. 362 ; *XCI.*, " Sopr'onne lengua amore," p. 474.

. the growing mystic does not always realise the partial
and transitory nature of his own experiences ; and is
often apt to give absolute value to a phase of feeling, or
glimpse of truth, which is merely a stage on the long
road to Reality. Jacopone's recommendations of " holy
madness " and passionate demands for suffering are
due to partial apprehensions of this kind. They are
the declarations of a spiritual adolescent ; and, taken
alone, give an entirely false impression of his teaching.
" Three-fold," says Dionysius the Areopagite, " is the
way to God. The first is the purgative way, wherein the
mind is inclined to learn true wisdom. The second is
the illuminative way, wherein the mind by pondering
is kindled to the burning of love. The third is the
unitive way, wherein the mind by understanding reason
and intellect is led up by God Alone." [1] This statement,
which profoundly impressed the imagination of the
Middle Ages, is based on a deep understanding of
human character: and has been found, again and again,
to elucidate the strange adventures of the mystics. The
law which it expresses is well seen in Jacopone's life, and
gives us a useful key to the many problems connected
with the dating and interpretation of his poems.

As a mystic, Jacopone is (1) Strictly practical: so
that his doctrine at any one moment is a true reflection
of his spiritual state. (2) Traditional: using first the
common formulæ of the Church, and afterwards the
great system of Christian mystical theology, to expound
his personal vision of truth. It follows that his work
will possess both original and acquired features ; and
will best be understood when we place his chief poems
in correct sequence and show them as milestones on
his road to God. This I have already tried to do. It
remains to examine first the main literary and other
sources on which he depends, and next the special
character of his own doctrines.

[1] *De Mystica Theologia,* Prologue.

In common with most of the mediæval mystics, Jacopone obtains many of his ruling conceptions from the New Testament, especially from the Fourth Gospel and the Pauline epistles, which are the true founts of Christian as distinct from Hellenic mysticism. From St. John comes, of course, his sanction for that identification of Jesus with the Platonic Logos of which he makes such magnificent use in " O Amor, divino amore," " Amor de caritate," " Troppo perde el tempo," and other poems.[1] The Fourth Gospel is also the ultimate source of the light-imagery, so dear to the mystics, which he employs in ·numerous *laude;*[2] and of the ideas—part mystical, part sacramental—of rebirth and of feeding on Christ.[3] The reminiscences of St. Paul are close and frequent ; and this we might expect, for the two great converts had much in common. In both we find a vehement temperament seeking expression, now in concrete action, now in exalted devotion. In both, vigorous criticism of man alternates with the mystical passion for Christ. From St. Paul comes the ruling conception of Jacopone's first period—that of the " fool for Christ's sake."[4] He has also been strongly influenced by the great passages in Romans vii. and viii.: the Pauline notions of the soul's inherent divinity,[5] and of redemption as the achievement of inward freedom.[6] The escape from law to liberty there promised to Christ's lovers is the supreme gift which Poverty offers to her friends ; and this Jacopone literally achieved.[7]

But perhaps he is nearest to St. Paul's thought and

---

[1] John, i., 1-4. Cf. *Laude LXXXI.*, p. 460; *XC.*, p. 362 ; and *CI.*, p. 342.
[2] John, i., 4-9, etc. Cf. *Laude XCI.*, " Sopr'onne lengua amore," p. 474 ; *XCII.*, " La fede e la speranza " ; *C.*, " Fiorito è Cristo," p. 406 ; and *CI.*, " Troppo perde el tempo," p. 342. But Jacopone's use of light symbols is deeply influenced by his study of Dionysius.
[3] John, iii., 3–8, and vi., 35. Cf. *Laude XXXIX.*, " O vita de *Iesú* Cristo," and *CI.*, " Troppo perde el tempo." [4] 1 Cor., iii., 18-19.
[4] Romans, viii., 16. Cf. *Lauda XXXV.*, " O anima mia," p. 388.
[5] Romans, viii., 2 ; Gal., v., 18. Cf. *Lauda XXXIV.*, " O libertá, subietta."
[7] *Lauda LX.*, " O amor de povertate," p 420.

feeling in his mystical doctrines of crucifixion with
Christ [1] and of Christ dwelling within the Soul: inter-
dependent ideas which, with the strange Pauline claim
to a share in his Master's wounds,[2] would be specially
dear to a Franciscan mystic of Jacopone's type. "Dying,
and behold we live!" "I live; yet not I." These
phrases he inserts unchanged into two of his most
characteristic poems.[3] In the great *lauda* of his middle
period, "Amor de caritate," the dependence on St.
Paul is specially marked; the whole Pauline concep-
tion of the soul's union with, and transmutation in
Christ, is adopted and woven with exquisite skill into
the framework of the poem.[4] The idea of the renovation
of the soul through Christ's vital dower of grace, so
dear and so actual to all "twice-born" spirits, Jaco-
pone takes intact from the first great convert, and uses
again and again.[5] In his own life he had learned, like
Saul of Tarsus, the difference between the "old Adam"
and the "new";[6] the nature of that mysterious gift
which the "vigorous Lover" makes to the soul.[7] We
may say generally that the experience and theory of
Divine union which governs his early and middle period
is Pauline; whereas that which he reached in his last
phase is characteristically Neoplatonic.

A thorough knowledge of the Bible and current
religious notions—for he was a strictly orthodox
Catholic, sharing the general reverence for the sacra-
ments, our Lady, and the Saints—will account for the
religious content of Jacopone's early poems; for these
poems are mainly inspired by his own deep heart-

---

[1] Gal., ii., 20. *Laude XLII.*, "Ensegnatime Iesú Cristo," p. 328;
LXIX., "Fede, spene e caritade"; and *LXXXIII.*, "O dolce amore," p. 286.
[2] 2 Cor., iv., 10; Gal., vi., 17.
[3] 2 Cor., vi., 9; Gal., ii., 20. *Laude LX.* and *LXXXIII.*
[4] *Lauda XC.*, p. 362. See especially the direct quotations from 2 Cor.,
v., 17; vi., 9; Gal., vi., 15; Eph., iv., 22-4; Coloss., iii., 10.
[5] Cf. *Laude LXXIV.*, "La Bontade se lamenta"; *XCI.*, "Sopr'onne
lengua amore," p. 474; *CI.*, "Troppo perde el tempo," p. 342.
[6] *Lauda XCII.*, "La fede e la speranza."
[7] *Lauda CI.*, "Troppo perde el tempo." Eph., ii., 4-5.

searchings and his crisp judgments of other men, and seldom probe beneath the surface of theology. But the characteristic works of his middle and last periods show that his life as a friar brought him into contact with a wider range of intellectual and emotional influences; and that his mysticism gained from them in richness and depth.

Chief among the influences which now affected his inner life we must reckon a closer contact with the spirit of St. Francis; as it was crystallised in his legend, and as it survived in his most loyal followers. Jacopone's knowledge of the Seraphic Father must have depended largely on oral tradition; especially on the legend then being built up by the Spirituals from Brother Leo's reminiscences. The early lives had been destroyed before he entered the Order,[1] and only the colourless work of St. Bonaventura was in open circulation. We have already noticed that his attitude to St. Francis was that of the extreme *zelanti;* and that he appears to have been acquainted with the *Sacrum Commercium*[2] and with that view of the Saint which inspires the *Speculum.* More important, however, was that initiation into the spirit of Franciscan mysticism which he would obtain through John of La Verna, and other great contemplatives of his type.[3] This mysticism, with its intense emotionalism, its passionate self-identification with the Crucified, its fervent and intimate devotion to the person of Christ, its cult of spiritual poverty, fed needs which his life-changing —whatever its cause—had brought to the surface of his consciousness, and inspired many of his most splendid poems.[4] Purely Franciscan are the complete

[1] See above, p. 158. [2] See above, p. 165. [3] See above, p. 151.
[4] Cf. among others *Laude XL.,* " O Cristo onnipotente "; *XLII.,* " Ensegnatime *Iesú* Cristo," p. 328; *LIX.,* " Povertade enamorata "; *LX.,* " O amor de povertate," p. 420; *LXXIII.,* " O derrata, guarda al prezo "; *LXXV.,* " Fuggo la croce," p. 356; *LXXXIII.,* " O dolce amore," p. 286; *CI.,* " Troppo perde el tempo," p. 342. Cf. above, ch. iv., p. 124, and ch. v., p. 165.

surrender to feeling which marks his middle period, and
his constant prayer for a share in the torments of the
Cross. So, too, are his treatment of the mysteries of
the Incarnation and Passion and his favourite conceit
of the Sacred Wounds as illuminations in the Book of
Life; legible according to their measure by the simplest,
yet transcending the comprehension of the wise.

> Io son libro de vita segnato de sette signi ;
> poi ch'io siraggio aperto, troverai cinque migni,
> son de sangue vermigni ove porran studiare. . . .
>   'Nante è la scrittura che omne studiante
> sí ce pò ben legere e proficére enante ;
> notace l'alifante e l'aino ce pò pedovare.[1]

(I am the Book of Life with seven seals ;
Mine open page five miniatures reveals
    Emblazoned with my blood, to all displayed. . . .
Thus is the Scripture all can make their own,
So plain to read, yet never wholly known ;
    Here elephants can swim, and lambs can wade.)

But although Jacopone's mature poems show a
complete sympathy with the spirit of Franciscan devo-
tion, this emotional surrender was balanced by vigorous
study of those Christian philosophers whom convent
life brought within his reach. His sharp intellect still
urged him to rationalise and explain his own experi-
ence ; and such an elucidation formed part of the
process of " ordering his love." He now begins to show
signs of dependence on literary sources ; an increasing
willingness to interpret his " infused knowledge " of
spiritual secrets by the help of acquired learning.
Among the books which we might expect him to meet
at San Fortunato are many of the Early Fathers, and
the works of Peter Lombard, Hugh and Richard of
St. Victor, St. Bernard, and other mediæval theologians.
The writings of St. Bonaventura were of course acces-
sible to him, though these would hardly be the favourite
reading of an advanced Spiritual ; but his knowledge
of the *Summa* of St. Thomas Aquinas is doubtful.

[1] *Lauda XL.* See also *Lauda LXXXIII.*, p. 286.

Some of Jacopone's correspondences with earlier mystics may be accidental. Thus the apparent identity of his own three stages of spiritual perception with the three degrees of contemplation described by Richard of St. Victor [1] can be explained by the fact that both men wrote from experience. But two writers at least have directly and deeply affected him; St. Augustine and Dionysius the Areopagite. From and through them the greater part of his Neoplatonism is undoubtedly derived; but since we find in his philosophy many conceptions which go back to Plato and to Plotinus, forming links in the strong chain which unites the Greek and the mediæval soul, it will be best to take together his principal correspondences with Hellenic thought.

First, we find that he has received from Plato—though probably at second-hand—several of the ideas and images prominent in his more philosophic *laude*; not only the "many-feathered soul" of the *Phædrus*,[2] but also the beautiful contrast between the "stormy sea" of passionate love and the deep tranquillity of love perfected, which illustrates his most characteristic doctrine of the spiritual life. "Love," says Plato, "produces peace among men and calm upon the sea; a stilling of the winds, and rest, and sleep even in grief." [3] The winds are here the soul's passions; the stillness is the quiet of contemplation. This is closely followed by Jacopone in his *lauda* on ecstatic union:

> son tranquillati i venti
> de li passati tempi,
> fatta è la pace del temporegiare.[4]

(The winds that were aforetime fall and cease,
The storms are over, all is peace.)

---

[1] *Mentis dilatatio*, a widening of the soul's vision which yet remains in the natural order; *mentis sublevatio*, in which the illuminated mind beholds things above itself; *mentis alienatio*, or the ecstatic vision of truth (R. of St. Victor, *Benjamin Major*).

[2] *Laude LIX.*, "Povertade enamorata," and *XXXIV.*, "O libertá, subietta." See above, p. 166.

[3] *Symposium*, 197a.   [4] *Lauda XCII.*, "La fede e la speranza."

Its influence can again be detected in the *lauda* on
Poverty, the " Kingdom of Tranquillity," with its de-
scription of the four winds—joy and sorrow, hope and
fear—which ruffle the surface of the mind that has not
achieved complete renunciation ; [1] and generally in the
sharp distinction—emphasised by his own experience—
between " tempestuous " and " transmuted " love.[2]
Ultimately Platonic also, though of course supported
by the Fourth Gospel and by numerous Christian
philosophers, is his majestic conception of the Logos-
Christ as the personification of Divine Wisdom, fount
of creation, source of all measure, form and beauty,[3]
and Conductor of the universe:

> Splendor che dona a tutto 'l mondo luce,
> amor, Iesú, de li angeli belleza,
> cielo e terra per te si conduce
> e splende in tutte cosc tua fattezza.[4]

Beauty, both eternal and successive, is for Jacopone—
as for Plato, Plotinus, and St. Augustine—a primal
attribute of God, Whom he calls, in Augustine's very
words, " belleza antiqua e nova."[5] So, too, in his picture
of Christ as the Artist-lover giving form to created
things,[6] we are reminded of Plotinus' " Beauty
Supreme," which " fashions its lovers to beauty and
makes them also worthy of love." [7]

> Onne altra creatura ha per niente
> enverso la bellezza de tua faccia,
> tu che de onne bellezza se' fattore.[8]

Here the identification of Christ with that Divine Love

---

[1] *Lauda LX.,* " O amor de povertate."
[2] *Lauda LXXXVII.,* " Amor che ami tanto."
[3] *Lauda XC.,* " Amor de caritate," p. 362.
[4] *Lauda CI.,* " Troppo perde el tempo," p. 342. Yet here Jacopone
comes very close to the Plotinian idea of Psyche, " whose counsel com-
prehends and conducts the heavens " (*En.,* vi., 2).
[5] *Lauda XC.,* " Amor de caritate." Cf. Aug., *Conf.,* x., 27, " O Beauty
so old and so new! too late have I loved thee."
[6] *Lauda LXXXI.,* " O Amor, divino amore, amor," p. 460.
[7] *En.,* i., 6, 7.   [8] *Lauda CI.,* p. 342.

which is the active Principle of creation, comes very
near the *Nous* of Plotinus ; for *Nous*, like Jacopone's
" Love," is at once Wisdom, Truth, and Spirit, the
manifestation and self-expression of the Godhead, the
object of religious passion, and King and Creator of
the World of Life.[1]

It is from Augustine, and through him from the
Platonists, that Jacopone seems to have obtained this
doctrine of love, which is the keystone of his philosophy.
For him, as for those mystics, Love is the " magic of
the universe " which draws all things to their own
place, and man's spirit to its home in the Absolute.

> Ché cielo e terra grida e sempre chiama,
> e tutte cose ch'io sí deggia amare ;
> ciascuna dice con tutto cuor : — Ama
> l'amor c'ha fatto briga d'abracciare ;
> ché quello amore, però che te abrama,
> tutti noi ha fatti per ad sé trare.[2]

Its function is two-fold. It inspires in God an
energy of creation, a passionate, outgoing quest of His
own, a " madness of love " which the Incarnation
dramatised in time ;[3] and in man a constant desire, a
tendency to God, never resting till the soul—stripped
of all partial loves and possessions—is " annihilated "
in Him.[4] These conceptions should be kept in mind
when we are reading the *laude* on love ; for we shall
mistake their meaning if we regard them as mere exer-
cises in religious emotionalism. They have a philo-
sophic basis, which Jacopone gets for the most part
from St. Augustine—mainly the *Confessions* and the
City of God, which he seems to have studied deeply—
and from Dionysius : the ultimate source in both cases
being Plotinus. Thus we read in the *Enneads :* " The

---

[1] Cf. Inge, *The Philosophy of Plotinus*, vol. ii., pp. 37 *et seq.*
[2] *Lauda XC.*, " Amor de caritate," p. 362.
[3] *Laude XXXIV.*, " O libertá, subietta " ; *LXV.*, " Ad l'amor ch'è
venuto " ; and *LXXXV.*, " O amor che m'ami."
[4] *Laude LXXX.*, " Sapete voi novelle de l'amore " ; *XC.*, " Amor de
caritate " ; *XCIX.*, " L'amor ch'è consumato," and many other places.

fullest life is the fullest love, and this love comes from
the celestial light which streams forth from the Abso-
lute One ";[1] in Augustine, " Thou hast made us for
Thyself and our heart can find no rest except in Thee ":
and in the *Divine Names* of Dionysius, " By all things
the Beautiful and Good is desired, loved, and chosen to
love. . . . The very cause of all things, through the
overflowing of His Goodness, makes and perfects all,
holds all together, draws all to Himself. Divine Love
is from the Good, and through the Good, and to the
Good."[2]

Here too we have that idea of the identity and
divine nature of all true love—that " word of which
the plural is unknown "[3]—which several times appears
in the *laude:*

> L' amor ch'io ademando si è 'l primo,
> unico, eterno e sta sublimo;[4]

> (The love I ask for is a single fire,
> And heaven and earth it fills with its desire)

and again:

> Amor tu se' quel ama
> donde lo cor te ama;[5]

a profound thought which underlies St. Augustine's
searching question, " Why do we not feel in ourselves
the love of that Love whereby we love whatsoever
good thing we love ? "[6] All these passages ultimately
depend on Augustine's central notion of love as a
gravitational force, drawing all things to their place
—an idea which profoundly affected Jacopone, and

[1] *En.*, vi., 7, 23. It is, however, unlikely that Jacopone knew Plotinus
at first hand. Even Aquinas has been shown to quote him only on the
authority of Macrobius. See Gardner, *Dante and the Mystics*, p. 82.

[2] Aug., *Conf.*, i., 1 ; *De Div. Nom.*, iv., 10.

[3] *Lauda LXXXV.*, " O amor che m'ami."

[4] *Lauda LXXX.*, " Sapete voi novelle de l'amore." Cf. Dionysius the
Areopagite, *De Div. Nom.*, iv., 12.

[5] *Lauda LXXXI.*, " O Amor, divino amore, amor," p. 460.

[6] *De Civ. Dei*, xi., 28. This seems to be the source of Jacopone's " amor,
che non se' amato," *Lauda LXXXI.*, p. 460.

after him Dante.[1] God, says St. Augustine again and
again, is the soul's resting-place; and love lifts us
thither. "The body by its own weight strives towards
its place: weight tends not downward only, but to its
own place. Fire tends up, a stone down. Urged by their
own weights, they seek their places. Out of order, they
are restless; restored to order, they are at rest. My
weight is my love; by this I am borne wheresoever I
go."[2] Here love, which first appeared to Jacopone
as a wildness, a fury, a dance, is declared to be the
very secret of stability, the rule of the Universe.[3] Here
lies the germ of that conception of the "ordering of
love" which was crucial for his spiritual development,
and distinguishes the poetry of his middle and last
periods from that which was inspired by the undiscip-
lined frenzy of his first convent years.[4] I have already
discussed the emergence of this idea,[5] which he uses
with such dramatic effect in the great poem "Amor de
caritate." This sense of the distinction between the
wild fervours of the *santa pazia* and the steady flame of
perfect charity—the whirl of a spiritual maelstrom and
the movement of the Infinite Sea—seems to have come
upon him with the force of a personal revelation; but
the form in which he expressed it was taken directly
from another celebrated passage in St. Augustine's
works:

"Every creature," says St. Augustine, "being good,
can be loved both well and ill; well when order is pre-
served, ill when order is violated. . . . For even Love
itself is to be loved in orderly fashion, so that what is to
be loved is loved well, whereby that virtue may be in

---

[1] On this see Gardner, *Dante and the Mystics*, p. 58.

[2] *Conf.*, xiii., 9.

[3] Cf. Dante—

Le cose tutte e quante
hann' ordine tra loro; e questo è forma
che l'universo a Dio fa simigliante.—(*Par.*, i., 103.)

[4] See above, ch. iv.   [5] Above, ch. iv, p. 132.

us through which we live well. Therefore it seems to me that a short and true definition of virtue is, the order of love." [1]

So Jacopone:

> Ordena questo amore, tu che m'ami,
> non è virtute senza ordene trovata,
> poiché trovare tanto tu m'abrami,
> ca mente con virtute è renovata
> a me amare, voglio che tu chiami
> la caritate qual sia ordenata ;
> arbore sí è provata
> per l'ordene del frutto
> el quale demostra tutto
> de onne cosa el valore.[2]

St. Augustine is again followed by him, even more exactly, in the important *lauda* on true and false love.[3] This gives us—though in rather dry and academic language—the substance of his doctrine, and re-echoes his definition of virtue as "love in order." Jacopone is here contrasting "natural love" of God, nourished on a merely intellectual knowledge, with "spiritual love," born of infused knowledge or intuition. The first seems spiritual to many, but it "has no wings and feathers." The second proves its authenticity by the order and balance which it imposes upon the faculties of the soul ; uniting power with a goodness in one single state and single aim, as the Trinity of Persons is united within the Being of God.[4]

> Scienzia acquisita
> assai può contemplare ;
> non può l'affetto trare
> ad essere ordenato ;
> scienzia enfusa,
> poi che n'hai a gustare,
> tutto te fa enfiammare
> ad essere enamorato ;

[1] *De Civ. Dei*, xv., 22.
[2] *Lauda XC.*, " Amor de caritate," p. 362.
[3] *Lauda XXXIV.*, " O libertá, subietta."
[4] *Op. cit.*, vv. 5-10.

con Dio te fa ordenato
el prossimo edificando
e te vilificando
ad tenerte en veritate.[1]

(Knowledge acquired may contemplate full well,
But ne'er affection set in order right ;
Knowledge infused His taste alone can tell,
But in the heart the flame of love can light.
With God it ranges thee,
Thy neighbour edifies,
Thy selfhood vilifies,
And in Truth holds the free.)

With this sense of the supreme place held by order in the life of spirit—" All's love, yet all's law "—is closely connected Jacopone's evident affection for that doctrine of emanations which Dionysius took and elaborated from the Neoplatonists.[2] This scheme of the graded celestial hierarchies or degrees of spiritual reality, bridging the apparent chasm between the world and the Godhead and each participating according to its measure in His life and light, seems to have appealed to the trained lawyer's instinct for order and form. For the Neoplatonists—here clearly followed by Dante in the *Paradiso*—the path of the soul's ascent is through these hierarchies, to its source and home in the beatific vision of the Absolute: " through virtue to the Divine Mind, through wisdom to the Supreme "[3]—a formula parallel to that mystic way of purification, illumination, and union which is associated by Dionysius with the functions of the angelic choirs.[4] With this three-fold office of the spiritual spheres, through which the mystic's soul mounts to its goal, are connected the three states of beginner, proficient, and perfect, and the three progressive forms of intercourse with God—meditation, contemplation, and union.[5]

[1] *Op. cit.*, v. 9.
[2] Dionysius the Areopagite, *De Cael. Hier.*
[3] Plotinus, *En.*, vi., 9, 11.
[4] *De Cael. Hier.*, iii., 2.   [5] *De Div. Nom.*, iii., 1.

All these triads are adopted by Jacopone, to whose
dynamic nature the whole idea of ordered growth and
movement was congenial.[1] In the most complete of his
autobiographical poems, he describes his own inward
development as a progress through the nine choirs and
three Heavens, successively achieving the Stellar
Heaven of perfect faith and the art of meditation, the
Crystalline Heaven of perfect hope and the art of con-
templation, and the Empyrean of perfect charity, where
the soul in ecstasy, " become a seraph, beholds the
Trinity, and dwells in God." [2] Plainly this chart of
transcendence, with its degrees of " do well, do bet,
do best," and its states of purification, of enraptured
vision, and of ecstatic union, is an apt allegory of the
soul's development as he had known it ; and his adop-
tion of it was due to something more than deference to
an established scheme. On it he was able to trace the
path he had followed, and through it to philosophise
and in some sort describe that ineffable vision or experi-
ence of the Godhead which crowned his spiritual life.
This experience, which can of course be matched by
many of the confessions of the mystics,[3] lifted him
beyond all the conceptions of an anthropomorphic
theology to the immediate apprehension of that Un-
conditioned and Absolute One who is for Neoplatonists
the sum and term of Reality. Here he found himself
plunged in that " radiant darkness " described by

---

[1] See especially *Laude LXIX.*,"Fede, spene e caritade," and *LXXXVIII.*,
" L'omo che può la sua lengua domare." Both these poems describe the
correspondences of the growing soul with the angelic choirs. Jacopone's
arrangement of the hierarchies, however, does not agree with Dionysius.
In *Lauda LXIX.* he comes nearest to the scheme used by St. Gregory the
Great in the *Moralia*, in *Lauda LXXXVIII.* to the same Father's homi-
lies: but there are small differences in each case.

[2] *Lauda LXIX.*

[3] See, for instance, Jacopone's contemporary, Angela of Foligno,
Visionum et Instructionum Liber, caps. xxvii., xxviii. Suso, *Leben*,
cap. lv. *The Cloud of Unknowing*, chs. iv., v., vi. Ruysbroeck, *Adornment
of the Spiritual Marriage*, bk. iii. *The Sparkling Stone*, ch. xii. *The Book
of Truth*, ch. xii.

Dionysius, in which all succeeding mystics found the symbol of their obscure yet vivid communion with the Divine.

"Leave," says Dionysius, "both sensual perceptions and intellectual effort, and all objects of sense and thought, and all things that are not, and are, and be raised aloft beyond knowledge to that union—so far as we may attain it—with Him who is above all being and knowledge. For when thou has cast away all and become free from all, thou shalt be lifted up by pure, irresistible, and absolute ecstasy from thyself and all things into the superessential radiance of the Divine Dark."[1] Again: "The Divine Dark is the inaccessible Light in which God is said to dwell: and in this Dark, invisible because of its surpassing radiance, and unapproachable because of the excess of the streams of supernal light, every one must enter who is deemed worthy to see or know God."[2]

It is needless to insist on the extent to which these passages, which so profoundly affected the development of mediæval mysticism, are reflected by Jacopone. We need not doubt that he found in them both sanction and description by his own experiences. They give him the philosophic basis of such poems as " Sopr' onne lengua amore " and " La fede e la speranza."[3] From them come his many references to contemplation *in caligine,* and that conception of the Third Heaven of negation which forms the climax of the poem on Poverty.

> Questo cielo ha nome none,
> moza lengua entenzione,
> o' l'amor sta en pregione
> en quelle luce ottenebrate,

---

[1] *De Myst. Theol.,* cap. i., 1.
[2] Dionysius the Areopagite, *Letter to Dorothy the Deacon.*
[3] *Laude XCI.,* p. 474, and *XCII.*

Omne luce è tenebría,
ed omne tenebre c'è dia,
la nova filosofia
gli utri vechi ha dissipate.[1]

We see, then, that on the intellectual side Jacopone
was deeply indebted to the Christian Platonists, and
especially to Dionysius the Areopagite; though his
use of their doctrines has been influenced by the Fran-
ciscan colour of his devotional life,[2] and is always
controlled by reference to experience. His claim to be
regarded as the first philosopher of the Primitive Rule
is based on this interaction of Platonic thought and
Franciscan feeling: for this enabled him to exhibit
Franciscan poverty as a new reading of Reality, and
show the "seraphic wisdom" of Francis as a key to
the universal plan. But it was his own experience and
intuition—knowledge "infused," not "acquired"—
which made this synthesis possible.

This experience was simply a gradual education in
love; steadily growing in purity, depth, and span
from the wild and almost erotic ardours of the *santa
pazia*, through the anguish of surrender to the Cross, to
a metaphysical conception of love as the primal attri-
bute of reality. We may take three *laude* as milestones
upon this road, which brought him first to the point
where the crucified Jesus is merged in the First and
only Fair, and finally to the vision of " the Wonder, the
One, to which in verity no name can be given." [3] He

---

[1] *Lauda LX.*, " O amor de povertate," p. 420.   Cf. a more popular
treatment of the same situation in *Lauda LXXI.*, " Omo che vol parlare ":

Cielo umano passa,
l'angelico trapassa,
ed entra en la caligine
col Figlio della Vergene.

[2] We have a small but significant instance of this dependence on Neo-
platonism in the poem " Fiorito è Cristo " (*Lauda C.*, p. 406), which seems
at first sight purely Franciscan in tone. It is apparently inspired by a
phrase in Dionysius: " The Lord Jesus and the Spirit are, if we may speak
thus, God-planted Shoots and Flowers, and super-essential Lights of the
God-bearing Deity " (*De Div. Nom.*, ii., 7).

[3] Plotinus, *En.*, vi., 9, 5.

has himself recognised the three distinct stages of
which they are representative expressions.

> Distinguese l'amore en terzo stato:
> bono, meglio, sommo, sublimato ;
> lo sommo sí vole essere amato
> senza compagnia.[1]

> (In perfect love three states I see:
> Good, better, best they seem to me.
> The best, the Ultimate, would be
> Loved undividedly.)

These three *laude* are " Senno me pare," the complete
expression of the " divine madness " ; " Amor de cari-
tate," the great poem of transition ;· and " Sopr'onne
lengua amore," the characteristic work of his ecstatic
period.[2] With them we may take "O amor de povertate,"
perhaps the best epitome of his mystical doctrine.[3]
Any one who has studied these four poems will have a
thorough grasp of Jacopone's mysticism, and a clue
wherewith to solve his contradictions and obscurities.

As Moses first knew God in the burning bush, and
only after long trial and experience was able to meet
Him in the stillness and solitude of Sinai ; so Jaco-
pone's first vision of reality was a vision instinct with
movement, ardour, and change, that matched his own
state of fervour and instability. Inducted into the
" Stellar Heaven " of multiplicity, lit by the scattered
splendour of the virtues,[4] he felt the onslaught of
Divine Love as a frenzy which transcended his own, and
invited him to his part in the love-dance of the uni-
verse.[5] All was in flux. The divine life itself partook of
the restlessness of the world of becoming. The Wisdom

---

[1] *Lauda LXXX.*, " Sapete voi novelle de l'amore."
[2] *Laude LXXXIV.*, p. 282 ; *XC.*, p. 362 ; and *XCI.*, p. 474.
[3] *Lauda LX.*, p. 420.
[4] *Ibid.*; also *Lauda LXIX.*, " Fede, spene e caritade."
[5] *Laude LXV.*, " Ad l'amor ch'è venuto," and *LXXIII.*, " O derrata
guarda al prezo " (see above, p. 233). Neoplatonists would say that
Jacopone now knew God in His third hypostasis, as Psyche, the divine
and eternal life of the created universe. Cf. Plotinus, *En.*, iv., 3.

Q

of God was crazed with love, and man could have no greater honour than a share in that insanity.[1]

> E la pazia
> gli par ritta via
> de gire empazato d'amore.[2]

The conception was imperfect: a phase in the soul's growth, rich in poetry, but which—like the ardours and unrest of physical adolescence—must be transcended if the self is to achieve a sane maturity. Many of Jacopone's finest poems were inspired by it, but we should wholly mistake the character of his doctrine if we accepted these *laude* as anything more than the expressions of a transitory state. We can detect the moment when he first suspected its validity, and tried to bridle his " impetuous love." [3] With the crisis which finally imposed order on this wild passion,[4] he entered on the second stage of his development, in which he produced his most characteristic works. These are remarkable for their constant insistence on order and measure,[5] their exaltations of the " golden mean " as the ideal of the spiritual life,[6] and a frequent condemnation of furious and tempestuous love [7] which cannot be reconciled with the *laude* of the first period. The storms are over ; Jacopone, no longer buffeted about by the winds of the passions, begins to perceive the great rhythms of the Divine Life behind the screen of succession, and the nature of that transcendence to which God invites the soul. He has entered the " Crystalline Heaven." [8] Neoplatonists would say of him

[1] *Lauda LXXIII.*, " O derrata, guarda al prezo."
[2] *Lauda LXXXIII.*, " O dolce amore," p. 286.
[3] *Lauda LXXIII.*
[4] See *Lauda XC.*, " Amor de caritate," p. 362, and above, ch. iv., p. 132.
[5] See above, *loc. cit.*; also *Laude XXXIV.*, " O libertá, subietta " ; *LXXIX.*, " La bontate enfinita " ; *LXXX.*, " Sapete voi novelle de l'amore."
[6] *Lauda XXXVIII.*, " O megio virtuoso."
[7] *Laude LXIX.*, " Fede, spene e caritade," v. 46, and *LXXXVII.*, " Amor che ami tanto."
[8] *Laude LX.*, " O amor de povertate," p. 420, and *LXIX.*

that he has achieved the second Divine Hypostasis, and looks into the "intelligible world" of spiritual realities.[1] The "vigorous Lover" who besieged his heart is now recognised as the Logos-Christ, shining in all loveliness, and leading life towards its bourne.[2]

In his last period, even this lofty sphere of spiritual apprehension is transcended. Jacopone reaches the goal of the contemplative life; the vision of that Ineffable One who is, say the Neoplatonists, "neither *Psyche* nor *Nous*"—neither God in Nature, nor the loving comrade of the enlightened soul—yet is the Sum which includes these partial manifestations of reality. He has reached the "hidden heaven" of divine union, where Love is known to be one with Truth; where moral struggle and intellectual effort alike are left behind, and the soul, bathed in the sea of Being, shares in the life of the whole. The *laude* in which he tries to tell the nature of this consummation,[3] though at first they baffle us by their strange language, repay the closest study; for they are among the few successful attempts in literature to express the secret of ecstasy. They begin with a confession that the Measureless Light, when at last it shone in his heart, disclosed the merely symbolic and approximate character of all his former religious conceptions. He goes on to describe that state of profound attention, "en Dio stando rapito," when all intellectual activity seems to be transcended, when even self-consciousness is obliterated; and the whole man, unified and lifted up to a "new condition," veritably tastes Eternal Life, and "enters into possession of all that is God." [4] This

---

[1] Cf. Inge, *The Philosophy of Plotinus*, vol. ii., pp. 37 *et seq.*

[2] *Laude LXXXI.*, "O Amor, divino amore, amor," p. 460, and *CI.*, "Troppo perde el tempo," p. 342.

[3] *Laude XCI.*, "Sopr'onne lengua amore," p. 474; *XCII.*, "La fede e la speranza"; and *XCV.*, "Que farai, morte mia."

[4] Cf. Plotinus: "The soul . . . can see only by completely possessing its object, that is, by becoming one within itself and one with the One: perfectly assimilated to the object of its contemplation, it recognises no

supreme fulfilment is the result and reward of supreme
renunciation: it is found only in the Third Heaven of
Poverty,[1] where desire is dead, and pleasure and dis-
pleasure are cast away:

> Però c'ha sé perduto
> tutto senza misura,
> possede quel'altura
> de summa smesuranza.[2]

Yet this apparent bareness and lostness, this com-
plete destitution, is in fact the consummation of love.
Without " the flame of love for what is there to know,
the passion of the lover resting on the bosom of his
love,"[3] Jacopone, like Plotinus, insists that the most
perfect virtue, the loftiest intellectual vision, will never
bring the soul to the heart of the Absolute.

> Mai trasformazione
> perfetta non può fare
> né senza te regnare
> amor, quanto sia forte.
> Ad sua possessione
> non può virtú menare
> né mente contemplare,
> se de te non ha sorte.[4]

It is the special glory of Christian mysticism that
the union with God to which it leads the self is not a
barren ecstasy, but a " life-giving life." Its final term
is creative. " The fourth degree of love," says Richard
of St. Victor, " is spiritually fruitful."[5] So Jacopone
says of the highest heaven: " Four-fold are the autumns
here; they are established, and they cannot pass."[6]

vision . . . consciousness of the One comes not by knowledge . . . the
soul therefore must rise above knowledge, above all its wandering from its
unity " (*En.*, vi., 9, 3-4).
  [1] *Lauda LX.*, " O amor de povertate," p. 420.
  [2] *Lauda XCI.*, vv. 31 and 7.
  [3] Plotinus, *loc. cit.*   [4] *Lauda XCI.*, v. 39.
  [5] *De quatuor gradibus violentiæ Charitatis*, col. 1216.
  [6] *Lauda XCII.*, " La fede e la speranza." I take this interpretation of
a peculiarly difficult passage from Tresatti's edition, p. 1046.

The soul has transcended the world-rhythm of growth
and decay, and achieved that experience of Eternity
which has been defined as " the total and perfect posses-
sion of unlimited life at a single moment." [1] Perfected
love, he says again, is fruitful love:

> Caritá increata
> ad sé lo fa salire,
> e falli partorire
> figlio d'amor beato.
>
> Questo figlio che nasce
> è amor più verace
> de onne virtú capace,
> copiosa.[2]

The intemperate ardours of the *santa pazia* are but
the soul's love-sickness, the preparation for the spiritual
marriage ; and that union itself is no merely private
beatitude. Its justification lies in the more abundant
life which it mediates to the world of time ; the vitality
with which the spirit transmuted in God dowers the
race. Thus the cycle of mystical love reproduces upon
higher levels the curve of human love ; a fact which
may give matter for reflection to philosopher, psycho-
logist, and poet.

Finally, if we try to extract from Jacopone's *laude*
the substance of his advice on the spiritual life, I think
we shall find it to be something like this:

Humility is the soul's central need, and the begin-
ning of its wisdom ; because it first sets man in his
right order, his due relation with God. When first
" fear of the fiend " brought Jacopone to the foot of
the Tree of Divine Love, and he gazed up its towering
bole to the majestic branches, they seemed inaccessible ;
but a little bough called humility hung down to the

[1] Boethius, *De consolatione philosophiæ*, v. 6. See Gardner, *Dante and
the Mystics*, p. 28.
[2] *Lauda XCIX.*, " L'amor ch'è consumato," p. 470.

ground, and by this he began his ascent.[1]   The next
need is poverty, humility's dramatic expression; for the
climb is long and hard, only to be managed by those
who cast away all encumbrances.   This idea of poverty
is stretched by Jacopone to cover every aspect of
human experience; [2] for he sees the whole path from
illusion to reality as a series of renunciations of our
proud, separate sense of self-hood and ownership, a
giving up of all personal claims upon the Universe
which makes us free of the whole.[3]   First in the cruder
forms of self-abasement, then in the deliberate sur-
render of personal feelings, preferences, intellectual
conceptions, progressive self-stripping to the point of
apparent "nothingness" alone makes man capable of
Eternal Life.   Even natural beauty and delight is best
possessed by those content to love and let it be: all the
green things of the earth, all its beasts and cattle, are
found on the Lady Poverty's farm.[4] Poverty, then, is a
mental and spiritual as well as a moral necessity; a
"three-fold heaven." [5]   The first heaven is found by
those who have killed the material desire for wealth,
the mental desire for learning, the heart's instinctive
love of reputation.   Quit of these, we may hope to reach
the Stellar Heaven of the virtues.   Yet even here we
remain at the mercy of the "four winds" of feeling.
These tempests of repulsion and desire will only be
quieted when we have "annihilated our separate
wills." This surrender brings us to the "second heaven"
of peaceful love, where we are conformed to the rhythm
of the Divine Life.   Then, become a part of all things—
"cosa d'onne cosa"—we are freed from the tyranny
of fragmentary desires.   So Dante:

[1] *Lauda LXXXIX.*, " Un arbore è da Dio plantato."
[2] Cf. *Lauda LX.*, " O amor de povertate," p. 420.
[3] So Plotinus: " We must stand alone in It and become It alone, after
stripping off all the rest that hangs about us " (*En.*, vi., 9).
[4] *Lauda LIX.*, " Povertade enamorata."
[5] *Lauda LX.*, " O amor de povertate," p. 420. For all that follows see
this poem and *XCII.*, " La fede e la speranza."

E la sua voluntate 'é nostra pace:
ella è quel mare, al qual tutto si move
· ciò ch'ella crea e che natura face.[1]

But still the busy intellect has not been put in its place.
It continues to possess its own ideas, and therefore to
be possessed by its own limitations. Entangled in these,
it ranges around, seeking to understand ; only to find
that the brick-built conceptual universe intervenes
between itself and reality. So, if the " third heaven " of
mystical union with God is to be achieved, all separate
thought must be " naughted," and the surrendered
mind must enter meekly into the " heaven of ignor-
ance," [2] where it is content to be still and know. There
wisdom transcends knowledge, and love transcends
desire.[3] This, says Jacopone, is the testing-house where
the academic and the real mystic part company. The
first is still held in the realm of speculation ; lofty
indeed, yet tethered to the earth, like a captive balloon.
The second has the free flight of a bird within the Being
of God, his native air. The wings of humility and
adoration hold him up. He needs not to see, because
he is at home. Yielding himself without reserve to that
Greater Life which is " present everywhere to those
who can receive it," [4] his small measure is swallowed
up in the measureless ; his little, ardent love that
burned so fiercely is found to be a spark of the single
fire. Within that furnace he receives again, pure of
illusion, all that he has renounced. His last stage is not
that of the bloodless dreamer, but of the " whole man."
" Cade, e cresce en vigore," says Jacopone ; powers
are perfected, defects are healed. Of such a man Blake
might say, speaking in another language, that he has
" put off the rotten rags of sense and memory, and put

---

[1] *Par.*, iii., 85.
[2] *Lauda LXXIX.*, " La bontate enfinita."
[3] *Laude XCII.* and *LX.*
[4] Plotinus, *En.*, vi., 9, 4.

on imagination uncorrupt." Surrendering one by one those graded falsehoods in which we live so comfortably lapped, he finds himself, at the moment of apparent destitution, inheritor of all the riches of the House of God.

BEATI PAUPERES SPIRITU,

QUONIAM IPSORUM EST

REGNUM CAELORUM

PART II

LAUDE: TEXT AND TRANSLATION

DE LA BEATA VERGINE MARIA E DEL PECCATORE

(LAUDA I)

O REG*I*NA cortese,
io so a voi venuto
ch'al mio cor feruto
deiate medecare.

Io so a voi venuto
com'omo desperato
da omn'altro aiuto ;
lo vostro m'è lassato ;
se ne fusse privato,
faríeme consumare.

Lo mio cor è feruto,
Madonna, nol so dire ;
ed a tal è venuto,
che comenza putire ;
non deiate soffrire
de volerm'aiutare.

Donna, la sofferenza
sí m'è pericolosa ;
lo mal pres'ha potenza,
la natura è dogliosa ;
siate cordogliosa
de volerme sanare.

Non aio pagamento,
tanto so anichilato ;
faite de me stromento,

OF THE BLESSED VIRGIN MARY, AND OF THE SINNER

(LAUDA I)

O QUEEN of all courtesy,
　　To thee I come and I kneel,
　　My wounded heart to heal,
　　　To thee for succour I pray—

To thee I come and I kneel,
　　For lo! I am in despair;
None other help can heal,
　　Thou only wilt hear my prayer:
　　And if I should lose Thy care,
　　　My spirit must waste away.

My heart is wounded more,
　　Madonna, than tongue can tell;
Pierced to the very core;
　　Rottenness there doth dwell.
　　Hasten to make me well!
　　　How canst Thou say me nay?

Madonna, so fierce the strain
　　Of this my perilous hour,
Nature is turned to pain,
　　So strong is evil's power;
　　Be gracious, O Ivory Tower!
　　　My anguish touch and allay.

All that I had is spent:
　　In nothingness am I drest;
Make me Thine instrument,

servo recomperato ;
donna, el prez'è dato ::
quel ch'avest'a lattare.

Donna, per quel amore
che m'ha avut'el tuo figlio
dever'aver en core
de darm'el tuo consiglio ;
succurrime, aulente giglio,
veni e non tardare.

Figlio, poi ch'èi venuto,
molto sí m'è 'n piacere ;
adomandimi aiuto,
dollote voluntere ;
ètte oporto soffrire
co per arte voglio fare.

Medecaro per arte
emprima fa la diita ;
guarda li sensi da parte
che non dien piú ferita
a la natura perita
che se possa aggravare.

E piglia l'oximello,
lo temor del morire ;
ancora si fancello,
cetto ce de' venire ;
vanetá lassa gire,
non pò teco regnare.

E piglia decozione
lo temor de lo 'nferno ;
pens'en quella prescione
non escon en sempiterno ;
la piaga girá rompenno
farallate revontare.

Thy servant ransomed and blest:
—He Who drank from Thy breast,
Madonna, the price will pay.

Thy Son, Who loved me first,—
By His dear love I entreat,
Madonna, pity my thirst,
Grant me Thy counsel meet!
Succour me, Lily most sweet!
Haste, and do not delay!

(*Madonna speaks*)

Come to Me, son most dear,
Thy coming is all my pleasure ;
Ask my help without fear,
Gladly I give in due measure ;
Yet, for my skill and treasure,
In suffering must thou pay.

If that thou wouldst be well,
Spare thy diet must be ;
Conquer thy senses and quell,
Teach them from peril to flee ;
Till they be chastened and free,
Lest nature ruin and slay.

Then take, for a healing draught,
Fear of the coming of death:
Though youth both sported and laughed,
That coming still hasteneth:
Let vanity, like a breath,
Fade from its ancient sway.

Then, for a potion, drink
The solemn terror of Hell:
In that dark prison, O think!
Lost souls forever must dwell.
So, surely, thy heart will swell,
And cast the poison away!

Denante al preite mio
questo venen revonta,
ché l'officio è sio ;
Dio lo peccato sconta ;
ca se 'l Nemico s'aponta,
non aia que mostrare.

Before my priest without fear,
    Void forth the venomous thing:
It is his office to hear,
    And God the ransom will bring:
    So the Enemy's triumphing
        Shall be hushed for ever and aye.

COMO CRISTO SE LAMENTA DELL'OMO PECCATORE

(LAUDA XXVI)

Omo, de te me lamento
che me vai pur fugendo
ed io te voglio salvare.

Omo, per te salvare
e per menarte a la via,
carne sí volse pigliare
de la Vergene Maria ;
ma non me ce val cortesia,
tant'è la sconoscenza
che ver' de me vol mostrare.

Se io te fosse signore
crudele e molto villano,
averia tua scusa valore
che me fugisse de mano ;
ma sempre vol esser ensano,
ché 'l ben che io t'ho fatto
non vole meditare.

Le creature ho create
che te degiano servire ;
e como sono ordenate
elle fon loro devere ;
haine recevuto el piacere,
e de me che l'ho create
non te voli recordare.

HOW CHRIST MOURNS OVER MAN THE SINNER

(LAUDA XXVI)

O MAN, I mourn for thee
Who still wouldst fly from me,
And I to save thee wait.

O Man, for thy soul's new birth,
To set thy feet in the Way,
I was incarnate on earth,
Of Mary, the Virgin May:—
And yet thou wilt not obey,
Unthankful art thou to Me,
Uncourteous and ingrate.

If I were a cruel lord,
An evil master to thee,
Well might'st thou then afford
Out of My hands to flee ;
Foolish indeed must thou be,
For on the good I do thee
Thou wilt not meditate.

All creatures my Hand hath made,
To serve thee in sequence true;
And all in order arrayed,
Each one his duty to do;
Pleasures before thee they strew,
Yet Me, the Maker of all,
Thou wilt not contemplate.

Como om ch'ama lo figlio
e quel è mal enviato,
menacciagli e dá consiglio
che da mal sia mendato,
de lo 'nferno t'ho menacciato,
e gloria t'ho empromessa
se a me te voi tornare.

Figlio, non gir pur fugenno!
tanto t'ho gito encalzanno,
che darte voglio el mio renno
e trarte fuor d'onne danno,
e vogliote remetter el banno
nel quale sei caduto,
ché non hai donde el pagare.

Non gire piú fugendo,
o dulcissimo frate!
ché tanto t'ho gito cheendo
che me ce manda el mio pate;
retorna en caritate,
ché tutta la corte t'aspetta
che con noi te degi alegrare.

El mio pate sí m'ha mandato
ch'io a la sua corte t'armine;
e co stai sí endurato
ch'a tanto amor non t'encline?
frate, or pone omai fine
a questa tua sconoscenza,
ché tanto m'hai fatto penare!

Fatt'ho per te el pelegrinagio
molto crudele ed amaro;
e vei le man quegne l'agio,
como te comparai caro!
frate, non m'esser sí avaro,
ca molto caro me costi
per volerte ariccare.

As a man may threaten a son,
   Beloved, but to error beguiled,
With the Courts, where justice is done,
   To heal his folly so wild ;
   So have I threatened thee, child,
      With hell, and have promised thee glory,
      If thou wilt turn to Me straight.

Son, cease thy restless flight,
   For long was My love's púrsuit ;
I would give thee a world of light,
   I would save thee from error's fruit :
   From the judgment absolute,
      That thy soul could never answer,
      I would keep thee inviolate.

Then flee no longer in fear ;
   O brother of Mine, so sweet!
My Father summoned me here,
   To follow thy flying feet.
   Return, for love I entreat!
      For all His court awaits thee
      In joys that are uncreate.

I was sent from My Father's throne,
   To summon thee to His court ;
Is thy heart as hard as a stone ?
   Untouched by love of such sort ?
   O brother, yield up thy fort!
      Cast off thine ingratitude,
      That hath crushed Me with its weight.

My pilgrimage on earth
   For thee was cruel and hard :
Dearly I bought thy worth ;
   See My hands that are scarred!
   Keep not back My reward,
      Brother, for great was the price
      Whereby I enriched thy state.

Aguarda a lo mio lato
co per te me fo afflitto!
de lancia me fo lanciato,
el ferro al cor me fo ritto ;
en esso sí t'agio scritto,
ché te ce scrisse l'amore,
che non me devesse scordare.

A la carne enganar·te lasse
perché de me te degi partire,
per un piacer t'abasse,
non pensi a que déi venire ;
figlio, non pur fugire,
ché caderai en mala via,
se da me departi l'andare.

El mondo si mostra piacente
per darte a veder che sia bono;
ma non dice com'è niente
e come te tolle gran dono ;
vedendo ch'io te corono
e ponote en sí grande stato,
se meco te voli acostare.

Le demonia te von pur guatanno
per farte cader en peccato ;
del ciel te cacciâro con gran danno
ed onte feruto e spogliato ;
e non voglion ch'arsalghi al stato
lo qual iustamente hai perduto ;
nante te von per engannare.

Cotanti nemici hai dentorno,
o misero, e non te n'adai ;
ch'hai la carne, el diavolo, el monno,
e contrastar non li porrai ;
e non te porrai aiutare ;
se meco non t'armi ed aiuti,
che non te possano sottrare.

Look on My wounded side,
  Pierced and wounded for thee ;
O look on the spear-thrust wide,
  Deep in the heart of Me!
  For there thy name thou shalt see,
    Writ on My heart for ever,
    By Love Insatiate.

Yet art thou snared by the flesh,
  Parted from Me, thy Home ;
Twisted in Pleasure's mesh,
  Careless of wrath to come :
  Son, thy footsteps that roam,
    Parted from Me, will lead thee
    In ways that are desolate.

Sweetly the world hath wrought,
  With seeming good to entice ;
She tells thee not she is nought,
  And takes of her lovers a price :
  I set thee in Paradise!
    And if thou wilt dwell beside Me
    I crown thee in royal state.

The demons who lurk and spy,
  To make thee fall into sin,
Would hunt thee from heaven on high,
  Spoil thee, and wound thee within;
  Nor would they have thee win
    That purer life thou hast lost:
    They trick thee early and late!

Thy foes are close convened,
  Poor wretch, thy soul is at stake,
The World, the Flesh, and the Fiend,
  And no defence canst thou make :
  Those forces thou canst not break,
    Save with Mine arms and equipment,
    Thy foes are so desperate!

Se tu signor trovassi
per te che fusse megliore,
scusa averíe che mostrassi,
ed io non averia tal dolore ;
ma lasse me per un traditore
lo qual te mena a lo 'nferno,
che te ce vol tormentare.

Fuggi da la man pietosa
e vai verso la man de vendetta;
molto será dolorosa
quella sentenza stretta,
ché la daraio si dretta
de tutto el mal c'hai fatto,
e non la porrai revocare.

Mal volentier te condanno,
tant'è l'amor ch'io te porto!
ma sempre vai pegioranno
e non me ce val conforto,
daragiote omai el botto
da ch'altro non me ce iova ;
ca sempre me voi contrastare.

If thou a master couldst find
  Better and kinder than I,
Excuse were thine, of a kind,
  And lighter my grief might lie:
  But thou hast left me, to hie
    Down to hell with a traitor,
      To torments inveterate.

Thou hast fled from my gentle hand
  To the hand of vengeance and death;
How dolorous wilt thou stand,
  When thy sentence hasteneth!
  Then shalt thou feel, in a breath,
    All thou hast wrought of evil,
      And never canst revocate.

Ah! to condemn am I loath!
  So dearly I love thee still;
Yet must I grieve at thy growth
  Deeper and deeper in ill:—
  The blow must fall when it will;
    Alas! for I cannot save thee
      Thy heart is so obdurate.

DE L'ANEMA CONTRITA DE L'OFFESA DI DIO

(LAUDA XI)

SIGNORE, damme la morte
nante ch'io piú te offenda ;
e lo cor se fenda
ch'en mal perseverando.

Signor, non t'è giovato
mostrarme cortesia ;
tanto so stato engrato,
pieno di villania!
pun' fin a la vita mia
ch'è gita te contrastando.

Megli'è che tu m'occidi,
che tu, Signor, sie offeso ;
ché non m'emendo, giá 'l vidi;
nante a far mal so acceso ;
condanna ormai l'appeso,
ché caduto è nel bando.

Comenza far lo iudicio,
a tollerme la santade,
al corpo tolli l'officio
che non agia piú libertade ;
perché prosperitade
gita l'ha mal usando.

A la gente tolli l'affetto,
che nul agi de me piatanza ;
perch'io non so stato deretto
aver a l'inferme amistanza ;
e toglieme la baldanza
ch'io non ne vada cantando.

OF THE SOUL, CONTRITE FOR ITS OFFENCES AGAINST GOD

(LAUDA XI)

LORD, wilt Thou grant me death,
  Lest I should grieve Thee more?
  Crush my heart to the core,
That in evil continueth.

Lord, it is all in vain
  Thy courtesy fair to show,
So black is my spirit's stain,
  So evil, thankless, and low.
  Nay, end my life at a blow,
    That hath spurned and resisted Thee.

Better to slay me, Lord,
  Than Thou to be grieved and defied:
I mend not in deed nor word,
  Thou seest, in sin I abide.
  Condemn the sinner, long tried;
    Pronounce Thy sentence on me.

Begin Thy judgment dread,
  By taking my health away;
Let my body be sore be-stead,
  No more in freedom to stray:
  Prosperity, in its day,
    It hath used most evilly.

And quench the kindness of man,
  That none may pity my state:
For wilful and cruel I ran,
  Leaving the sick at the gate.
  Lord, leave me disconsolate,
    That hushed my singing may be.

Adunense le creature
a far de me la vendetta ;
ché mal ho usate a tutture
contra la legge deretta ;
ciascuna la pena en me metta
per te, Signor, vendecando.

Non è per tempo el corotto
ch'io per te deggo fare ;
piangendo continuo el botto
dovendome de te privare,
o cor, co 'l poi pensare
che non te vai consumando ?

O cor, co 'l poi pensare
de lassar turbato amore,
facendol de te privare
o' patéo tanto labore ?
or piagne 'l suo descionore
e de te non gir curando.

Then gather all creatures for this:—
　Vengeance on me to wreak:
I have used them all amiss,
　　Thy righteous laws to break;
　　Let each, O Lord, for Thy sake,
　　　Trouble and torture me.

O deathless shall be the lament
　My heart shall make for my Love!
By ruin and anguish rent,
　　Deprived of my God above!
　　My heart, canst thou think thereof,
　　　Unconsumed by misery?

Canst thou think thereof, my heart?
　That Sorrowful Love to forsake?
From Him to turn and depart,
　　Who suffered all for thy sake?
　　Weep, not for thine own heart-break,
　　　But for His dishonour in thee!

DE LA CONTEMPLAZIONE DE LA MORTE ED INCINERAZIONE CONTRA LA SUPERBIA

(LAUDA XXV)

QUANDO t'alegri, omo de altura,
va', pone mente a la sepultura.

E loco poni lo tuo contemplare,
e pensa bene che tu de' tornare
en quella forma, che tu vedi stare
l'omo che iace ne la fossa scura.

— Or me responde tu, omo sepelito,
che cusí ratto de sto mondo e' scito!
o' so i bei panni de que eri vestito,
ch'ornato te veggio de molta bruttura?

— O frate mio, non me rampognare,
ché lo fatto mio a te può iovare ;
poi che i parente me fiero spogliare,
de vil cilicio me dier copretura.

— Or ov'è 'l capo cusi pettenato?
con cui t'aragnasti che 'l t'ha sí pelato?
fo acqua bullita che t'ha sí calvato?
non te c'è oporto piú spicciatura.

— Questo mio capo ch'avi si biondo,
cadut'è la carne e la danza d'entorno ;
nol me pensava quand'era nel monno
ca entanno a rota facea portatura.

— Or ove son gli occhi cusí depurati?
fuor del lor loco sono gettati ;
credo che i vermi glie son manecati ;
del tuo regoglio non áver paura.

OF THE CONTEMPLATION OF DEATH AND BURIAL, TO COUNTER PRIDE

(LAUDA XXV)

WHEN thou art merry, and thy head is high,
Think on the grave, O Man, where thou must lie.

Come here, thy sepulchre to contemplate,
And think, thou too must share this heavy fate;
Like his in this dark ditch shall be thy state,
    Thou too must bear the grave's indignity.

—Now answer me, thou man entombed and dead,
Thou who so swiftly from this world art sped;
Where are thy clothes, once gay with gold and red?
    I see thee here adorned full loathsomely.

—Nay, blame not, nor rebuke me, brother mine,
My evil state may warn and profit thine;
My kindred stripped me of my raiment fine,
    And then with sackcloth did they cover me.

—Where is the head, with tresses once so fair?
Who struggled with thee, and tore out thy hair?
Was't scalding water left thy skull so bare?
    No need to brush or comb that nudity!

—This head of mine that was so blond and gay,
Its curls are gone, its flesh is fall'n away;
How little did I think upon this day,
    When I was flaunting in my revelry!

—Where are the eyes that were so clear and bright?
From out their sockets they are put to flight;
The worms have gnawed them, and have quenched
    their light;
    Worms do not fear thy pride and majesty.

— Perduto m'ho gli occhi con que gía peccanno,
guardando a la gente, con essi accennanno ;
oimè dolente, or so nel malanno,
ché 'l corpo è vorato e l'alma en ardura.

— Or ov'è 'l naso ch'avevi per odorare ?
quegna enfermetate el n'ha fatto cascare ?
non t'èi potuto dai vermi aiutare,
molto è abassata sta tua grossura.

— Questo mio naso, ch'avea per odore,
caduto se n'é con molto fetore ;
nol me pensava quand'era en amore
del mondo falso pieno de vanura.

— Or ov'è la lengua tanto tagliente ?
apre la bocca : non hai niente ;
fone troncata o forsa fo el dente
che te n'ha fatta cotal rodetura ?

— Perdut'ho la lengua con la qual parlava,
e molta discordia con essa ordenava ;
nol me pensava quand'io mangiava
lo cibo e lo poto ultra misura.

— Or chiude le labra per li denti coprire ;
par, chi te vede, che 'l vogli schirnire ;
paura me mette pur del vedire,
caggionte i denti senza trattura.

— Co chiudo le labra ché unqua non l'agio ?
poco pensava de questo passagio ;
oimè dolente, e come faragio
quand'io e l'alma starimo en ardura ?

— Or o' son glie braccia con tanta forteza
menacciando la gente, mostrando prodeza ?
ráspate 'l capo, se t'è ageveleza !
scrulla la danza e fa portadura !

—Mine eyes destroyed me with their trespassing,
Enticing others, looking, languishing:
And now, alas! I dwell in suffering,
  My form devoured, my soul in agony.

—Where is the nose thou hadst, that once could smell?
What ailment dragged it from its bony shell?
Thou canst not chase the worms therein that dwell,
  Abased are now thy pride and luxury.

—This nose that once was mine, so keen of scent,
In search of fetidness a-wandering went;
I thought not, when on lust my thoughts were bent,
  How false the world, how full of vanity!

—Where is the tongue that was so sharp and keen?
Open thy mouth: no tongue can there be seen:
Perchance 'twas cut away; perchance, I ween,
  Thy teeth have gnawed it thus corrosively!

—The tongue wherewith I talked is lost and gone;
Discord and wrath were dwellers thereupon;
To meat and drink it made its orison,
  I feasted careless, lapt in gluttony.

—Close now thy lips, to cover up thy teeth;
Their grin of scorn from all men's sight to sheath;
I fear to look upon these fangs of death,
  That crack and fall, fast-rooted though they be!

—How can I close my lips that are no more?
I little thought to enter at this door;
What shall I do, alas! for on that shore,
  My soul and I must dwell in agony.

—Where are the arms that once were straight and strong
To threaten others, and to further wrong?
Now scratch thy head, now flaunt amid the throng!
  Now toss thy curling locks in vanity!

— La mia portadura giace ne sta fossa ;
cadut'è la carne, remaste so gli ossa :
ed omne gloria da me s'é remossa
e d'omne miseria en me è empietura.

— Or lèvate en piedi, ché molto èi iaciuto;
acónciate l'arme e tolli lo seuto ;
en tanta viltate me par ch'èi venuto,
non comportar piú questa afrantura.

— Or co so adagiato de levarme em piede?
forsa chi 'l t'ode dir, mo lo se crede ;
molto è pazo chi non provede
en la sua vita la sua finitura.

— Or chiama li parenti che te venga aiutare
e guarden dai vermi che te sto a devorare ;
ma fuor piú vivacce a venirte a spogliare,
partierse el poder e la sua mantatura.

— No i posso chiamare, ché so encamato ;
ma fálli venire a veder mio mercato!
che me veggia giacer colui ch'é adagiato
a comparar terra e far gran chiusura.—

Or me contempla, o omo mondano, .
mentre èi nel mondo, non esser pur vano ;
pènsate, folle, che a mano a mano
tu serai messo en grande strettura.

—My vanity is lying in the tomb ;
My flesh decayed, my bones take little room ;
Now all my glorying is turned to gloom,
I dwell in fullness of all misery.

—Now stand upon thy feet, nor lie concealed:
Buckle thine armour and take up thy shield ;
No longer to this vile oppression yield,
No longer bear this dolorous infamy.

—And am I loth to stand upon my feet ?
A man might deem it, hearing thee entreat!
How crazed is he, that in his life so fleet
Provides not for his own mortality.

—Now call thy kindred, bid them help thy need,
And save thee from the worms that on thee feed ;
Yet stay!—to snatch thy raiment will they speed,
And rob thee of thy power and mastery.

—I cannot call them ; here I lie in chains ;
Yet bid them come to see my bitter gains!
Yea, show me to each mortal who refrains
From selling earth, to gain eternity.—

Now look on me, O man of worldly mind ;
No longer in this world thy pleasures find ;
For step by step, bethink thee, fool and blind!
Thou wilt be bound and shackled cruelly!

DE LA GUARDA DE SENTIMENTI

(LAUDA VI)

GUARDA che non caggi, amico,
              guarda!

Or te guarda dal Nemico,
che se mostra esser amico ;
no gli credere a l'iniquo,
              guarda!

Guarda 'l viso dal veduto,
ca 'l coragio n'é feruto ;
ch'a gran briga n'è guaruto,
              guarda!

Non udir le vanetate,
che te traga a su' amistate ;
piú che visco apicciarate,
              guarda!

Pon' al tuo gusto un frino,
ca 'l soperchio gli è venino ;
a lussuria è sentino,
              guarda!

Guárdate da l'odorato,
lo qual ène sciordenato ;
ca 'l Signor lo t'ha vetato,
              guarda!

OF WATCHFULNESS OVER THE SENSES

(LAUDA VI)

FR*I*END, beware lest thou fall:
>   Beware!

First, beware thy ghostly foe,
Who in friend's disguise doth go,
Trust him not, he brings thee woe:
>   Beware!

Turn thine Eyes away from ill,
Evil sights may wound thy will;
Healing hurt thee deeper still:
>   Beware!

Evil tongues a snare will set;
Stop thine Ears: nay, closer yet!
Lest they catch thee in a net:
>   Beware!

Put a bridle on thy Taste:
Plenty turns to poisonous waste,
Then comes Luxury in haste:
>   Beware!

Scents and savours perilous,
Fragrances insidious—
God hath set them far from us:
>   Beware!

Guárdate dal toccamento,
lo qual a Dio è spiacemento,
al tuo corpo è strugimento,
                    guarda!

Guárdate da li parente
che non te piglien la mente ;
ca te faran star dolente,
                    guarda!

Guárdate da molti amice,
che frequentan co formice ;
en Dio te seccan le radice,
                    guarda!

Guárdate dai mal pensiere,
che la mente fon ferire,
la tua alma enmalsanire,
                    guarda!

God is grieved by sinful Touch ;
Set thy guard and keep thy watch!
Thou may'st perish in its clutch :
                                Beware!

From thy kindred dwell apart,
Lest they shake thy steadfast heart,
Lest they cause thee dole and smart ;
                                Beware!

Watch! thy friends will throng around,
Run like ants, like ants abound,
Dry thy roots in God's own ground:
                                Beware!

O beware! lest evil thought
Wound and bring thy mind to naught ;
Sicken all thy soul distraught:
                                Beware!

DEL IUBILO DEL CORE CHE ESCE IN VOCE

(LAUDA LXXVI)

O IUB*I*LO del core,
che fai cantar d'amore!

Quando iubilo se scalda,
sí fa l'uomo cantare;
e la lengua barbaglia
e non sa que parlare,
dentro non pò celare,
tanto è grande el dolzore!

Quando iubilo è acceso,
sí fa l'omo clamare;
lo cor d'amore è preso
che nol pò comportare,
stridendo el fa gridare
e non vergogna allore.

Quando iubilo ha preso
lo cor enamorato,
la gente l'ha en deriso,
pensando suo parlato,
parlando smesurato
de que sente calore.

O iubil, dolce gaudio,
ched entri ne la mente,
lo cor deventa savio
celar suo convenente,
non può esser soffrente
che non faccia clamore.

OF THE JUBILUS OF THE HEART, THAT BREAKS FORTH IN THE VOICE

(LAUDA LXXVI)

Thou, Jubilus, the heart dost move;
And makst us sing for very love.

The Jubilus in fire awakes,
  And straight the man must sing and pray,
His tongue in childish stammering shakes,
  Nor knows he what his lips may say·;
  He cannot quench nor hide away
    That Sweetness pure and infinite.

The Jubilus in flame is lit,
  And straight the man must shout and sing;
So close to Love his heart is knit,
  He scarce can bear the honeyed sting;
  His clamour and his cries must ring,
    And shame for ever take to flight.

The Jubilus enslaves man's heart,
  —A love-bewildered prisoner—
And see! his neighbours stand apart,
  And mock the senseless chatterer;
  They deem his speech a foolish blur,
    A shadow of his spirit's light.

Yea, when thou enterest the mind,
  O Jubilus, thou rapture fair,
The heart of man new skill doth find
  Love's own disguise to grasp and wear,
  The suffering of Love to bear,
    With song and clamour of delight!

Chi non ha costumanza
te reputa empazito,
vedendo svalianza
com omo ch'é desvanito,
dentro lo cor ferito
non se sente de fuore.

And thus the uninitiate
  Will deem that thou art crazed indeed ;
They see thy strange and fevered state,
  But have not wit thy heart to read ;
  Within, deep-pierced, that heart may bleed,
    Hidden from curious mortal sight.

COMO È SOMMA SAPIENZIA ESSERE REPUTATO PAZO PER L'AMOR DE CRISTO

(LAUDA LXXXIV)

SENNO me pare e cortesia
empazir per lo bel Messia.

Ello me sa sí gran sapere
a chi per Dio vol empazire,
en Parige non se vidde
ancor sí gran filosofia.

Chi per Cristo va empazato,
par afflitto e tribulato ;
ma è maestro conventato
en natura e teologia.

Chi per Cristo ne va pazo,
a la gente sí par matto ;
chi non ha provato el fatto
pare che sia fuor de la via.

Chi vol entrare en questa scola,
troverá dottrina nova ;
la pazia, chi non la prova,
giá non sa que ben se sia.

Chi vol entrar en questa danza,
trova amor d'esmesuranza ;
cento di de perdonanza
a chi li dice villania.

HOW IT IS THE HIGHEST WISDOM TO BE REPUTED MAD FOR THE LOVE OF CHRIST

(LAUDA LXXXIV)

Wisdom 'tis and Courtesy,
Crazed for Jesus Christ to be.

No such learning can be found
In Paris, nor the world around;
In this folly to abound
    Is the best philosophy.

Who by Christ is all possessed,
Seems afflicted and distressed,
Yet is Master of the best,
    In science and theology.

Who for Christ is all distraught,
Gives his wits, men say, for naught;
—Those whom Love hath never taught,
    Deem he erreth utterly.

He who enters in this school,
Learns a new and wondrous rule:—
" Who hath never been a fool,
    Wisdom's scholar cannot be."

He who enters on this dance,
Enters Love's unwalled expanse;
—Those who mock and look askance,
    Should do penance certainly.

Ma chi va cercando onore,
non è degno del suo amore,
ché Iesú fra doi latrone
en mezo la croce staia.

Ma chi cerca per vergogna,
ben me par che cetto iogna ;
iá non vada piú a Bologna
a 'mparar altra mastria.

He that worldly praise achieves,
Jesus Christ his Saviour grieves,
Who Himself, between two thieves,
  On the Cross hung patiently.

He that seeks for shame and pain,
Shall his heart's desire attain:
All Bologna's lore were vain,
  To increase his mastery.

DE L'AMORE DE CRISTO IN CROCE, E
COMO L'ANIMA DESIDERA DE MORIR CON LUI

(LAUDA LXXXIII)

O DOLCE amore
c'hai morto l'amore,
prego che m'occidi d'amore.

Amor c'hai menato
lo tuo enamorato
ad cusi forte morire,
perché 'l facesti
ché non volesti
ch'io dovesse perire?
Non me parcire,
non voler soffrire
ch'io non moia abracciato d'amore.

Se non perdonasti
a quel che sí amasti,
como a me vòi perdonare?
Segno é, se m'ami,
che tu me c'enami
como pesce che non pò scampare.
E non perdonare,
ca el m'è en amare
ch'io moia anegato en amore.

L'amore sta appeso,
la croce l'ha preso
e non lassa partire.
Vocee currendo
e mo me cce appendo,
ch'io non possa smarrire.

OF THE LOVE OF CHRIST ON THE CROSS, AND HOW THE SOUL DESIRES TO DIE WITH HIM

(LAUDA LXXXIII)

O Gentle Love,
Who died for Love,
I pray Thee, slay me for Love!

Love, Who didst lead
To death indeed,
Thy Lover upon the Cross,
O tell me why
Thy Dear must die?
—'Twas to redeem my loss.
Then try me by fire,
For 'tis all my desire
To die in the arms of Love.

If Thou didst not spare
Thy Beloved there;
How should I escape from Thee?
Thy Love hath took
Me with an hook,
Thy fish from out of the sea:
Then spare me not,
For 'tis all my thought
To perish, immersed in Love.

The Cross hath lifted
Love, Heaven-gifted,
Never to let it go:
And the Cross shall take me,
Lift me, break me,
For all the world to know.

Ca lo fugire
faríame sparire,
ch'io non seria scritto en amore.

O croce, io m'apicco
ed ad te m'aficco,
ch'io gusti morendo la vita.
Ché tu ne se' ornata,
o morte melata ;
tristo che non t'ho sentita!
O alma sí ardita
d'aver sua ferita,
ch'io moia accorato d'amore.

Vocce currendo,
en croce legendo
nel libro che c'è ensanguinato.
Ca essa scrittura
me fa en natura
ed en filosofia conventato.
O libro signato
che dentro se' aurato,
e tutto fiorito d'amore!

O amor d'agno,
magior che mar magno,
e chi de te dir porría?
A chi c'è anegato
de sotto e da lato
e non sa dove sia,
e la pazia
gli par ritta via
de gire empazato d'amore.

If I shrink and flee,
My name shall be
Blotted out from the Book of Love.

To the Cross I sprang,
On the Cross to hang
To taste true life as I die:
How sweet is thy breath,
O honied Death!
For thee I long and I sigh.
Mine ardent soul
Would pay its toll,
And perish, heart-rent by Love.

Lo! the world shall heed:
On the Cross I read
This scroll that in blood is writ
That giveth to me
God's own degree
In philosophy, science and wit:
And each golden line
Bears God's own sign,
Emblazoned and bordered with Love.

O Love of the Lamb!
O Ocean calm!
Of thy depths what tongue can tell?
In Thee am I drowned,
For Above and Around,
Thy fathomless waters well!
And the straightest road,
To the Heart of God,
Is the Swirl and the Folly of Love.

COMO L'ANIMA PIANGE LA PARTITA DEL SUO AMORE

(LAUDA LXV*III*)

PIANGI, dolente anima predata,
che stai vedovata de Cristo amore.

Piangi, dolente, e getta suspiri,
ché t'hai perduto el dolce tuo Sire ;
forsa per pianto mo 'l fai revenire
a lo sconsolato tristo mio core.

Io voglio piangere, ché m'agio anvito,
ché m'ho perduto pate e marito ;
Cristo piacente, giglio fiorito,
èsse partito per mio fallore.

O Iesú Cristo, ed o' m'hai lassata
enfra nemici cusi sconsolata ?
ònme assalita le molte peccata,
de resistenzia non aggio valore.

O Iesú Cristo, co 'l puoi sofferire
de si amara morte farme morire ?
Damme licenzia de me ferire,
ché mo m'occido con gran desiore.

O Iesú Cristo, avessi altra morte
che me donassi che fosse piú forte !
Sèmmeti tolto, serrate hai le porte,
non par che c'entri a te mio clamore.

HOW THE SOUL LAMENTS THE PARTING FROM ITS LOVE

(LAUDA LXV*III*)

WEEP, sorrowful Soul, despoiled of thine Adored,
Widowed of Christ, thy Lover and thy Lord.

Lament and mourn, and shed full many a tear,
For thou hast lost thy Lord, so fair, so dear ;
Perchance such bitter sighs may bring Him near,
  Back to my mourning heart disconsolate.

Deep cause is mine to mourn, and sore my cost,
Father and Husband both my soul hath lost ;
Christ, gracious flowering Lily, Christ my Trust,
  Hath left me, for my sins that are so great.

O Jesus Christ, why hast Thou left me so?
Disconsolate, beset by many a foe,
Besieged by sins that fain would bring me low!
  I am too weak to strive against my fate.

O Jesus Christ, how canst Thou suffer me
By such a cruel death destroyed to be?
Grant me to wound myself, and so be free,
  Quenching in Death my thirst insatiate.

O Jesus Christ, hast Thou no other death,
Less harsh, less dreadful for my failing breath?
Vain is my cry,—in vain it clamoureth,
  For Thou hast left me, and hast locked the gate.

O cor tapino, e que t'ha emprenato,
che t'ha el dolor cusi circondato?
recerca de for, ché 'l vaso è acolmato,
non hai dannagio da non far clamore.

O occhi miei, e como finati
de pianger tanto che 'l lume perdati?
Perduto avete la gran redetate
de resguardare al polito splendore.

Orecchie miei, e que ve deletta
de udir pianto de amara setta?
non resentiti la voce diletta
che ve facea canto e iubilore?

O trista mene, que vo recordando!
La morte dura me va consumando,
né vivo né muoio cusi tormentando,
vo sciliata del mio Salvatore.

Non voglio mai de om compagnia,
salvaticata voglio che sia
enfra la gente la vita mia,
da c'ho perduto lo mio Redentore.

O wretched heart, who hath imprisoned thee,
Surrounded thee with pain and misery?
Thy cup's too full:—present thy piteous plea,
　And let thy clamour be intemperate!

O eyes of mine, how can ye cease to weep,
To mourn the vanished light ye could not keep?
Your birthright have ye lost, in darkness deep,
　—Of gazing on the Splendour Uncreate.

O ears of mine, and can ye listen so
To these my sad complaints of bitter woe?
Have ye forgot that Voice that lovers know,
　That once did make me sing and jubilate?

O grief! O cruel pangs of memory!
Fierce death devours and gnaws me steadily,
So tortured, I can neither live nor die,
　While from my Saviour I am separate.

Now in no comrade's heart will I confide,
My life shall be a desert wild and wide;
Lonely I dwell, with crowds on every side;
　I have lost my Lord, and I am desolate!

COMO L'ANEMA SE LAMENTA DE L'AMORE DIVINO PARTITO

(LAUDA LXVII)

AMOR, diletto amore,
perché m'hai lassato, amore?

Amor, di' la cagione
de lo tuo partimento,
che m'hai lassata afflitta
en gran dubitamento;
se da schifeza èi vento,
vogliote satisfare;
s'io me voglio tornare,
non te ne torne amore?

Amor, perché me desti
nel cor tanta dolceza,
da poi che l'hai privato
de tanta alegreza?
non chiamo gentileza
om che dá ed artoglie;
s'io ne parlo co folle,
io me n'ho anvito, amore.

Amor, tua compagnia
tosto sí m'è falluta,
non saccio do' me sia,
facendo la partuta;
la mente mia smarruta
va chedendo 'l dolzore,
che gli è furato ad ore
che non se nn'è adato, amore.

HOW THE SOUL MOURNS FOR DIVINE LOVE THAT HATH DEPARTED

(LAUDA LXVII)

(The Soul speaks)
> LOVE, O dearest Love,
> Why hast Thou left me, Love?

> Tell me, Love, if Thou wilt,
> Tell me why Thou hast fled,
> Leaving me wrapt in doubt,
> Grieved and uncomforted.
> If Thou art angry, I said,
> Fain would I make Thee content;
> If *I* then turn and repent,
> Wilt *Thou* not repent Thee, Love?

> Love, why give to my heart
> Sweetness so deep, so fair,
> Only to snatch away
> The joy that was nestling there?
> That man is not debonair,
> Who gives, and taketh again:
> If my complaint be vain,
> Not mine is the fault, O Love!

> Love, Thy company sweet
> Soon was taken away:
> When I am parted from thee,
> I know not the night from the day;
> My mind, forlorn and astray,
> Wanders, seeking its bliss;
> Robbed in a moment of this,
> It loseth its being, Love.

Amore, om che fura
ad altri gran tesoro,
la corte si lo piglia,
fagli far lo ristoro ;
denante a la corte ploro
che me faccia ragione
de te, grande furone,
che m'hai sottratto, amore.

Amor, lo mercatante,
ch'è molto pregiato,
e nascoso fa 'l sottratto
a chi li s'é tutto dato,
da poi che è spalato,
perde la nomenanza ;
onon ha dubitanza
de crédergliese, amore.

Amor, li mercatanti
c'han fatta compagnia,
e l'un fa li sottratti,
non li se par chi sia ;
tutta moneta ria
lassa nello taschetto,
la bona se n'ha scelto,
si la rapisce, amore.

Amor, om c'ha mercato
e véndolo volentire,
vedendo quel che brama,
deve da lui fugire ?
Non lo deveria dire:
Io vogl vender mercato ?
Ed en cor tien celato,
ché nogl vol dar, amore.

Love, if a wicked man
    Stealeth another's store,
The Court will arraign him straight,
    Make him repay and restore:
    So the Court I implore
    For justice full and free
    Thou terrible Robber, on thee,
        Who hast stolen away my Love!

Love, if a merchant-man,
    Honoured by great and small,
Should secretly rob the friend
    Who trusted him with his all,
    In the dust his honour must fall,
    When his sin is visible made ;
    And every one is afraid
        To trust him again, O Love.

Love, there be merchant-men,
    Who are joined in a company:
If one take thievish profits—
    No matter which one it be,
    None of their hoard is free ;
    Tainted is all their wealth
    By him who hath snatched in stealth,
        In secret robbery, Love.

Love, if a man be willing
    To sell of his merchandise,
And seeth one that hath need,
    Should he flee from him who buys ?
    Should he speak to him on this wise:
    " Here are goods to be bought! "—
    The intent to give him naught
        Hid in his heart, O Love?

Amor, lo tuo mercato
era tanto piacente,
nol m'avessi mostrato,
non siria si dolente ;
lassasteme ne la mente
la lor remembranza,
facestilo a sutiglianza
per farme morir, amore.

Amor, om ch'è ricco
ed ha moglie 'narrata,
tornagli a grande onore
s'ella va mendicata ?
Ricchezza hai smesurata,
non trovi a chi ne dare,
e pòimene satisfare
e non par che il facci, amore.

Amor, tu se' mio sposo,
haime per moglie presa,
tórnate a grande onore,
vetata m'è la spesa ?
sòmmete en mano mesa
ed haime en le tue mane ;
la gente desprezata m'hane,
sí so denigrata, amore.

Amore, chi mostrasse
lo pane a l'afamato,
e nolli volesse dare,
or non siria blasmato ?
Da poi chel m'hai mostrato
e vedemi morire,
pòimene sovenire
e non par chel facci, amore.

Love, it was very fair—
    Fair was thy merchandise!
If Thou hadst never shown it,
    These tears were not in mine eyes.
    Thou hast planted memories
Of its beauty in my mind,
With anguish of death entwined:
    Thou hast woven them subtly, Love!

Love, if a man be rich,
    And a gentle wife should wed,
Would it be for his honour
    That she should beg her bread?
    Thy wealth is un-measurèd,
Thou couldst give to all a part,
Thou couldst satisfy my heart,
    Yet Thou wilt not do it, Love!

Love, my husband Thou art,
    Thou hast taken me for Thy bride:
Can it be for Thine honour
    That I should starve at Thy side?
    My all to Thee I confide,
Thou hast my life in Thy hand;
—And I am scorned in the land,
    Despised and dishonoured, Love!

Love, Who hast shown the starved
    Bread that he longs to claim,
Yet giv'st it not to his hunger,
    Art Thou not sore to blame?
    —Hungry and dying I came,
To me Thou hast shown Thy bread:
I too, I too, would be fed!
    Yet Thou wilt not feed me, Love!

Amor, lo mio coraggio
sí l'hai stretto ligato,
voglilo far perire,
ché gli hai el cibo celato ;
forse ch'en tal stato
mo me ne vuoi poi dare,
ch'io nol porrò pigliare,
però tel recordo, amore.

Amor, om c'ha l'albergo
ed hal tolto a pescione,
sel lassa 'nante el tempo,
que ne vol la ragione ?
Ca torni a la magione
e paghi tutta la sorte,
giá non vol cose torte
a chi me ne rechiamo, amore.

— Omo che te lamenti,
brevemente responno :
tollendo lo tuo albergo,
crèdici far sogiorno ;
albergastice 'l monno
e me cacciasti via ;
donqua fai villania,
se tu mormori d'amore.

Tu sai, mentre ce stetti,
quegne spese ce feci ;
non te puoi lamentare,
sí te ne satisfeci,
ch'a nettarlo me misi,
ch'era pieno de loto ;
fecel tutto devoto
per abitarci amore.

Love, my strength and my will
    Thou hast so straitly bound,
Taking their nurture away,
    They perish without a sound;
    So wretched now I am found,
Perchance I could not receive,
E'en wert Thou willing to give;
    I bid Thee remember it, Love!

Love, if one dwell at an inn,
    Renting a lodging there,
And leave it before the time,
    Is he not judged unfair?
    All the costs he must bear,
Back to that house must hie,
Nor cherish an enmity
    To the claimant who calls him, Love.

(*Love Speaks*)
    O Man, lamenting thy lot,
    Swift in answer I say:
When I came to dwell in thine inn,
    Long did I hope to stay;
    Alas! I was chased away—
'Twas the world who sojourned there.
Unjust thy murmuring prayer
    When thou mak'st complaint of Love.

Thou knowest, while I was there,
    What treasure for thee I spent;
How canst thou then complain,
    If now thou art not content?
    To cleanse thy house was I bent—
Thy house that was foul with mire!
I strove with devout desire,
    To make it a home for Love.

Quando me ne partie,
se ne portai lo mio,
como lo puoi tu dire
ch'io ne portassi el tio?
tu sai ch'ell'è sí rio,
ch'a me non è em piacere;
ergo, co lo puoi dire
che te tolesse amore?

Quando alcuna cosa
ad alcuno è prestata,
e non glie dá entrasatto,
non déi esser blasmata
se la tolle a la fiata,
essendo colui villano,
non conoscente de mano
de que gli ha prestato amore.

Tu sai molte fiate
s'io ce so albergato,
e sai con gran vergogna
si me n'hai fuor cacciato;
forse non t'é a grato
che ce deggia abitare,
facendo vituperare
sí nobilissimo amore.

— Amor, ditt'hai la scusa,
ch'ella sí può bastare
a lo mormoramento
ch'agio voluto fare;
voglio 'l capo enchinare
che ne facci venditta;
non me tener piú afflitta
de celarmete, amore.

When I was forced to depart,
  Bearing away what was Mine,
How canst thou dare to say
  That I robbed thee of what was thine?
  Thou know'st how soiled was that shrine—
I could not linger nor stay ;
Then how dost thou dare to say,
    That I robbed thee of thy Love?

If a precious thing and a fair,
  Be granted a man in loan,
—No sudden and certain gift—
  What wrong hath he to bemoan,
  If the lender take back his own,
From one so thankless and cold?
Who spurns the Hand he might hold,
    Of Him Who hath lent His Love.

Thou know'st how many a time,
  When I dwelt within thy door,
Thou hast fiercely chased Me forth,
  Scorning Me more and more.
  When I lodged with thee before,
Thine enemy sure I seemed,
Since thou hast thus blasphemed
    So fair and noble a Love.

(*The Soul speaks*)
  Love, Thou hast made excuse,
    Therewith am I satisfied:
Yea, I will silence the murmur
    I made in error and pride.
    I bow my head at Thy side ;
  Accept my penitent pain,
  Nor crush and wound me again,
    By hiding Thyself, my Love.

—Vedendote pentuta,
sí ce voglio artornare,
ancor me fosse fatto
villano allecerare ;
non voglio che tuo pare
facesse lamentanza
ch'io facesse fallanza
de lo legale amore.

(*Love speaks*)
Yea, I will straight return,
    Now that I see thee repent;
Though by thy pride and anger
    Far from thee I was sent.
    Nor can I let thee lament
That *I* was faithless or cold;
I, who eternally hold
    To the loyalty of Love.

COMO LA VITA DI IESÛ È SPECCHIO DE L'ANIMA

(LAUDA XXXIX)

O vita de Iesú Cristo,
specchio de veritate,
o mia deformitate
en quella luce vedere!

Pareame essere chevelle,
chevelle me tenea,
l'opinion ch'avea
faceame esser iocondo ;
guardando en quello spechio,
la luce che n'uscia
mostrò la vita mia
che giacea nel profondo ;
venneme pianto abondo,
vedendo smesuranza :
quant'era la distanza
fra l'essere e 'l vedere.

Guardando en quello spechio,
vidde la mia essenza :
era, senza fallenza,
piena de feditate ;
viddece la mia fede :
era una diffidenza,
speranza, presumenza,
piena de vanitate ;
vidde mia caritate,
amor contaminato ;
poi ch'a lui me so specchiato,
tutto me fa stordire.

HOW THE LIFE OF JESUS IS THE MIRROR OF THE SOUL

(LAUDA XXXIX)

O LIFE of Jesus Christ!
　　Mirror of Verity!
　　Mine own deformity
　　　I see in that clear Light.

Somewhat, methought, I was ;
　　Somewhat, methought, I seemed ;
　　The Self of which I dreamed
　　　I gladly did survey.
But gazing on that Glass,
　　The light thenceforth that streamed
　　On my true nature gleamed :—
　　　Down in the depths it lay!
　　　Needs must I weep and pray ;
　　For, far as earth from skies,
　　Seeing from Being lies—
　　　Distant as day from night.

And in that Looking-Glass
　　I saw myself indeed,
　　All cruelty and greed,
　　　I read my nature clear.
I saw my faith revealed
　　A halting, doubting creed,
　　A hope, a guess indeed,
　　　A vanity, a fear.
　　　I saw my love appear
　　Corrupt, contaminate,
　　And, all around me, wait
　　　Amazement and affright.

Guardando en quello spechio,
iustizia mia appare
che sia un deguastare
de virtute e de bontate ;
l'onor de Dio furato,
lo innocente dannare,
lo malfattor salvare
e darglie libertate ;
o falsa iniquitate,
amar me malfattore
e de sottrar l'amore
a quel ch'io deve amare.

Guardandò en quello spechio,
vidde la mia prudenza :
era una insipïenza
d'anemalio bruto,
la legge del Signore
non avi en reverenza,
puse la mia entendenza
al mondo c'ho veduto ;
or, ad que so venuto,
omo razionale,
de farme bestiale
e peggio se può dire!

Guardando en quello spechio,
vidde mia temperanza :
era una lascivanza
esfrenata senza frino ;
gli moti de la mente
non ressi en moderanza,
lo cor prese baldanza
voler le cose em pino ;
copersese un mantino,
falsa discrezione,
somerse la ragione
a chi fo data a servire.

And in that Looking-Glass
  My justice I behold;
  A waste, a shame untold,
    Virtue and kindness dead.
The innocent condemned,
  God's honour bought and sold;
  The wicked uncontrolled,
    The good uncomforted—
    Shame on my sinful head!
I held ill-doers dear,
And turned away in fear
    From love and truth and right.

And looking in that Glass,
  My prudence did I view
  Senseless and useless too—
    The folly of the brute.
For laws that God had made,
  No reverence I knew;
  I turned away to woo
    The world, and world's repute.
    I tore up reason's root;
From man's estate I turned,
For bestial life I burned,
    Yea, worse than beast's my plight!

And looking in that Glass,
  My temperance I saw,
  Unreined by any law,
    Lascivious and unwise.
I could not rule my heart
  To modesty and awe;
  Towards evil must I draw—
    Look licence in the eyes.
    In false discretion's guise,
Reason—to whom I knew
My loyalty was due—
    I scorned and put to flight.

Guardando en quello spechio,
vidde la mia forteza:
pareame una matteza
de volerne parlare,
ca non glie trovo nome
a quella debeleza ;
quanta è la fieveleza
non so donde me fare ;
retornome ad plorare
el mal non conosciuto,
virtute nel paruto
e vizia latere.

O false opinione,
como presumevate
l'opere magagnate
de venderle al Signore ?
En quella luce divina
poner deformitate
seria grande iniquitate
degna de gran furore ;
partanne da sto errore,
ché non glie piace el mio,
'nante li sconza el sio
quando 'l ce voglio unire.

Iustizia non può dare
ad om ch'è vizioso
lo regno glorioso,
ché ce seria splacente ;
ergo chi non si sforza
ad esser virtuoso,
non será gaudioso
con la superna gente ;
e non varria niente
buon loco a lo 'nfernale,
ed al celestiale
luoco nogl può nuocere.

And looking in that Glass
  I saw my fortitude:—
  'Twere folly twice renewed
    To say one word of it!
Far worse than words can tell,
  Unfit for aught of good,
  Infirm and poor, it stood,
    My frailty infinite!
  Once more I weeping sit,
  Lamenting sins unknown,
  Virtues all falsely shown,
      Vice crouching out of sight.

O false esteem of self!
  How couldst thou dare to bring,
  As offerings to thy King,
    These worthless works of thine?
Thy nature, all deformed,—
  Ah, what an evil thing
  To urge it, tottering,
    Before that Light Divine!
  These errors that are mine,
  Must loose me from their sway;
  Disorder must away,
      Ere God with man unite.

Justice can never give
  To men contaminate
  That glorious realm and great
    Where nothing base can grow.
So he who will not strive
  To enter virtue's gate,
  Would find the paths too strait
    Where heavenly peoples go.
  Not even Hell below
  To his despair is kind;
  Nor gladness will he find
      In Heaven's radiance bright.

Signore, haime mostrata
nella tua claritate
la mia nichilitate
ch'è meno che niente;
da questo sguardo nasce
sforzata umilitate
legata de vilitate,
voglia non voglia sente;
l'umiliata mente
non è per vil vilare,
ma en virtuoso amare
vilar per nobilire.

Non posso esser renato
s'io en men non so morto,
anichilato en tutto,
el esser conservare
del nichil glorioso;
nul om ne gusta frutto
se Dio non fa 'l condutto,
ché om non ci ha que fare;
o glorioso stare:
en nihil quietato,
lo 'ntelletto posato,
e l'affetto dormire!

Ciò c'ho veduto e pensato
tutto è feccia e bruttura,
pensando de l'altura
del virtuoso stato;
nel pelago ch'io veggio
non ce so notatura,
farò somergitura
de l'om ch'é anegato;
sommece inarenato
'n'onor de smesuranza,
vinto da l'abundanza
del dolce mio Sire.

Lord, Thou hast shown me now,
In Thy fair holiness,
Mine utter nothingness ;
Yea, less than nothing I!
And from this gazing springs
An eager humbleness ;
Prisoned in wretchedness,
My will but lives to die.
My mind's humility
Is not made vile by ill,
But, loving virtue still,
Through vileness, gains Thy height.

I cannot be re-born
Till mine own self be dead ;
My life out-poured, out-shed,
Sheer essence to renew:
On glorious Nothingness
He only can be fed,
Whom God Himself hath led ;—
Here man hath naught to do.
O glorious state and true!
In Nothingness to cease,
Desire and mind at peace
In calmness infinite.

Ah! how my earth-bound thoughts
Are hideous and mean,
Beside those heights serene,
Where virtue's treasures be.
That Deep whereon I gaze,
I cannot swim therein,
I must be swallowed clean,
Like men who drown at sea.
Shoreless Infinity!
I sink in Thee, the Whole ;
Thy fullness storms my soul,
Thou Sweetness and Thou Light!

COMO LA RAGIONE CONFORTA L'ANIMA CHE RETORNI A DIO

(LAUDA XCV*III*)

PERCHÉ m'hai tu creata,
o creatorc Dio,
e poi recomperata
per Cristo Iesú mio?

Amor, tu m'bai creata
per la tua cortesia,
ma so villana stata
per la mia gran follia,
fuor de la mia contrata
smarrita aggio la via,
la vergine Maria
me torni all'amor mio.

Anima peccatrice,
co l'hai potuto fare,
o falsa meretrice,
senza lo sposo stare?
Ché sai che esso lo dice:
Chi a me vorrá tornare,
farollo delettare
nello dolce amor mio.

Occhi miei, piangete,
non cessate a tutte ore,
ché fare lo dovete
per trovar l'amore;

HOW REASON COMFORTS THE SOUL THAT RETURNS TO GOD

(LAUDA XCVIII)

(The Soul speaks)

O WHY didst Thou create me,
　Great God of Heaven above?
Redeem me, and await me,
　Through Jesus Christ my Love?

Thou, Love, didst give me life,
　In tender graciousness;
But guilt in me was rife,
　So great my foolishness;
In misery and strife,
　I roamed the wilderness,
　Till Mary bent to bless,
　　And turned me to my Love.

O sinful, erring Soul!
　Thy life how couldst thou bear,
O harlot false and foul,
　Without thy Bridegroom fair?
" Return to Me, thy Goal,"
　He whispers soft; " and there,
　My sweetness shalt thou share,
　　Wrapt in My tender Love."

Weep, eyes of mine, and mourn,
　Cease not to weep and pray;
Repent, and Love will turn,
　Thine anguish to allay.

ch'io n'aggio sí gran sete,
che me strugge el core,
de Cristo Salvatore,
ché esso è l'amor mio.

O Pier, Paulo e Giovanni,
lo dolce Evangelista,
Gregorio ed Augustino,
e l'amante Battista,
rendeteme l'amore
ch'io non sia sí trista,
morragio s'io sto in quista
ch'io non aggia l'amor mio.

O umile Francesco,
de Dio tutto enfiammato,
che Cristo crucifisso
portasti in cor formato,
priega el mio gran Signore,
ch'io ho tanto aspettato,
che tosto a l'apenato
soccorra l'amor mio.

O crucifisso amore,
recòrdati la lancia,
che te fo data al core
per me trar de pesanza;
donqua ritorna, amore,
non far piú demoranza,
fallami la speranza
s'io non t'ho, amor mio.

Non posso piú soffrire
li tuoi lamenti,
gli amorosi languire
che tu fai spessamente;

So fierce my thirst doth burn,
  It wastes my heart away,
For Christ, my Dawn, my Day,
  For Christ who is my Love!

O Peter, Paul, and John,
  Fore-runners of the Word,
Gregory, and Augustine,
  And John who loved the Lord,
Bring back my Love that's gone!
  Grief cuts me like a sword,
  My life will snap her cord,
    Still straining towards my Love.

O Francis sanctified!
  Inflamed by Love Divine!
Who bore the Crucified,
  Deep in that heart of thine,
Entreat my Lord Who died,
  That Lord for Whom I pine,
  To heal this grief of mine,
    To think upon my Love.

O Love the Crucified!
  Dost Thou remembering see
The spear that pierced Thy side?
  That pang was borne for me!
Return, my Love, my Guide!
  Return all speedily!
  All hopeless must I be,
    Possessing not my Love.

(*Christ speaks*)
  Ah! I can bear no longer
    Thy tender mournful cry;
  Thy yearning and thy hunger,
    Thy faint impassioned sigh.

or briga de venire,
lieva in alto la mente,
farrotte esser gaudente
del dolce Iesú mio.

Or te diletta, sposa,
de me quanto tu voli,
ché ben sei gloriosa,
tanto d'amor tu oli!
Non esser vergognosa,
non c'è perché te duoli,
trovato hai quel che voli,
cioè el dolce amor mio.

Haste, for thy soul grows stronger,
   Lift up thy mind on high!
And laugh, for He is nigh,
   Thy Jesu and thy Love.

Come to My Heart, My bride,
   So radiant and so fair ;
Cling closer to My side,
   Love's fragrance in thy hair ;
No need thine eyes to hide,
   No shame can touch thee there ;
   Hast found thy Hope, thy Prayer,
   The sweetness of My Love!

COMO L'ANIMA PER FEDE VIENE A LE COSE INVISIBILE

(LAUDA XLVI)

Con gli occhi ch'agio nel capo
la luce del di mediante
a me representa denante
cosa corporeata.

Con gli occhi ch'agio nel capo
veggio 'l divin sacramento,
lo preite me mostra a l'altare,
pane sí è en vedemento ;
la luce ch'é de la fede
altro me fa mostramento
agli occhi mei c'ho dentro
en mente razionata.

Li quattro sensi dicono:
Questo si è vero pane.
Solo audito resistelo,
ciascun de lor fuor remane,
so' queste visibil forme
Cristo occultato ce stane,
cusi a l'alma se dáne
en questa misteriata.

Como porría esser questo ?
vorríal veder per ragione,
l'alta potenzia divina
somettiriti a ragione ;
piacqueglie lo ciel creare
e nulla ne fo questione ;
voi que farite entenzone
en questa sua breve operata ?

HOW THE SOUL COMES, THROUGH FAITH, TO THINGS INVISIBLE

(LAUDA XLVI)

THROUGH these two eyes set in my head,
  Daylight transmits, and pencils clear
Within my mind, the image here,
  Of each corporeal thing.

So with these eyes set in my head,
  I see the Sacrament divine
Shown by the priest, and visible
  As Bread from out the altar shrine.
But by the mystic light of faith,
  Other the vision that is mine,
  Eyes of my mind behold it shine,
    My mind, whose power is reasoning.

Four of my senses say to me:
  " This that thou seest is simple bread."—
Yea, all save Hearing are deceived,
  Nor can they enter, and be fed.
For lo! beneath these visible forms
  Stands Christ, hid deep in lowlihead,
  And to the soul, O mystery dread!
    He gives Himself for nourishing.

And dost thou ask, " How can this be? "
  By reason wouldst thou see, and show?
And wouldst thou force the Power divine
  In reason's narrow yoke to go?
He for His pleasure made the heavens,
  Unquestioned:—yet thy queries flow,
  The secret of this Act to know,
    Though swift it be in vanishing.

A lo 'nvisibile cieco
vien con baston de credenza,
a lo divin sacramento
vienci con ferma fidenza ;
Cristo che li ce sta occulto
dátte la sua benvolenza,
e qui se fa parentenza
de la sua grazia data.

La corte o' se fon ste noze
sí è questa chiesa santa,
tu vien' a lei obedente
ed ella de fé t'amanta ;
poi t'apresenta al Signore,
essa per sposa te planta,
loco se fa nova canta
ché l'alma per fé è sponsata.

E qui se forma un amore
de lo envisibile Dio ;
l'alma non vede, ma sente
che glie despiace onne rio ;
miracol se vede infinito :
lo 'nferno se fa celestío,
prorompe l'amor frenesío
piangendo la vita passata.

O vita mia maledetta,
mondana, lussuriosa,
vita de scrofa fetente,
sozata en merda lotosa,
sprezando la vita celeste
de l'odorifera rosa,
non passerá questa cosa
ch'ella non sia corrottata.

Come, with the staff of faith, approach
  This mystery thou canst not see;
Come to this holy Sacrament,
  In confidence and certainty;
For Christ, who hides Himself therein,
  His sweet goodwill bestows on thee,
  And knits thee to this mystery—
    This grace that He is offering.

Our holy Church shall be the court,
  Wherein these nuptials shall be made:
Then come to her obediently,
  In faith she'll cloak thee, undismayed:
She will present thee to thy Lord,
  His bride, beloved and unafraid;
  Thy wedded soul, in faith arrayed,
    Shall hear new songs around her ring.

And here a wondrous love is formed,
  A love of God invisible:
And that He grieves at every sin,
  The soul not sees, but feels full well.
Yea, miracle is infinite!—
  A Heaven is made of deepest Hell:
  And frenzied love her grief must tell
    For bygone days of wandering.

O evil life that I have led,
  In worldly revel and repose!
O life all fetid and diseased!
  O mire, that for my couch I chose!
I scorned the heavenly life—I scorned
  The sweetness of that Fragrant Rose:—
  Now I must bear these bitter throes,
    And mourn with cruel sorrowing.

O vita mia maledetta,
villana, engrata, soperba,
sprezando la vita celeste
a Dio stata so sempre acerba,
rompendo la lege e statuti,
le sue santissime verba,
ed esso de me fatt'ha serba,
ché non m'ha a lo 'nferno dannata.

Anima mia, que farai
de lo tuo tempo passato?
non è dannagio da gioco
ch'ello non sia corrottato;
planti, sospiri e dolori
sirágione sempre cibato;
lo mio gran peccato
ch'a Dio sempre so stata engrata.

Signor, non te veio, ma veio
che m'hai en altro om mutato;
l'amor de la terra m'hai tolto,
en cielo sí m'hai collocato;
te dagetor non vegio,
ma vegio e tocco 'l tuo dato,
ché m'hai lo corpo enfrenato
ch'en tante bruttur m'ha sozata.

O castitate, que è questo
che t'agio mo en tanta placenza?
ed onde speregia esta luce
che data m'ha tal conoscenza?
vien de lo patre de lumi
che spira la sua benvoglienza
e questo non è fallenza
la grazia sua c'ha spirata.

O evil life that I have led!
  Ungrateful, haughty, cruel, base!
Scorning the fair and heavenly life,
  And hateful to the God of grace.
I broke His statutes:—from His word
  I turned away my stubborn face;
  Yet hath He saved me from the place
  Of Hell's eternal perishing.

O soul of mine, what wilt thou do?
  How canst thou bear thine evil past?
My sins were neither jest nor sport;
  Corrupt I was from first to last.
Yea, tears and sighs shall be my meat,
  Behold me mourning and aghast,
  My thanklessness to God, how vast!
  How great my guilt and trespassing!

Lord, though I see thee not, I know
  That Thou hast changed me utterly;
My love of Earth Thou hast destroyed,
  That my desire to Heaven may be:
I see Thee not, O Giver fair;
  It is Thy gift I touch and see,
  That curbs my flesh, and sets it free
  From all its taint and sullying.

O Chastity, what power is here,
  That makes so fair thy lovely face?
This light, that makes me wise and pure,
  Whence comes it, from what hidden place?
It cometh from the Lord of light,
  It breathes His sweetness and solace;
  It is no dream, this healing grace,
  Blown through our souls for strengthening.

O povertate, que è questo
che t'agio mo en tanto piacire,
ca tutto lo tempo passato
orribel me fosti ad udire?
piú m'affligea che la freve
quando venea 'l tuo pensire,
ed or t'agio en tanto desire,
che tutta de te so enamata.

Venite a veder meraveglia
che posso mo el prossimo amare,
e nulla me dá mo graveza
poterlo en mio danno portare;
e de la iniuria fatta
lebbe sí m'è el perdonare;
e questo non m'è bastare
se non so en suo amor enfocata.

Venite a veder meraveglia
che posso mo portar le vergogne,
che tutto 'l tempo passato
sempre da me fuor da logne;
or me dá un'alegreza,
quando vergogna me iogne,
però che con Dio me coniogne
nella sua dolce abracciata.

O fede lucente, preclara,
per te so venuto a sti frutti;
benedetta sia l'ora e la dine
ch'io credetti a li toi mutti;
parme che questa sia l'arra
de trarme a ciel per condutti;
l'affetti mei su m'hai redutti
ch'io ami la tua redetata.

O Poverty, what power is here,
  That makes me love thee now so well?
For to mine ears, in days gone by,
  Thy very name was horrible.
More grievous far than fever-fires,
  Thine image made my heart rebel;
  But, now, beneath thy tender spell,
    I long for thy sweet fostering.

Come, see a miracle! for now
  My neighbour to my heart is dear;
The very thought of harm to him,
  Fills me with trouble and with fear.
How easily I can forgive
  The injury or bitter sneer!
  Nor is this all,—with heart sincere,
    A fervent love to him I bring.

Come, see a miracle! for now
  Shames and dishonours I can bear;
Those things that ever, in the past,
  My burdens and my torments were:
But now, when I am scorned and mocked,
  My heart is glad, without a care:
  I am made one with God, and there
    Fast to His sweet embrace I cling.

O lucent Faith, so clear, so pure!
  Through thee alone these fruits I gain.
O blest the day, and blest the hour
  When I believed thy teaching plain!
And this the pledge, that into heaven
  Shall draw me with resistless rein;
  For, taught by thee, my heart is fain
    To love thy fair inheriting.

COMO L'ANIMA PRIEGA LI ANGELI
CHE L'INSEGNINO AD TROVAR IESÚ CRISTO

(LAUDA XL*II*)

— ENSEGNATIME Iesú Cristo,
ché lo voglio trovare ;
ch'io l'aggio udito contare
ch'esso è de me 'namorato.

Prego che m'ensegnate
la mia 'namoranza,
faccio gran villania
de far piú demoranza ;
fatta n'ha lamentanza
de tanto che m'ha 'spettato.

— Se Iesú Cristo amoroso
tu volessi trovare,
per la val de vilanza
t'è oporto d'entrare ;
noi lo potem narrare,
ché molti el ci on albergato.

— Prego che consiglite
lo cor mio tanto afflitto,
e la via m'ensignite
ch'io possa tener lo dritto ;
da poi ch'ad andar me mitto
ch'io non pos'esser errato.

HOW THE SOUL ENTREATS THE ANGELS TO TEACH IT HOW TO FIND JESUS CHRIST

(LAUDA XLII)

(Soul speaks)
O SHOW me Jesus Christ,
 Him would I find and hold ;
For I have heard it told
 He loves me tenderly.

(Soul)
Teach me and lead me on
 To find my Love so sweet ;
No longer would I grieve my Lord
 By pause, or by retreat :
Sore hath He mourned the tarrying of my feet,
 Hath waited long for me.

(Angels)
If thou wouldst find thy Love,
 Christ Jesus, sweet and fair,
Behold, Humility's dark vale !
 Thou needs must enter there :
Many have breathed that Valley's heavy air ;—
 We tell thee faithfully.

(Soul)
O counsel me, I pray !
 My heart is sore be-stead ;
Show me the path, that stedfastly
 Right onward I may tread :
That I may hold my way, nor turn my head,
 Nor stray confusèdly.

— La via per entrar en vilanza
è molto stretta l'entrata ;
ma poi che dentro serai,
lebbe t'è poi la giornata ;
serain' assa' consolata,
se c'entrera' en quello stato.

— Opriteme la porta,
ch'io vogli' entrar en viltate,
ché Iesú Cristo amoroso
se trova en quelle contrate ;
decetel ch'en veritate
molti el ci on albergato.

— Non te lassamo entrare ;
iurato l'avem presente
che nullo ce può transire
ch'aia veste splacente ;
e tu hai veste fetente,
l'odor n'ha conturbato.

— Qual è 'l vestir ch'i' aggio
el qual me fa putigliosa ?
ch'io lo voglio gettare
per esser a Dio graziosa,
e como deventi formosa
lo cor n'ho 'nanemato.

— Ora te spoglia del mondo
e d'onne fatto mondano ;
tu n'èi molto encarcata,
el cor non porti sano ;
par che l'aggi sí vano
del mondo ove se' conversato.

(*Angels*)
Humility's dark path
    Hath but a narrow gate ;
Yet, entered there, thy journey lies
    More easy and more straight:
    Thou shalt find consolation in that state,
        Yea, comfort fair and free.

(*Soul*)
Then open wide the gate,
    That I may enter there ;
Because it is His dwelling-place,
    Jesus, my Love most fair.
    Many have breathed that Valley's heavy air:—
        Ye say it verily.

(*Angels*)
We cannot let thee in,
    For we have straitly sworn
That none shall enter at that gate
    With raiment stained and worn:
    Thy robe is evil-smelling, coarse and torn,
        All soiled and foul to see.

(*Soul*)
What is this robe I wear,
    That makes me rank and vile ?
Fain would I fling it far, that God
    Might turn to me, and smile.
    Fain would my heart be lovely, pure from guile,
        Fair in its poor degree.

(*Angels*)
Then strip the world away,
    And every worldly thing ;
These heavy burdens load thy heart—
    'Tis sick and suffering.
    The world where thou hast dallied, loitering,
        Hath brought thee misery.

— Del mondo ch'agio· 'l vestire,
vegente voi, me ne spoglio.
e nul encarco mondano
portar meco piú voglio ;
ed omne creato ne toglio
ch'io en core avesse albergato.

— Non ne pari spogliata
como si converría ;
del mondo non se' desperata,
spene ci hai falsa e ria ;
spògliate e gettala via,
ché 'l cor non sia reprovato.

— Ed io me voglio spogliare
d'omne speranza ch'avesse,
e vogliomene fugire
da om che me sovenesse ;
megli'è se en fame moresse
che 'l mondo me tenga legato.

— Non ne pari spogliata
che glie ne sia 'n piacemento,
de spirital amistanza
grande n'hai vestimento ;
usate ché getta gran vento
e molti sí ci on tralipato.

— Molto m'è duro esto verbo
lassar loro amistanza ;
ma veggio che lor usamento
m'arieca alcuna onoranza ;
per acquistar la vilanza
siragio da lor occultato.

(*Soul*)
Ah! see me tear it off,
  This vain and worldly dress!
No more the burden will I bear
  Of dark world-weariness:
    Far, far from out my heart, all shelterless,
      Created things shall flee!

(*Angels*)
Not yet thy soul is stript,
  As faithful spirits are:
Still worldly hopes entangle thee
  With lies, thy course to mar:
    Then tear them off, and hurl them all afar,
      Lest they should ruin thee.

(*Soul*)
I strip myself of hopes,
  Those hopes so false and vain ;
And I will flee from any man
  Who would restore their reign ;
    Better to die in hunger and in pain,
      Than bound so cruelly.

(*Angels*)
Not yet thy soul is stript ;
  Not yet all fair 'tis found:
In pious friendships art thou clad,
  Enveloped and enwound:
    Strong winds may blow, and fling thee to the ground;
      Many so tripped there be.

(*Soul*)
Bitter is this command,
  To leave these friendships true ;
And yet I see, that from their use
  Honours and pride ensue:
    I will obey, and hide me from their view,
      To gain humility.

— Non t'è oporto fugire
lor usamento a stagione,
ma ètte oporto fugire
de non oprir tua stacione ;
per uscio entra latrone
e porta el tuo guadagnato.

— Opriteme la porta,
pregove en cortesia,
ch'io possa trovar Iesú Cristo
en cui aggio la spene mia ;
respondemi, amor, vita mia,
non m'eser ormai straniato.

— Alma, poi ch'èi venuta
respondote volontire:
la croce è lo mio letto,
lá 've te poi meco unire ;
sacci si vogl salire
haveráme po' albergato.

— Cristo amoroso, e io voglio
en croce nudo salire ;
e voglioce abracciato
Signor, teco morire ;
gaio seram' a patire,
morir teco abracciato.

(Angels)
Nay, use these friendships fair,
　In their due place and hour:
But open not thy door to them,
　Distrust their charm and power.
　　Through open doorways, thieves may gain thy tower,
　　And sack thy treasury.

(Soul)
Now open wide the gate,
　That I my Love may seek:
My Life, my Hope, yea, Jesus Christ:
　Love, turn to me and speak!
　　Nor longer be estranged from one so weak,
　　Who prays in courtesy.

(Christ speaks)
Soul, thou art come to Me:
　Now hear what I have said:
Thou canst be Mine upon the Cross:—
　There only is My Bed.
　　There only canst thou lay thy weary head
　　With Mine eternally.

(Soul)
O Christ, my Love, I climb
　Thy Cross, I will not shrink:
Naked, and wrapt in Thine Embrace,
　Death's cup with Thee to drink.
　　Joyful in anguish, in Thine Arms to sink,
　　Dying in ecstasy.

COMO L'ANIMA DIMANDA PERDONANZA DE L'OFFENSIONE E GUSTO D'AMORE

(LAUDA LXXXVI)

AMOR dolce senza pare
sei tu, Cristo, per amare.

Tu sei amor che coniugni,
cui piú ami spesso pugni;
onne piaga, poi che l'ugni,
senza unguento fai sanare.

Amor, tu non abandoni
chi t'offende, sí perdoni;
e de gloria encoroni
chi se sa umiliare.

Signor, fanne perdonanza
de la nostra offensanza,
e de la tua dolce amanza
fanne um poco assagiare.

Dolce Iesú amoroso,
piú che manna saporoso,
sopra noi sie pietoso,
Signor, non n'abandonare.

Amor grande, dolce e fino,
increato sei divino,
tu che fai lo serafino
de tua gloria enflammare.

HOW THE SOUL ASKS PARDON FOR THE OFFENDING AND TRYING OF LOVE

(LAUDA LXXXVI)

Jesus, Lover dear and fair,
Sweet Thou art beyond compare.

Thou art Love: in Thee we rest.
Whom Thou lov'st Thou chastenest,
Yet Thine ointments heal the breast,
 Wounded by Thy sacred spear.

Thou, O Love, wilt never leave us:
Though we sin, Thou wilt forgive us,
Crowned with glory wilt receive us,
 If our lot we humbly bear.

Pardon, Lord, we sinners pray,
Our offences purge away,
Let us taste, if so we may,
 Of Thy love a little share.

Jesu, dear, we kiss Thy feet ;
Manna were not half so sweet ;
Leave us never, we entreat,
 Orphaned of Thy pitying care.

Love, so great, so sweet, so fine,
Uncreate, and all Divine,
Seraphs in Thy splendour shine ;
 Flames Thy glory in their hair!

Cherubin ed altri cori,
apostoli e dottori,
martiri e confessori,
vergene fai iocundare.

Patriarche e profete
tu tragisti da la rete ;
de te, amor, áver tal sete,
non se crèdor mai saziare.

Dolce amor, tanto n'ame,
al tuo regno sempre clame,
saziando d'onne fame,
tanto sei dolce a gustare.

Amor, chi de te ben pensa,
giammai non déi far offensa ;
tu sei fruttuosa mensa
en cui ne devem gloriare.

Nella croce lo mostrasti,
amor, quanto tu n'amasti ;
ché per noi te umiliasti
e lassasti cruciare.

Amor grande fuor misura,
tu promission secura,
de cui nulla creatura
d'amar non se può scusare.

Dáite a chi te vol avere,
tu te vien a proferire,
amor, non te puoi tenere
a chi te sa ademandare.

Ademando te amoroso,
dolce Iesú pietoso, ·
che me specchi el cor gioioso
de te solo, amor, pensare.

Angel choirs, Apostles too,
Doctors, Saints, Confessors true,
Virgins, Martyrs, not a few,
   Joyful sing, and debonair.

Patriarchs, and Prophets great,
Thou hast caught them in Thy net;
Deep their thirst, and deeper yet,
   Love to drink, and not to spare.

Sweet, O Love, so sweet Thou art!
Towards Thy realm aspires my heart;
Thirst and hunger straight depart,
   Love, when once I taste Thy fare.

He who turns his thoughts to Thee
Sinful sure can never be;
Thou, the Fruitful Table, see
   Feasts of love Thou dost prepare.

On the Cross Thou once didst show,
Love, that Thou couldst love us so,
That for us Thou wast brought low,
   Crucified in anguish there.

Love unmeasured, Thou didst gain
Pardon for us sinful men,
So our debt is very plain,
   Love and fealty to declare.

Give Thy Self to all who will;
Thou art come our hearts to fill;
Thou wilt give us good for ill,
   If we come to Thee in prayer.

See Thy longing, loving child,
Jesus, pitiful and mild;
Lull my stormy heart and wild,
   Let Thy face be mirrored there.

Lo pensar de te, amore,
fa enebriar lo core,
vol fugir onne rumore
per poterte contemplare.

Contemplando te, solazo,
pargli tutto 'l mondo laccio,
regemento fa de pazo
a chi non sa el suo affare.

Tu se' amor de cortesia,
en te non è villania,
dámmete, amor, vita mia,
non me far tanto aspettare.

Love, the thought of Thee so great,
Makes my heart inebriate,
Leaving all to contemplate
  Thee, my Lord, divinely fair.

Gazing on the Only Pure,
All the world seems but a lure,
And a madness with no cure,
  For the soul that lingers there.

Thou art Love and Courtesy,
Nought ungracious dwells in Thee ;
Give, O Love, Thyself to me,
  Lest I perish in despair!

COMO IL VERO AMORE NON È OZIOSO

(LAUDA C*I*)

Troppo perde el tempo chi non t'ama,
dolce amor Iesú, sopra ogni amore.

Amore, chi t'ama non sta ozioso,
tanto li par dolce de te gustare,
ma tutta ora vive desideroso,
como te possa stretto piú amare;
ché tanto sta per te lo cor gioioso,
chi nol sentisse, nol porría parlare
quanto è dolce a gustare lo tuo sapore.

Sapor che non si trova simiglianza,
oh lasso, ché 'l mio cor poco t'assagia!
Nulla altra cosa a me è consolanza,
se tutto el mondo avesse e te non aggia;
o dolce amor Iesú, in cui ho speranza,
tu regge lo mio cor che da te non caggia,
ma sempre piú strenga lo tuo amore.

Amor che tolli forza ed onne amaro,
ed onne cosa muti in tua dolcezza,
e questo sanno i santi che 'l provâro,
che fecero dolce morte in amarezza;
ma confortolli il dolce lattuaro
de te, Iesú, che vensero onne asprezza,
tanto fusti suave nei lor core!

Cor che te non sente, ben pò esser tristo;
Icsú, letizia e gaudio de la gente,
solazzo non puote esser senza Cristo;

HOW TRUE LOVE IS NEVER IDLE

(LAUDA CI)

His time is lost indeed who loves not Thee,
 Jesu, sweet love, most dear and most divine.

Love, whoso loves Thee doth not idle stand,
 For, tasting Thee, he finds so sweet a bliss,
That day and night his longing still is fanned
 To love Thee more, make Thee more wholly his;
So blest the heart that shelters 'neath Thy hand!
 Nor can he tell, who knoweth naught of this,
  The honeyed taste, the savour that is Thine.

Thy savour with none other can compare,
 Alas, my heart! whose portion is so scant!
Naught else consoles me,—nothing can I care
 For all the world, if Thee I needs must want.
Sweet love of Jesus! all my hope is there!
 Rule Thou my heart, lest I should fall, and grant
  That I may knot Thy love more close to mine.

Love, to Thy sweetness Thou dost change the whole
 Of life, and force and bitterness dost kill:
Yea, every Saint doth prove it in his soul,
 And cruel death with sweetness dost Thou fill:
Thy sweet electuary can console
 And strengthen them, O Christ, for every ill,
  So gently with their heart dost Thou combine.

The heart that hath not Thee must needs be sad;
 Jesu, Thou joy and solace of mankind:
Christ, without Thee no spirit can be glad,

tapino, ch'io non t'amo sí fervente!
Chi far potesse ogni altro acquisto
e te non aggia, de tutto è perdente,
e senza te sarebbe in amarore.

Amaro nullo core puote stare
cui de tua dolcezza ha condimento;
tuo sapore, Iesú, non può gustare
chi lassa te per altro entendimento,
non sa né può el cor terreno amare;
sí grande è el cielestial delicamento,
che non vede te, Cristo, in tuo splendore.

Splendor che dona a tutto 'l mondo luce,
amor, Iesú, de li angeli belleza,
cielo e terra per te si conduce
e splende in tutte cose tua fattezza,
ed ogni creatura a te s'aduce,
ma solo el peccator tuo amor despreza
e partese da te, suo creatore.

Creatura umana sconoscente
sopra qualunche altra creatura,
como te puoi partir sí per niente
dal tuo Fattor de cui tu sei fattura?
Elli te chiama sí amorosamente,
che torni a llui, ma tu li stai pur dura,
e non hai cura del tuo Salvatore.

Salvator, che de la Vergen nascesti,
del tuo amor darme non ti sia sdegno;
ché gran segno d'amor allora ce desti
quando per noi pendesti su in quel legno,
e nelle tue sante mano ce scrivisti
per noi salvare e darce lo tuo regno;
legge la tua scrittura buon scrittore.

Ah, wretched me! whose love is chill and blind!
Yea, if a man all other treasure had
   Save Thee, he loseth all, and naught shall find,
   And far from Thee, in bitterness must pine.

No bitterness can dwell in heart or brain
   That with Thy sweetness hath been seasonèd ;
Thy savour, Jesu, none can ever gain,
   Who leaveth Thee, to feast on other bread:
Love in the earth-bound heart can never reign,
   Though heavenly glories all around it spread,
      Christ, if it sees not Thee in splendour shine.

Thy splendour gives to all the world its light ;
   Love! Jesu! Thou the angels' beauty art:
Yea, heaven and earth in Thee are led aright,
   Of each fair thing Thy features are a part ;
All creatures follow Thee, and own Thy might,
   —Only the sinner scorns Thee in his heart:—
      Thou mad'st him—yet he only is not Thine.

O human creature, that art more ingrate
   Than any other creature that is wrought,
How canst thou from thy Maker separate ?
   From thy fair Pattern flee, and all for naught ?
How tenderly He calls thee, early and late,
   To turn to Him, hard heart that hearkenest not ;
      For thou art careless of thy Saviour's sign.

O Saviour, of the gentle Virgin born,
   Great were Thy proofs of love, and great Thy loss ;
Then let me not requite that love with scorn,
   For Thou didst hang for us upon the Cross,
And in Thy sacred Hands, that nails have torn,
   The deed of our salvation didst engross ;
      Good Writer, read that blood-emblazoned line.

Scritti sul santo legno de la vita
per tua pietá, Iesú, ci representa;
la tua scrittura giá non sia fallita,
el nome che portam de te non menta;
la mente nostra sta di te condita,
dolcissimo Iesú, fa che te senta
e strettamente t'ami con ardore.

Ardore che consumi ogni freddura,
e sí purghi ed allumini la mente,
onne altra cosa fai parere oscura,
la quale non vede te presente,
che omai altro amor non cura
per non cessar l'amor da te niente,
e non ratepidar lo tuo calore.

Calor che fai l'anima languire,
ed el core struggi de te infiammato,
che non è lengua che 'l potesse dire,
né cuor pensare, se non l'ha provato;
oimè, lasso, fammete sentire,
deh! scalda lo mio cor de te gelato!
Che non consumi in tanto freddore!

Freddi peccatori, el gran fuoco
nello inferno v'è apparecchiato,
se in questo breve tempo, che è sí poco,
d'amor lo vostro cor non è scaldato;
però ciascun se studie in onne luoco
dell'amor di Cristo essere abrasciato
e confortato dal suave odore.

Odor che trapassi ogni aulimento,
chi ben non t'ama, bene fa gran torto;
chi non sente lo tuo odoramento,
o elli è puzzolente o elli è morto;
o fiume vivo de delettamento,
che lavi ogni fetore e dái conforto
e fai tornare lo morto in suo vigore!

Thy writing, Jesu, on life's sacred Tree,
   Through Thy sweet pity, clearly may be seen:
Thy holy Writ in error cannot be,
   The name Thou giv'st, from all untruth is clean:
Our souls are 'stablished and built up in Thee,
   Upon Thy love, sweet Jesu, let me lean,
      And to fresh ardours let my heart incline.

Ardour of Love, that burns away all cold,
   That purges and illumines all the heart,
All other things in darkness dost Thou fold,
   Save, Love, Thyself, that ever present art;
All other loves I cast away, to hold
   Thyself more close, that we may never part,
      And that Thy fervour never may decline.

Fervour that makes the soul Thou dost inflame,
   To melt away in daily languishing;
There is no tongue can give this wonder name,
   Nor heart conceive, that hath not felt its sting.
Alas! my frozen soul denies Thy claim:
   O warm my heart, ice-bound and perishing!
      Lest in this cold forever I should pine.

Cold-hearted sinners, lo! the fires of Hell,
   Strong fires and fierce, for you shall lie in wait,
Unless the love of Christ stand sentinel
   O'er this your life, that is so brief a state.
Then hasten, every soul, and strive to dwell
   In Christ's embrace of love compassionate,
      That comforts you with fragrance fair and fine.

O Fragrance that surpasseth every scent!
   Who loves Thee not, committeth grievous wrong.
Who with that perfume cannot be content,
   Is dead, or to corruption doth belong.
O Living River of Enravishment!
   That brings the dead to life, and makes him strong;
      And laves his sin in waters crystalline.

Vigoros'amante, li amorosi
en cielo hanno tanta tua dolcezza,
gustando quelli morselli saporosi
che dá Cristo ad quelli c'hanno sua contezza,
che tanto sono suavi e delettosi;
chi ben li assagia, tutto el mondo sprezza
e quasi in terra perde suo sentore.

Sentítivi, o pigri e negligenti,
bastevi el tempo ch'avete perduto!
Oh quanto simo stati sconoscenti
al piú cortese che si sia veduto!
El qual promette celestial presenti,
e mai nullo non ne vien falluto;
chi l'ama, sí li sta buon servidore.

Servire a te, Iesú mio amoroso,
piú sei suave d'ogni altro diletto;
non può sapere chi sta de te ozioso
quanto sei dolce ad amar con affetto;
giamai el cor non trova altro reposo
se non in te, Iesú, amor perfetto,
che de tuoi servi sei consolatore.

Consolar l'anima mia non può terrena cosa,
però ch'ella è fatta a tua sembianza;
che piú de tutto el mondo è preziosa
e nobile e sopr'onne altra sustanza;
solo tu, Cristo, li puoi dar puosa
e puoi empire de tutta sua bastanza,
però che tu sei solo suo maggiore.

Maggiore inganno non mi par che sia
che volere quello che non se trova,
e pare sopra onne altra gran follia
de quel che non può esser farne prova;
cusí fa l'anima che è fuor de la via,
che vuol che 'l mondo li empia legge nova,
e non può essere, ché 'l mondo è minore.

O Lover strong! Thy sweetness cherisheth
  Thy followers and friends in Paradise.
Christ gives to those whom He enlighteneth,
  Sweet morsels for their taste—an honeyed prize,
Delicious fare, to whoso savoureth,
  And he who tries it doth the world despise,
    —No taste he finds in earthly food and wine.

O taste and see, ye careless sluggards all!
  Too long, too long, your time hath wasted been:
Ungrateful are ye to His tender call,
  He, the Most Courteous that was ever seen:
To you He offers gifts most prodigal,
  Unfailing gifts, of fair and heavenly sheen;
    Then be ye faithful servants at His sign.

To be Thy servant, Jesu, my Delight,
  Than any other joy is sweeter far;
The sluggish soul that longs not for Thy light
  Knows not how sweet those passionate ardours are;
—No rest the heart can find by day nor night,
  Save, Jesu, in Thy love, that naught can mar:—
    Consoler of the servants that are Thine!

Nothing of earth my spirit can console,
  For in Thy likeness is that spirit wove;
Yea, fairest of all Substance is the Soul,
  More precious than the whole world's treasure-trove;
Thou only, Christ, art her eternal goal,
  For only Thou canst satisfy her love,
    Since Thou alone art greater, more divine.

This is the greatest error man can make,
  To long for something that can never be:
Most foolish and most desperate mistake,
  To strive for this impossibility!
O soul that from this world thy law wouldst take,
  How dost thou err!—the world is less than thee;
    Her power and compass smaller far than thine.

Menorar sí vuole lo cor villano
che del mondo chiamasi contento,
che te vuole, Iesú, amor soprano,
per terrene cose cambiare intendimento;
ma se el suo palato avesse sano,
che assagiasse lo tuo delettamento
sopra ogni altro li parría el migliore.

Migliore cosa di te, amore Iesú,
nissuna mente può desiderare;
però deverebbe el cor teco lá su
con la mente sempre conversare,
ed onne creatura de qua giú
per tuo amore niente reputare,
e te solo pensare, dolcissimo Signore.

Signor, chi ti vol dare la mente pura,
non te déi dare altra compagnia;
ché spesse volte, per la troppa cura,
da te la mente si svaga ed esvia;
dolce cosa è amar la creatura,
ma 'l Creatore piú dolce che mai sia,
però che è da temere onne altro amore.

Amore e gilosia porta la mente
che ama Iesú che non li dispiaccia,
e partesi al tutto da onne altra gente,
e te, dolce Iesú, suo cuore abraccia;
onne altra creatura ha per niente
enverso la bellezza de tua faccia,
tu che de onne bellezza se' fattore.

De te solo, Iesú, me fa pensare
ed onne altro pensier dal cor mi caccia,
ch'en tutto el mondo non posso trovare
creatura chi a me satisfaccia;
o dolce Creatore, fammite amare
e dammi grazia che 'l tuo amor mi piaccia,
tu che d'onne grazia sei datore.

The heart that with this world is well content,
    Makes itself small and shrivels up thereby;
Ah, Jesu, he that on Thy love is bent,
    Can give to all things earthly the go-by.
And if his palate be not impotent,
    Thy sweetness, when he tastes, 'twill satisfy,
      —More sweet than earthly fare, more pure, more fine.

For never could the heart of man desire,
    O Love of Christ, than Thee a better thing;
Therefore man's heart and soul should never tire
    Of converse in the heights with Thee his King.
No creature of this world must he admire,
    But only to Thy love eternal cling,
      And think of none but Thee, sweet Lord Divine.

And he, O Lord, who would be Thine for ever,
    Must give Thee no companion in his heart;
For other cares and hopes will oft-times sever
    The soul from Thee, and lead it far apart:
Sweet is the love of creatures, but yet never
    So sweet as Thou, that their Creator art;
      Let other loves be feared and held malign.

This jealous love the soul of man shall bring,
    Through love of Christ, to please Him night and day;
Shall set him free from every other thing,
    To clasp Thee, Jesu, to his heart alway:
All other creatures in the reckoning
    Are naught, Thy face is fairer far than they;
      Thou Beauty's Maker art, and Beauty's shrine.

Then, Jesu, make me think of Thee alone,
    All other thoughts afar I fain would chase;
For in this world no creature have I known,
    To satisfy my soul with all solace:
O sweet Creator, make me all Thine own!
    Thou Who the Giver art of every grace,
      Let Thy love satisfy this heart of mine.

Damme tanto amore di te che basti
ad amarte quanto so tenuto,
del grande prezzo che per me pagasti,
sia per me da te reconosciuto;
o Iesú dolce, molto me obligasti
a piú amarte, ch'io non ho potuto
né posso senza te conforto avere.

Conforta el mio cor che per te languesce,
che senza te non vole altro conforto;
se 'l lassi piú degiuno, deliquesce,
ché 'l cor che tu non pasci vive morto;
se 'l tuo amore assaggia, revivesce;
or n'aiuta, Cristo, in questo porto,
tu che sei sopra ogni altro aiutatore.

Aiutami, amor, ch'io non perisca,
amor dolce per amor t'adomando;
pregoti che 'l tuo amor non mi fallisca,
recevi i gran sospiri ch'io te mando;
ma se tu voli ch'io per te languisca,
piaceme, ch'io vo' morire amando
per lo tuo amore, dolce Redentore.

O Redentore, questo è 'l mio volere:
d'amarte e de servir quanto io potesse;
o dolce Cristo, deggiati piacere
che 'l mio core del tuo amor si empiesse,
quella ora, buon Iesú, mi fa vedere
ch'io te solo nel mio core tenesse
e tu me fussi cibo e pascitore.

Pascime de pane celestiale,
e famme ogni altra cosa infastidire;
cibo de vita sempre eternale,
chi ben t'ama, mai non può perire;
famme questo gran dono speziale
che te, dolce amor, possa sentire
per pietate largo donatore.

And give me love, yea, love enough, I pray,
  Wherewith to love Thee even as I am bound ;
—Thou Who so great a price for me didst pay—
  Fain would my heart in gratitude abound ;
Dear and sweet Jesu, Thou Thy claim dost lay
  To all my heart, nor ever have I found
    Comfort in aught, save in Thy love benign.

Comfort my heart, that languisheth for Thee ;
  Afar from Thee, none other comforteth ;
I faint, if thus to starve Thou leavest me ;
  The heart, unfed by Thee, must live in death :
To taste Thy love is my vitality ;
  Then help me, Christ, to draw my painful breath !
    None other help prevails save only Thine.

Then help me, Love, lest I should perish straight,
  Yea, love for love I ask, for love is sweet :
Ah, let Thy love not fail me where I wait,
  Accept the sighs I lavish at Thy feet :
Yet, if for Thee Thou'dst have me desolate,
  Glad would I give for love my heart's last beat,
    And die for love of Thee, Redeemer mine.

O my Redeemer, this is all my prayer ;
  To love Thee and to serve Thee all I may ;
O Christ most sweet, to please Thee is my care,
  And with Thy love to fill my heart of clay
So full, good Jesu, that I then may bear
  Within that heart Thee only, night and day,
    And Bread and Giver in one Feast combine.

Then give me, Saviour, of Thy heavenly bread,
  And let all else to me be weariness ;
With food of life eternal I am fed,
  He cannot die, whose love is measureless :
Thy greatest, choicest gift upon me shed,
  Bountiful Giver, in Thy tenderness,
    —To feel the love and sweetness that are Thine.

Doname de te, dolcissimo, assaggiare ;
per te sopr'onne cibo delicato
voglio de tutto degiunare ;
chi ben t'assagia la lengua e 'l palato
tutto latte e mele li fai stillare,
e d'onne altro amore el fai levato
e renovar la mente en tuo fervore.

Fervente amor di te li dá', Iesú,
chi canta el detto di sí grande alteza,
mentre che vive en terra de qua giú,
tu reggi la sua vita en gran netteza,
e poi gli dá' el solazzo de lá su,
che prenda gioia de la tua conteza
e sempre regni teco, vero amore.

So of Thyself, O Sweetest, let me taste:
　　More delicate Thou than any other meat,
From all things else how gladly will I fast:
　　—The tongue, the palate that of Thee shall eat,
With fragrant milk and honey are solaced:
　　Then quench all other loves, and with the heat
　　　　Of all Thy fervours let my spirit shine.

Lord Jesu, give a fervent love of Thee
　　To him who sings this story of Thy might ;
And whilst on this low earth his path must be,
　　Rule Thou his life in purity most white ;
And after, peace and solace let him see,
　　And in Th wisdom let him take delight,
　　　　And evey reign with Thee, True Love Divine.

DE LA DIVERSITÁ DE CONTEMPLAZIONE
DE CROCE

(LAUDA LXXV)

— Fuggo la croce che me devora,
la sua calura non posso portare.

Non posso portare sí grande calore
che getta la croce, fuggendo vo amore ;
non trovo loco, ca porto nel core
la remembranza me fa consumare.

— Frate, co fuggi la sua delettanza ?
io vo chirendo la sua amistanza ;
parme che facci grande vilanza
de gir fugendo lo suo delettare.

— Frate, io fuggo, ché io son ferito ;
venuto m'è 'l colpo, e 'l cor m'ha partito ;
non par che senti de quel c'ho sentito,
però non par che ne sacci parlare.

— Frate, io sí trovo la croce fiorita,
de soi pensieri me sono vestita,
non ce trovai ancora ferita,
'nante m'è gioia lo suo delettare.

OF DIFFERENCES IN THE CONTEMPLATION OF THE CROSS

(A Dialogue between two Brothers in Religion)

(LAUDA LXXV)

(First Brother speaks)

I FLEE the Cross that doth my heart devour,
I cannot bear its ardour and its power.

I cannot bear this great and dreadful heat;
Far from the Cross, from Love, on flying feet
I haste away; my heart at every beat
    Consumes me with that burning memory.

(Second Brother)

Brother, why dost thou flee from this delight?
This is the joy I yearn for, day and night:
Brother, this is but weakness in my sight,
    To flee from joy and peace so cravenly.

(First Brother)

Brother, I flee, for I am wounded sore,
My heart is pierced and sundered to the core;
—Thou hast not felt the anguish that I bore,
    Else wouldst thou speak in other words to me.

(Second Brother)

Brother, I find the Cross all garlanded,
And with its blossoms do I wreathe my head;
It wounds me not;—nay, I am comforted;
    The Cross is all delight and joy to me.

— Ed io la trovo piena de sagitte
ch'escon del lato ; nel cor me son fitte,
el balestrier en ver me l'ha diritte,
on arme ch'aggio me fa perforare.

— Io era cieco ed or veggio luce,
questo m'avenne per sguardo de cruce ;
ella me guida, ché gaio m'aduce,
e senza lei son en tormentare.

— E me la luce sí m'ha acecato ;
tanto lustrore de lei me fo dato,
che me fa gire co abacinato,
c'ha li bel occhi e non pote mirare.

— Io posso parlar, ché stato so muto,
e questo ella croce sí m'è apparuto ;
tanto de lei sí aggio sentuto,
ch'a molta gente ne pos predicare.

— E me fatt'ha muto che fui parlatore,
en sí grande abisso entrat'è el mio core,
ch'io non trovo quasi auditore
con chi ne possa de ciò ragionare.

— Io era morto ed or aggio vita,
e questo e la croce sí m'è apparita ;
parme esser morto de la partita
ed aggio vita nel suo demorare.

(*First Brother*)

I find it full of arrows sharp, that dart
Forth from its side: they reach, they pierce my heart!
The Archer aims His shafts that tear and smart;
    And through my armour He hath wounded me.

(*Second Brother*)

I once was blind, but now I see the light;
Gazing upon the Cross I found my sight.
Beneath the Cross my soul is glad and bright;
    Far from the Cross, I am in misery.

(*First Brother*)

Not so with me: this Light hath made me blind!
So fierce the lustre that around me shined,
My head is giddy, and confused my mind,
    Mine eyes are dazzled that I cannot see.

(*Second Brother*)

Now can I speak, I that was once so dumb;
'Tis from the Cross that all my powers come;
Yea, by that Cross, of Thought and Love the Sum,
    Now can I preach to men full potently.

(*First Brother*)

The Cross hath made me dumb, who spoke so well;
In such a deep abyss my heart doth dwell,
I cannot speak, and nothing can I tell;
    And none can understand nor talk with me.

(*Second Brother*)

Lo, I was dead, and now new life is mine,
Life that was given me by the Cross Divine:
Yea, parted from the Cross, in death I pine,
    Its Presence gives me all vitality.

— Ed io non so morto, ma faccio el tratto,
e Dio lo volesse ch' el fosse ratto!
star sempremai en estremo fatto
e non poterme mai liberare!

— Frate, la croce m'è delettamento,
nollo dir mai ch'en lei sia tormento ;
forsa non èi al suo giognemento
che tu la vogli per sposa abracciare.

— Tu stai al caldo, ma io sto nel fuoco ;
a te è diletto, ma io tutto cuoco ;
con la fornace trovar non pò loco,
se non c'èi entrato non sai quegn'è stare.

— Frate, tu parli che io non t'entendo,
como l'amore gir vòi fugendo,
questo tuo stato verria conoscendo
se tu el me potessi en cuore splanare.

— Frate, el tuo stato è en sapor de gusto,
ma io c'ho bevuto, portar non pò el musto,
non aggio cerchio che sia tanto tusto
che la fortura non faccia alentare.

(*First Brother*)

I am not dead, but dying day by day,
Would God that I were dead and passed away!
Eternally I struggle, gasp, and pray,—
 And nothing that I do can set me free.

(*Second Brother*)

Brother, to me the Cross is all delight ;
Beneath it dwells no torment nor affright:
Perchance thou hast not felt that Union's might,
 Nor that Embrace, that clasps so tenderly?

(*First Brother*)

Ah, thou art warmed ; but I am in the Fire:
Thine the delight, and mine the flaming Pyre ;
I cannot breathe within this furnace dire!
 Thou hast not entered There, It burns not thee.

(*Second Brother*)

Brother, thy words I cannot understand:
Why dost thou flee from gentle Love's demand?
Tell me thy state, and let me take thy hand,
 The while I listen to this mystery!

(*First Brother*)

Brother, thou breath'st the perfume of the Wine;
But I have drunk It, and no strength of mine
Can bear the onslaught of that Must Divine,
 That ruthless, ceaseth not to torture me!

COMO L'ANIMA SE LAMENTA CON DIO DE LA
CARITÁ SUPERARDENTE IN LEI INFUSA

(LAUDA XC)

AMOR de caritate,
perché m'hai sí ferito?
lo cor tutt'ho partito
ed arde per amore. ·

Arde ed incende, nullo trova loco,
non può fugir però ched è legato,
sí se consuma como cera a foco ;
vivendo more, languisce stemperato,
demanda de poter fugire um poco,
ed en fornace tròvase locato ;
oimè, do' so menato?
A sí forte languire?
Vivendo sí, è morire,
tanto monta l'ardore!

'Nante che el provasse, demandava
amare Cristo, credendo dolzura ;
en pace de dolceza star pensava,
for d'ogni pena possedendo altura ;
pruovo tormento qual non me cuitava,
che 'l cor se me fendesse per calura ;
non posso dar figura
de que veggio sembianza,
ché moio en delettanza
e vivo senza core.

Aggio perduto el core e senno tutto,
voglia e piacere e tutto sentimento,

HOW THE SOUL COMPLAINS TO GOD OF THE OVER-ARDENT LOVE INFUSED IN HER

(LAUDA XC)

LOVE, that art Charity,
Why hast Thou hurt me so?
My heart is smote in two,
And burns with ardent love.

Glowing and flaming, refuge finding none,
  My heart is fettered fast, it cannot flee;
It is consumed, like wax set in the sun;
  Living, yet dying, swooning passionately,
It prays for strength a little way to run,
  Yet in this furnace must it bide and be:
  Where am I led, ah me!
    To depths so high?
    Living I die,
  So fierce the fire of Love.

Before I knew its power, I asked in prayer
  For love of Christ, believing it was sweet;
I thought to breathe a calm and tranquil air,
  On peaceful heights, where tempests never beat.
Torment I find, instead of sweetness there!
  My heart is riven by the dreadful heat:
  Of these strange things to treat
    All words are vain;
    By bliss I am slain,
  And yet I live and move.

For I have lost my heart, my will, my wit,
  My hopes, desires, my pleasures and my taste;

onne belleza me par loto brutto,
delize con riccheze perdimento ;
un arbore d'amor con grande frutto,
en cor piantato, me dá pascimento,
che fe' tal mutamento
en me senza demora,
gettando tutto fòra,
voglia, senno e vigore.

Per comperar amor tutto aggio dato,
lo mondo e mene, tutto per baratto ;
se tutto fosse mio quel ch'è creato,
daríalo per amor senza onne patto ;
e trovome d'amor quasi engannato,
ché, tutto dato, non so dove so tratto ;
per amor so desfatto,
pazo sí so tenuto;
ma, perché so venduto,
de me non ho valore.

Credeame la gente revocare,
amici che me fuoro, d'esta via ;
ma chi è dato piú non se può dare,
né servo far che fugga signoria ;
prima la pietra porríase amollare
ch'amor che me tien en sua bailia ;
tutta la voglia mia
d'amor si è enfocata,
unita, trasformata :
chi tollerá l'amore ?

Fuoco né ferro non li può partire,
non se divide cosa tanto unita ;
pena né morte giá non può salire
a quella alteza dove sta rapita ;
sotto sé vede tutte cose gire

Beauty seems vile, corruption crawls on it,
　Riches, delights and honours all are waste:
—A Tree of Love, with fruits both fair and fit
　To feed me, in my heart is rooted fast,
　It flings away in haste
　　　All it can find,
　　　Will, strength, and mind:
　With Love in vain I strove.

All that I had, to purchase Love I gave,
　Yea, all myself, and the whole world in fee;
And had Creation been all mine to have,
　For Love would I have given it willingly:
Now Love hath tricked and caught me, woful slave;
　Emptied of all, I know not where I be;
　Yea, Love hath ruined me,
　　　All crazed my thought;
　　　I am sold for naught,
　Beggared and stript by Love.

My friends, who loved me, called me oft away,
　Far from this bitter path, this arid track;
But how can kingship sink to serfdom? nay—
　Who gives himself hath given, and takes not back.
Marble may sooner melt and turn to clay,
　Than Love, my Jailer, loose me from His rack;
　My Will, a broken wrack,
　　　Love hath ignited,
　　　Transformed, united;
　Who can endure Thee, Love?

Now are we one, we are not separate;
　Fire cannot part us, nor a sword divide;
Not pain nor death can reach these heights so great
　Where Love hath snatched and set me by His side:
Far, far below, I see the worlds gyrate,

ed essa sopra tutte sta gradita ;
alma, co se' salita
a posseder tal bene ?
Cristo, da cui te vene,
abraccial con dolzore.

Giá non posso vedere creatura,
al Creatore grida tutta mente ;
cielo né terra non me dá dolzura,
per Cristo amore tutto m'è fetente ;
luce de sole sí me pare oscura,
vedendo quella faccia resplendente,
cherubin son niente,
belli per ensegnare,
serafin per amare,
chi vede lo Signore.

Nullo donqua ormai piú me reprenda
se tale amore me fa pazo gire,
giá non è core che piú se defenda
d'amor sí preso che possa fugire ;
pensi ciasuno co el cor non se fenda,
cotal fornace co possa patire ;
s'io potesse envenire
alma che m'entendesse
e de me cordoglio avesse,
ché se strugge lo core!

Ché cielo e terra grida e sempre chiama,
e tutte cose ch'io sí deggia amare ;
ciascuna dice con tutto cuor :— Ama
l'amor c'ha fatto briga d'abracciare ;
ché quello amore, però che te abrama,
tutti noi ha fatti per ad sé trare ;
veggio tanto arversare
bontade e cortesia
de quella luce pia
che se spande de fuore.—

Far, far above, my heart is satisfied:
My soul, who is thy Guide
    To this strange bliss?
    'Tis Jesu's kiss,
All sweetness far above.

Now on no creature can I turn my sight,
    But on my Maker all my mind is set;
Earth, sea, and sky are emptied of delight,
    For Christ's dear love all else I clean forget:
All else seems vile, day seems as dark as night;
    Cherubim, seraphim, in whom are met
    Wisdom and Love, must yet
        Give place, give place,
        To that One Face
    To my dear Lord of Love.

Therefore let none reprove me evermore,
    If Love so wondrous craze me utterly;
How can my heart withstand these onslaughts sore?
    Besieged and taken thus, how can I flee?
My heart must break; think, friends, what pains it bore!
    Can I endure this furnace patiently?
    All you who list to me,
        And pity take,
        Your hearts would ache,
    If I my woes could prove.

For heaven and earth and all things else do cry,
    That Love is all my task, my life, my place;
Their heartfelt voices cry aloud—" Draw nigh!
    The Love that made thee, hasten to embrace!
That Love that thirsts for thee eternally,
    Commands us, to His arms thy soul to chase;
    He pours His light and grace,
        And courtesy,
        All, all on thee,
    In spreading streams of Love!"

Amare voglio piú, se piú potesse,
ma, co piú ami, lo cor giá non trova ;
piú che me dare con ciò cche volesse
non posso, questo è certo senza prova ;
tutto l'ho dato perché possedesse
quel amador che tanto me renova ;
belleza antiqua e nova,
da poi che t'ho trovata,
o luce smesurata
de sí dolce splendore!

Vedendo tal belleza, sí so tratto
de for de me, non so dove portato ;
lo cor se strugge como cera sfatto,
de Cristo se retrova figurato ;
giá non si trova mai sí gran baratto :
vestirse Cristo, tutto sé spogliato ;
lo cor sí trasformato
amor grida che sente,
anegace la mente,
tanto sente dolzore!

Ligata sí la mente con dolceza,
tutta se destende ad abracciare ;
e, quanto piú reguarda la belleza
de Cristo, fnor de sé piú fa gettare
en Cristo tutta possa con riccheza ;
de sé memoria nulla può servare,
ormai a sé piú dare
voglia nulla né cura,
né può perder valura
de sé onne sentore.

En Cristo trasformata, quasi è Cristo ;
con Dio gionta tutta sta divina ;
sopr'onne altura è sí grande acquisto
de Cristo e tutto lo suo star regina ;
or donqua co potesse star piú tristo

More would I love, if more were possible ;
   Yet can I give no more than all my heart ;
I give my all,—my life, my soul, my will,
   Nor needs it proof that all is more than part.
I give Thee all, O Lover Terrible,—
   Take all, fresh life for ever to impart ;
   So old, so new, Thou art;
      Yea, I have found Thee,
      Soft light around Thee,
   And whiter than the Dove.

Gazing on Thee, Thou Bright and Morning Star,
   I am led far, I know not where I be ;
My heart is melted like a waxen bar,
   That moulded in Christ's likeness it may be ;
O Christ, Thy barters keen and wondrous are!
   I am stript naked, to be drest in Thee:
   My heart transformed in me,
      My mind lies dumb,
      To see Thee come,
   In sweetness and in Love.

So linkèd with that sweetness is my mind,
   It leans and strains, its Lover to embrace:
And all in Him, and naught in self to find,
   It learns, by gazing ever on His face.
Riches, and powers, and memories strong to bind,
   It casts away, as burdens in the race ;
   It hath no resting-place,
      No will, no care ;
      It mounts the stair,
   Towards which its being strove.

In Christ transformed, almost my soul is Christ;
   Conjoined with God, all, all is now divine,
So great, so high, its marvellous acquist,—
   —Possessing, Jesu, all that once was Thine:
Nor need I now, set free from mortal mist,

2 A

de colpa demandando medicina
nulla c'è piú sentina;
dove trovi peccato,
lo vecchio m'è mozato,
purgato onne fetore.

En Cristo è nata nova creatura,
spogliato lo vechio, om fatto novello;
ma tanto l'amor monta con ardura,
lo cor par che se fenda con coltello,
mente con senno tolle tal calura,
Cristo me tra' tutto, tanto è bello!
Abracciome con ello
e per amor sí chiamo:
— Amor, cui tanto bramo,
famme morir d'amore! —

Per te, amor, consumome languendo,
e vo stridendo per te abracciare;
quando te parti, si moio vivendo,
sospiro e piango per te retrovare;
e, retornando, el cor se va stendendo,
ch'en te se possa tutto trasformare;
donqua, piú non tardare:
Amor, or me soviene,
ligato sí me tiene,
consumame lo core!

Resguarda, dolce amor, la pena mia!
tanto calore non posso patire;
l'amor m'ha preso, non so do' me sia,
que faccio o dico non posso sentire;
como stordito sí vo per la via,
spesso trangoscio per forte languire;
non so co sofferire
possa tal tormento,
emperò non me sento
che m'ha secco lo core.

Ask medicine for the guilt that once was mine;
No more in grief I pine,
    My sinful soul
    Is purged and whole,
Yea, it is cleansed and shrove.

Now, a new creature, I in Christ am born,
    The old man stripped away ;—I am new-made;
And mounting in me, like the sun at morn,
    Love breaks my heart, even as a broken blade:
Christ, First and Only Fair, from me hath shorn
    My will, my wits, and all that in me stayed,
    I in His arms am laid,
        I cry and call,—
        " O Thou my All,
    O let me die of Love! "

For Thee, O Love, my heart consumes away,
    I cry, I call, I yearn for Thy caress ;
Living, I perish when Thou dost not stay,
    Sighing and mourning for my Blessedness:
Dost Thou return, I strain and strive and pray,
    To lose amidst Thine All my Nothingness:
    Then tarry not to bless,
        Love, think on me ;
        Bind me to Thee,
    Consume my heart with Love!

O Love most gentle, look upon my pain,
    How can I suffer all Thy dreadful heat?
All crazed I am, close fettered by Love's chain,
    I know not what I say, nor Whom I greet:
Fevered, amazed, to wander I am fain,
    In anguish oft, and dragging weary feet ;
    I have no strength to meet
        This torment's tide ;
        My heart is dried,
    And like an empty glove.

Cor m'è furato, non posso vedere
que deggia fare o que spesso faccia ;
e, chi me vede, dice che vol sapere
amor senza atto se a te, Cristo, piaccia ;
se non te piace, que posso valere ?
de tal mesura la mente m'alaccia
l'amor che sí m'abraccia,   .
tolleme lo parlare,
volere ed operare,
perdo tutto sentore.

Sappi parlare, ora so fatto muto ;
vedea, mò so cieco deventato ;
sí grande abisso non fo mai veduto:
tacendo parlo, fugo e so legato,
scendendo salgo, tengo e so tenuto,
de fuor so dentro, caccio e so cacciato ;
amor esmesurato,
perché me fai empazire,
en fornace morire
de sí forte calore ?

Ordena questo amore, tu che m'ami,
non è virtute senza ordene trovata,
poiché trovare tanto tu m'abrami,
ca mente con virtute è renovata
a me amare, voglio che tu chiami
la caritate qual sia ordenata ;
arbore sí è provata
per l'ordene del frutto
el quale demostra tutto
de onne cosa el valore.

— Tutte le cose qual aggio ordenate
sí so fatte con numero e mesura,
ed al lor fine son tutte ordenate
conservanse per orden tal valura,
e molto piú ancora caritate

My wits are stolen away: I cannot grasp
  What things I ought to do, or may have done;
The world, a-wonder, deems I strive to clasp
  Love bodiless, if Christ but lead me on :
If not, my joy were but a venomous asp ;
  My mind, entangled, loseth all it won,
  Yea, Love hath left me none
        Of all my skill,
        My speed, my will ;
      He taketh all for Love.

I once could speak, but now my lips are dumb ;
  My eyes are blind, although I once could see:
In this abyss my soul is stark and numb,
  Silent, I speak ; cling, yet am held by Thee:
Falling, I rise ; I go, and yet I come:
  Pursue, and am pursued ; I am bound yet free ;
  O Love that whelmeth me!
        Maddened I cry:
        "Why must I die,
      Thy fiery strength to prove ? "

(*Christ speaks*)
Order this love, O thou who lovest Me,
  For without order virtue comes to naught ;
And since thou seekest Me so ardently,
  —That virtue may be ruler in thy thought
And in thy love—summon that charity
  Whose fervours are by gentle Order taught :
  A tree to proof is brought
        By ordered fruit ;
        Bole, branch, and root,
      All thrive in Order's grove.

For see, with number and with measure fit,
  All things I have ordered in this world that are:
From end to end fair Order ruleth it,
  That all may move in peace, and not in war ;
Then should not Love in ordered sweetness sit ?

sí è ordenata nella sua natura.
Donqua co per calura,
alma, tu se' empazita?
For d'orden tu se' uscita,
non t'è freno el fervore.

— Cristo, che lo core sí m'hai furato,
dici che ad amor ordini la mente,
come da poi ch'en te sí so mutato
de me remasta, fusse convenente?
Si com'è ferro ch'é tutto enfocato,
aurora da sole fatta relucente,
de lor forma perdente
son per altra figura,
cusi la mente pura
de te è vestita, amore.

Ma, da che perde la sua qualitate,
non può la cosa da sé operare;
como formata sí ha potestate,
opera con frutto sí puote fare;
donqua si è transformata en veritate
en te sol, Cristo, che se' dolce amare;
a te si può imputare
non a me quel che faccio;
però, se non te piaccio,
tu a te non piaci, amore.

Questo ben sacci che, s'io so empazito,
tu, somma sapienzia, sí el m'hai fatto;
e questo fo da che io fui ferito
e quando con l'amor feci baratto,
che, me spogliando, fui de te vestito,
ad nova vita non so co fui tratto;
de me tutto desfatto
or so per amor forte,
rotte sí son le porte
e giaccio teco, amore.

Love, of her nature stedfast as a star?—
This frenzy sore doth mar
    Thy fervours, Soul,
    And brings thee dole;
  Thou hast not reined thy love.

(*The Soul answers*)
Christ, Who hast stolen my heart, Thou biddest me
  In order fair my trembling mind to set;
But am I still mine own, though one with Thee?
  —Never was such a bargain driven yet!
As skies at sunrise, shining lucently,
  Or iron that the piercing flame hath met,
  Their native form forget,
    In wondrous change,
    —So I, O strange!
  Am dipped and clothed in Love.

So, when a soul its self-hood quite hath lost,
  Of its own will no action can it take;
Of all its deeds that Power must pay the cost
  Who hath re-made it, and doth still re-make;
Then, if my soul upon Thy bridge hath crossed,
  O Christ, from Self's false dream in Thee to wake,
  I do all for Thy sake,
    And if Thou rue
    Aught that I do,
  'Tis Thine own doing, Love.

And this I tell Thee, Love, if I be crazed,
  Thou, Wisdom's self it is, that crazeth me:
'Twas Thou that pierced me, Thou on Whom I gazed,
  The bargain that we made is all my plea:
On that new life I entered, all amazed,
  Stript of myself, to be enwrapt in Thee;
  Undone, from self I flee;
    Strong for Thy sake,
    The doors I break,
  And reach Thy breast, O Love!

Ad tal fornace perché me menavi,
se volevi ch'io fossi en temperanza?
Quando sí smesurato me te davi,
tollevi da me tutta mesuranza;
poi che picciolello me bastavi,
tenerte grande non aggio possanza;
onde, se c'è fallanza,
amor, tua è, non mia,
però che questa via
tu la facesti, amore.

Tu da l'amore non te defendesti,
de cielo en terra fecete venire;
amore, ad tal basseza descendesti
co omo despetto per lo mondo gire;
casa né terra giá non ce volesti,
tal povertate per noi arricchire
la vita e nel morire
mostrasti per certanza
amor de smesuranza
ch'ardea nello core.

Como per lo mondo spesso andavi,
l'amor sí te menava co venduto;
en tutte cose, amor, sempre mostravi
de te quasi niente perceputo,
che stando nello tempio sí gridavi:
— Ad bever venga chi ha sostenuto,
sete d'amor ha 'vuto,
ché gli dirá donato
amore smesurato
qual pasce con dolzore. —

Tu, sapienzia, non te contenesti
che l'amor tuo spesso non versasse,
d'amor non de carne tua nascesti,
umanato amor che ne salvasse;
per abracciarne en croce tu salesti,

Why didst Thou lead me to this bed of fire,
  If Thou wouldst have me calm and temperate?
Thou giv'st Thyself, Thyself, to my desire!
  And so my transports never can abate:
To clasp Thee little, Love, I did aspire,
  How can I bear it when I clasp Thee great?
    If this a fault Thou rate,
      The fault is Thine,
      Beloved, not mine,
    Thou mad'st my path, O Love.

Thyself from Love Thy Heart didst not defend,
  From Heaven to earth it brought Thee from Thy
    throne;
Beloved, to what sheer depths didst Thou descend,
  To dwell with man, unhonoured and unknown:
In life and death to enrich us without end,
  Homeless and poor, with nothing of Thine own,
    Thou here didst come alone,
      For Thou wert called
      By Love unwalled,
    That all Thy heart did move.

—And as about the world Thy feet did go,
  'Twas Love that led Thee, always, everywhere;
Thy only joy, for us Thy love to show,
  And for Thyself no whit at all to care;
Thou, in the Temple standing, calledst " Ho!
  All ye who thirst, come hither; come and share
  The living waters fair;
    For I will give
    To all who live
  Unending draughts of Love! "

O Deepest Wisdom, counting all things dross,
  Save love of us, so wretched and forlorn;
O Love Incarnate, counting gain for loss,
  Sharing our life, yet of the Spirit born;
Uplifted to embrace us on the Cross,

e credo che perció tu non parlasse,
né te amor scusasse
davanti da Pilato
per compier tal mercato
en croce de l'amore.

La sapienza, veggio, se celava,
solo l'amore se potea vedere ;
e la potenza giá non se mostrava,
che era la virtute en dispiacere ;
grande era quel amor che se versava,
altro che amor non potendo avere,
né l'uso nel volere,
amor sempre legando
en croce ed abracciando
l'omo con tanto amore.

Donqua, Iesú, s'io so sí enamorato,
enebriato per sí gran dolceza,
ché me reprendi s'io vo empazato,
ed onne senno perdo con forteza ?
Poi che l'amore te sí ha legato,
quasi privato d'ogne tua grandeza,
co seria mai forteza
en me di contradire,
ch'io non voglia empazire
per abracciarte, amore ?

Ché quel amore che me fa empazire
a te par che tollesse sapienza,
e quel amor che sí me fa languire,
a te per me sí tolse la potenza ;
non voglio ormai né posso sofferire,
d'amor so preso, non faccio retenza,
daramme la sentenza
che io d'amor sia morto,
giá non voglio conforto
se non morire, amore.

Love spared Thee not, Thy hands with nails were torn,
Enduring Pilate's scorn,
  That dreadful Day,
  Our debt to pay,
 Upon Thy Cross of Love!

For see, how Wisdom hid herself away,
 And Love alone was to our vision plain :
Omnipotence sate shrouded on that Day,
 When strength and power were turned to bitter pain;
No gift but Love upon that Altar lay,
 Love, that for us was spent, for us was slain ;
 Custom and will were vain ;
  Love, crucified,
  Fettered and tied,
 Embraced mankind for Love.

Then, Jesu, if I be inebriate,
 Enamoured of Thy sweetness and Thy woe,
From all reproach I stand inviolate,
 Though foolish and distracted I should grow ;
Thou too wert bound by Love, Who was so great,
 That He was strong to bring Thy greatness low;
 Nor would I scatheless go,
  Though all amazed,
  My wits be dazed,
 With Thy caress, O Love.

For that same Love, that drives me all distraught,
 Took all Thy wisdom, Lord, away from Thee ;
That Love, that dips in languor all my thought,
 Destroyed Thy powers too, and all for me:
And I will keep back nothing ; I am caught
 By Love Himself: I yield, I would not flee ;
 O let my sentence be
  For Love to die,
  No succour nigh,
 O grant me death, my Love!

Amore, amore che sí m'hai ferito,
altro che amore non posso gridare ;
amore, amore, teco so unito,
altro non posso che te abracciare ;
amore, amore, forte m'hai rapito,
lo cor sempre se spande per amare ;
per te voglio pasmare,
amor, ch'io teco sia,
amor, per cortesia,
famme morir d'amore.

Amor, amor, Iesú, so gionto a porto,
amor, amor, Iesú, tu m'hai menato ;
amor, amor, Iesú, damme conforto,
amor, amor, Iesú, sí m'hai enflammato ;
amor, amor, Iesú, pensa lo porto,
fammete star, amor, sempre abracciato,
con teco trasformato
en vera caritate,
en somma veritate
de trasformato amore.

Amor, amore grida tutto 'l mondo,
amor, amore, onne cosa clama ;
amore, amore, tanto se' profondo,
chi piú t'abraccia sempre piú t'abrama.
Amor, amor tu se' cerchio rotondo,
con tutto 'l cor chi c'entra sempre t'ama,
ché tu se' stame e trama
chi t'ama per vestire,
cusi dolce sentire,
che sempre grida amore.

Amore, amore, tanto tu me fai,
amor, amore, nol posso patire ;
amor, amore, tanto me te dái,
amor, amore, ben credo morire ;

Love, Love, of naught but Love my tongue can sing,
  Thy wounded Hand hath pierced my heart so deep:
Love, Love, with Thee made one, to Thee I cling,
  Upon Thy breast, my Jesu, let me sleep;
Love, Love, with love my heart is perishing;
  Love, like an Eagle snatching me Thy sheep,
  For Thee I swoon, I weep,
      Love, let me be,
      By courtesy,
  Thine own in death, O Love!

Love, Love, O Jesu, I have reached the goal,
  Love, Love, O Jesu, whither Thou hast led;
Love, Love, O Jesu, comfort Thou my soul,
  Love, Love, O Jesu, on her fiery bed.
Love, Love, O Jesu, Thou Who art my Goal,
  O set Thy gentle hands about my head!
  To Thee my soul is wed,
      In Love most sure,
      In Truth most pure,
  In Thy transforming Love.

Love, Love, O Love, the world's wild voices cry,
  Love, Love, O Love, the clamorous echoes spread;
Love, Love, O Love, so deep Thy treasures lie,
  We hunger more, the more we taste Thy bread:
Love, Love, O Love, Thou Circling Mystery,
  Who enters Thee at Love's deep heart is fed;
  Thou'rt Loom, and Cloth, and Thread:
      O sweet to be
      Clad all in Thee,
  And ceaseless chant of Love.

Love, Love, O Love, Thy touch so quickens me,
  Love, Love, O Love, I am no longer I:
Love, Love, O Love, Thyself so utterly
  Thou giv'st me, Jesu, that I can but die.

amor, amore, tanto preso m'hai,
amor, amor, famme en te transire;
amor, dolce languire,
amor mio desioso,
amor mio delettoso,
anegame en amore.

Amor, amor, lo cor sí me se speza,
amor, amore, tal sento ferita ;
amor, amor, tramme la tua belleza,
amor, amor, per te sí so rapita ;
amor, amore, vivere despreza,
amor, amor, l'alma teco è unita ;
amor, tu se' sua vita:
giá non se può partire;
perché lo fai languire
tanto stregnendo, amore ?

Amor, amor, Iesú desideroso,
amor, voglio morire te abracciando ;
amor, amor, Iesú, dolce mio sposo,
amor, amor, la morte t'ademando ;
amor, amor, Iesú sí delettoso,
tu me t'arendi en te transformando,
pensa ch'io vo pasmando,
Amor, non so o' me sia,
Iesú, speranza mia,
abissame en amore.

O Love, O Love, I am possessed of Thee,
  Love, Love, my Love, O take me in a sigh!
Love, glad and spent I lie.
    O Love, my Bliss!
    O Lover's Kiss!
    O quench my soul in Love!

Love, Love, my heart is broken in its pride,
  Love, Thou hast hurt me, I am wounded sore:
Love, Love, Thy beauty draws me to Thy side,
  Love, Thou hast ravished me for evermore:
O Love, despised and scorned let me abide,
  Love, Love, my soul hath entered at Thy door;
  O Love, my Sea, my Shore!
    No more we part:
    Why bind my heart
In cords so ruthless, Love?

Love, Love, my Jesu, O my heart's Desire!
  Love, Love, within Thine arms to die were sweet:
Jesu, my Love, I climb the Bridal Pyre,
  Love, Love, among the flames my Spouse to meet.
O Jesu, Lover, Husband, Tempest, Fire!
  Take me, transform me in Thine utmost heat:
Visions around me fleet:
    I swoon, I grope:
    Jesu, my Heart, my Hope,
    O shatter me in Love!

DE LA IMPAZIENZIA CHE FA TUTTI LI BENI PERDERE

(LAUDA XXVIII)

Assai me sforzo a guadagnare
se 'l sapesse conservare.

Relioso sí so stato,
longo tempo ho procacciato ;
ed aiolo sí conservato,
che nulla ne pos mostrare.

Stato so en lezione,
esforzato en orazione,
mal soffrir a la stagione
ed al pover satisfare.

Stato so en obedenza,
povertate e sofferenza ;
castetate abbe en placenza
secondo 'l pover mio afare.

E molta fame sostenía,
freddo e caldo soffería ;
peregrino e longa via
assai m'è paruto andare.

Assai me lievo a matutino
ad officio divino,
terza e nona e vespertino
po' compieta sto a veghiare.

OF IMPATIENCE, WHICH BRINGS ALL OUR GAINS TO NOTHING

(LAUDA XXVIII)

I LABOURED long, I strove with might and main:
    And yet I cannot keep the good I gain.

Yea, I have been a monk full many a year,
Have suffered much, and wandered far and near,
Have sought and found,—yet held not,—till I fear
    That nothing can I show for all my pain.

In calm retreats my truest joy I found;
I strove in prayer, with no uncertain sound:
I fed the poor for many miles around:
    In sickness, very patient have I lain.

In uttermost obedience did I dwell,
In suffering and poverty as well;
Yea, I was chaste and happy in my cell,
    So far as my poor powers could attain.

Famished and weak, I fasted many a day;
Dried up by heat and pinched by cold I lay;
I was a pilgrim on a weary way,
    Or so it seemed, in sunshine and in rain.

To pray, I daily rose before the sun;
Mass did I hear before the dark was done;
To tierce and nones and vespers would I run,
    And, after compline, still to watch was fain.

2 B

E vil cosa me sia ditta,
al cor passa la saitta ;
e la lengua mia sta ritta
ad voler fuoco gettare.

Or vedete el guadagnato,
co so ricco ed adagiato!
ch'un parlar m'ha sí turbato
ch'a pena posso perdonare.

And then was said to me a scornful word!
—Deep in my heart the poisoned arrow stirred,—
At once my tongue was ready when I heard,
   With fierce and burning fury to complain.

Now see how great and wealthy I must be!
I heap my gains for all the world to see ;
Yet one poor word so fiercely angers me,
   That I must strive to pardon it in vain!

ESORTAZIONE A L'ANIMA PROPRIA CHE, CONSIDERATA LA SUA NOBILITÁ, NON TARDI LA VIA A L'AMOR DIVINO

(LAUDA XXXV)

O ANIMA mia
creata gentile,
non te far vile
enchinar tuo coragio,
ch'en gran baronagio
è posto el tuo stato.

Se om poveretto
gioietta te dona,
la mente sta prona
a darli el tuo core ;
con gran disio
de lui se ragiona,
con vile zona
te lega d'amore ;
el gran Signore
da te è pelegrino,
fatt'ha 'l camino
per te molto amaro ;
o core avaro,
starai piú endurato ?

Se re de Francia
avesse figliola
ed ella sola
en sua redetate,
giria adornata
de bianca stola,

EXHORTATION TO HIS OWN SOUL, THAT, CON-SIDERING HER GREAT NOBILITY, SHE SHOULD NOT DELAY TO TAKE THE WAY OF DIVINE LOVE

(LAUDA XXXV)

O SOUL of mine, how noble wert thou made!
Be not afraid,
    Nor deem thy natúre low:
    Thou art not so,
High is thy birth, and lordly thine estate.

If a poor man a gift to thee should bring,
Thy heart would cling
    To him, and there abide,
With love and gratitude unfaltering ;
—So slight a thing
    Would bind thee to his side.
    —Thy Lord, thy Guide,
Makes pilgrimage for thee,
Treads painfully
    His toilsome path alone:
    O heart of stone!
        To stand thus obdurate.

The King of France might have a daughter fair,
His only Heir,
    His pride and his delight.
The fame of her would travel everywhere,
Gems would she wear,

sua fama vola
en omne contrate ;
s'ella en viltate
entendesse, en malsano,
e désseise en mano
a sé possedere,
que porría om dire
de questo trattato?

Piú vile cosa
è quello c'hai fatto :
darte 'ntransatto
al mondo fallente :
lo corpo per servo
te fo dato atto,
ha' 'l fatto matto
per te dolente ;
signor negligente
fa servo regnare
e sé dominare
en rea signoria ;
hai presa via
ca questo c'è entrato.

Lo tuo contato
en quinto è partito :
veder, gusto, udito,
odorato e tatto ;
al corpo non basta
che 'l tuo vestito
lo mondo ha dimplito
tutto ad ha fatto ;
ponam questo atto :
veder bella cosa ;
l'udir non ha posa,
né l'occhio pasciuto
en quarto frauduto
qual vòi te sia dato.

And robes of spotless white.
But should she plight
Her troth, in marriage base,
Her tender grace
    To infamy betray,
    —What should men say
      Of bonds so profligate?

The thing that thou hast done is worse than this,
—To clasp and kiss
    The treacherous world abhorred!
Thy body, that thy humble servant is,
Thou'st used amiss,
    Given him the ruler's sword.
    Ah, careless lord,
To set a slave to reign!
—So doth he gain
    A lordship criminal:
    And to this thrall
      'Tis thou hast oped the gate.

Thy kingdom of five parts is composite;
—Hearing and Sight,
    And Taste, and Touch, and Scent.
This Body, that the world hath ruled outright,
Resents her plight,
    Restless in discontent.
    Her gaze is bent
To seek the Beautiful;
Naught else can lull
      Her ear, nor feed her eye:
      Earth's fragments die,
        Her makeshifts come too late.

El mondo non basta
a l'occhio vedere,
che possa empire
la sua smesuranza ;
se mille i ne mostri,
faralo enfamire,
tant'è 'l sitire
de sua desianza ;
lor delettanza
sottratto en tormento
reman lo talento
fraudato en tutto ;
placer rieca lutto
al cor desensato.

Lo mondo non basta
a li toi vasalli ;
parme che falli
de dargli el tuo core ;
per satisfare
a li toi castalli,
mori en travalli
a gran dolore ;
retorna al core
de que viverai ;
tre regni c'hai,
per tuo defetto
moron negetto,
lor cibo occultato.

Tu se' creata
en sí grande alteza,
en gran gentileza
è tua natura ;
se vedi e pensi
la tua belleza,
starai en forteza

This World sufficeth not thine Eye to feed,
Because her need
    Must still be measureless.
She of a thousand Worlds would take no heed,
—So strange her greed,
    So deep her thirstiness.
    The World's caress
  Is turned to torment so:
  The mind must go
    Defrauded of her gain ;
    Joy becomes pain,
     The heart to penetrate.

This World feeds not thy senses, nor thy mind,
Nor canst thou bind
    Thy heart in her control.
Joy for these vassals if thou strive to find,
That task will grind
    Thy struggling, suffering soul.
    Then seek thy goal
  There, where thy heart must be ;
  Thy kingdoms three
    Now lie, though once so fair,
    All parched and bare,
     Famished and desolate.

So high and in such honour wert thou born,
Thy nature's morn
    Awaked in gentlehood.
Ponder the grace and beauty thou hast worn,
So shalt thou scorn

servandote pura ;
ca creatura
nulla è creata
che sia adornata
d'aver lo tuo amore ;
solo al Signore
s'affá el parentato.

Se a lo specchio
te voli vedere,
porrai sentire
la tua delicanza ;
en te porti forma
de Dio gran Sire ;
ben pòi gaudire,
c'hai sua simiglianza ;
o smesuranza
en breve redutta :
cielo terra tutta
veder en un vascello ;
o vaso bello,
co mal se' trattato !

Tu non hai vita
en cose create,
en altre contrate
t'è opo alitare ;
salire a Dio
che è redetate,
che tua povertate
pò satisfare ;
or non tardare
la via tua a l'amore ;
se li dái el tuo core,
datese en patto
se el suo entrasatto
è 'n tuo redetato.

All else, with fortitude.
Naught here is good—
No creature fair enough ;
No earthly stuff
    Deserves thy heart's desire ;
    God is thy Sire,
      To Him be consecrate.

Look in thy mirror for a little space,
And thou shalt trace
    Thy delicate beauty there.
Thou bear'st thy Father's image on thy face:
O joy! O grace!
    His likeness thus to wear!
    The Eternal Fair,
Poured in thy little cup,
Floats trembling up,
    —There Earth and Heaven meet.
    O Vessel sweet!
      So spoiled, so desecrate!

Thou art not nourished by created things;
Thy nature's wings
    To other realms must fly.
Thou art God's heir,—towards Him thy being
    springs,
His largess brings
    Wealth to thy poverty ;
    Pause not, nor sigh ;
Swift on Love's journey start:
Give Him thy heart,
    And let the pact be fair ;
    —Thou art His Heir,
      —Lay hold on thine Estate.

O amor caro,
che tutto te dái
ed omnia trai
en tuo possedere,
grande è l'onore
che a Dio fai
quando en lui stai
en tuo gentilire ;
che porría om dire :
Dio n'empazao,
se comparao
cotal derata,
ch'è sí esmesurata
en suo dominato.

O Love, thou givest all, and for Love's sake
All dost thou take,
    To have and hold for aye.
Ah, to thy God great honour dost thou make,
All to forsake,
    To find in Him thy Way!
    —What should man say?
E'en God were sure unwise,
If when He buys
    This treasure fathomless,
    He should give less,
        Bargain or hesitate.

COMO LI ANGELI SI MARAVIGLIANO DE LA PEREGRINAZIONE DE CRISTO NEL MONDO

(LAUDA XLI)

— O CRISTO onnipotente,
ove sete enviato?
perché poveramente
gite pelegrinato?

— Una sposa pigliai
che dato gli ho 'l mio core;
de gioie l'adornai
per averne onore;
lassòme a descionore,
famme gire penato.

Io sí l'adornai
de gioie e d'onoranza,
mia forma l'assignai
a la mia simiglianza;
hame fatta fallanza,
famme gire penato.

Io glie donai memoria
ne lo mio piacemento,
de la celeste gloria
glie diei lo 'ntendemento,
e voluntá en centro
nel core gli ho miniato.

HOW THE ANGELS ARE AMAZED AT CHRIST'S PILGRIMAGE IN THIS WORLD

(LAUDA XLI)

(*Angels speak*)
> O JESUS CHRIST Omnipotent
> Where are Thy footsteps wandering?
> Why art Thou thus a pilgrim sent,
> In poverty and suffering?

(*Christ speaks*)
> I took a young and gentle bride,
> And gave My heart into her care;
> I decked her, for My joy and pride,
> With jewels very bright and fair:
> —She left Me in dishonour there,
> And I must wander sorrowing.

> With beauty and with reverence
> I decked her out so lovingly,
> That on her tender innocence
> My likeness blossomed visibly;
> —Yet now her heart is false to Me,
> And I must wander sorrowing.

> I gave her Memory, pure and clear,
> To be of Love the guide and chart;
> And Understanding, bringing near
> Celestial glory's lore and art:
> And in the centre of her heart
> I blazoned Will, all-conquering.

Puoi glie donai la fede
ch'adempie entendanza,
a memoria diede
la verace speranza,
e caritate amanza
al voler ordenato.

A ciò che l'esercizio
avesse compimento,
lo corpo per servizio
diéglie per ornamento ;
bello fo lo stromento,
se non l'avesse scordato.

Acciò ch'ella avesse
en que esercitare,
tutte le creature
per lei volse creare ;
donde me deve amare,
hame guerra menato.

A ciò ch'ella sapesse
como sé esercitare,
de le quattro virtute
sí la volsi vestire ;
per lo suo gran fallire
con tutte ha adulterato.

— Signor, se la trovamo
e vole retornare,
voli che li dicamo
che gli vol perdonare,
ché la possam retrare
del pessimo suo stato ?

And after that, I gave her Faith,
　　Her Understanding to fulfil ;
And Hope I gave, that knows not death,
　　To teach and mould her Memory's skill ;
　　And to her sweet and ordered Will
　　　I gave her Love, long-suffering.

And that her energies might have
　　Their organs and their complement,
For service and delight I gave
　　Her body for an ornament :
　　And lovely was the instrument,
　　　If discords had not wrenched the string.

Her thirst for life and joy to slake,
　　Her energies to task and train,
I made all creatures for her sake,
　　That she might use them or refrain ;
　　—The love she owes I ask in vain ;—
　　　She wars on me in everything.

To let her heart and conscience know
　　How best their skill to exercise,
I wrapped and clothed her, pure as snow,
　　In the four Virtues' draperies.
　　—By her adulterous treacheries,
　　　She makes of each an outcast thing.

(*Angels speak*)
　　Dear Lord, if we can find Thy bride,
　　　And if she will return to Thee,
　　O may we tell her, Thou wilt guide
　　　And pardon her most tenderly ?
　　　That we may snatch her from the sea
　　　　Of sin where she is perishing ?

2 C

— Dicete a la mia sposa
che deggia revenire ;
tal morte dolorosa
non me faccia patire ;
per lei voglio morire,
sí ne so enamorato.

Con grande piacemento
facciogli perdonanza,
rendogli l'ornamento,
donoglie mia amistanza ;
de tutta sua fallanza
sí me serò scordato.

— O alma peccatrice,
sposa del gran marito,
co iaci en esta fece
lo tuo volto polito ?
co se' da lui fugito
tanto amor t'ha portato ?

— Pensando nel suo amore
sí so morta e confusa ;
poseme en grande onore,
or en que so retrusa !
O morte dolorusa,
co m'hai circundato !

— O peccatrice engrata,
retorna al tuo Signore,
non esser desperata
ca per te muor d'amore ;
pensa nel suo dolore
co l'hai d'amor piagato.

(*Christ*)
    Yea, find and hold My love, and say
        That she must hear Me, and return ;
    Nor make Me suffer, day by day,
        A death so dolorous and dern ;
        For her I die, for her I burn,
          My love is so unreasoning!

    I shall rejoice, if she repents,
        To pardon freely all her debt ;
    To give her back her ornaments,
        My friendship round her path to set,
        And all her frailty to forget,
          That once so sore My heart did wring.

(*Angels*)
    O wandering and sinful soul,
        Bride of a Husband fair and great,
    How canst thou soil in dregs so foul
        Thy face that was immaculate?
        How canst thou flee in fear and hate,
          From Love so deep, so mastering?

(*The Soul*)
    Ah, when upon His love I think,
        I am confused, I die with shame:
    He gave me grace and joy to drink,
        And see the mire to which I came!
        O dolorous death, undying flame,
          That clips me in a fiery ring!

(*Angels*)
    O erring and ungrateful soul,
        Go back to thy dear Lord again:
    Be hopeful in thy bitter dole,
        Nor let Him die for thee in vain.
        His heart is pierced by thy disdain:
          —O think upon His suffering!

— Io aggio tanto offeso,
forsa non m'arvorría;
aggiol morto e conquiso;
trista la vita mia!
Non saccio ove me sia,
sí m'ha d'amor legato.

— Non aver dubitanza
de la recezione;
non far piú demoranza,
non hai nulla cagione;
clame tua entenzione
con pianto amaricato.

— O Cristo pietoso,
ove te trovo, amore?
Non esser piú nascoso,
ché moio a gran dolore;
chi vide el mio Signore?
narrel chi l'ha trovato.

— O alma, noi el trovammo
su nella croce appiso;
morto lo ce lassamo
tutto battuto e alliso;
per te a morir s'è miso,
caro t'ha comparato!

— Ed io comenzo el corrotto
d'un acuto dolore:
amore, e chi t'ha morto?
se' morto per mio amore;
o enebriato amore,
ov'hai Cristo empicato?

(The Soul)
   Nay, I have given such deep offence,
     Perchance He will not take me back ;
   I wounded Him and drove Him hence ;
     My life is turned to woe and wrack!
     I see no pathway and no track ;
      For Love hath bound me shuddering!

(Angels)
   Doubt not, nor pause upon thy way,
     He will receive thee, and will hear.
   O tarry not, nor make delay!
     Thou hast no cause to doubt or fear.
     Call on His name, cry out, draw near,
      With bitter plaint and clamouring.

(The Soul)
   O ruthful Christ, where art Thou fled?
     Where shall I find Thee, Love most fair?
   Hide not away Thy lovely Head ;
     I die of sorrow and despair.
     O who hath seen my Lord, and where?
      Tell me where He is tarrying!

(Angels)
   O soul, we found Him where He hangs,
     Nailed high upon the Cross is He ;
   Forsaken in His mortal pangs,
     Scourged and tormented cruelly,
     He tastes of death, and all for thee!
      —For thou wast dear in purchasing!

(The Soul)
   The bitter grief that must be mine,
     Exhales in tears and sobbing breath:
   O what hath slain Thee, Love Divine?
     For love of me He perisheth!
     O Love, Inebriate in death,
      Where hast thou hung my Lord and King?

DE LA INCARNAZIONE DEL VERBO DIVINO

(LAUDA C)

FIORITO è Cristo nella carne pura,
or se ralegri l'umana natura.

Natura umana, quanto eri scurata,
ch'al secco ficno tu eri arsimigliata!
Ma lo tuo sposo t'ha renovellata,
or non sie ingrata
de tale amadore.

Tal amador è fior de puritade,
nato nel campo de verginitade,
egli è lo giglio de l'umanitade,
de suavitate
e de perfetto odore.

Odor divino da ciel n'ha recato,
da quel giardino lá ove era piantato,
esso Dio dal Padre beato
ce fo mandato
conserto de fiore.

Fior de Nazzareth si fece chiamare,
de la Giesse Virgo vuols pullulare,
nel tempo del fior se volse mostrare,
per confermare
lo suo grande amore.

Amore immenso e caritá infinita
m'ha demostrato Cristo, la mia vita ;
prese umanitate in deitá unita,
gioia compita
n'aggio e grande onore.

OF THE INCARNATION OF THE DIVINE WORD

(LAUDA C)

REJOICE, O Human Nature! Christ hath flowered
From virgin flesh, in purity embowered.

O Human Nature, dark and poor and low,
Like withered grass, a-droop for Death to mow,
Thy Bridegroom lifts thee up from sin and woe;
Then bloom and grow,
    And thank thy Love and Lord.

Thy Lord and Love, the Flower of Purity,
Born in the field of fair Virginity,
He is the Lily of Humanity,
All sweetness He,
    All fragrant and adored.

Adored the fragrance that from Heaven He bore,
Heaven, the fair garden where He bloomed of yore;
Yea, God the Father sent Him through this Door,
Wreathed o'er and o'er,
    And twined with many a flower.

A Flower of Nazareth was first His Name,
Who from the Rod of Jesse blooming came,
Springing in time of flowers; and all his aim
Love, like a flame,
    Upon mankind to shower.

To shower His Charity most infinite:
This have I seen in Christ, that is my Light;
Mankind to God He draws, and doth unite,
And all delight
    He gives, and all reward.

Onor con umilitá volse recepere,
con solennitá la turba fe' venire,
la via e la cittade refiorire
tutta, e reverire
lui como Signore.

Signor venerato con gran reverenza,
poi condannato de grave sentenza,
popolo mutato senza providenza,
per molta amenza
cadesti in errore.

Error prendesti contra veritade
quando lo facesti viola de viltade,
la rosa rossa de penalitate
per caritade
remutò el colore.

Color natural ch'avea de bellezza
molta in viltade prese lividezza,
con suavitade portò amarezza,
tornò in bassezza
·lo suo gran valore.

Valor potente fo umiliato,
quel fiore aulente tra piè conculcato,
de spine pungente tutto circundato,
e fo velato
lo grande splendore.

Splendor che illustra onne tenebroso,
fo oscurato per dolor penoso,
e lo suo lume tutto fo renchioso
en un sepolcro
nell'orto del fiore.

Lo fior reposto giacque e sí dormio,
renacque tosto e resurressío,
beato corpo e puro refiorío
ed apparío
con grande fulgore.

Reward He doth receive with lowliness,
The people come with pomp, His name to bless,
City and wayside wear a flowery dress,
All, all confess
    And greet Him as their Lord.

Their Lord He is, they give Him reverence,
Yet when He is condemned, for none offence,
The changeful populace would drive Him hence,
With no defence,
    Such blindness holds their sight.

Their sight is veiled, the Truth they will not see ;
The crimson rose of suffering Charity,
Empurpled by their cruel blows must be,
Its hues must flee,
    And lose their colours bright.

Colours so bright and fair, that Nature gave,
Are now brought low, made livid as the grave,
And yet that pain He bears, most sweet, most brave,
Nor seeks to save
    His valour and His might.

His might and strength are all humiliate ;
That fragrant Flower is crushed and desolate ;
Encircled by the pungent thorns of hate,
His splendour's state
    Is dimmed and veiled in night.

In night is drowned that Splendour of the Day,
While suffering holds her melancholy sway ;
And in a sepulchre is hid away
The Light, the Way,
    Hid in a flowery place.

A place wherein that Flower may sleep and rest,
And rise again, re-born from Darkness' breast,
In bodily form and bodily pureness drest,
The Visible Blest,
    In radiance and in grace.

Fulgore ameno appario nell'orto
a Magdalena che 'l piangea morto,
e del gran pianto donògli conforto,
sí che fo absorto
l'amoroso core.

Lo core confortò agli suoi fratelli,
e resuscitò molti fior novelli,
e demorò nello giardin con elli,
con quelli agnelli
cantando d'amore.

Con amor reformasti Tomaso non credente,
quando li mostrasti li tuoi fiori aulente,
quali reservasti, o rosa rubente,
sí che incontinente
gridò con fervore.

Fervore amoroso ebbe inebriato,
lo cor gioioso fo esilarato;
quando glorioso t'ebbe contemplato,
allora t'ebbe vocato
Dio e signore.

Signor de gloria sopra al ciel salisti,
con voce sonora degli angeli ascendesti,
con segni di vittoria al Padre redisti,
e resedisti
in sedia ad onore.

Onor ne donasti a servi veraci,
la via demostrasti a li tuoi sequaci,
lo spirito mandasti acciò che infiammati
fussero i sequaci
con perfetto ardore.

Grace, radiance, in that garden did He shed,
Upon the Magdalen, who mourned Him dead;
And in her sorrow she was comforted,
Her love was fed,
    Her tender heart consoled.

Consoled the hearts of His disciples too,
And from their grief fresh flowers of love He drew;
There in the Garden, with His servants true,
His sheep He knew;
    They sing as they behold!

Behold, e'en doubting Thomas didst Thou gain,
Showing Thy wounds, sweet flowers without a stain,
He gazed, O blushing Rose, and gazed again;
And he was fain
    To cry out fervently.

Fervently loving, all inebriate,
His heart was joyous and exhilarate,
And gazing on Thy Glory Uncreate,
He knew Thee straight,
    His God, His Lord to be.

To be the King of Glory in the skies,
Back to Thy Father, crowned with victories,
Hailed by the sound of angels' harmonies,
Thou didst arise
    In Honour's Seat to sit.

To sit, and share Thine honour with Thine own,
Who follow in the Way that Thou hast shown;
To send Thy Fiery Spirit streaming down,
Their hearts to crown
    With ardours infinite.

CANTICO DE LA NATIVITÁ DE IESÚ CRISTO

(LAUDA LXIV)

O novo canto,
c'hai morto el pianto
de l'uomo enfermato.

Sopre el « fa » acuto
me pare emparuto
che 'l canto se pona ;
e nel « fa » grave
descende suave
che 'l verbo resona.
Cotal desciso
non fo mai viso
sí ben concordato.

Li cantatori
iubilatori
che tengon lo coro,
son gli angeli santi,
che fanno li canti
al diversoro,
davante 'l fantino,
che 'l Verbo divino
ce veggio encarnato.

Audito è un canto :
« Gloria en alto
a l'altissimo Dio ;
e pace en terra,
ch'è strutta la guerra
ed onne rio ;
onde laudate
e benedicete
Cristo adorato! »

SONG OF THE NATIVITY OF JESUS CHRIST

(LAUDA LXIV)

O NEW Song, of heavenly strain,
Man's lamenting Thou hast slain,
  Raised him from his misery.

In a piercing major key,
Yet with soft timidity,
  Sweetest singing charms the ear ;
Now ensues a minor strain,
Gently floating down again,
  Sweeter still, and still more clear.
Such a descant, pure and keen,
Never sure was heard or seen,
  So divine in harmony.

And the Singers, glad and fair,
Making in the wintry air,
  Strains so sweet, and so sonorous,
—Ah, the blessèd Angels they,
Chanting thus in parts their lay,
  Singing in a varied chorus,
To the Babe, th' Incarnate Word ;
And the little Babe hath heard,
  Lovely in His Infancy.

Music fills the midnight sky
" Glory be to God on high! "
  Say the voices resonant.
" And on earth there shall be peace,
" Strife shall die and wars shall cease,
  All the world be jubilant! "
Then together let us sing,
Laud and honour to our King,
  Christ, adored and blest is He.

En carta ainina
la nota divina
veggio ch'è scritta,
lá 'v'è 'l nostro canto
ritto e renfranto
a chi ben ci afitta;
e Dio è lo scrivano
c'ha 'perta la mano,
che 'l canto ha ensegnato.

Loco se canta
chi ben se n'amanta
de fede formata;
divinitate
en sua maiestate
ce vede encarnata;
onde esce speranza
che dá baldanza
al cor ch'é levato.

Canto d'amore
ce trova a tutt'ore
chi ce sa entrare;
con Dio se conforma
e prende la norma
del bel desiare;
co serafino,
deventa divino
d'amor enflammato.

El primo notturno
è dato a lo sturno
de martirizati:
Stefano è 'l primo,
che canta sublimo
con soi acompagnati,
ch'on posta la vita,
en Cristo l'ò insita
ch'è fior de granato.

On an earthly parchment writ
Is this music infinite,
   Blazoned firm, and fair, and clear.
We who stand on earth-bound feet,
We may claim this music sweet,
   If we listen, we may hear.
God's own hand the scroll hath given,
For He writes the notes in heaven,
   Teacheth us the melody.—

There, where Love the heart hath stirred,
There that singing shall be heard,
   Faith shall hear it and shall know.
For God's great Divinity,
In its wondrous Majesty,
   Is incarnate here below.
Hence comes Hope, both fair and true,
Lifts our hearts to God anew,
   Gives us courage joyously.

He that enters at this door,
He shall hear for evermore,
   Songs of love within his heart:
To God's image he aspires,
Of the Beauty he desires,
   He shall now become a part.
Like the heavenly seraphim,
Love shall flame so high in him,
   He shall gain divinity.

Hark! the first nocturn is given
To the valiant troop from heaven,
   To the noble martyr band:
Stephen singing at their head,
Risen from his stony bed,
   And his comrades round him stand.
Jesus Christ their life doth give,
Grafted in His Stem they live,
   Red Pomegranate flower is He.

El secondo sequente
è dato a la gente
de li confessori;
lo Vangelista
la lengua ci ha mista
ch'adorna li cori;
ché nullo con canto
volò tanto ad alto
si ben consonato.

El terzo sequente
a li innocenti
par che se dia;
ché col Garzone
ad ogne stagione
so en sua compagnia:
« Te Dio laudamo,
con voce cantamo,
ché Cristo oggi è nato! »

O peccatori,
ch'a li mal signori
avete servito,
venite a cantare
che Dio pò om trovare,
ch'en terra è apparito
en forma de garzone,
e tiello en prigione
chi l'ha desiato.

Uomini errati,
che site vocati
a penetenza,
la quale onne errore
ve tolle dal core,
e dá entellegenza
da veritade
per pietade
a chi è umiliato;

The Confessors following,
Do the second nocturn sing,
   On their voices it is borne;
And the great Evangelist,
He must be their rhapsodist,
   For His words their notes adorn,
Treble notes, and clearer far
This their strain, than others are,—
   Rare it is in harmony.

Next the Innocents are heard,
For their nocturn is the third;
   Sweetly do they take their part.
They around the Holy Child,
Ages-long have knelt and smiled,
   Sweet companions for His Heart.
" Christ is born," their voices say;
" Jesus Christ is born to-day,
   Praise, O God, we sing to Thee! "

O ye sinners, erring throng,
Serving evil lords so long,
   Come and hail this Infant Birth!
Come, and make a joyful sound;
God with Man henceforth is found,
   He is come to dwell on earth.
As a Little Boy He's here;
Long-desired, we hold Him dear;
   Very precious shall He be.

Erring men, on evil bent,
He hath called you to repent,
   Come to Him in penitence.
Penitence your hearts shall stay,
Driving every sin away,
   Purging heart, and soul, and sense.
Verily the humble mind
Penitent, the truth shall find,
   Blessedness and piety.

2 D

uomini iusti,
che sete endusti,
venite a cantare,
ché sete envitati,
a Dio vocati
a gloriare,
a regno celesto,
che compie onne festo
che 'l core ha bramato,

Humble men, and innocent,
Upright men, and diligent,
   Come before Him, come and sing.
Let Him not in vain entreat,
Come and kneel before His feet,
   Giving glory to your King.
Ye shall have your hearts' desire,
Tasting, with the heavenly choir,
   Feasts of Love eternally.

DE LA SANTA POVERTÁ E SUO TRIPLICE CIELO

(LAUDA LX)

O AMOR de povertate,
regno de tranquillitate!

Povertate, via secura,
non ha lite né rancura,
de latron non ha paura
né de nulla tempestate.

Povertate muore en pace,
nullo testamento face,
lassa el mondo como iace
e le gente concordate.

Non ha iudece né notaro,
a corte non porta salaro,
ridese de l'uomo avaro
che sta en tanta ansietate.

Povertá, alto sapere,
a nulla cosa soiacere,
en desprezo possedere
tutte le cose create.

Chi despreza si possede,
possedendo non se lede,
nulla cosa i piglia 'l pede
che non faccia sue giornate.

Chi desia è posseduto,
a quel ch'ama s'é venduto;
s'egli pensa que n'ha 'vuto,
han' avute rei derrate.

OF HOLY POVERTY, AND HER THREEFOLD HEAVEN

(LAUDA LX)

O Love of Holy Poverty!
Thou kingdom of Tranquillity!

Poverty, whose path is safe and clear,
Hath no griefs, nor rancour, sheds no tear,
Nor of robber hands hath any fear,
 Tempests cannot trouble Poverty.

Poverty can die in perfect peace ;
Maketh neither will, nor bond, nor lease,
Leaves the world behind, and lies at ease,
 And around her strife can never be.

Needs no judge, nor scribe, nor lawyer sort,
Brings no fees to notary nor court,
And can turn the miser into sport,
 Who is ever in anxiety.

Poverty, High Wisdom deep and sure,
Unsubdued by earth and earthly lure,
Scorns created things, detached and pure,
 Scorning, yet possessing utterly.

Who despiseth, surely doth possess,
Owning all things without bitterness,
—Nothing trips him up, his feet can press
 On their daily journey faithfully.

He whose wants are master, is a slave,
Sells himself for what his longings crave,
Him his purchased riches cannot save,
 He hath bargained very foolishly.

Tropo so de vil coragio
ad entrar en vasallagio,
simiglianza de Dio ch'agio
deturparla en vanitate.

Dio non alberga en core stretto,
tant'è grande quant'hai affetto,
povertate ha si gran petto,
che ci alberga deitate.

Povertate è ciel celato
a chi en terra è ottenebrato ;
chi nel terzo ciel su è 'ntrato,
ode arcana profunditate.

El primo ciel è 'l fermamento,
d'onne onore spogliamento,
grande porge empedimento
ad envenir securitate.

A far l'onor en te morire,
le ricchezze fa sbandire,
la scienzia tacere
e fugir fama de santitate.

La richeza el tempo tolle,
la scienzia en vento estolle,
la fama alberga ed acolle
l'ipocresia d'onne contrate.

Pareme cielo stellato
chi da questi tre è spogliato.
ècce un altro ciel velato:
acque chiare solidate.

Quattro venti move 'l mare
che la mente fon turbare,
lo temere e lo sperare,
el dolere e 'l gaudiare.

Mortal courage sure must hesitate,
Shrink and turn from such a vassal state,
Where God's image, beautiful and great,
   Is debased, and changed to vanity.

In a narrow heart God cannot bide;
Where the love is great, the heart is wide;
Poverty, great-hearted, dignified,
   Entertains and welcomes Deity.

Poverty is highest Heaven revealed,
—Yet to darkened souls on earth concealed:
Those who reach this Third Heaven read, unsealed,
   Every deep and hidden mystery.

And the first Heaven is the Firmament,
Pride and glory there are past and spent,
Are but hindrance and impediment
   To the soul that seeks security.

That thy glory and thy pride may die,
Give to all earth's riches the go-by;
Bid all learning dead and silent lie;
   Flee from all repute of sanctity.

Riches will but steal thy time away;
Learning vanish like the winds at play;
Fame will nurse and nourish, day by day,
   Every form of vile hypocrisy.

Steadfast in the Stellar Heaven is he
Who hath rid his being of these three;
Then another Heaven shall he see,
   Crystalline, of highest purity.

Four great winds upon man's sea that blow
Waste his mind with constant ebb and flow;
Hope and Fear, that ceaseless come and go;
   Joy, and Grief, that vary endlessly.

Queste quattro spogliature
piú che le prime so dure ;
se le dico, par errure
a chi non ha capacitate.

De lo 'nferno non temere
é del ciel spem non avere ;
e de nullo ben gaudere
e non doler d'aversitate.

La virtú non è perchene,
ca 'l perchene è for de tène ;
sempre encognito te tène
a curar tua enfermitate.

Se son nude le virtute
e le vizia son vestute,
mortale se don ferute,
caggio en terra vulnerate.

Puoi le vizia son morte,
le virtute son resorte
confortate de la corte
d'onne empassibilitate.

Lo terzo ciel è de piú altura,
non ha termen né mesura,
fuor de la magenatura
fantasie mortificate.

Da onne ben sí t'ha spogliato
e de virtute spropriato,
tesaurizi el tuo mercato
en tua propria vilitate.

Questo cielo è fabricato,
en un nihil è fondato,
o' l'amor purificato
vive nella veritate.

And these four his soul shall strip and spoil,
Worse than wealth, or fame, or learning's toil;
This is truth, that error cannot soil,
  Though the foolish will not credit me.

Even deepest Hell thou must not fear;
Hopes of Heaven must never charm thine ear;
No delight must rouse thy heart, nor cheer;
  No distress must cause thee misery.

Virtue cannot be by causes bought,
Incorruptible, she comes unsought;
All unknown and veiled, her power hath brought
  Healing to thy deep infirmity.

If the virtues all are bare and nude,
And the vices clothed, an evil brood,
In the mortal strife 'twixt ill and good,
  Borne to earth and wounded must thou be.

When the vices are destroyed and dead,
Every virtue lifts a lovely head,
By divinest banquet comforted,
  Raised to God's Unchangeability.

This Third Heaven is highest and most fair;
Limit, no, nor measure enters there;
Man's imagination must despair,—
  So doth it transcend his fantasy.

Emptied when thou art of Good and Right,
Dispossest of Virtue and Delight,
Prize that bargain, clasp thy treasure tight,
  In thy lowness and humility:

—For this Heaven is built and 'stablished fast,
In the Nothingness where First is Last,
Where Pure Love, whence all alloy hath past,
  Dwelleth with Eternal Verity.

Ciò che te pare non é,
tanto è alto quello che è,
la superbia en cielo se'
e dannase l'umilitate.

Entra la vertute e l'atto
molti ci ode al ioco « matto »,
tal se pensa aver buon patto
che sta en terra alienate.

Questo cielo ha nome none,
moza lengua entenzione,
o' l'amor sta en pregione
en quelle luce ottenebrate.

Omne luce è tenebria,
ed omne tenebre c'è dia,
la nova filosofia
gli utri vechi ha dissipate.

Lá 've Cristo è ensetato,
tutto lo vechio n'è mozato,
l'un ne l'altro trasformato
en mirabile unitate.

Vive amor senza affetto
e saper senza entelletto,
lo voler de Dio eletto
a far la sua volontate.

Viver io e non io,
e l'esser mio non esser mio,
questo è un tal trasversío,
che non so diffinitate.

Povertate è nulla avere
e nulla cosa poi volere ;
ed omne cosa possedere
en spirito de libertate.

What thou seest is not What is There,
That which Is, is high beyond compare,
Pride must faint upon that heavenly air,
  Melt and die into humility.

For between the Visible and Real,
Strangest transports do man's reason steal,
Happy they, this deepest truth who feel,
  Crazed on earth they are content to be.

And this Heaven, the Nought, is deep and strange,
Far beyond our tongue's faint stammering range,
Love is prisoned there, and cannot change,
  In that Light, to us Obscurity.

Light is Darkness in that wondrous state,
Darkness is the Dawn for which we wait,
This new wine shall break and dissipate
  The old bottles of philosophy.

Ah! where Christ is grafted on the spray,
All the withered wood is cut away;
See the freshness springing from decay!
  Changing to a wondrous Unity,—

Love, that lives and breathes without Desire;
Wisdom, freed from Thought's consuming fire;
Will, at one with God, that doth aspire
  But to obey Him in simplicity.

Lo, I live! yet not my self alone ;
I am I, yet am I not mine own ;
And this change, cross-wise, obscure, unknown,
  —Language cannot tell its mystery.

Poverty has nothing in her hand,
Nothing craves, in sea, or sky, or land:
Hath the Universe at her command!
  Dwelling in the heart of Liberty.

EPISTOLA A CELESTINO PAPA QUINTO, CHIAMATO PRIMA PETRO DA MORRONE

(LAUDA LIV)

Que farai, Pier da Morrone?
èi venuto al paragone.

Vederimo el lavorato
che en cella hai contemplato;
se 'l mondo de te è 'ngannato,
sèquita maledizione.

La tua fama alt'è salita,
en molte parte n'è gita;
se te sozzi a la finita,
agl buon sirai confusione.

Como segno a sagitta,
tutto 'l mondo a te affitta;
se non tien bilanza ritta,
a Dio ne va appellazione.

Se se' auro, ferro o rame
proveráte en esto esame;
quegn'hai filo, lana o stame
mostreráte en est'azone.

Questa corte è una fucina
che 'l buon auro se ci afina;
se llo tiene altra ramina,
torna en cenere e carbone.

Se l'officio te deletta,
nulla malsania piú è 'nfetta;
e ben è vita maledetta
perder Dio per tal boccone.

EPISTLE TO POPE CELESTINE V., FORMERLY CALLED PETRO DA MORRONE

(LAUDA LIV)

PIERO DA MORRON', what wilt thou do?
Thou art brought to trial and touchstone too.

We shall see, perchance, at last achieved
What within thy cell thy heart believed:
If in thee the world should be deceived,
    Maledictions deep will follow thee.

Very high and noble is thy fame,
Far and wide the folk revere thy name;
If at last thou soil thyself with shame,
    Strange confusion must the righteous see.

As a mark for arrows is thy state,
All the world is watching for thy fate;
If thou dost not hold the balance straight,
    From thy rule to God appeal shall be.

By this test thy metal shall be told,
Be it copper, iron, or pure gold;
Be thou thread, or fleece, or cloth—behold!
    Now thine acts shall tell us certainly.

'Tis a forge, this court, to try thy mind,
In its fires pure gold shall be refined;
—Nought but ashes will be left behind,
    If from dross thy metal be not free.

If in office thou shouldst take delight,
Evil will infect thee with its blight,
And a heavy curse thy life shall smite,
    Losing God, for bribes of empery.

Grande ho aúto en te cordoglio
co te uscio de bocca:— Voglio;—
ché t'hai posto iogo en coglio
che t'è tua dannazione.

Quando l'uomo virtuoso
è posto en luoco tempestoso,
sempre el trovi vigoroso
a portar ritto el gonfalone.

Grand'è la tua degnitate,
non è meno la tempestate;
grand'è la varietate
che troverai en tua magione.

Se non hai amor paterno,
lo mondo non girá obedenno;
ch'amor bastardo non è denno
d'aver tal prelazione.

Amor bastardo ha 'l pagamento
de sotto dal fermamento;
ché 'l suo falso entendemento
de sopre ha fatto sbandegione.

L'ordene cardenalato
posto è en basso stato;
ciaschedun suo parentato
d'ariccar ha entenzione.

Guárdate dagl prebendate
che sempre i trovera' afamate;
e tant'è la lor siccitate;
che non ne va per potagione.

Guárdate dagl barattere
che 'l ner per bianco fon vedere;
se non te sai ben schirmere
canterai mala canzone.

Anxious grief for thee my heart did fill,
When thou didst pronounce the words,—" I will! "
Lest that yoke should damn thy soul to ill,
　　Laid upon thy neck thus heavily.

When the virtuous man, whose heart is sound,
To a hard and storm-tost task is bound,
Vigorous and faithful is he found,
　　He will bear his banner steadfastly.

Great thy rank and great thy worthiness,
But the tempest round thee is no less,
And within thy mansion, questionless,
　　Thou shalt find most strange variety.

If a father's love thou dost not feel,
Never will the world obedient kneel ;
Bastard love is empty and unreal,
　　All unworthy of thy prelacy.

Bastard love knows naught of heavenly aid;
For with earthly coin that love is paid,
False of heart, deceitful and afraid,
　　Banished far from heavenly purity.

And the cardinals are fallen low,
In an evil course their longings flow,
Never one his kinsmen will forgo
　　To enrich them all by perfidy.

Of the prebends, too, thou must beware,
Great their hunger for unlawful fare,
Fierce their thirst, fierce even to despair,
　　For no draught can quench its cruelty.

And beware the cheats, who'd have thee think
Black is white, and white as black as ink ;
If, unguarded, in their snares thou sink,
　　Thou wilt sing thy song full evilly.

DEL PIANTO DE LA CHIESA REDUTTA
A MAL STATO

(LAUDA LIII)

P*i*ange la Ecclesia, piange e dolura,
sente fortura di pessimo stato.

— O nobilissima mamma, que piagni?
mostri che senti dolur molto magni;
narrame 'l modo perché tanto lagni,
ché sí duro pianto fai smesurato.

— Figlio, io si piango ché m'aggio anvito;
veggiome morto pate e marito;
figli, fratelli, nepoti ho smarrito,
omne mio amico è preso e legato.

So circundata da figli bastardi,
en omne mia pugna se mostran codardi,
li mei legitimi spade né dardi
lo lor coragio non era mutato.

Li mei legitimi era en concorda,
veggio i bastardi pien de discorda,
la gente enfedele me chiama la lorda
per lo reo exemplo ch'i'ho seminato.

Veggio esbandita la povertate,
nullo è che curi se non degnetate;
li mei legitimi en asperitate,
tutto lo mondo gli fo conculcato.

LAMENT OF THE CHURCH REDUCED TO EVIL STATE

(LAUDA LIII)

THE Church is weeping, weeping bitterly,
Feeling the torments of her evil state.

O Mother, noble Mother, wherefore weep?
Surely the sorrow of thy heart is deep;
Tell me the griefs that call thee from thy sleep,
    To anguish measureless and desolate?

(*The Church speaks*)
My son, good cause have I these tears to shed,
I see my Spouse, my Father, lying dead:
Sons, brothers, kinsmen, all alike are fled;
    My friends are prisoned and disconsolate.

Now none but bastard sons around me press,
False cowards, who desert me in my stress;
My true sons, in their fervent tenderness,
    Feared neither sword nor dart nor foeman's hate.

My true sons dwelt in peace and amity;
These bastard sons in wrath and discord be;
The faithless name me vile, because they see
    These evil growths I cannot extirpate.

Now holy Poverty they scorn and slay;
For pomp and place alone they strive and pray;
My true sons lived austerely, in their day,
    And trampled on the world, and world's estate.

2 E

Auro ed argento on rebandito,
fatt'on nemici con lor gran convito,
omne buon uso da loro è fugito,
donde el mio pianto con grande eiulato.

O' sono li patri pieni de fede?
nul è che curi per ella morire ;
la tepedeza m'ha preso ed occede,
el mio dolore non è corrottato.

O' son li profeti pien de speranza?
nul è che curi en mia vedovanza ;
presunzione presa ha baldanza,
tutto lo mondo po' lei s'é rizato.

O' son gli apostoli pien de fervore?
nul è che curi en lo mio dolore ;
uscito m'è scontra el proprio amore
e giá non veggio ch'egl sia contrastato.

O' son gli martiri pien de forteza?
non è chi curi en mia vedoveza ;
uscita m'è scontra l'agevoleza,
el mio fervore si è anichilato.

O' son li prelati iusti e ferventi,
che la lor vita sanava la gente?
uscit'è la pompa, grossura potente,
e sí nobel orden m'ha maculato.

O' son gli dottori pien de prudenza?
molti ne veggio saliti en scienza ;
ma la lor vita non m'ha convenenza,
dato m'on calci che 'l cor m'ha corato.

O religiosi en temperamento,
grande de voi avea piacemento ;
or vado cercando omne convento,
pochi ne trovo en cui sia consolato.

Silver and gold with ardour they have sought,
By pride and state, fierce enmity have bought ;
Have driven away all pious use and thought ;
    And therefore must I mourn my wretched fate.

Where are the Fathers, once so filled with faith ?
Not one to-day is steadfast unto death :
Lukewarm I grow, and faintly draw my breath,
    How can my sorrow soften or abate ?

Where are the Prophets, filled with hope and praise ?
Not one is left to cheer my widowed days ;
Now Impudence takes courage, and displays
    The whole world at his back, importunate.

And where are the Apostles, filled with zeal ?
Not one is left to hear my sad appeal ;
Self-love draws near, to ravage and to steal,
    And none steps forth, his fury to frustrate.

Where are the Martyrs, filled with fortitude ?
Not one is left to cheer my widowhood :
Softness and ease upon my strength intrude,
    And all my fervour is annihilate.

Where are the Prelates, just and vehement ?
To feed their flocks their ardent lives were spent :
False pomp and ostentation now are bent
    This noble order to attenuate.

Where are the Doctors, filled with wisdom's grace ?
Many I see, whose science grows apace,
Yet from their evil lives I veil my face ;
    They strike and pierce my heart unfortunate.

O ye Religious, whose austerities
In days gone by gave pleasure to mine eyes,
Vainly I seek a cloister whence arise
    The virtues that I love to contemplate.

O pace amara co m'hai si afflitta !
mentre fui en pugna si stetti dritta,
or lo riposo m'ha presa e sconfitta,
el blando dracone si m'ha venenato.

Nul è che venga al mio corrotto,
en ciascun stato si m'è Cristo morto ;
o vita mia, speranza e deporto,
en omne coraggio te veggio afocato!

O bitter peace, despair's ambassador!
I stood upright, the while I was at war:
Now ease destroys me, through my conqueror,
   —The flattering serpent's poisoned opiate!

Not one comes near to raise my drooping head;
In each condition, Christ our Lord is dead;
Thou, O my Life, my Joy, my Hope, art fled!
   In every heart I see Thee suffocate.

EPISTOLA A PAPA BONIFAZIO OTTAVO

(LAUDA LVI)

O PAPA Bonifazio,
io porto el tuo prefazio
e la maledizione
e scomunicazione.

Colla lengua forcuta
m'hai fatta sta feruta,
che colla lengua ligni
e la piaga me stigni.

Ché questa mia feruta
non può esser guaruta
per altra condizione
senza assoluzione.

Per grazia te peto
che me dichi:— Absolveto —
e l'altre pene me lassi
fin ch'io del mondo passi.

Puoi, se te vol provare
e meco esercitare,
non de questa materia,
ma d'altro modo prelia.

Se tu sai si schirmire
che me sacci ferire,
tengote bene esperto
se me fieri a scoperto.

EPISTLE TO POPE BONIFACE VIII

(LAUDA LVI)

O BON*I*FACE, who art the Pope,
Thy ban is heavy on my hope;
Thy malediction and thy hate
Have made me excommunicate.

Thy forky tongue, so like a snake's,
This wound upon my spirit makes:
There let thy tongue again be laid,
To staunch the hurt itself hath made.

None other power but thine can heal
This gaping wound I still must feel;
None other can my griefs dispel;
If thou absolve me, I am well.

By God's dear grace I humbly pray,
Speak but the words " Absolvo te ":
All else I'll bear with steadfast mind,
Until I leave the world behind.

If thou wouldst struggle with me still,
And set against me all thy will,
Take other weapons for the strife,
Turn not this sword against my life.

If thou so brilliantly wouldst fence,
And wound my dauntless innocence,
Unmatched indeed thy skill must be,
If thou canst pink me openly.

Ch'aio doi scudi a collo
e, se io non me li tollo,
per secula infinita
mai non temo ferita.

El primo scudo sinistro,
l'altro sede al diritto ;
lo sinistro scudato
lo diamante ha provato.

Nullo ferro ci aponta,
tanto c'è dura pronta !
Questo è l'odio mio,
ionto a l'onor di Dio.

Lo diritto scudone
d'una pietra en carbone,
ignita como fuoco
d'uno amoroso iuoco.

Lo prossimo en amore
d'uno enfocato ardore ;
se te vuoli fare enante,
puòlo provare 'nestante.

E, quanto vol, t'abrenca,
ch'io co l'amar non venca ;
volentiere te parlára,
credo che te iovára.

Vale, vale, vale,
Dio te tolla omne male,
e díelome per grazia
ch'io 'l porto en lieta facia.

Finisco lo trattato
en questo loco lassato.

For on my breast two shields I bear,
And whilst I hold them firm and fair,
I fear nor wound nor foeman's might,
Through all the ages infinite.

On my left shoulder one is hung,
The other from my right is swung ;
The left of adamant is made
Not to be pierced by keenest blade.

No sword can break its steely strength,
It baffles every thrust at length ;
From love of God, from strong self-scorn,
This flawless diamond shield is born.

The other shield, upon my right,
Shines with a brave and fiery light,
Of ruby is this buckler cut,
And flames of love therein are shut.

And that I love my neighbour well,
This ardent flaming shield must tell ;
Come, tilt, and try if either yields ;
Come to the fray and prove my shields!

Though fierce and sharp be thine attack,
By Love I'll beat thine onslaught back;
I'll speak to thee with right good will,
And gladly shalt thou listen still.

Farewell, farewell, farewell to thee!
From every ill God set thee free:
And may He grant me, by His grace,
My ills to bear with cheerful face.

Herewith I end my case
Abandoned in this place.

COMO L'ANIMA TROVA DIO IN TUTTE
CREATURE PER MEZO DE SENSI

(LAUDA LXXXII)

O AMOR, divino amore,
perché m'hai assediato?
Pare de me empazato,
non puoi de me posare.

Da cinque parte veggio
che m'hai assediato:
audito, viso, gusto,
tatto ed odorato;
se esco, so pigliato,
non me te pos' occultare.

Se io esco per lo viso,
ciò che veggio è amore,
en onne forma èi pento,
ed en onne colore;
represèntime allore
ch'io te deggia albergare.

Se esco per la porta
per posarme en audire,
lo sono e que significa?
Representa te, sire;
per essa non può useire
ciò cche odo è amare.

Se esco per lo gusto,
onne sapor te clama:
— Amor, divino amore,

HOW THE SOUL FINDS GOD IN ALL CREATURES
BY MEANS OF THE SENSES

(LAUDA LXXXII)

O Love Divine and Great,
 Why dost thou still besiege my heart?
Of me infatuate thou art,
 From me thou canst not rest!

My five engirdling battlements
 Are all besieged by Thee ;
The Ear, the Eye, Taste, Smell, and Touch,
 By Love, mine Enemy:
  If I come forth I cannot flee,
  Nor hide me from Thy quest.

If I come forth by way of Sight,
 Love, Love is all around ;
In radiance painted on the skies,
 In colour on the ground:
  They plead with me, in beauty drowned,
  To take Thee to my breast.

If I come forth by Hearing's gate,
 O what is this I hear?
What is this woven mist of sound
 That breaks upon mine ear?
  Here's no escape! Thy voice is clear,—
  'Tis Love, in music drest.

If I come forth by way of Taste,
 In savours Thou art set ;
That Love Divine, Who craves for me,

amor pieno de brama ;
amor preso m'hai a l'ama
per potere en me regnare. —

Se esco per la porta
che se chiama odorato,
en onne creatura
te ce trovo formato ;
retorno vulnerato,
prendime a l'odorare.

Se esco per la porta
che se chiama lo tatto,
en onne creatura
te ce trovo retratto ;
amor, e co so matto
de volerte mucciare ?

Amor, io vo fugendo
de non darte el mio core,
veggio che me trasformi
e faime essere amore,
si ch'io non son allore
e non me posso artrovare.

S'io veggio ad omo male
o defetto o tentato,
trasformome entro en lui
e face 'l mio cor penato ;
amore smesurato,
e chi hai preso ad amare ?

Prendeme a Cristo morto,
traime de mare al lito,
loco me fai penare
vedendol sí ferito ;
perché l'hai sofferito ?
Per volerme sanare.

And snares me in His net,
Prisons me close, and closer yet,
　　To be His child and guest.

If I come forth by way of Smell,
　　Thine odours sweet and fine
In every creature I perceive,
　　And every one divine ;
　　Thy spears they are, to make me Thine,
　　They wound at Thy behest.

If I come forth by way of Touch,
　　On every creature fair
In sacred awe I lay my hands,
　　For Thou art sculptured there ;
　　'Twere madness, Love, this way to dare
　　Escape Thy sweet conquest.

O Love, why do I flee from Thee ?
　　Why should I fear to yield ?
Because Thou wouldst re-make my heart,
　　In fires of love annealed ?
　　No more myself, in Thee concealed,
　　And by Thy love possessed.

I, if I see another moved
　　The downward step to make,
I am made partner of his loss,
　　I suffer for his sake :
　　Whom, Love Unmeasured, dost *Thou* take
　　To Thy compassion blest ?

Lead me to Christ, Who died for me,
　　Draw me from sea to shore :
And make me mourn in penitence
　　The wounds and griefs He bore :
　　Why did He suffer pains so sore ?
　　That I might be at rest.

COMO DIO APPARE NE L'ANIMA EN CINQUE MODI

(LAUDA XLV)

En cinque modi appareme
lo Signor en esta vita ;
altissima salita
chi nel quinto è entrato.

Lo primo modo chiamolo
stato timoroso,
lo secondo pareme
amor medecaroso,
lo terzo amore pareme
viatico amoroso,
lo quarto è paternoso,
lo quinto è desponsato.

Nel primo modo appareme
nell'alma Dio Signore ;
da morte suscitandola
per lo suo gran valore,
fuga la demonia
che me tenean 'n errore,
contrizion de cuore
l'amor ci ha visitato.

Poi vien como medico
ne l'alma suscitata,
confortala ed aiutala,
ché sta sí vulnerata ;
le sacramenta ponece
che l'hanno resanata,
ché l'ha cusi curata
lo medico ammirato.

HOW GOD APPEARS TO THE SOUL IN FIVE WAYS

(LAUDA XLV)

In this our life the Lord appears
    In five ways to me ;
And he who gains the fifth way,
    High in grace is he.

And this I call the first Way,
    The state of Holy Fear ;
The second Way seems to me
    A Love to heal and cheer ;
The third Love seems to me
    A Comrade year by year ;
    The fourth Love, a Father dear:
    —The fifth weddeth me.

The first Way, God comes to me,
    My soul's only Lord ;
Raising her from deepest death,
    By His mighty word ;
Drives afar the demons,
    False and abhorred !
    —Wounds me with contrition's sword,
    Love's harbinger to be.

Comes He as doctor then,
    The soul to sustain ;
Comforting and helping her
    In her wounds and pain:
Brings her the Sacraments,
    Cleansing every stain,
    Healing all her hurts again ;
    —The Good Physician He!

Como compagno nobile
lo mio amor apparuto,
de trarme de miseria
donarme lo suo aiuto,
per le virtute mename
en celestial saluto ;
non degio star co muto,
tanto bene occultato.

Lo quarto modo appareme
como benigno pate,
cibandome de donora
de la sua largitate ;
da poi che l'alma gusta
la sua amorositate,
sente la redetate
de lo suo paternato.

Lo quinto amore mename
ad esser desponsata,
al suo Figliol dolcissimo
essere copulata ;
regina se' degli angeli,
per grazia menata,
en Cristo trasformata
en mirabel unitato.

As a noble Comrade,
  Comes my Love once more ;
Draws me forth from misery,
  Gives me of His store ;
Through the virtues leadeth me
  To the Heavenly shore:
  Let me tell His mercies o'er,
    Nor hide His charity!

The fourth Way, He comes to me,
  A Father, kind and good:
Decks me with ornaments,
  Nourishes with food:
My soul tastes the tenderness
  Of His Fatherhood,
  Gives Him her gratitude ;
    His child and heir is she.

The fifth Love leadeth me
  To the marriage bed ;
To God's Son, honey-sweet,
  Joyful to be wed:
Queen among the angels,
  By grace to be led,
  One with Christ, my Spouse, my Head,
    To all Eternity.

DELLA BONTÁ DIVINA E VOLONTÁ CREATA

(LAUDA LXXIX)

La bontate enfinita
vol enfinito amore,
mente, senno e core
lo tempo e l'esser dato.

Amor longo fidele,
in eterno durante,
alto de speranza,
sopra li ciel passante,
amplo en caritate,
onne cosa abracciantc,
en un profondo stante
de core umiliato.

La volontá creata,
en infinitate unita,
menata per la grazia
en sí alta salita,
en quel ciel d'ignoranzia
tra gaudiosa vita,
co ferro a calamita
nel non veduto amato.

Lo 'ntelletto ignorante
va entorno per sentire,
nel ciel caliginoso
non se lassa transire,
che fôra grande eniuria
la smesuranza scire,
siria maior sapire
che lo saper ch'è stato.

OF DIVINE GOODNESS AND CREATED WILL

(LAUDA LXXIX)

THE Goodness that is Infinite
    Infinite love demands again ;
It claims the soul, the heart, the brain,
    All time, all being, for its own.

It asks a patient, faithful love,
    Enduring through Eternity:
A love instinct with highest hopes,
    Beyond Heaven's utmost mystery:
A love embracing everything,
    And generous in charity,
    That on the heart's humility
        Hath built her dwelling and her throne.

Created Will, the will of man,
    Must with Infinity unite ;
So, led by grace, this earth-born will
    Shall mount to regions infinite:
And in that Heaven of Ignorance
    Shall dwell in joy and in delight,
    As iron by the loadstone's might,
        Drawn into Love, unseen, unknown.

The mind, unlearned and ignorant,
    Gropes, thinking thus to comprehend,
And towards that Heaven, so dark, so strange,
    Its stubborn steps it will not bend.
Yet, beyond utmost injury,
    Infinity to apprehend,
    Were deeper wisdom, in the end,
        Than all the lore the mind hath known.

Lo 'ntelletto ignorante
iura fidelitate,
sotto l'onnipotenza
tener credulitate,
de mai ragion non petere
a la difficultate,
vive en umilitate
en tal profondo anegato.

O savia ignoranza,
en alto loco menata,
miracolosamente
se' en tanto levata,
né lengua né vocabulo
entende la contrata,
stai co dementata
en tanto loco ammirato.

— O alma nobilissima,
dinne que cose vide!
— Veggo un tal non veggio
che onne cosa me ride ;
la lengua m'è mozata
e lo pensier m'ascide,
miracolosa side
vive nel suo adorato.

— Que frutti reducene
de esta tua visione ?
— Vita ordinata
en onne nazione ;
lo cor ch'era immondissimo,
enferno inferione,
de trinitá magione
letto santificato.

The mind, unlearned and ignorant,
  Must swear a steadfast faithfulness,
And, sheltered by Omnipotence,
  A trust unswerving must confess.
No help in Reason must it seek
  For difficulty and distress ;
  But it must dwell in Humbleness
    In that Abyss o'erwhelmed and prone.

O fresh and healthful Ignorance!
  Led up to such a lofty place ;
How marvellous the miracle,
  That sets so high thy humble face ;
Thou hast no tongue, no words, to tell
  The secret of that country's grace,
  Senseless and speechless for a space
    In this fair dwelling art thou grown.

(*The Auditor questions*)
  " Most noble and majestic Soul,
    O tell me, tell me, what you see ? "
(*Soul*) " I see such Dark, so deep, so blind,
    That all things, ever, smile on me.
  My tongue may stammer and may fail,
    My thought may stark and lifeless be,
    Yet Faith, that wondrous mystery,
      Can live in the Adored alone."

(*Auditor*)
  " And what the fruits that thou shalt pluck
    Of this thy vision sweet and fair ? "
(*Soul*) " The fruit shall be an ordered life,
    Redeemed and lovely everywhere.
  The heart that was impure and vile,
    More deep than Hell in its despair,
    Shall be a home for love and prayer,—
      A mansion for the Three in One."

Cor mio, se' te venduto
ad alto emperatore,
nulla cosa creata
m'archieda omai d'amore,
ché non è creatura
posta en tanto onore,
a me è 'n gran descionore
se en mio cor fosse entrato.

Se creatura pete
per lo mio amor avere,
vadane a la bontade
che l'ha distribuire,
ch'io non aggio que fare,
ella ha lo possedere,
può far lo suo piacere,
ché lo s'ha comparato.

Lo tempo me demostra
ch'io gli ho rotta la legge,
quando l'aggio occupato
en non servire de rege ;
o tempo, tempo, tempo,
en quanto mal sommerge
a chi non te correge
passando te oziato!

O heart of mine, if thou be sold
  To such a noble Emperor,
My love and trust I must bestow
  On things created, never more!
For of the honour of thy love
  No creature may be heritor,
  And should they enter at thy door,
    Thou wert disgraced and overthrown.

O Creatures, if ye now should come
  For my affection clamouring,
Go to that Goodness, Whose it is,
  Who holds it for distributing.
He all my being doth possess,
  I am not lord of anything;
  For He may do His pleasuring
    With what He bought to be His own.

Ah, I have broken all His laws,
  Have spent my time in vain, I wis;
I have not served Him as my King,
  'Tis Time's own self that shows me this.
O Time, Time, Time! laid waste by sloth!
  In what an evil, dark abyss
  He sinks, who useth thee amiss:
    —He dreams, he wakes, and thou art flown!

DE L'AMOR MUTO

(LAUDA LXXVII)

O AMORE muto
che non vòi parlare,
che non sie conosciuto!

O amor che te celi
per onne stagione,
ch'omo de fuor non senta
la sua affezione,
che non la senta latrone
per quel c'hai guadagnato,
che non te sia raputo.

Quanto l'om piú te cela,
tanto piú foco abundi;
om che te ven occultando
sempre a lo foco iugne,
ed omo c'ha le pugne
de voler parlare,
spesse volte è feruto.

Omo che se stende
de dir so entendimento,
avenga che sia puro
el primo comenzamento;
vience da fuor lo vento
e vagli spaliando
quel ch'avea receputo.

OF THE LOVE THAT IS SILENT

(LAUDA LXXVII)

LOVE, silent as the night,
  Who not one word wilt say,
That none may know thee right!

O Love that lies concealed,
  Through heat and storm and cold,
That none may guess nor read
  Thy secrets manifold ;
  Lest thieves should soon grow bold
    To steal away thy treasure,
      Snatch it and take to flight!

Deep-hid, thy secret fires
  More ardently shall glow ;
And he who screens thee close,
  Thy fiercest heat shall know ;
  But he who fain would show
    Thy mysteries, will be wounded,
      Scorched by thy fiery might.

The man who strives to tell
  That secret joy within,
In vain he babbles thus :—
  Before his words begin
  The bitter winds of sin
    Will storm and whirl around him,
      And wreck his treasure bright.

Omo che ha alcun lume
en candela apicciato,
se vol che arda en pace,
mettelo a lo celato;
ed onne uscio ha enserrato
che nogl venga lo vento
che 'l lume sia stenguto.

Tal amor ha posto
silenzo a li suspiri,
èsse parato a l'uscio
e non gli lascia uscire;
dentro el fa partorire
che non se spanda la mente
da quel che ha sentuto.

Se se n'esce el suspiro,
esce po' lui la mente,
va po' lui vanegiando,
lassa quel c'ha en presente:
poi che se ne resente,
non puote retrovare
quel ch'avea receputo.

Tal amor ha sbandito
da sé la ipocrisia,
che esca del suo contado
che trovata non sia;
de gloria falsa e ria
sí n'ha fatta la caccia
de lei e del suo tributo.

The man who sets his torch
　High on a candlestick,
To let it shine in peace,
　Shields it with shutters thick,
　Lest winds should catch the wick,
　　—Through open casements blowing—
　　And quench its flick'ring light.

'Tis Silence, at thy door
　Holds captive all thy sighs:
Mute Love hath set him there,
　He will not let him rise;
　So shalt thou hold thy prize
　　That it may live within thee,
　　Not scattered left and right.

For if thy sighs come forth,
　Therewith comes forth thy mind,
To wander far from home,
　And leave her joy behind,
　Nor can she ever find
　　The Good, bestowed upon her,
　　That Treasure Infinite.

Mute Love hath thrust away
　False Seeming from his side,
In Love's fair land and realm
　No longer to abide.
　Hypocrisy and Pride,
　　And all that do them homage
　　Are chased to outer night.

DE L'AMOR DIVINO E SUA LAUDE

(LAUDA LXXXI)

O AMOR, divino amore,
amor, che non se' amato.

Amor, la tua amicizia
è piena de letizia
non cade mai en tristizia
lo cor che t'ha assagiato.

O amor amativo,
amor consumativo,
amor conservativo
del cuor che t'ha albergato!

O ferita gioiosa,
ferita dilettosa,
ferita gaudiosa,
chi de te è vulnerato!

Amore, unde entrasti,
ché sí occulto passasti?
Nullo signo mostrasti
unde tu fusse entrato.

O amor amabile,
amor delettabile,
amor encogitabile
sopr'onne cogitato!

Amor, divino fuoco,
amor de riso e gioco,
amor non dái a poco,
ché se' ricco smesurato.

OF DIVINE LOVE, AND THE PRAISES THEREOF

(LAUDA LXXXI)

O LOVE, divine and Lord,
That asks for no reward!

O Love, O Love, Thy tender amity
    Is full of joy and gladness,
    . And into grief and sadness
That heart shall never fall that tasteth Thee.

O Love, O Love, Thou dearest art and best:
    Love that with fire consumes,
    Yet safeguards and illumes
The heart that houseth Thee, belovèd Guest.

Dulcet as honeyed stings those wounds must be,
    Sweet wounds of rapture bright,
    All joy, and all delight,—
The wounds of him whose heart is pierced by Thee!

Love, Thou didst enter very softly in
    To hold this heart of mine.
    No sound, no stir, no sign!
How couldst Thou cross my threshold all unseen?

O Love adorable, with sweetness fraught,
    O Love delectable,
    Love inconceivable,
Outstripping knowledge and surpassing thought!

O Love, Thou fire divine, of laughter spun ;
    Love that art smile and jest,
    Thou giv'st us of Thy best,
Thy wealth unmeasured that is never done.

Amor, con chi te poni?
con delette persone,
e lassi gran baroni,
ché non fai lor mercato.

Tale non par che vaglia
en vista una medaglia,
che quasi como paglia
te dái en suo tratto.

Chi te crede tenere,
per sua scienzia avere,
nel cor non può sentire
che sia lo tuo gustato.

Scienzia acquisita
mortal si dá ferita,
s'ella non è vestita
de core umiliato.

Amor, tuo magisterio
enforma el desiderio,
ensegna l'evangelio
col breve tuo ensegnato.

Amor che sempre ardi
e i tuoi coraggi inardi,
fai le lor lengue dardi
che passa onne corato.

Amore grazioso,
amore delettoso,
amor suavetoso,
che 'l core hai saziato.

Amor ch'ensegni l'arte
che guadagni le parte,
de cielo fai le carte,
en pegno te n'èi dato.

Where wilt Thou enter, Love, and make Thy home?
    The lowly and the poor
    May draw Thee through their door:
To lords of high estate Thou wilt not come.

All such Thou setst not at a farthing's fee;
    Like straw where reapers bind,
    Thou giv'st them to the wind,
They get no promise and no pledge from Thee.

Science is vain, and knowledge but a cheat:
    He who by learning's skill
    Would hold Thee at his will,
His heart shall never taste Thy savour sweet.

For store of science is a deadly dart;
    'Twill slay herself at length,
    Save if she clothe her strength
In the fair garment of an humble heart.

Thy mastery, O Love, can softly steal
    Deep-hid desires to reach,
    The Gospel's lore to teach,
And stamp the heart with Thine all-powerful seal.

O Love, forever glowing and aflame,
    Kindle Thy warriors' hearts,
    And turn their tongues to darts,
To pierce each soul that hears Thy sacred name.

O Love, with Thee doth all delight abide;
    Love, that most gracious art,
    Love, sweetest to the heart,
The heart whose longings Thou hast satisfied.

Love, Thou dost teach us, and Thy gentle skill
    Gains all that God hath given,
    Maps out the path to Heaven,
Keeps it a pledge forever by His will.

Amor, fidel compagno,
amor, che mal se' a cagno,
de pianto me fai bagno
ch'io pianga el mio peccato.

Amor dolce e suave,
de cielo, amor se' chiave;
a porto meni nave
e campa el tempestato.

Amor che dái luce
ad omnia che luce,
la luce non è luce,
lume corporeato.

Luce luminativa,
luce demostrativa,
non viene a l'amativa
chi non è en te luminato.

Amor, lo tuo effetto
dá lume a lo 'ntelletto,
demóstrali l'obietto
de l'amativo amato.

Amor, lo tuo ardore
ad enflammar lo core
uniscil per amore
ne l'obietto encarnato.

Amor, vita secura,
riccheza senza cura,
piú ch'en eterno dura
ed ultra smesurato.

Amor che dái forma
ad omnia c'ha forma,
la forma tua reforma
l'omo ch'è deformato.

Love, faithful Comrade, change mine evil state;
 Blot out my sinful years,
 And bathe my soul in tears,
Yea, floods of tears, my sins to expiate.

O sweet and gentle Love, Thou art the key
 Of heaven's city and fort:
 Steer Thou my ship to port,
And from the tempest's fury shelter me.

Love, Giver of light to all that fain would shine,
 Thy light alone is bright,
 There beams none other light,
Save with a sullen glow that is not Thine.

Thou light, so vivid and so luminous,
 Thy lover cannot know
 Pure radiance, steadfast glow,
Save in Thy rays, that lighten all of us.

O Love, Thy keen and piercing brilliancy
 Illumes and guides the mind
 That Object fair to find,
—The end and aim of all her fervency.

O Love, Thine ardours pure and passionate
 Wake and inflame the heart,
 To dwell no more apart,
With the Adored made One and incarnate.

Love, Thou art life, in certain safety set,
 Eternal art Thou there ;
 Thou'rt wealth, unspoilt by care,
And measureless beyond our utmost debt.

Love, all things that have form are formed by Thee;
 And man, whose form is bent
 In vile disfigurement,
Thou dost re-form in Thine own majesty.

2 G

Amore puro e mondo,
amor saggio e iocondo,
amor alto e profondo
al cor che te s'é dato.

Amor largo e cortese,
amor con larghe spese,
amor, con mense stese
fai star lo tuo affidato.

Lussuria fetente
fugata de la mente,
de castitá lucente,
mundizia adornato.

Amor, tu se' quel ama
donde lo cor te ama,
sitito con gran fama
el tuo enamorato.

Amoranza divina,
ai mali se' medicina,
tu sani onne malina,
non sia tanto agravato.

O lengua scotegiante,
come se' stata osante
de farte tanto enante
parlar de tale stato?

Or pensa que n'hai detto
de l'amor benedetto,
onne lengua è en defetto
che de lui ha parlato.

Se onne lengue angeloro
che stanno en quel gran coro
parlando de tal foro,
parlaran scelenguato.

O Love, how stainless and how pure Thou art!
How jocund and how wise,
How high, how deep Thy guise,
To him who gives Thee gladly all his heart!

Love, that art bountiful and courteous,
Great gifts Thou dost divide,
Thy table's long and wide:
How welcome is Thy servant in Thy house!

Chase luxury, of foulness redolent,
Far forth from out my mind;
Leave chastity behind,
To bloom, and purity for ornament.

Love, it was Thou Thyself that didst inspire
My heart to love Thee first;
—An-hungered and athirst,
Thy lover longed, with very great desire.

O Love divine, Thou that art charity,
Thy medicine giveth ease;
Thou healest all disease,
Yea, all—though fierce and terrible it be.

O stammering, trembling tongue, so far astray
How dost thou dare to speak,
So bold, and yet so weak?
Of this strange state what words hast thou to say?

Now think, for all that thou hast said is vain,
Of Love, so fair, so blest:
—Imperfect and distrest
Is every tongue, to make that secret plain.

If all the tongues of angels strove to tell
—Yea, all the heavenly choir—
Of Love, and of His fire,
Even their tongues would stammer and rebel.

Ergo co non vergogni?
nel tuo parlar lo pogni,
lo suo laudar non giogni,
'nante l'hai blasfemato.

— Non te posso obedire
ch'amor deggia tacire,
l'amor voglio bandire,
fia che mo m'esce 'l fiato.

Non è condizione
che vada per ragione,
che passi la stagione
ch'amor non sia clamato. —

Clama la lengua e 'l core:
Amore, amore, amore!
chi tace el tuo dolzore
lo cor li sia crepato.

E ben credo che crepasse
lo cor che t'assagiasse;
se amor non clamasse,
trovárese afogato. —

Then art not *thou* ashamed, Love's praise to sing?
    Thou wrong'st Him with thy speech,
    —So high thou canst not reach,
Thou who didst once blaspheme fair Love thy King.

(*The Tongue saith*)
    Nay, how can I obey thee and be mute?
        For silence would be death;
        And while I draw my breath
Of love I still must sing, and of love's fruit.

My season's changed, love's tempests o'er me blow;
    Reason, no more my guide,
    Her baffled head must hide,
And I must shout and cry, my love to show.

The heart, the tongue, must song and clamour make:
    " Love, love, O love! "—they cry;
    Of thy sweet ecstasy
He that is silent, sure his heart will break.

For he that tastes Thy sweetness, well I wot,
    His heart may break indeed,
    And in its sorest need
May stifle, if to love he clamour not.

CONDIZIONE DEL PERPETUO AMORE

(LAUDA XCIX)

L'AMOR ch'è consumato
nullo prezzo non guarda,
né per pena non tarda
d'amar co fo amato.

Consumato l'amore,
si va pene cercando,
se ama sé dilettando,
sta penoso.
E con grande fervore
al diletto dá bando,
per viver tormentando
angoscioso.
Allora sta gioioso
e sé conosce amare,
se fugge el delettare
e sta en croce chiavato.

Servo che prezzo prende,
ch'ama sempre diletto,
si porta nell'affetto
pagamento.
Per lo prezzo vendere
lo prezzo, gli è difetto;
non è anco perfetto
lo stormento.
Se amor non fo tormento,
sí non fo virtuoso,
né sirá glorioso
se non fo tormentato.

THE CONDITION OF PERPETUAL LOVE

(LAUDA XCIX)

LOVE that is perfect made
    Seeketh for no reward,
    Findeth no toil too hard
Till Love with love be paid.

Love that is perfected,
    Searcheth for pain and night,
    And if it find delight,
      It grieveth sore.
And with a fervent dread,
    It puts all joy to flight,
    To bide in bitter plight,
      Tortured and poor:
      Rejoicing more and more,
To love so steadfastly,
And from all joys to flee,
      Nailed to the bitter Cross.

A servant that takes wage
    Of comfort and of cheer,
    Sells his affection dear,
      On profit bent:
In trade he doth engage,
    Ah, what a fault is here!
    Imperfect to God's ear
      This instrument:
      For, save by torture rent,
No man can be victorious,
Cannot be strong, nor glorious,
      Unless he suffer loss.

L'amor vero, liale
odia sé per natura,
vedendosi mesura
terminata.
Perché puro, leale
non ama creatura,
né se veste figura
mesurata.
Caritá increata
ad sé lo fa salire,
e falli partorire
figlio d'amor beato.

Questo figlio che nasce
è amor piú verace
de onne virtú capace,
copiosa.
Dove l'anima pasce
fuoco d'amor penace,
notrícasi de pace
gloriosa.
È sta sempre gioiosa
e si 'namora tanto,
che non potrebbe el quanto
esser considerato.

Love that is true and leal,
    Itself must needs despise,
    Piteous in its own eyes,
      So poor, so small:
If it be pure and real,
    No creature doth it prize;
    It wears no mortal guise,
      But scorns them all.
    Love uncreate doth call;
It hears, and mounts above,
To bring the child of Love
    To birth most rapturous.

This child that shall be born
    Is Love, most fair, most true,
    Dowered with virtues due,
      Plenteous and rare.
There, by Love's tortures torn,
    The soul shall feed anew,
    All peaceful through and through,
      All glad, all fair.
    And Love shall hover there,
So great, so sweet a treasure,
That none shall dare to measure
    A Love so marvellous.

COME L'ANIMA PER SANTA NICHILITÁ E CARITÁ PERVIENE A STATO INCOGNITO ED INDICIBILE

(LAUDA XCI)

Sopr'onne lengua amore,
bontá senza figura,
lume fuor de mesura
resplende nel mio core.

Averte conosciuto
credea per entelletto,
gustato per affetto
viso per simiglianza.
Te credendo tenuto
averte si perfetto
provat'ho quel diletto,
amor d'esmesuranza.
Or, parme, fo fallanza,
non se' quel che credea,
tenendo non avea
vertá senza errore.

O infigurabil luce,
chi te può figurare,
ché volesti abitare
en la seura tenebria?
Tuo lume non conduce
chi te veder gli pare
potere mesurare
de te quel che sia.
Notte veggio ch'é dia,
virtute non se trova,
non sa de te dar prova
chi vede quel splendore.

HOW THE SOUL BY HOLY ANNIHILATION AND LOVE REACHES A CONDITION THAT IS UNKNOWN AND UNSPEAKABLE

(LAUDA XCI)

INEFFABLE Love Divine!
　　Sweetness unformed, yet bright,
　　Measureless, endless Light,
Flame in this heart of mine!

Well did I know Thee, meseemed,
　　Through intellect and through awe;
　　Thy visible semblance saw,
Tasted Thy savour sweet:
And perfectly, so I deemed,
　　I held Thee without a flaw,
　　Close to Thy Heart could I draw,
—Love, timeless, measureless, great!—
Yet now, all seemeth a cheat:
　　I hold Thee less and less;
　　I grasped, yet not possess
　　　Thee, Uttermost Verity.

O Inconceivable Light!
　　Who can Thy secrets tell?
　　Thou Who wast fain to dwell
In darkness deep and obscure!
No more is Thy lantern bright
　　To guide the soul who would spell,
　　Measure, and mark Thee well,
And seize on Thine Essence pure.
Virtue nor strength is sure;
　　The night is turned to the day,
　　No words, no language have they
　　　Thy splendour and light that see.

Virtute perde l'atto
da poi che giogne a porto,
e tutto vede torto
quel che dritto pensava,
Trova novo baratto
dove lume è aramorto,
novo stato gli è porto
de quel non procacciava;
e quel che non amava
e tutto ha perduto
quel ch'avea posseduto
per caro suo valore.

Se l'atto de la mente
è tutto consopito,
en Dio stando rapito,
ch'en sé non se retrova,
de sé reman perdente
posto nello 'nfinito,
ammira co c'è gito,
non sa como se mova.
Tutto sí se renova,
tratto fuor de suo stato,
en quello smesurato
dove s'anega l'amore.

En mezo de sto mare
essendo sí abissato,
giá non ce trova lato
onde ne possa uscire.
De sé non può pensare
né dir como è formato,
però che, trasformato,
altro sí ha vestire.
Tutto lo suo sentire
en ben si va notando,
belleza contemplando
la qual non ha colore.

For Virtue's strength is weak,
 When once it hath reached the goal.
 The paths are quicksand and shoal,
That seemed so firm and so fair.
A new abyss and a bleak,
 Quenches the light of the soul;
 A change comes over the whole,
Unsought for, yet it is there.
The soul is stript and bare
  Of all that it once possessed,
  And all that it loved the least,
  It yearns for ardently.

When the mind's very being is gone,
 Sunk in a conscious sleep,
 In á rapture divine and deep,
Itself in the Godhead lost:—
It is conquered, ravished and won!
 Set in Eternity's sweep,
 Gazing back on the steep,
Knowing not how it was crossed—
To a new world now is it tossed,
  Drawn from its former state,
  To another, measureless, great—
  Where Love is drowned in the Sea.

In the midst of this Ocean's tide
 Whelmèd for evermore
 It cannot find a shore,
Gone is the solid ground:
Thought it hath laid aside,
 Transformed to its inmost core
 It knows not its own heart's lore;
New-clad the soul is found:
Its feeling is sunk and enwound
  In the Good that is ultimate,
  The Beauty to contemplate
  That is colourless, formless, free.

De tutto prende sorte,
tanto ha per unione
de trasformazione,
che dice:— Tutto è mio. —
Aperte son le porte
fatta ha coniunzione,
ed è en possessione
de tutto quel de Dio.
Sente que non sentío,
que non cognove vede,
possede que non crede,
gusta senza sapere.

Però c'ha sé perduto
tutto senza misura,
possede quel'altura
de summa smesuranza.
Perché non ha tenuto
en sé altra mistura,
quel ben senza figura
receve en abondanza.
Questa è tal trasformanza
perdendo e possedendo,
giá non andar chirendo
trovarne parladore.

Perder sempre e tenere
amare e delettare,
mirare e contemplare,
questo reman en atto.
Per certo possedere
ed en quel ben notare,
en esso reposare
ove se vede tratto.
Questo è un tal baratto,
atto de caritate,
lume de veritate
che remane en vigore.

It welcometh any fate:
    Transformed so wondrously
    By union profound and free,
It whispereth " All is mine! "
Wide open standeth the gate—
    The soul is joined to Thee,
    Endlessly, utterly,
    Possessing all that is Thine.
It feels what it cannot divine,
      Sees what it may not discern,
      Grasps more than Faith can learn,
      Tastes God unknowingly.

It hath found the measureless way
    Itself to lose and to spend,
    And so it can comprehend
The Immeasurable Height:
And purifying its clay
    From all alloy or blend,
    It drinks without pause or end
Ineffable Delight.
Loosing, yet holding tight,
      No longer the soul doth seek
      Power to tell and to speak,
      Transformed so utterly.

To lose, and yet to keep,
    To love, and in joy to wait,
    To gaze and to contemplate,
This is the True and the Real.
To possess in certainty deep ;
    To float in that blessed state,
    Anchored, yet early and late,
Nearer, nearer to steal ;
—Deeper than woe or weal
      Is the Act of Heavenly Love,
      And the Light of Truth from above,
      Strong, eternal and free.

Altro atto non ci ha loco,
lá su giá non s'apressa,
quel ch'era si se cessa
en mente che cercava.
Calor, amor de fuoco,
né pena non c'è admessa,
tal luce non è essa
qual prima se pensava.
Quel con que procacciava
bisogno è che lo lassi,
a cose nòve passi
sopr'onne suo sentore.

Luce gli pare oscura
qual prima resplendea,
que virtute credea,
retrova gran defetto.
Giá non può dar figura
como emprima facea,
quando parlar solea
cercar per entelletto.
En quello ben perfetto
non c'è tal simiglianza,
qual prese per certanza
e non è possessore.

Emprima che sie gionto
pensa che è tenebría,
que pensi che sia dia,
que luce oscuritate.
Se non èi en questo ponto
che niente en te non sia,
tutto sí è falsía,
que te par veritate.
E non è caritate
en te ancora pura,
mentre de te hai cura,
pènsete far vittore.

None other Act can be there,
    Naught other can ever draw nigh,
    And all that is past must die,
In the mind that restlessly sought.
The loves that scorch and flare,
    And the sorrows, must all pass by;
    That Light in the flooded sky,
Is other than once we thought:
And the things for which we fought,
      We must leave them all behind,
      New, wonderful things to find,
      Other than eye can see.

The light that was once so clear
    Now seems as dark as night:
    All that we thought was right,
Imperfect and poor we find:
Nor can we see and hear
    In figures, as once we might,
    When we could speak and write,
With the searching, curious mind.
The perfect Good to bind,
      The symbols we fancied true,
      Are useless, through and through;
      So prisoned she cannot be.

Before the goal is attained,
    The light that is clear as day,
    Seems darkness upon the way ;
The sun seems gloomy as night.
Before the Ocean is gained,
    Where Self is noughted for aye,
    'Tis but Falsehood's glimmering ray,
We take for Truth's own light.
Not yet unstained and bright,
      Is Charity in thy soul,
      If thou yield not up the whole,
      If victor thou still wouldst be.

Se vai figurando
imagine per vedere
e per sapor sapere
que è lo smesurato,
credi poter cercando
enfinito potere,
sí come è possedere,
molto parmi engannato.
Non è que hai pensato,
que credi per certanza,
giá non se' simiglianza
de lui senza fallore.

Donqua te lassa trare
quando esso te toccasse,
se forsa te menasse
a veder sua veritate.
E de te non pensare,
non val che procacciassi
che lui tu retrovassi
con tua vanitate.
Ama tranquillitate
sopra atto e sentimento,
retrova en perdimento
de te el suo valore.

En quello che gli piace
te ponere, te piaccia,
perché non val procaccia
quando te afforzassi.
En te sí aggi pace,
abraccial se t'abraccia,
se nol fa, ben te piaccia,
guarda non te curassi.
Se como déi amassi,
sempre serie contento,
portando tal talento
luce senza timore.

If thou in images fair,
    In types and figures, wouldst see,
    And the Unconditioned, the Free,
  Wouldst measure and mark and taste:
If thou thinkest, by searching and care,
    To encompass Infinity,
    To enclose and clasp It to thee,
  —Vain are thy hopes and thy haste!
Thy thoughts are error and waste!
    Thy faith, so strong and certain,
    Is but a dissolving curtain,
      Hiding the Perfect from thee.

When the Unknown takes thy hand,
    Let Him lead thee where He will;
    Perchance He may guide thee still
  To the vision of His Truth.
Stript of thy self must thou stand,
    Vain are thy searchings until
    Vanity's cup thou spill;
  It never can quench thy drouth.
Love Calm, that is tranquil and smooth,
    Beyond all feeling and deed;
    It will satisfy thy need,
      Sink thyself in that Sea!

Be happy in any place
    Where He pleaseth to set thy feet;
    'Tis in vain the bars to beat,
  Effort and struggle are vain.
If He offer thee His embrace,
    Run His caress to meet!
    —If not, His withholding is sweet,—
  Reck not of loss nor of gain.
If thy love be pure from stain,
    Thou wilt be ever content,
    Thy longings only bent
      To shine more fearlessly.

Sai che non puoi avere
se non quello che vol dare,
e q_ua_{ndo} nol vol fare,
giá non hai signoria.
Né non puoi possedere
quel c'hai per afforzare,
se nol vuol conservare
sua dolce cortesia.
Perché tutta tua via
sí fuor de te è posta,
ch'en te non è reposta,
ma tutta è nel Signore.

Donqua se l'hai trovato,
cognosci en veritate
che non hai potestate
alcun ben envenire.
Lo ben che t'è donato
fal quella caritate
che per tua primitate
non se può prevenire.
Tutto lo tuo desire
donqua sia collocato
en quello smesurato
d'ogne ben donatore.

De te giá non volere
se none que vuol esso,
perdere tutto te stesso
en esso trasformato.
En tutti i suoi piaceri
sempre te trova messo,
vestito sempre d'esso,
de te tutto privato.
Però che questo stato
onne virtute passa,
ché te Cristo non lassa
cader mai en fetore.

What thou art willing to give,
　　That only is thine indeed:
　　If thou canst not rule thy need,
　　Thou canst have no mastery.
Nothing can bloom and live
　　That is clutched by force and greed:
　　Fair Courtesy must thou heed,
　　And guard her tenderly.
Thy pathway is not in thee;
　　Far away doth it bend,
　　In the Lord, thy Way and thy End,
　　Voyage and Harbour is He.

So if thou hast found thy Lord,
　　Verily shalt thou know
　　Thou canst not discover nor show,
　　Any good of thine own.
'Twas Love, the Eternal Word,
　　All good on thee did bestow,
　　Ere Creation's primal flow,
　　Ere the seeds of the world were sown.
The Ineffable, the Unknown,
　　Filleth thy cup to the brim;
　　Set all thy desires on Him,
　　The Giver of all is He.

Ask nothing to be thine own,
　　Save to be one with thy Lord,
　　To lose thy note in His chord,
　　To be transformed in Him:
—Thy will, contented and prone,
　　Accepting all His award,
　　Robed all in His accord,
　　Stript of thy self-hood dim.
This state overfloweth the brim
　　Of virtues and merits all;
　　Nor will Christ let thee fall
　　Into sin and misery.

Da poi che tu non ami
te, ma quella bontate,
cerca per veritate
ch'una cosa se' fatto.
Bisogno è che te reami
sí con sua caritate,
en tanta unitate
en esso tu sie attratto.
Questo si è baratto
de tanta unione,
nulla divisione
pò far doi d'un core.

Se tutto gli t'èi dato
de te non servando,
non te, ma lui amando
giá non te può lassare.
Quel ben che t'é donato,
en sé te commutando,
lasserá sé lassando
en colpa te cascare.
Donqua co sé lassare
giá non può quella luce,
sí te, lo qual conduce
per sí unito amore.

O alta veritate
cui è la signoria,
tu se' termine e via
a chi t'ha ben trovato.
Dolce tranquillitate
de tanta magioría,
cosa nulla che sia
può variar tuo stato ;
però che è collocato
en luce de fermeza,
passando per laideza
non perde el suo candore.

When thou lov'st thyself no longer,
    But only that Good and Fair,
    Utterly strive and dare
Therewith One Thing to be made.
Thine answer must aye be stronger
    To thy Lover's tender prayer,
    Drawn into His Essence there,
Towards His Being swayed.
This One-head can never fade ;
    Division must strive in vain,
    To make One Heart into twain,
    So deep is this Unity.

If thou hast served Him well,
    Given Him all that was thine,
    Loved only the Divine,
He never will part from thee.
Wholly in Him shalt thou dwell,
    Thy being with His combine :
    If sin should sully that shrine,
Sharer in sin would He be !
From Himself how can He flee ?
    His light can never be quenched,
    So thou, in that glory drenched,
    Shalt be His to Eternity.

O loftiest Verity !
    All, all is under Thy sway ;
    Thou art the End and the Way,
For all who can seek Thee and find.
O gentle Tranquillity !
    Whose greatness endureth for aye,
    Who knowest not change nor decay,
Whom naught can vary nor bind.
Thy Light with Thy Strength is twined;
    Thy Infinite Essence and Soul
    Can pass through all that is foul,
    Nor sully Its purity.

Monda sempre permane
mente che te possede,
per colpa non se lede,
ché non se può salire.
En tanta alteza stane
ed en pace resede,
mondo con vizio vede
sotto sé tutto gire.
Virtute non ha sentire,
né caritá fervente,
de stato sí possente
giá non possede onore.

La guerra è terminata,
de le virtú battaglia,
de la mente travaglia,
cosa nulla contende.
La mente è renovata,
vestita a tal entaglia,
de tal ferro è la maglia,
feruta no l'offende.
Al lume sempre intende
nulla vuol piú figura,
però che questa altura
non chiede lume de fuore.

Sopra lo fermamento
lo qual sí è stellato
d'ogne virtute ornato
e sopre al cristallino
ha fatto salimento,
puritate ha passato,
terzo ciel ha trovato,
ardor de serafino.
Lume tanto divino
non se può maculare
né per colpa abassare
né en sé sentir fetore.

White without spot or stain,
  Is the mind that possesseth Thee,
  From smutch of sin is it free,
Sin cannot reach that height.
High on its heavenly plane,
  It dwells in tranquillity ;
  Evil and good can it see,
Below it in circling flight.
It recks not of Wrong nor Right ;
    The virtues it soars above,
    Feels not its own fervent love,
    Distinctions vanish and flee.

The battle is over now,
  The travail that drains the blood,
  The spirit's struggle for good,—
Peace hath ended the war.
With his helmet on his brow,
  Behold the spirit renewed,
  With tempered armour endued,
Wound cannot hurt him nor scar.
He looks on the radiance afar,
    Asks not for symbol nor sign ;
    No tapers of sense may shine,
    On those heights of Eternity.

Far over the firmament,
  Where the stellar Heaven is bright,
  Adorned by virtues white,
To the Third Heaven's ecstasy,
The soul hath made its ascent!
  Beyond the Crystalline Height
  To the seraphs' Fire and Light ;
Far, far above purity!
That light, divine and high,
    Can never be stained nor spoiled,
    Never by sin be soiled,
    No evil therein can be.

Onne fede sí cessa,
ché gli è dato vedere
speranza, per tenere
colui che procacciava.
Desiderio non s'apressa
né forza de volere,
temor de permanere
ha piú che non amava.
Veder ciò che pensava
tutto era cechitate,
fame de tempestate,
simiglianza d'errore.

En quello cielo empiro
sí alto è quel che trova,
che non ne può dar prova
né con lengua narrare.
E molto piú m'amiro
como sí se renova
en fermeza sí nova,
che non può figurare.
E giá non può errare,
cadere en tenebria,
la notte è fatta dia,
defetto grande amore.

Como aere dá luce,
se esso lume è fatto,
como cera desfatto
a gran foco mostrata,
en tanto sí reluce
ad quello lume tratto,
tutto perde suo atto,
volontate è passata.
La forma che gli è data
tanto sí l'ha absorto,
che vive stando morto,
è vinto ed è vittore.

Faith no longer is here,
   For faith is lost in sight ;
   Hope is changed to delight,
  Grasping what once it sought.
Desire no more draws near,
   Nor force of will, nor affright
   Lest the Treasure should take to flight;
The soul by Love is taught:
All his beliefs and his thought
    Were foolish and poor and blind,
    Tumult and tempest and wind,
    Error and falsity.

High in that Empyrean,
   The soul finds treasure so great,
   No place it hath, and no date,
Nothing for tongue to tell.
And wonder groweth more keen,
   At the soul, thus re-create,
   In a new and stronger state,
Where images cannot dwell,
Where illusions melt and dispel;
    It cannot be lost in night,
    Darkness is turned to light,
    In a love so great and free.

As air becomes luminous,
   When filled with the light of day;
   —As wax dissolveth away,
In the heat and glow of fire:
So the soul grows glorious,
   Fused in that Heavenly Ray;
   No action can it essay,
Gone are its Will and Desire.
The Height that is ever higher
    Absorbs its heart and its breath,
    It is living, yet lives in death,
    Is vanquished in victory.

Non gir chirendo en mare
vino se 'l ce mettessi,
che trovar lo potessi
che 'l mar l'ha recevuto;
e che 'l possi preservare
e pensar che restesse
ed en sé remanesse
par che non fosse suto.
L'amor sí l'ha bevuto,
la veritá mutato,
lo suo è barattato,
de sé non ha vigore.

Volendo giá non vole,
ché non ha suo volere,
e giá non può volere
se non questa belleza.
Non demanda co suole,
non vuole possedere,
ha sí dolce tenere,
nulla c'è sua forteza.
Questa sí somma alteza
en nichilo è fondata,
nichilata, formata,
messa nello Signore.

Alta nichilitate,
tuo atto è tanto forte,
che apre tutte le porte,
entra nello 'nfinito.
Tua è la veritate
e nulla teme morte,
dirize cose torte,
oscuro fai chiarito.
Tanto fai core unita
en divina amistanza,
non c'è dissimiglianza
de contradir chi ha amore.

For wine poured into the sea,
    A man may search in vain,
    There is left of it not a stain,
In the ocean waves that roll.
Itself no more can it be,
    Nor doth it ask to regain
    Its former essence again ;
It must give its being in toll.
So Love hath drunk the Soul,
    And Truth hath changed it so,
    All that it was must go,
    It giveth its self in fee.

It yearns, yet desireth not,
    For its will is not its own ;
    It longs for naught that is known,
Except that Beauty so fair.
Its longings are all forgot,
    It asks nor bread nor a stone ;
    Nothingness is its throne ;
Sweet is its holding there.
This state, so lofty and rare,
    On Nothingness is it built,
    In the Lord it is noughted and spilt,
    Formed and stablished to be.

O Noughting mysterious!
    So strong thou art and so great,
    Thou openest every gate,
That leads to the Infinite.
Thou art Very Truth for us,
    We fear not death nor fate,
    Thou guidest evil and hate,
Thou makest the darkness bright.
The heart of man thou canst plight
    So close to the Heart Divine,
    There is left no dividing line,
    To trouble Love's ecstasy.

Tanta è tua sutiglicza,
che onne cosa sí passi,
e sotto te sí lassi
defetto remanere.
Con tanta legereza
a la veritate passi,
che giá non te rabassi
po' te colpa vedere.
Sempre tu fai gaudere,
tanto se' concordata,
e, veritá portata,
nullo senti dolore.

Piacere e dispiacere
fuor da te l'hai gettato,
en Dio se' collocato
piacer ciò che gli piace.
Volere e non volere
en te si è anegato,
desiderio remortato,
però hai sempre pace.
Questa è tal fornace
che purga e non incende,
a la qual non se defende
né freddo né calore.

Merito non procacci,
ma merito sempre trovi,
lume con doni nuovi
gli quali non ademandi.
Se prendi, tanto abracci
che non te ne removi
e gioie sempre trovi
ove tutta despandi.
Tu curri, se non andi,
sali, co piú descendi,
quanto piú dái, sí prendi,
possedi el Creatore.

So subtle thy wisdom and deep,
    The world that passeth away
    Below thy sphere must stay,
Imperfect, shadowy, vain.
So light, so swift canst thou leap
    To that unclouded day,
    Thou needst not stoop nor delay,
To gaze upon guilt or stain.
Forever that joyful strain
      Rings in concord and peace;
      All pain and sorrow shall cease,
      Uplifted to Verity.

There pleasure and trouble are naught,
    Far from thee they are flung;
    Fast to God thou hast clung,
Thy pleasure with His to entwine.
Liking and loathing are brought
    To nothingness on thy tongue;
    No more dost thou crave or long,
In the peace that forever is thine.
This is that fire divine
      That purges, but doth not burn;
      Where heat and cold unlearn
      Their arrogant mastery.

Thou seekest not any reward,
    And yet reward thou dost find,—
    New gifts, new light for the mind,
More than heart could demand.
What thou tak'st, thou dost safely guard,
    And fast to thy being bind:
    Give all, for more is behind,
Fresh joys for thine emptied hand.
Thou dost run, though thou canst not stand;
      Dost mount, although thou descend;
      Hast more, the more thou dost spend,
      Possessing the Deity.

Possedi posseduta,
en tanta unione
non c'è divisione
che te da lui retragga.
Tu bevi e se' bevuta
en trasformazione,
da tal perfezione
non è chi te distragga,
onde sua man contragga,
non volendo piú dare,
giá non si può trovare,
tu se' donna e signore.

Tu hai passata morte,
se' posta en vera vita,
né non temi ferita
né cosa che t'offenda.
Nulla cosa t'è forte,
da te po' t'èi partita,
en Dio stai enfinita,
non è chi te contenda.
Giá non è chi t'entenda,
veggia co se' formata,
se non chi t'ha levata
ed è de te fattore.

Tua profonda basseza
sí alto è sublimata,
en sedia collocata
con Dio sempre regnare.
En quella somma alteza
en tanto se' abissata,
che giá non è trovata
ed en sé non appare.
E questo è tal montare
onde scendi, e salire,
chi non l'ha per sentire,
giá non è entendetore.

Possessed of Him, He is thine,
 In union so intimate,
 That nothing shall separate—
Nothing draw thee away.
Thou drink'st, and thou art the Wine;
 Transformed to that perfect state,
 So holy, so pure and great,
Nothing can lead thee astray.
Never His hand can delay,
  Never His gifts shall cease,
  Thou hast entered His central peace
  Beloved and Lover to be.

Death thou hast left behind,
 The centre of life is here;
 No wounding needst thou fear
Nothing can hurt thee more.
Nothing can force thee nor bind,
 Thy Self is no longer near;
 No hostile voice canst thou hear,
Upon this infinite shore.
God, Who taught thee to soar,
  He only can understand
  Thee, the work of His hand;
  Thy Maker and Lord is He.

Thou who wert once so low,
 Art now exalted so high,
 To God thou art ever nigh,
Dost reign with Him in content.
Thy baseness is noughted so,
 In the heights of His Majesty,
 It needs must vanish and die,
Like mist, 'tis scattered and spent.
This is that wondrous ascent,
  Whose depth is one with its height,
  They only can grasp it aright,
  Who dwell in its secrecy.

Riccheza che possedi
quando hai tutto perduto,
giá non fo mai veduto
questo simel baratto.
O luce che concedi
defetto essere aiuto,
avendo posseduto
virtú fuor de suo atto,
questo è novel contratto
ove vita s'enferma,
enfermando se ferma,
cade e cresce en vigore.

Defetti fai profetti,
tal luce teco porti,
e tutto sí aramorti
ciò che puoi contradire.
Tuoi beni son perfetti
tutti altri si son torti,
per te sí vivon morti,
gl'infermi fai guarire.
Perché sai envenire
nel tosco medicina,
fermeza en gran ruina
en tenebre splendore.

Te posso dir giardino
d'ogne fiore adornato,
dove sí sta piantato
l'arbore de la vita.
Tu se' lume divino,
da tenebre purgato,
ben tanto confermato
che non pati ferita.
E, perché se' unita
tutta con veritate,
nulla varietate
ti muta per timore.

When all that was thine is lost
　　The riches thou countedst o'er—
　　—Never was known before
So great and rare an exchange!
O Light that gives without cost
　　A Lack that shall be a store,
　　A Want that is able to pour
Power beyond action's range!
O Covenant new and strange!
　　　　Where life doth sicken and fade,
　　　　Yet in sickness is stronger made,
　　　　Mounts and falls like the sea!

So deep, so pure is thy light,
　　It turns a fault to a gain;
　　All that would hinder and pain,
Lieth defeated and dead.
Thy gifts are perfect and right,
　　All others are useless and vain,
　　The dead thou raisest again,
The sick to health thou hast led.
Thou hast skill, the healing to shed
　　　　In the poison's venomous bite;
　　　　Splendour to hide in the night,
　　　　And in ruin, constancy.

Thou art a garden in bloom,
　　Adorned with many a flower;
　　And there, thro' sun and thro' shower,
The Tree of Life shall be green.
Purged of shadows and gloom,
　　Thou art Light divine, and Power,
　　Firmness and strength are thy dower,
From maiming and taint made clean.
And since to the truth unseen
　　　　Eternally thou art wed,
　　　　Change cannot touch thee, nor dread,
　　　　Nor any diversity.

Mai trasformazione
perfetta non può fare
né senza te regnare
amor, quanto sia forte.
Ad sua possessione
non può virtú menare
né mente contemplare,
se de te non ha sorte.
Mai non si serran porte
a la tua signoria,
grande è tua baronia,
star co l'emperadore.

De Cristo fusti donna
e de tutti gli santi,
regnar con doni tanti
con luce tutta pura.
Però pregam Madonna
ched essa sí n'amanti,
davanti a lei far canti,
amar senza fallura.
Veder senza figura
la somma veritate
con la nichilitate
del nostro pover core.

Love cannot transform the soul,
   How strong so ever He be,
   Save hand in hand with thee,
  To make it perfect and fair.
To gain that ultimate goal,
   Virtue and Intellect flee;
   Love's face they never may see,
Save with thy shelter and care.
No gates shall be bolted there,
    Against the touch of thy hand;
    Thou art the lord of that land,
    Reigning in majesty.

Sweetheart of Christ wast thou,
   To every saint thou wast dear;
   Pure is thy Light and clear,
Great the gifts of thy reign.
We plead with Our Lady now,
   —Who dwelt in thy holy sphere,—
   Our singing and prayers to hear,
To grant us Love without stain,
Vision unveiled and plain
    Of Truth, supreme and apart;—
    And the Noughting of our own heart,
    In uttermost Poverty.

APPENDIX I

MANUSCRIPTS OF THE *LAUDE*

EXISTING manuscripts of Jacopone's *laude* fall with few exceptions into three distinct groups: those of Umbrian, Tuscan, and Venetian origin.

A. Umbrian Manuscripts.—These form at once the smallest and the most important class. They usually resemble each other closely in the text and arrangement of the *laude;* and readings obtained from them are generally regarded as more authentic than those from the Tuscan or Venetian groups. Between ninety and a hundred *laude* are common to the principal Umbrian manuscripts, and these invariably include Jacopone's most violent political poems. Nine *laude* are peculiar to this group and seldom found outside it, namely:

Frate Ranaldo	(Bonaccorsi	XVII.)
O me lasso, dolente	(„	XX.)
Fede, spene e caritate	(„	LXIX.)
Que farai, morte mia	(„	XCV.)
Troppo m'è grande fatica	(„	XCVI.)
O peccator dolente	(„	XCVII.)
Perché m'hai tu creata	(„	XCVIII.)
Fiorito è Cristo	(„	C.)
Troppo perde el tempo	(„	CI.)

Umbrian manuscripts usually begin with "La Bontade se lamenta," followed by "Fuggo la croce"; this arrangement not occurring in the other groups. The great *lauda*, "Sopr' onne lengua amore," is seldom found in them. These texts were probably written by and for the use of the Spiritual friars in Umbria and the March of Ancona, and constituted part of the propaganda of the Spiritual movement in the fourteenth century. The most ancient and important surviving examples are the MSS. in the Angelica Library at Rome (No. 2216), with 29 *laude*, and in the Biblioteca Oliveriana at Pesaro, with 83 *laude;*

one probably spurious. Both these are of the first half of the
fourteenth century. Next in interest are two MSS. written at
Todi, probably early in the fifteenth century: namely, No. 2306
in the Angelica Library, with 104 *laude* ("Signore, damme la
morte" being twice repeated), and No. 194 in the Communal
Library at Todi, with 160 *laude*, of which the first 99 are in-
cluded in Jacopone's accepted text. These are regarded by
Signor Brugnoli as probable copies of the "ancient Todi manu-
scripts" from which Bonaccorsi obtained the text for his edition
of the *laude*;[1] since 99 of the 102 poems which he prints occur
in them, and he expressly states that the three which are
absent were obtained by him from other sources. With these
two MSS. should be mentioned the interesting and hitherto un-
described MS. of the *laude* in the British Museum (Add. 16567).[2]
This is a duodecimo, written on vellum by several hands in the
fifteenth century. It contains some miscellaneous religious
pieces, the prose sayings of Jacopone in Latin, and 86 *laude*, all
authentic; "Signore, damme la mo.te" being twice repeated, as
in Angelica 2306. An entry on the last page, from which the
proper names have been imperfectly erased, says:

    "Iste liber est ad usum mei fratris [Bernardini Johannis de
Toridunis?] de Bevanea ordinis fratrum minorum: quem emi a
uenerabili uiro magistro herculano olim domini Clementis de
tuderto pro pretio trium florenorum coram fratre luca de acqua
sperta eiusdem ordinis minorum."

    This, together with the fact that the *laude* begin, in proper
Umbrian fashion, with "La Bontade se lamenta" and "Fuggo
la croce," sufficiently establishes the *provenance* of the MS.;
and further creates a strong presumption that it belongs to the
small and authoritative group written at Todi. The text does
not always support the readings in Bonaccorsi or Brugnoli.[3]
Among the omitted *laude* are the two satires on the new learn-
ing—"Frate Ranaldo" and "Tale qual è"—and the four great
mystical poems, "Amor de caritate," "Sopr'onne lengua
amore," "La fede e la speranza," and "Troppo perde el tempo."

---

[1] Brugnoli, *Le Satire*, pp. xvi *seq.* See Preface to Bonaccorsi's edition,
and above, ch. i., p. 11.

[2] I am indebted to Mr. J. A. Herbert, Assistant Keeper of MSS., for
drawing my attention to this book.

[3] Wide discrepancies, for instance, in No. lvii., "Audite una tençone
kera fra diu persone" (Bonaccorsi, *Lauda XXII.*, Brugnoli, p. 200).

All the minatory pieces, and those written during imprisonment, are included.

Finally, the rather late Umbrian MS. described by Tobler in *Zeitschrift für Romanische Philologie*, 1878, may be mentioned here as the source of the legendary life of Jacopone from which I have given quotations. This manuscript, probably of the late fifteenth or early sixteenth century, came from the Communal Library of Assisi, and is now in the Spithöver collection. It contains 241 *laude*, of which more than half are doubtful and many certainly spurious. All appear to be of Umbrian origin, and are probably collected from among the numerous local imitations of Jacopone's songs. The *laude* purport to be arranged in chronological order; but this claim has no foundation in fact.

B. Tuscan Manuscripts.—The Tuscan manuscripts of the *laude* have been separated by Signor Brugnoli into two classes, according to the order in which the poems are arranged.[1]

(*a*) Of the first class, only two examples are known; No. I., VI. 9 of the Communal Library of Siena, and No. II., VI. 63 of the Magliabecchi collection in the Biblioteca Nazionale, Florence. Both are of the fourteenth century; the Sienese MS. —which is the oldest known text of Jacopone—dating from its first years, the Florentine from the second half. The Sienese MS. contains 46 *laude*, its cousin 63. Both begin with " O Cristo onnipotente," and end with " L'omo che può la sua lengua domare ": an order not observed in any other known text. The poems which they have in common are given, with trifling exceptions, in the same sequence.

(*b*) The second class, which is very large, consists mainly of MSS. of the fifteenth century; the oldest example, No. 1049 in the Biblioteca Riccardiana at Florence, being of the late fourteenth. This, however, contains only 30 *laude*. Another MS. in the same collection, Riccardi 1049—probably of the early fifteenth century—is more typical of the family. It contains 115 *laude*, beginning with " Amor de caritate," which is followed by " Sopr'onne lengua amore." None of the *laude* already mentioned as special to the Umbrian MSS. are included; but several of doubtful authenticity, never found in that group, appear in their place. The order observed is characteristic of a large number of Tuscan MSS. of this class.

Tuscan MSS. contain as a rule about 112 *laude :* rather more

[1] *Op. cit.*, p. liv.

than are found in good Umbrian texts. Five are special to this group:

> Ad te mi son data.
> Dolce amor de povertate.
> Venite a veder meraviglia.
> Disiar, Iesú amore.
> Vorrei in alto gridare.

The authenticity of these poems is doubtful; though it is possible that " Dolce amor de povertate " may be a genuine work.[1]

Tuscan MSS. of the *laude* are seldom of conventual origin, but seem often to have been made for private owners. It is probable that many were written for the use of fervent Tertiaries, such as we know flourished in Florence and Siena in the fourteenth century. The text does not always agree with that of the Umbrian group, and the dialect and spelling are modified to those current in Tuscany between 1300 and 1325. We find many of Jacopone's *laude* in the collections of hymns used by the Tuscan flagellants and *laudesi* in the first half of that century.

C. Venetian Manuscripts.—Venetian MSS. of the *laude* form a large class ; but, owing to the number of doubtful and spurious poems which they generally contain, and the many alterations, interpolations, and corruptions of the text, they are of small value to students. The oldest appears to be Canonici 240 in the Bodleian, of the late fourteenth or early fifteenth century. It contains 36 *laude*, of which 33 are authentic. Next to this comes an early fifteenth-century text, A.7, 15 in the Convent of S. Maria delle Grazie at Bergamo. It contains 140 *laude*, and agrees closely with the edition printed at Venice in 1514.

Venetian MSS. usually contain more *laude* than either Umbrian or Tuscan texts. They begin almost invariably with the poems on Poverty; and the general order and selection suggests that they were written by and for the Spiritual friars, and used as party weapons in their war with the *relaxati*. Nearly all are of conventual origin. Among the many doubtful and spurious pieces special to this group, the following are peculiarly characteristic:

> Iesú faccio lamente.
> O vergine chiara luce.
> Voi che avete fame de l'amore.
> Volendo acomençare.[2]

---

[1] See Brugnoli, pp. lxiv and 402.   [2] *Id.*, p. lxxxii.

APPENDIX II

CHRONOLOGY OF THE *LAUDE*

Since all students are agreed as to the impossibility of fixing the chronological order of the *laude*, the following arrangement must be regarded merely as tentative. It is based upon that view of Jacopone's life and development which I have set out in previous chapters, and is supported by all that we know of the interior growth of other mystics of his type. But even so, many poems—especially those inspired by his recurrent states of spiritual darkness, or by the varying moods of his intercourse with Divine Love—are appropriate to more than one period of his life; and some readers will probably disagree with the dating which I suggest. Such poems are marked by a query. The difficulty of this task is much increased by our ignorance of Jacopone's poetic past, and his metrical skill at the time of his conversion. My arrangement differs considerably from that adopted by Signor Brugnoli, who does not seem to me to have paid sufficient attention to the close connection between the poems and the successive stages of Jacopone's spiritual life.

A. Poems of the Penitential Period. 1268-1278

Personal

Peccator, chi t'ha fidato.
O Regina cortese.
O alta penitenza.
Omo de te me lamento.
Signore, damme la morte.
O me lasso, dolente.
Cinque sensi mess'on pegno.
O Signor, per cortesia.
Amor diletto, Cristo beato.
O iubilo del core.

Senno me pare.
O dolce amore.
O derrata, guarda al prezo.
Piangi, dolente anima predata. (?)
Or chi averá cordoglio?
Amor, diletto amore. (?)
Molto me so delongato. (?)

Didactic

Omo, tu sè engannato.
Omo, mettete a pensare.
O frate mio.
Figli, nepoti e frati.
O frate, guarda 'l viso.
Si como la morte face.
O corpo enfracedato.
Troppo m'è grande fatica.
O vita penosa.
O femene, guardate.
Audite una 'ntenzone—ch'è 'nfra l'anima e 'l corpo.
Audite una entenzone—ch'era fra doi persone.
Quando t'alegri.
O Cristo pietoso.
L'anema ch'è viziosa.
Vorría trovare chi ama.
Guarda che non caggi.

B. Poems of the Conventual Period. 1278–1293

Personal

La Bontade se lamenta.
O vita de Iesú Cristo.
Perché m'hai tu creata.
Con gli occhi ch'agio nel capo.
O Cristo onnipotente—ove sète enviato?
Ensegnatime Iesú Cristo.
Amor dolce senza pare.
Troppo perde el tempo.
Fuggo la croce.

Amor de caritate
O megio virtuoso.
En cinque modi appareme. (?)
Un arbore è da Dio plantato. (?)
Assai me sforzo a guadagnare.
A fra Ianne de la Verna.
Amor contrafatto.
Or udite la battaglia.

Impersonal and Didactic

En sette modi.
Alte quattro virtute.
La superbia de l'altura.
O castitate, fiore.
Anima che desideri.
L'omo fo creato virtuoso.
Omo che vol parlare.
Que fai, anema predata?
O libertá, subietta.
L'amor lo cor sí vòl regnare.
Udite una entenzone—ch'è fra Onore e Vergogna.
O peccator dolente.
O Cristo onnipotente—dove se' enviato. (?)
O anima mia.
O novo canto.
O Vergine piú che femina.
Ad l'amor ch'è venuto.
Fiorito è Cristo.
Donna del paradiso. (?)

Poems related to the Spiritual Movement

O anema fedele.
Solo a Dio ne possa piacere.
Tale qual è.
O Francesco povero.
O Francesco, da Dio amato.
Povertade enamorata.
O amor de povertate. (?)

C. Poems of the Political Period. 1294-1303

Que farai, Pier da Morrone?
Or se parrá chi averá fidanza.
La Veritade piange.
Iesú Cristo se lamenta.
Piange la Ecclesia.
O papa Bonifazio—molt'hai iocato al mondo.
Que farai, fra Iacovone?
O papa Bonifazio—io porto el tuo prefazio.
Lo pastor per mio peccato.
Frate Ranaldo, dove se' andato?

D. Poems of the Last Period. 1303-1306

O amor, divino amore—perché m'hai assediato.
O amore muto.
La bontate enfinita.
L'omo che può la sua lengua domare.
Fede, spene e caritade.
Sapete voi novelle de l'amore.
O Amor, divino amore—amor che non se' amato.
O amor che m'ami.
Amor che ami tanto.
O coscienza mia.
L'amor ch'è consumato.
Sopr'onne lengua amore.
La fede e la speranza.
Que farai, morte mia.

BIBLIOGRAPHY

ALVARUS PELAGIUS. De Planctu Ecclesiæ. Venice, 1560.

ALVI, P. Jacopone da Todi: cenni storici. Todi, 1906.

ANGELA DA FOLIGNO. Beatæ Angelæ de Fulginio Visionum et Instructionum liber. Cologne, 1849.
> *Trans.* The Book of Divine Consolations of the Blessed Angela of Foligno. Trans. by M. Steegman. (New Mediæval Library.) London, 1908.

ANGELO CLARENO. Historia septem tribulationum. (Archiv für Litt. und Kirschengesch. des Mittelalters, Bd. ii., 1886.)

AUGUSTINE, ST. Opera omnia. (Migne, Pat. lat., vols. xxxii.-xxxiv.) Paris, 1844.
> *Trans.* Works (Library of Nicene and Post-Nicene Fathers, vols i.–viii.). New York, 1888–92.

BARTOLOMMEO OF PISA. De Conformitate Beati Francisci ad vitam Domini Jesu. (Analecta Franciscana, vol. iv. and v. Quaracchi, 1906, 1912.)

BELCARI, FEO. Prose edite ed inedite. Rome, 1843.

BOEHMER, E. Jacopone da Todi, Prosastücke von ihm, nebst Angaben über Manuscripte, Drucke und Uebersetzungen seiner Schriften. (Romanische Studien, Bd. i., 1871.)

BONAVENTURA, ST. Opera omnia. 10 vols, ed. P. P. Collegii S. Bonaventuræ. Quaracchi, 1882–1902. Legendæ duo de vita S. Francisci Seraphici. Quaracchi, 1898.
> *Trans.* Life of St. Francis by St. Bonaventura. Trans. by E. G. Salter. (Temple Classics.) London, 1904.

BRUGNOLI, B. Le satire di Jacopone da Todi. Florence, 1914.
Fra Jacopone da Todi. Assisi, 1907.

BRUNNER, S. Jacopone da Todi. Würtzberg, 1889.

CALLAEY, P. FRÉDÉGOND. L'idéalisme franciscain spirituel au XIVe siècle: Ubertin de Casale. Louvain, 1911.

CASINI, T. Le forme metriche italiane. Florence, 1900.

CATHERINE OF SIENA, ST. Opere. 5 vols., Lucca, 1721.
> *Trans.* The Divine Dialogue. Trans. by A. Thorold. London, 1896.

Chronica XXIV. Generalium O.M. (Analecta Franciscana, vol. iii.) Quaracchi, 1897.

Cloud of Unknowing, The. Edited from B. M. Harl. 674, by Evelyn Underhill. London, 1912.

CORNELIUS A LAPIDE. Commentarium in Ecclesiasticum. Venice, 1717.

COSMO, U. Frate Pacifico Rex versuum. (Gior. stor. della lett. italiana, vol. xxxviii. 1901.)

COULTON, G. G. From St. Francis to Dante. London, 1908.
> Christ, St. Francis, and To-day. Cambridge, 1919.

CUTHBERT, FR. Life of St. Francis of Assisi. London, 1914.

D'ANCONA, A. Jacopone da Todi, il Giullare di Dio del secolo XIII. Todi, 1914.
> Studi sulla Letteratura Italiana dei primi secoli. 2nd ed., Milan, 1891.
> Origini del Teatro in Italia. 2nd ed., 2 vols., Turin, 1891.

D'ANCONA, A., e O. BACCI. Manuale di Letteratura Italiana. 6 vols., Florence, 1904–6.

DANTE ALICHIERI. Tutte le opere. Rived. nel testo da Dr. E. Moore. Oxford, 1894.
> *Trans.* The Divine Comedy. Text with translation by Carlyle, Okey, and Wicksteed. 3 vols. (Temple Classics.) London, 1900.

DELLA GIOVANNA, I. S. Francesco d'Assisi Giullare. (Gior. stor. della lett. italiana, vol. xxv. 1895.)

DENIFLE, H. Die Denkschriften der Colonna gegen Bonifaz VIII. (Archiv für Litt. und Kirschengesch. des Mittelalters, Bd. v. 1889.)

DIONYSIUS THE AREOPAGITE. Opera omnia. (Migne, Pat. græc., vols. iii., iv.) Paris, 1855.
> *Trans.* The works of Dionysius the Areopagite. Trans. by the Rev. J. Parker. London, 1897.

EHRLE, F. Die Spiritualen, ihr Verhältnis zum Franciscaner-orden, etc. (Archiv für Litt. und Kirschengesch. des Mittel-aiters, Bd. i. 1885, ii. 1886, iii. 1887, iv. 1888.
> Petrus Johannes Olivi, sein Leben und seine Schriften. (*Loc. cit.*, Bd. iii. 1887.)

Fava, A. Jacopone da Todi e S. Francesco. Naples, 1910.

Ferrers-Howell, A. G. S. Bernardino of Siena. London, 1913.

Finke, H. Aus den Tagen Bonifaz VIII. Munster, 1902.

Fioretti di San Francesco. Rome, 1900.
   Trans. The Little Flowers of St. Francis. Trans. by T. W. Arnold. (Temple Classics.) London, 1903.

Galli, G. I disciplinati dell' Umbria nel 1260. (Gior. stor. della lett. italiana, Supp. ix. 1906.)

Gardner, Edmund. Dante and the Mystics. London, 1913. The Poet of the Franciscan Movement: Fra Jacopone da Todi. (Constructive Quarterly, vol. ii. pt. 6. June, 1914.)

Gaspary, A. History of Early Italian Literature. Trans. by H. Oelsner. London, 1901.

Gebhart, E. L'Italie Mystique. 6th ed., Paris, 1908.

Gregory the Great, St. Opera omnia. (Migne, Pat. lat., vols. lxxv.–lxxix.) Paris, 1855.
   Trans. Works. (Library of Nicene and Post-Nicene Fathers, vols. xii., xiii.) Oxford, 1895–98.

Hannay, J. O. The Spirit and Origin of Christian Monasticism. London, 1903.

Holzapfel, H. Handbuch der Geschichte des Franciscanerordens. Freiburg, 1909.

Huck, J. C. Ubertin von Casale und dessen Ideenkreis. Freiburg, 1903.

Inge, W. R. The Philosophy of Plotinus. 2 vols., London, 1918.

Jacopone da Todi. Laude di frate Jacopone da Todi, impresse per Ser Francesco Bonaccorsi. Florence, 1490.
   [From this are derived Modio's edition of 1588 and the Neapolitan edition of 1615.]
   Laude del beato frate Jacopone del sacro ordine di frati minori de observantia. Brescia, 1495.
   [From this are derived the Venetian editions of 1514 and 1556.]
   Li Cantici del Beato Jacopo da Todi, con diligenza ristampati con la gionta di alcuni discorsi del Padre Modio, e con la vita sua. Rome, 1588.
   Le poesie spirituali del B. Jacopone da Todi . . . accresciute di molti altri suoi cantici nuovamente ritrovati, con le scolie et annotationi del Fra Francesco Tresatti. Venice, 1617.
   Laude di frate Jacopone da Todi secondo la stampa fioren-

tino del 1490 ; con prospetto grammaticale e lessico, a cura di Giovanni Ferri. (Società Filologica Romana.) Rome, 1910.

[Reprinted with small modifications in the series *Scrittori d'Italia*, Bari, 1915.]

Trans. Jacopone da Todi: Choix et traduction des poèmes, par J. Pacheu. Paris, 1917.

JOHN OF THE CROSS, ST. Obras. 2 vols. Toledo, 1912.

Trans. The Ascent of Mount Carmel. Trans. by David Lewis. London, 1889.

The Dark Night of the Soul. Trans. by David Lewis. London, 1908.

JONES, RUFUS. Studies in Mystical Religion. London, 1909.

MACDONELL, ANNE. Sons of Francis. London, 1902.

MANDONNET, P. Les Règles et le Gouvernement de l'Ordo de Pœnitentia au XIII siècle. 1901.

MAZZONI, G. Esercitazioni sulla letteratura religiosa in Italia. Florence, 1905.

NANTES, RENÉ DE. Histoire des Spirituels. Paris, 1909.

NOVATI, F. Freschi e Minii del Dugento. Milan, 1908.

OLIGER, L. Jacopone da Todi. (Catholic Encyclopædia, vol. viii.)

OZANAM, A. F. Les poètes franciscains en Italie au XIIIᵉ siècle. 6th ed., Paris, 1882.

PLATO. Opera. Ed. J. Burnet. 5 vols., Oxford, 1899–1907.

Trans. The Dialogues. Trans. by B. Jowett. 3rd ed., 5 vols., Oxford, 1892.

PLOTINUS. Enneades. Edidit R. Volkmann. 2 vols., Leipzig, 1883-4.

Trans. The Ethical Treatises, etc. Trans. by Stephen Mackenna. London, 1917.

POSSEVINO, G. Vite de' Santi e Beati di Todi. Perugia, 1597.

RENIER, R. Un codice di Flagellanti della Biblioteca di Cortona. (Gior. stor. della lett. italiana, vol. xi., 1888.)

RICHARD OF ST. VICTOR. Opera. (Migne, Pat. lat., vol. cxcvi.) Paris, 1855.

ROLLE, RICHARD. The Incendium Amoris of Richard Rolle of Hampole. Ed. M. Deanesly. Manchester, 1915.

Trans. The Fire of Love and the Mending of Life. Trans. by Richard Misyn. Ed. F. M. Comper. London, 1914.

Rossetti, Dante Gabriel. Italian Poets, chiefly before Dante. Text with translation. Stratford-on-Avon, 1908.

Ruysbroeck. Werken. Ed. J. David. 6 vols., Ghent, 1858-68.

  Trans. The Adornment of the Spiritual Marriage, The Book of Truth, The Sparkling Stone. Trans. by P. A. Wynschenk Dom. Ed. Evelyn Underhill. London, 1916.

  The Book of the Twelve Béguines. Trans. by J. Francis. London, 1913.

Sacrum Commercium: the Converse of Francis and his Sons with Holy Poverty. Text and translation. (Temple Classics.) London, 1904.

Salimbene. Cronica fratris Salimbene de Adam Ordinis Minorum. Ed. O. Holder-Egger. (Mon. Germ. Historica, vol. xxxii.) Hanover, 1905-8.

Schmitt, J. La metrica di Fra Jacopone. (Studii medievali, I. 4, 1905.)

Speculum Perfectionis. Ed. P. Sabatier. (Collection des documents pour l'histoire du moyen age, I.) Paris, 1898.

  Trans. The Mirror of Perfection. Trans. by R. Steele. (Temple Classics.) London, 1903.

Suso. Die Schriften des seligen H. Seuse. Ed. H. S. Denifle. Munich, 1876.

  Trans. Life of the Blessed Henry Suso. Trans. by T. F. Knox. London, 1913.

Tamassia, N. San Francesco d'Assisi e la sua leggenda. Padua, 1906.

  Trans. St. Francis of Assisi and his Legend. Trans. by Lonsdale Ragg. London, 1910.

Tenneroni, A. Inizii di antiche poesie italiane religiose e morali. Florence, 1909.

  Lo Stabat Mater e Donna del Paradiso. Florence, 1887.

  Due antiche Laude a S. Francesco. (Raccolta Monaci.) Rome, 1901.

Thode, H. Franz von Assisi und die Anfänge d. Kunst d. Renaissance in Italien. 2nd ed., Berlin, 1904.

Thomas à Kempis. De Imitatione Christi. Ed. P. E. Puyal. Paris, 1886.

  Of the Imitation of Christ. Trans. by C. Bigg. London, 1901.

THOMAS OF CELANO. S. Francisci Assisiensis vita et miracula.
Ed. Fr. E. Alençon, O.F.M. Rome, 1906.
  Trans. The Lives of St. Francis of Assisi. Trans. by A. G.
Ferrers Howell. London, 1908.
TOBLER, A. Vita del Beato Fra Jacopone da Todi. (Zeitschrift
für Romanische Philologie, Bd. ii.) Halle, 1878.
TOCCO, F. DI. L'eresia nel medio evo. Florence, 1884.
  Studi Francescani. Naples, 1909.
UBERTINO DA CASALE. Arbor Vitæ Crucifixæ Jesu. Venice, 1485.
WADDING, LUKE. Annales Minorum. 19 vols. 2nd ed., Rome,
  1731-45.

INDEX

THE TEMPLE PRESS LETCHWORTH ENGLAND

WS - #0039 - 140723 - C0 - 229/152/29 - PB - 9781333651862 - Gloss Lamination